The Sword,
the Cross, and the Eagle

The Sword, the Cross, and the Eagle

The American Christian Just War Tradition

Davis Brown

ROWMAN & LITTLEFIELD PUBLISHERS, INC.

Lanham • Boulder • New York • Toronto • Plymouth, UK

ROWMAN & LITTLEFIELD PUBLISHERS, INC.

Published in the United States of America
by Rowman & Littlefield Publishers, Inc.
A wholly owned subsidiary of The Rowman & Littlefield Publishing Group, Inc.
4501 Forbes Boulevard, Suite 200, Lanham, Maryland 20706
www.rowmanlittlefield.com

Estover Road
Plymouth PL6 7PY
United Kingdom

British Library Cataloguing in Publication Information Available

Library of Congress Cataloging-in-Publication Data

Brown, Davis.
  The sword, the cross, and the eagle : the American Christian just war tradition / Davis
Brown.
    p. cm.
  Includes bibliographical references (p.   ) and index.
  ISBN-13: 978-0-7425-6259-2 (cloth : alk. paper)
  ISBN-10: 0-7425-6259-X (cloth : alk. paper)
  ISBN-13: 978-0-7425-6560-9 (electronic)
  ISBN-10: 0-7425-6560-2 (electronic)
  1. War—Religious aspects—Christianity. 2. Just war doctrine. 3. United States—
Military policy—Moral and ethical aspects. I. Title.
  BT736.2.B77 2008
  241'.6242--dc22

                                                                              2008012661

Printed in the United States of America

(∞)^TM   The paper used in this publication meets the minimum requirements of
American National Standard for Information Sciences—Permanence of Paper
for Printed Library Materials, ANSI/NISO Z39.48-1992.

DEDICATION

This book is dedicated to Thomas Franck, but for whose early tutelage my life might very well have taken a different path, and to Annette Brown, for her extraordinary perseverance through many adversities.

Contents

Acknowledgments

The events that culminated in the writing of this book began in June 2005. I was a panelist at the annual meeting of the Academic Council on the United Nations System (ACUNS), giving a presentation on a tort-based analytical approach to the use of force in international law that I had been developing. One of the spectators, Kendall Stiles of Brigham Young University, came up to me afterward and invited me to speak on the same topic at BYU's Kennedy Center Global Issues Series, which I did. While I was there, I took the opportunity to study the approach to war in the Mormon Church, to complement my ongoing study of the just war tradition across cultures and faiths, which Ken greatly facilitated by arranging a series of interviews with other BYU faculty. So my first acknowledgment goes to Ken Stiles, for setting in motion the events that led to this book.

My next major acknowledgment goes to Mark Miller, the pastor at Ebenezer United Methodist Church in Stafford, Virginia, where I am a member. Having been spooked a bit by the treatment of Jan Hus at the Council of Constance, I felt it prudent to enlist a member of the professional clergy to keep me out of heresy by looking over the initial draft. As busy as Mark is, he agreed to undertake this project and needed very little coaxing either before or during the process.

My third major acknowledgment goes to James Turner Johnson, professor of religion at Rutgers University, himself a major and prolific contributor to modern just war thinking. In addition to his wisdom on the substance of this work, Jim has offered invaluable advice in the preparation of proposals and in seeking a publisher.

I would also like to acknowledge several individuals, who know far more about their own respective faiths than I, and who also took time out of their busy schedules to talk to (i.e. enlighten) me. These persons include, in alphabetical order:

James Childress, Darrell Cole, Steven Harper, Valerie Hudson, Susan Karamanian, John Langan, Allan Parrent, Charles Raynal, James Siebach, Robert Smylie, Alexander Webster, Milton Winter, Robert Wood and three anonymous reviewers.

I would like further to express my deepest appreciation to Ana Cristina Alves, a Ph.D. student in international relations at the University of Virginia, for her invaluable assistance in the lengthy and cumbersome final editing and revision of the manuscript. I truly could not have accomplished it without her.

And finally, my highest acknowledgement goes to my wife Annette and my children for their patience with the long hours I spent cooped up in the office instead of being with them.

I shall close with the standard disclaimer, which is certainly true in this case, that my conclusions do not necessarily reflect the opinions of the persons mentioned above (indeed, some definitely do not), and that any omissions are strictly my own.

Davis Brown
Charlottesville, Virginia

Cast of Major Characters
(in chronological order)

Jesus of Nazareth, Jesus Christ—founder of Christianity

Paul of Tarsus, Saint—spread Christianity to the Gentiles; wrote Letter to the Romans, which is the foundation of Christian political theory

Quintus Septimius Florens Tertullianus [Tertullian] (c. 160-c. 240)—most influential theologian of his day; espoused total pacifism

Flavius Valerius Constantinus [Constantine] (c. 274-337)—first Roman emperor to convert to Christianity

Ambrose, Saint, Bishop of Milan (c. 340-397)—first major purveyor of the concept of *bellum justum* in Christian doctrine

Aurelius Augustinus, Saint, Bishop of Hippo [Augustine] (354-430)—founder of the just war tradition in its Christian form

Gratianus [Gratian] (?-c. 1160)—author of the first systematic treatment of canon law, the *Concordia Discordantium Canonum*, also known as *Decretum Gratiani*

Raymond of Peñafort, Saint (c. 1175-1275)—church canonist

Henry of Segusio, Blessed, Cardinal, Bishop of Ostia [Hostiensis] (c. 1200-1271)—church canonist

Tommaso d'Aquino, Saint [Thomas Aquinas] (c. 1225-1274)—author of the venerated *Summa Theologica* and the three classic just war criteria

Tommaso de Vio, Cardinal, Bishop of Gaeta [Cajetan] (1469-1534)—author of the celebrated *Commentary to the* Summa Theologica

Martin Luther (1483-1546)—founder of Protestant movement and the Lutheran Church

Franciscus de Victoria [Francisco de Vitoria] (1483-1546)—Jesuit priest and professor of theology at the University of Salamanca, author of *De Indis* and *De Iure Belli*, the first treatments of modern international law

Jean Chauvin [Johannes Calvinus, John Calvin] (1509-1564)—founded the Calvinist branch of the Protestant movement, author of *Institutes of the Christian Religion*, the first systematic treatise of Protestantism

Francisco Suarez (1548-1617)—Jesuit priest and professor of theology at the University of Coimbra, author of *De Bello* and other works influential in the early formation of modern international law

Huig de Groot [Hugo Grotius] (1583-1645)—Dutch jurist and statesman, author of *De Jure Belli ac Pacis*, the first systematic treatise of international law; often regarded as the "father of international law"

Samuel Pufendorf (1632-1694)—German jurist and leader in the post-Grotian tradition in natural law

Emmerich de Vattel (1714-1767)—Swiss jurist whose treatise on international law, *Le Droit de Gens* was highly influential in America

Joseph Smith (1805-1844)—founder of the Mormon Church

Reinhold Niebuhr (1892-1971)—founder of Christian Realism

Paul Ramsey (1913-1988)—pioneer of the rediscovery of the just war tradition in the 1960s, and fellow Mississippian

I

INTRODUCTION

· 1 ·

Introduction

Those who wage war justly aim at peace, and so they are not opposed to peace, except to the evil peace.—Thomas Aquinas[1]

[O]ne may deny that war is opposed to an honorable peace; rather, it is opposed to an unjust peace, for it is more truly a means of attaining peace that is real and secure.—Francisco Suarez[2]

What else is war but the punishment of wrong and evil? Why does anyone go to war, except because he desires peace and obedience?—Martin Luther[3]

And thus he was preparing to support their liberty, their lands, their wives, and their children, and their peace, and that they might live unto the Lord their God.—Book of Mormon[4]

DOES GOD TAKE SIDES IN WAR?

$\mathcal{I}$ was seated at the dinner table when my host announced his characteristically imponderable table topic for the evening: "Does God take sides in war?" I looked up and could not miss the twinkle in his eye; he had obviously already given the question some thought and was ready to pounce on whatever response I gave. If I answered yes he would demand, why do righteous people sometimes lose wars? If I answered no he would repost, how could a just and loving God be neutral toward a hateful belligerent that opposes him? The Pharisees trying to entrap Jesus with the question about paying taxes to Rome must have worn the same facial expressions.

I declined the bait and proceeded with my dinner.

3

But having had a few years to think about it, I have concluded that the question is not so imponderable after all. God does take an interest in war, but no greater interest than in all other manifestations of human brokenness. War is but an extreme symptom of an extreme sin, whether that sin be greed, lust, hatred, pride, or something else. Since God deplores sin, he favors the side that opposes it. When the sin has drawn the sinner into war, God most definitely takes sides.

But even though God takes sides in wars, he does not fight them for us,[5] nor does he guarantee the outcome. War is a human condition that God allows Man to suffer for reasons Man cannot fully comprehend in the temporal world. Humanity suffers the calamity of war for the same reason that we suffer the calamities of natural disasters, broken relationships, pain, and death. To a Christian, these are but a few of the many challenges of faith and spiritual maturation that must be overcome en route to the Afterlife. As a one-time church pastor of mine is fond of saying, God is more interested in our development than our comfort.

Consequently war *qua* war is neither good nor evil. War can be God's way of answering prayers; just as the Hebrew slaves groaned under the weight of their bondage in Egypt, millions of people today groan under the oppression of authoritarianism and corruption, along with all of the woes that they bring, such as poverty, indignity, terror, murder, rape, plunder, and hopelessness. Rebellions and interventions to remove such regimes from power do entail some suffering, but are also often regarded as a welcome relief—just ask anyone who once languished in the killing fields of Cambodia, survived or escaped the barbarism of Idi Amin, or suffered a thousand injuries at the hands of Iraqi occupation forces in Kuwait. Yet it cannot be denied that war itself can, and almost always does, bring forth similar woes of death, injury, destruction, suffering, and poverty, as well as wars' unintended consequences of occasional murders, rapes, and plundering committed by unprofessional and undisciplined soldiers. This lamentable reality induces some pragmatic pacifists and reluctant just war theorists to wrongly label war a "lesser evil." In that line of reasoning, war is an evil act yet a necessary one in this fallen and broken world, needed in order to avoid or alleviate some greater evil. But treating war as a "lesser evil" is no better than a hypothetical movement to rid the world of snake venom, despite its medicinal value, on the basis that it is a dangerous substance and lethal if abused. War *qua* war is not a sin or an evil, but rather a tool, as Martin Luther pointed out:

> [W]e must distinguish between an occupation and the man who holds it, between a work and the man who does it. An occupation or a work can be good and right in itself and yet be bad and wrong if the man who does the work is evil or wrong or does not do his work properly.[6]

The classic military strategist Carl von Clauswitz defined war as simply the use of force to compel one's adversary to do one's bidding.[7] This amoral definition is not especially appealing to the pacifists who find all war to be evil, nor to the jihadists who consider all that their opponent is and does to be evil, nor even to the just war theorists who reluctantly admit the occasional necessity of war to achieve some greater good. However, precisely because it is mutually *un*satisfactory, Clauswitz's definition is the most universally acceptable definition of war and its function in a multicultural, reasonably enlightened human society.

In this ideologically neutral respect, war is much like money. Both are the means toward an end that can be truly great or truly wicked. Rather than money itself being the root of evil, it is the *love* of money.[8] The same holds true for war; when human depravity wins over human decency, war is an instrument of considerable evil. But as a tool in the hands of the charitable and well-meaning, war can produce enormous good. As Augustine put it, the *love* of war is evil, not war itself.[9]

THE DUALITY OF WAR, LOST IN TRANSLATION

What so complicates the topic of war in modern discourse is that the word itself is so imprecise. The English word *war*, along with the French word *guerre* and the Spanish, Portuguese, and Italian word *guerra*, are all derived from the proto-Germanic root *werra*, which means confusion, discord, or strife. The German word *krieg*, the Dutch word *krijg*, and the Swedish word *krig* are derived from the Old High German word *chreg*, which means stubbornness, exertion, or fight. Most of these meanings have negative connotations; discord and strife are specifically mentioned in the *Summa Theologica* as sins contrary to peace[10] and stubbornness can be synonymous with sinful pride. None of these words convey any distinction between a "good" war and a "bad" war. The lack of such a distinction in the Western lexicon leads naturally to the *a priori* conclusion, especially among Christians, that all wars are bad.

The ancient Greeks, on the other hand, understood the dichotomy between "good" and "bad" wars quite well. In pre-Christian Greek mythology, the god of war, Ares, was a brutish lover of discord and strife, thriving on destruction, who kept his offspring Phobos (fear) and Deimos (terror) as his constant companions. In contrast to Ares stood Athena, the Greek goddess of war, who was also the goddess of wisdom and justice. Although fierce and ruthless in battle, she was loved and respected. Athena is also reputed to have created the olive tree[11]; today the olive branch is a universal symbol of peace. These diametrically opposed personifications of war are reflected in Homer's depiction of the Trojan War in the *Iliad*; in the heat of battle Ares and his companions incite the combatants to savagery, rejoicing in the slaughter, blood, and misery. Enraged at finding Ares stirring such trouble among the mortals, Athena strikes him down and forces him to withdraw, whimpering cowardly.[12]

It is perhaps significant to the ill reputation of the concept of war that Ares's counterpart in Roman mythology, Mars, was far more respectable to the Romans than Ares was to the Greeks. The Romans were conquerors and in their ethos the warrior profession was honorable. The high regard for military prowess in Roman ethics is evident in the praise bestowed on Mars and in the desire to die in battle.[13] The Latin word *bellum* denotes simply a contest between equals. As Latin displaced Greek as the language of learning in Western culture, it became the native language of Western—and Christian—ethics and political philosophy. It follows that the meaning of "war" in the Latin language would dominate the Western frame of reference for studying the concept of war. By the time this displacement occurred, however, the old Republican concept of the *bellum justum* (just war) in Roman law was, along with the Republic itself, supplanted by Roman imperialism.

The *bellum justum* was restored to political theory by the Christian church and thus the church deserves the credit for restoring the dual concept of war, through the classic just war tradition. Pioneered by Augustine and developed into its modern expression by Thomas Aquinas, that concept was fundamental to the approaches of the early fathers of international law. Francisco Suarez distinguished between "good" and "bad" wars with terms such as *offensive* and *defensive* wars.[14] Defensive wars were unquestionably just and offensive wars could be just if they were provoked by some grave injury. Because no legal structure existed to regulate the activities of sovereign states, the early fathers of international law built their conclusions upon the foundation of natural law, which is that innate sense of justice and reason that exists in all persons.

After the Enlightenment and the wane of the church's influence in international affairs, the distinction between "good" and "bad" wars began to erode once again. In the nineteenth century age of colonialism and imperialism, virtually any use of force could be considered legitimate in international law. In contrast to the faithful expositions of the just war tradition in seventeenth and eighteenth century works, nineteenth century treatises of international law often denied the very validity of the doctrine and some treatises even omitted mentioning it altogether. In the twentieth century, especially after World War II and the rise of the United States as a superpower, the concept of the just war eroded in international law in a different but no less insidious way: by failing to distinguish a "good" war from an offensive (as opposed to defensive) war. International law has thus imposed a definition of just war that is too restrictive for military force to fully realize its function in statecraft, which is to hold states accountable for their misconduct. In the United Nations Charter and the 1974 Definition of Aggression, the terms *aggression* and *armed attack* encompass any use of force against another state that is not self-defense, regardless of cause or provocation. This interpretation has resulted in a tendency to label *any* offensive war as aggression, however charitably motivated it may be. In addition, it enables genuinely aggressive states to manipulate circumstances to make themselves appear as innocent victims of "aggression" by genuinely peace-loving states that seek only to contain the mischief of the former. The marvelously cynical complaints of damages from military force by Nicaragua against the United States, Yugoslavia against the European members of NATO, and Iran against the United States in the International Court of Justice provide ample witness to this:[15] Nicaragua was fomenting revolution in its neighbors; Yugoslavia was engaged in ethnic cleansing in Kosovo; and Iran was mining the Persian Gulf. Modern international law has, in effect, turned on its ancestors and twisted the meaning of aggression into something nearly unrecognizable.

CONTRIBUTION OF THIS WORK

The purpose of this book is thus twofold. One purpose is to push back, from the perspective of Christian political theory, against the perversities that international law (aided by the forces of propaganda, moral equivalency, and political correctness) has imposed on generally law-abiding states, states that decline to comply with the letter of international law when its spirit, or its morality, demand otherwise. Darrell Cole and Daryl Charles have both picked up on this point, the former warning of the danger of idolizing peace (taken as the absence of war)[16] and the latter arguing that tyranny has been an even greater scourge on mankind than war.[17] No state of affairs that allows the evils of absolute corruption, lust for power, genocide, and other crimes against humanity to thrive with impunity should be permitted to stand. No war should be characterized as legitimate and yet illegal, as the Kosovo War has been.[18]

Since the just war tradition is the bedrock upon which modern *jus ad bellum* (the law regulating the decision to go to war) is constructed, that tradition must be the tool of choice in restoring the balance of justice and accountability that has been lost. We must, metaphorically, return to the nest and reevaluate the role of the just war tradition in modern statecraft. In doing so, we must consider just war theory within the larger precepts of the Christian faith. Religion is an integral part of any culture's ethical values that govern the resort to military force, as Quincy Wright observed in 1947[19] and which political scientists and theorists have begun to rediscover in the last two decades. Barry Rubin follows Samuel Huntington's seminal proposition of a "clash of civilizations"[20] in arguing that religion, as a dimension of statecraft, transcends all other interests.[21] Even the late pacifist John Howard Yoder argues persuasively that the teachings of Christ are relevant not only to a modern social and personal ethic, but also to political theory and statecraft.[22] I will go even further and submit, as Alexander Webster does,[23] that the Christian ethic is not merely relevant to the task set before us, but indispensable. The just war tradition that spawned modern *jus ad bellum* is largely a Christian creation. In Christian thought the core human ethic is charity, i.e. loving one's neighbor as oneself,[24] and therefore charity must occupy a central place among the norms of human interaction—including statecraft in general and the just war tradition in particular. That thread of logic has endured from Augustine all the way through the Middle Ages and the Modern Age, with only a (comparatively brief) respite after the Enlightenment. The values that drive the just war tradition cannot be divorced from the values of Christianity as a whole.

But the Christian Bible does not reveal everything needed to fully comprehend the just war tradition; one must also draw from natural law. Charles writes, "The very premise on which just war rests is that there is a universal moral sense that informs human beings on what is good and just over what is evil and unjust."[25] In this respect I take issue with the assertion of James Turner Johnson that natural law does not render the principles of just war theory "self-evident"; even Johnson accepts the possibility that there do actually exist universal values that are accessible to Man, if only Man can find them.[26] Natural law is divine in origin but it is neither Christian nor non-Christian and Johnson rightly reminds us that we must dig deeper than Christian ideology to find it.[27] Christian philosophers from the time of Paul to the present have sought precisely that, and every step of reasoning brings humanity closer to discovering those values, as Johnson points out when he advocates a "regular and continuing systematic moral analysis" of the just war tradition.[28]

For this reason I submit that the just war tradition, although Western and Christian in origin, has universal application. The most fundamental tenet of modern international law, that war is prohibited in all cases except self-defense, is directly traceable to the just war tradition. Indeed, modern international law is itself a Western creation, and distinctly Christian in origin, for two of its intellectual progenitors, Franciscus de Victoria and Francisco Suarez, were Jesuit priests and the "father of international law," Hugo Grotius, also wrote learned treatises on religious matters. The rest of the world has, for the most part, subscribed to the Western system of international law and consequently it is appropriate for that system to draw upon one of its foundations, the Christian just war tradition.

This brings us to the second purpose of this book, which is to instill an understanding of how the just war tradition drives the military ethos and statecraft of the United States. Just as Christian principles are essential to a philosophical and ethical understanding of the legitimacy of war, the practice of the United States is essential to an applied understanding of the same Christian principles. The United States is the world's only superpower and the world's standard-bearer for democracy, and has more armed forces stationed or deployed outside its borders than all other countries combined. The conduct of the United States, for good or ill, has enormous impact on the development of norms of international law and statecraft. It therefore behooves the international community to appreciate what values the United States seeks to advance when it resorts to military force. Those values are essentially those sought in the just war tradition, which as Johnson notes, runs deep in the American normative thought.[29] Indeed, Johnson goes as far as describing American thought as the "principal locus" of the recovery of the just war tradition.[30] The international community needs to know and understand the ethos that drives America's seeming propensity toward using force; the "method behind the madness," so to speak. In turn, the key to understanding American values in statecraft is to understand American Christianity (recall the observation of Rubin about the importance of religion to statecraft). According to the *CIA World Factbook*, 78 percent of the American population claims to be Catholic, Protestant, or Mormon.[31] Forty percent of the U.S. population are members of one of sixteen major denominations.[32] Although the United States has a secular government, religious freedom was one of the *raisons d'être* of the original American colonies, and since that time the church has occupied a central place in American life. Every American president has been Christian and the vast majority of the American political leadership is Christian, along with the vast majority of the American military itself.

Thus this book is directed toward two audiences. In a broad sense, it is directed toward the global community of international affairs, Christian and non-Christian, in all relevant disciplines, including politics, law, philosophy and ethics, and religion. For this reason, the book draws from all of these fields and assumes no prior knowledge of any of them on the part of the reader. It is hoped that this book will instill a greater understanding and appreciation of the value of the classic just war tradition to modern statecraft, where I submit it is direly needed.

In a narrower sense, this book is addressed to the American clergy and lay leadership, particularly those with a role in forming official policy of their respective denominations on the legitimacy of the use of military force. In this respect the United States is hardly united. Even among the churches that recognize the validity of the just war tradition (and not all of them do), there are many differences of opinion as to what constitutes a just war. Worse still, as a result of the way in which interest in the just war tradition was rekindled among the American clergy (i.e., the specter of nuclear Armageddon), many denominations have adopted positions on war that are illogical, impractical, or ill-conceived. For this reason, we will often stop along the way to examine and challenge many statements and positions of the American churches, and to draw from the best of them, with the design of forging a common, even ecumenical framework for judging recourse to force in the twenty-first century.

Many readers will be surprised to see a treatment of the Church of Jesus Christ of Latter-day Saints (the LDS or Mormon Church)[33] alongside the Catholic and Protestant churches, given that a very substantial portion of the Catholic and Protestant (and Orthodox) population does not regard the Mormon faith as compatible with mainstream Christian theology. I have elected to include the Mormon approach for several reasons. First, the Mormon Church self-identifies as part of the Christian community and its members claim to follow Jesus Christ. Because this work is not the proper place for evaluating the merits of that assertion, their claim to membership in Christendom will be accepted. Second, and as a corollary to the first reason, this work is devoted to a study of American Christian just war theory and it is thus fitting to include a denomination that is decidedly American in origin, even if it is radically different from the rest. Third, there is a growing sense in American society that Mormons enjoy a disproportionately large degree of political influence. There is only anecdotal evidence to support this proposition but given the present number of Mormon senators, governors, federal employees, and military members, as well as a major contender for the 2008 Republican presidential nomination, that anecdotal evidence is strong indeed. Fourth, regardless of whether or not basic Mormon beliefs are compatible with the other branches of Christianity, the positions of Mormon elders and scholars on war and peace specifically are generally not incompatible with those of the other branches and they do not conflict with the just war traditions of the Catholic and Protestant churches (at least not any more than the other two branches conflict with each other). Indeed, as we shall see in the chapters ahead, several Mormon articulations are quite useful and have the potential to contribute to the development of a common Christian just war tradition for the modern age.

STRUCTURE OF THIS BOOK

The next step in getting our arms around this elephantine topic is to recognize and appreciate the distinction between just war and two other flawed moral trajectories of war. Chapter 3 will place the just war tradition in historical context, taking notice of its development and major contributors in Catholic, Protestant, and Mormon doctrine (the Orthodox presence in the U.S. is too small to exert significant influence and therefore it will not be studied).

Part II, consisting of chapters 4 through 10, will be a systematic exploration of each of the criteria that any armed conflict must satisfy for it to be just, as stated by the various American churches. For each criterion we shall present its origin and development, study the differences in the way it is articulated by each denomination, and reexamine its validity. In some cases I will conclude that the criterion should be disavowed. After exploring six criteria of *jus ad bellum* (the law regulating the decision to go to war), we shall then briefly explore the relationship of *jus ad bellum* with *jus in bello* (the law regulating the execution of the war).

Part III, consisting of chapters 11 through 13, will examine several problem areas of the just war tradition, some of which are modern, others of which are age-old quandaries. This part will begin with a survey of Christian doctrine on rebellion against tyranny. That study will serve as a springboard for tackling the vexing controversy of humanitarian intervention, which is the use of military force to stop another state from inflicting gross violations of fundamental human rights. Finally, we shall reexamine the question of when, if ever, just war permits the use of weapons of mass destruction. Since it was the prospect of nuclear annihilation during the Cold War that rekindled public interest in the just war tradition, it is only fitting that this work conclude by revisiting that prospect, this time with the benefit of hindsight.

The Place of War in
Modern Christian Thought

MORAL TRAJECTORIES OF WAR

$\mathcal{I}$n 1944, Reinhold Niebuhr defined evil as "the assertion of some self-interest without regard to the whole" and good as "the harmony of the whole on various levels."[1] We therefore begin with the premise that the many theories on the use of force (war) can be classified into various degrees of morality and immorality by evaluating self-interest in the decision to use force, that is the degree to which a motive for war is charitable (good) or selfish (evil). This taxonomy is able to complement, rather than supplant, the traditional classification of Christian theories of war by degree of propensity (at one extreme, militancy; at the other extreme, restraint). If these two continuums are superimposed, the result is the double-axis shown in figure 2.1. The various moralities, or "trajectories," to borrow a term from Eastern Orthodoxy,[2] are now more readily identifiable. Every war (or use of force) can be pinpointed somewhere on this double continuum, between the extremes of militancy and restraint, and charity and self-centeredness.

The four quadrants are loosely equivalent to four distinct moral trajectories of *jus ad bellum*. On the upper right, where restraint and charity converge, lies pacifism, which is the forbearance of force motivated by the desire to not inflict harm on anyone. When charity is replaced with selfishness, the use of force occupies the lower right quadrant that is the domain of isolationism. In this trajectory, the regime elites refrain from using force purely out of concern for their own well-being or ill-being, that is, lack of interest in the rest of the world and/or reluctance to devote any resources to any cause other than their own advancement. On the upper left quadrant is holy war, which is the confluence of charity and militancy. In this trajectory, the belligerents are not concerned about

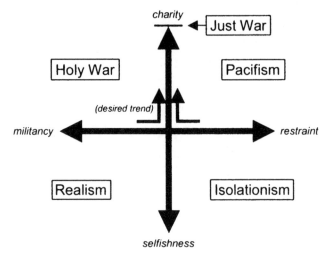

Figure 2.1.

the physical harm they inflict, as long as that harm furthers their cause. But the cause itself lies on the "charitable" side because the belligerents act not for themselves but for a higher calling, including God. The combination of militancy and self-centeredness produces realism, which occupies the lower left quadrant. Once again, the belligerents are unconcerned about the suffering they inflict on others, as long as it benefits their cause. The distinction from holy war is that in realism the cause is the belligerents' own advancement. Of these four moral trajectories, two are commonly recognized as having some basis in Christianity: holy war and pacifism.

Christianity also forms the basis for a third trajectory that does not fit neatly into any of the four quadrants. That third trajectory is just war and it occupies the top of the double continuum along the vertical axis; that is, at the equilibrium of militancy and restraint and at the high end of charity (the ideal just war would be at the extreme end). What makes a just war charitable is that the regime elites respond to an injury to the state, that is the people and collective good for which they are responsible for protecting; they respond not for themselves but for their charges. This feature is what distinguishes a modern hostage-rescue operation from, for example, the Trojan War, which was fought over the wife of one of the regime elites. What pulls the just war trajectory toward the center of the horizontal axis, between militancy and restraint, is that the just war shares characteristics with both extremes. The same holy war motivation to do what is "righteous" in God's eyes is also the driving factor in the decision to embark on a just war. In both trajectories, the belligerents believe the objective pleases God—the difference being that in holy war that viewpoint is shared by only the warriors themselves, instead of the community of Man as a whole. Thus, even as the holy war trajectory is repudiated (in the following section), its contribution to the mainstream must be recognized, namely that God is on the side of those who must fight in order to preserve his values. The just war trajectory also has commonalities with pacifism, in that they share a reluctance for war and preference of peace. The difference is that pure pacifism strives for peace as the *absence* of war, whereas just war seeks to achieve a broader, more comprehensive peace that incorporates justice. In every just warrior resides a bit of Crusader and a bit of peacenik.

THREE THEORIES OF WAR IN CHRISTIAN THOUGHT

Holy War

Holy war is fought at the command of, or on behalf of, God specifically. An often accompanying concept is that the war is actually being fought *by* God, through the warriors. Holy war is not fought for any earthly objective or motive, but rather to bring about a situation that its warriors believe to be pleasing to God, however illogical, incomprehensible, or unfair the objective may be in the minds of those who are not attuned to the divine nature of the warriors' mandate. As Edward Long puts it, the so-called duty in holy war to make war against evil "is considered more important than holding coercive techniques under critical judgment."[3] In holy war, any amount of destruction, death, and suffering is permissible, for God's purpose cannot be questioned.

The Judeo-Christian basis for this trajectory is grounded in God's covenant with Abraham to give Canaan (the Promised Land) to Abraham's descendants.[4] When Israel emerges as a nation and is freed from bondage in Egypt, God fulfills that covenant by instructing the Israelites to conquer Canaan completely, leaving no survivors.[5] Furthermore, the history of ancient Israel is depicted in the Old Testament as one in which faith and obedience to God guarantees victory, a point not lost on Pope Gregory I who considered righteous the extermination of heretical sects,[6] or Pope Urban II who preached in favor of holy war to liberate the Holy Land from the Muslims during the Crusades.[7]

The flaw in holy war is that it does not differentiate between sins against God and sins against Man. The first portion of the Ten Commandments defines Christendom's (and Judaism's) relationship with God and violations of those commandments are offenses against God, not Man. For Man to punish Man for these offenses is to trespass upon God's purview. In the temporal world, God the Father and Christ the Son reign only over those who choose to be subservient to them. This is evidenced by the fact that religions other than Christianity not only exist but thrive. Christendom cannot claim superiority over non-Christian peoples and faiths in their relations with them, merely by virtue of their not being Christian.

Holy war, on the other hand, is based on the premise that one culture or faith is *ipso facto* superior to another, and therefore has no obligation to adhere to universal rules of good conduct. Such a premise is illegitimate, not to mention grossly unfair, because it violates the principle that all persons are equal before God. It allows a culture to "trump" otherwise universal norms, such as the right to defense, by appealing to an authority that is recognized by *that* culture and no other. Unfettered by universal norms of civilized relations, the self-styled superior culture abandons such norms, with disastrous consequences in warfare. In holy war, the cause transcends all other considerations, brooking no compassion, mercy, humanity, or charity, and often is directed against an enemy not in response to their actions, but in response to their identities and religious choices. Like the just war trajectory, holy war purports to export a virtue, but holy war carries that logic too far, without duly considering other norms of justice and righteousness. When holy war is viewed through the lens of its results—the horrors perpetrated by the Nazis, Serb nationalists in Bosnia and Kosovo, and what radical Islamist groups aspire to today—it is revealed to be antithetical to all the divine virtues.

Holy war deserves a broader definition than the modern idiom has given it. In the 1960s, Edward Long identified four characteristics of holy war, namely: (1) the war is solely or primarily motivated by religion; (2) the promise of a spiritual reward for making war; (3) the erosion of restraint in the methods and means of war, for example, protection of noncombatants; and (4) an absolutism that justifies any and all means, however immoral that might be in any other context.[8] It is granted that Long's characteristics accurately describe the ethic that drove the Crusades, as well as that which drives radical Islamist militarism today. But any militaristic ethic that idolizes a single objective or ideology at the expense of the larger moral framework is properly grouped into the same category as holy war. John Howard Yoder warns against idolizing "defense of 'the free world'" and "liberation of 'the working class.'"[9] But while Yoder is correct in arguing, indirectly, that promoting such ideologies does not justify some of the excesses of Soviet and American militarism during the Cold War, he makes the overbroad generalization that *all* use of force to defend democracy, or to alleviate oppression, must be condemned.

A unique doctrine of the Mormon Church must be mentioned here, chiefly because of its holy war dimension. In Mormon doctrine, the U.S. Constitution is regarded as hallowed, even sacred. The Mormon Church regards America as the Promised Land[10] and the Constitution as instituted by

God.[11] For this reason, the Mormon Church directly supported the U.S. government during the Mexican War[12] even as it suffered persecution by local governments. The Mormon Church also went out of its way to demonstrate support for the federal government during the Spanish-American War.[13] In both cases, the church lent its support without any serious debate on the merits of the conflicts. This outlook is evident at the highest echelons of the LDS Church in the twentieth century as well; a member of the First Presidency wrote in 1940 of the virtues of America, its constitution, its democracy, and its role in promoting freedom worldwide[14] and in 1962, Ezra Taft Benson, who would later become the president and prophet of the church, described America as "the Lord's base of operations."[15] The extolment of the United States' system of governance in this manner has the potential to transform a rational preference for democracy into a dogma.

Indeed, Yoder is highly critical of the Protestant denominations for this very reason, arguing that by incorporating the just war tradition into their confessional creeds, the early Protestant churches dogmatized it.[16] By affixing such a label to the just war tradition, Yoder advances the claim that the tradition itself is but a less-virulent form of holy war, on the basis that it cannot be derived by reason but only by faith. This argument has many flaws. First, just war theory has already been derived by reason, by none other than the Doctors of the Catholic Church. Second, the just war tradition is also included in the *Catechism of the Council of Trent* (a Catholic document),[17] which was written around the same time, or before, many of the confessional creeds of which Yoder complains; Yoder would have to object to the Catholic Church's memorialization of the tradition too, and he does not. Third, Yoder's characterization of just war theory as "dogma," on the basis of its inclusion in the creeds, would serve to expose other, more faith-based tenets of Christianity (e.g. the Trinity) to similar criticism. While Yoder is correct to caution against dogmatizing the causes of war, a proper application of the just war tradition satisfies those concerns.

Pacifism

At the opposite extreme from holy war is pacifism, which embodies the proposition that no destruction, death, or suffering is permissible regardless of the cause or provocation. In this trajectory, the use of force must be avoided at *any* cost. From time immemorial Western philosophers have decried war as a scourge of and upon mankind and it is conceded that war does destroy people's lives, homes, and prosperity, which is something that the pacifist trajectory can never support. The ethic of pacifism lies at the heart of the Christian outlook not merely on war, but in all levels of interaction between persons and peoples. Prophesied as the "Prince of Peace,"[18] Jesus offers a compelling alternative to the debauchery and depravity of the Roman ethic:

> But I say to you, Love your enemies and pray for those who persecute you.[19]
> [I]f anyone strikes you on the right cheek, turn the other also.[20]
> Blessed are the peacemakers . . . Blessed are those who are persecuted.[21]

That Jesus is extolling the virtue of nonviolent personal interaction, even at the cost of enduring personal injustice, is quite clear and is further attested by Christ's willingness to be arrested, tortured, and crucified without offering any resistance.

The earliest post-Biblical purveyors of Christian thought extended Jesus's teachings of nonviolence to the corporate level. Since Christ had ruled out the legitimacy of violence against others, the argument went, any participation in war was illegitimate also.[22] Consequently, the early church's condemnation of war was complete and unequivocal. Its most influential proponent, Tertullian, advocated complete and total submission, even to persecution and execution of Christians, even though in his heyday Christendom's numbers were sufficient to put successful revolt within the realm of possibility.[23] To Tertullian, the defining moment of pacifism is Jesus's response to Peter's attempt to prevent the Roman guards from arresting him. In rebuking Peter for cutting off a soldier's ear, he claims, Jesus "cursed the works of the sword for ever after."[24] The ramifications of this interpretation to war doctrine are thus predictable; in contrast to some of his contemporaries who were ambivalent about military service, Tertullian actively advises Christians to leave the army.[25] "In disarming Peter," he writes, "[Christ] unbelted every soldier."[26]

Just War

Just war is a war of vindication, whereby force is used to impose or restore justice to a situation in which injustice would otherwise prevail. Like holy war, just war is fought for an objective that is pleasing to God, but only to the extent that the greater good outweighs the destruction, death, and suffering that will almost inevitably take place in pursuit of it. Like pacifism, the just war trajectory has peace as its ultimate objective, but the war is fought in order to promote accountability, an essential component of a good, real, and durable peace.

At first glance, however, pacifism seems like a more appealing ethic to the followers of Christ; it is the pacifist ethic that Jesus taught and which defines the ideal Christian. Quotations such as "Turn the other cheek" and "Blessed are the meek" would, by their plain meaning and removed from their context, depict Jesus as a total pacifist who silently endured the insults and injuries at the hands of others and instructed his followers to do the same

Christian realism also espouses this view. Notwithstanding his condemnation of earthly pacifism as an impossible ideal, Niebuhr is quick to affirm what he regards as the Gospel's injunction of all nonresistance whatsoever (including nonviolent resistance).[27] Hence, Niebuhr is forced into a position that requires Christians to momentarily put aside the Christian ethic in order to fight. The problem with such an approach, as pointed out by Darrell Cole,[28] is that it makes no provision for discerning good and evil. Niebuhr attacks the just war tradition because "it assumes that obvious distinctions between 'justice' and 'injustice,' between 'defence' and 'aggression' are possible."[29] If, as Niebuhr contends, there is no obvious distinction, then it would follow that all just wars are also unjust and all unjust wars are also just. This incoherent approach leads to one of two results. The first is the "shun the leper" ethic; because any and all war is evil, it must never be undertaken no matter what injustice may prevail otherwise. The other result is the "in for a penny, in for a pound" ethic; since any and all war is evil, once it is undertaken, the limitations of ethical conduct are lifted. Caught between two mutually exclusive results, the righteous warrior is left confused or worse, paralyzed into inaction. In Christian realism, no one in a Christian society could ever prosecute a just war without deliberately choosing to abandon Christianity, even momentarily. This is an unconscionable predicament for a Christian statesman. The pacifist would respond with the solution that Christians must disassociate themselves with any matters of state. However, such a resolution is neither practical, due to the large number of Christians today, nor desirable, for it would be illogical for a Christian to oppose the instillment of Christian values such as charity into governance.

To apply the pacifism of Jesus, as depicted in the New Testament, to matters of state is to remove Jesus's message from its proper context. In *The Politics of Jesus*, Yoder shows the relevance of Jesus's teachings to the temporal world, partly by arguing that Romans 13:1–7 cannot be interpreted properly outside of the context of the entire exposition on love in Romans 12 and 13.[30] The same standard of biblical exegesis must also apply to the rest of the New Testament as well. For example, the Sermon on the Mount was directed to how the common folk (the poor, disenfranchised, and oppressed) should live their lives, not how regime elites should conduct statecraft. The injunction to "turn the other cheek" instructs Christians to restrain themselves from reacting with anger or pride to a minor injury at the hands of another. In many cultures a backhanded cuff on the cheek is more of an insult than a serious injury.[31] Jesus is simply telling his followers to "get over it." As Augustine puts it, turning the other cheek is a disposition "not in the body but in the heart."[32]

Jesus's admiration of the "meek" has a modern connotation that is often equated with excessive submission. The word also means gentle or soft, slow to anger, and able to keep one's power under control. It may also be that Jesus was using hyperbole as a teaching tool, which was a common rabbinical style in ancient Eastern cultures.

The primary fallacy of total pacifism is that it abdicates the responsibility to defend others. Christians are taught to love their neighbors as themselves, and to love their enemies, and perhaps even to voluntarily submit to injury and death in doing so, as Jesus did. Jesus did not teach his followers to allow *others* to submit to suffering. James writes, "Anyone, then, who knows the right thing to do and fails to do it, commits sin."[33] This is the core principle of the entire Christian just war tradition—that a Christian must be empowered to use force, and indeed has a *duty* to use it, when justice demands it.[34] Thus Paul Ramsey embraces the Augustinian view of force as an act of charity, but couches it in terms of defending others; on the parable of the Good Samaritan he quips, "[W]hat do you think Jesus would have made the Samaritan do if he had come upon the scene while the robbers were still at their fell work?"[35] Michael Walzer further points out that pacifism, which he decries as a form of radicalism, is for those who expect never to wield power, and therefore will never be burdened with the choice to use it or not.[36]

The ethic of force to defend or protect others from harm is well-grounded in both Catholicism and Protestantism. Church law, as compiled in the *Decretum Gratiani*, takes the position that "He who does not ward off an injury done to his fellow-man is like him who does the injury. . . . They are not immune from crime who do not liberate those whom in fact they have the power to free."[37] The modern Catholic and Presbyterian catechisms allude to this principle in setting forth a duty to defend others from harm:

> Legitimate defense can be not only a right but a grave duty for one who is responsible for the lives of others. [Catholic][38]
>
> The duties required in the Sixth Commandment are: . . . protecting and defending the innocent. [Presbyterian][39]

The Lutheran catechism goes further, echoing Gratian's position that having the ability to defend the innocent and willfully failing to do so is equivalent to murder: "[N]ot only is he guilty who does evil to his neighbor, but he also who can do him good, prevent, resist evil, defend and save him, so that no bodily harm or hurt happen to him, and yet does not do it."[40]

Pacifism is based on an unfounded assumption that because Jesus did not directly support the use of force, he must have condemned it. Such a premise does not explain why Jesus went out of his way to heal the Roman soldier, or to praise the centurion for his faith, rather than rebuking him for his choice of profession.[41] It also does not explain why he urged his disciples, after the Last Supper, to sell their cloaks in order to buy swords.[42] Even the assumption itself is not fully supported by the Gospels; Jesus's use of a whip to cleanse the Temple (John 2:15) serves as a potent counter-example.

A Christian war ethic is more visible in the letters of Paul, chiefly his letter to the Romans. Paul wrote, "For rulers are not a terror to good conduct, but to bad. Do you wish to have no fear of the authority? Then do what is good, and you will receive its approval."[43] This necessarily implies some use of the sword to accomplish God's will. Paul's letters are also noteworthy for their militaristic imagery:

> Therefore take up the whole armor of God . . . Stand therefore, and fasten the belt of truth around your waist, and put on the breastplate of righteousness . . . take the shield of faith, with which you will be able to quench all the flaming arrows of the evil one. Take the helmet of salvation, and the sword of the Spirit, which is the word of God.[44]
>
> Share in suffering like a good soldier of Christ Jesus.[45]

Although no fan of the Roman central government or of its armed soldiers, Paul appreciated the higher purpose that the power of the sword can realize.

At this point the pacifist protests, pointing out that in the same letter Paul wrote, "Do not repay anyone evil for evil."[46] And further:

> [N]ever avenge yourselves, but leave room for the wrath of God; for it is written, "Vengeance is mine, I will repay, says the Lord." No, "if your enemies are hungry, feed them; if they are thirsty, give him something to drink; for by doing this you will heap burning coals on their heads." Do not be overcome by evil, but overcome evil with good.[47]

Surely, remonstrates the pacifist, Paul could not have considered war to be compatible with such love and compassion. But Paul also wrote, "hate what is evil, hold fast to what is good."[48] This world is replete with evils to be hated, but nowhere in the New Testament are Christ's followers instructed to hate *those persons who are* evil, or *those persons who do* evil things, as opposed to the evil acts themselves. Lisa Sowle Cahill argues that the meaning of the instruction not to resist the evildoer[49] is to "not approach the enemy or evildoer in hard, resistant, alienating, and self-righteous judgment, but in a compassionate desire to meet the needs of wrongdoers and victims as well as possible in the circumstances."[50] As shown in chapter 6, "Right Intention," one indicator of a just war is whether its motivation is sinful or charitable. Just as it is possible to love one's country but hate what it does, it is also possible—even mandated—to deplore evil acts. At times it may be necessary to overcome evil with force. Paul alluded to this possibility when he wrote, "*If it is possible*, so far as it depends on you, live peaceably with all."[51] The passage "Vengeance is mine" should not be taken as a suggestion, as Yoder does,[52] that no Christian should ever take part in a just war or punishment; Paul makes no distinction between a pagan and Christian authority, implying that even a pagan government can unwittingly serve as an instrument of God's justice. If God can work through a pagan authority, he can certainly work through a Christian one, which is Paul's point in writing, "We have gifts that differ according to the grace given to us: prophecy, in proportion to faith; ministry, in ministering; the teacher, in teaching . . . *the leader, in diligence*."[53] The phrase "do not repay evil for evil" means exactly that: Do not respond with *evil*. It does not preclude responding with good, and that good may, out of necessity, be the use of force in all lovingness toward the evildoer on behalf of the victims of the evil act. Nowhere in the New Testament did Jesus, or Paul, or anyone else declare all war to be evil, nor that any use of force to restrain the wicked is itself wicked. This is why church doctrine, beginning with Augustine,[54] omits killing in a just war from the list of transgressions that violate the Ten Commandments.

But, replies the pacifist, did not Jesus rebuke Peter for defending him at Gethsemane, saying "Put your sword back into its place; for all who take the sword will perish by the sword"?[55] Was Jesus thus not condemning all violence everywhere and regardless of cause or provocation, as Tertullian claims? Yoder treats this vignette as the clincher for the argument that Jesus renounced all violence, even in legitimate defense, reasoning that "His disavowal of Peter's well-intentioned effort to defend him cannot be taken out of the realm of ethics by the explanation that he had to get himself immolated in order to satisfy the requirements of some metaphysically motivated doctrine of atonement."[56] Yet in the text of the book of Matthew, Jesus very plainly states that that is precisely his intention. "Do you think I cannot appeal to my Father, and he will at once send me more than twelve legions of angels?" he asks Peter. "But how then would the scriptures be fulfilled, which say it must happen in this way?"[57] Jesus declined Peter's aid because he was fulfilling *his* duty to die on the cross. Thus an ethic of absolute pacifism cannot be generalized from this specific, unique instance. The other way in which this episode is distinguishable from the just war trajectory is that, by the law of the Jews, the Roman occupation, and today's modern state, Peter had no legal right to resist the arrest, not even on a trumped-up charge. Peter was not leading an organized revolt against tyranny, but assaulting a police officer who was discharging his duty. Jesus's metaphor of "those who live by the sword" refers to private persons acting on their own or for their own selfish purposes, and does not refer to force undertaken by the duly constituted authorities in the discharge of their civic duties.[58]

Those who are in a position of authority *do* have the right, even duty, to use force when necessary to defend the common good. Paul alluded to this as well, writing, "[Authority] is God's servant for your good. . . . It is the servant of God to execute wrath on the wrongdoer."[59] As James Turner Johnson points out, the positive responsibilities of good government include ensuring the common good, protecting against threats, and maintaining civil order.[60] Law enforcement and duly constituted armed forces and militias exist specifically for these public purposes. As long as they discharge their duties with love instead of hatred, they exercise charity in using force to defend the nation, or more fundamentally, the *people* of the nation. The tendency of churches to rail against the expense of building up military forces when that money could be used for humanitarian and social purposes is unpersuasive for this reason. The proponents of such arguments misconstrue the divinely ordained role of the civil magistrate, which is to *protect*. Responsibility for defense lies *exclusively* with the government, which would be derelict in its duty if it did not exercise its right to defend the people.

But wait a minute, the pacifist demurs: Did not Jesus explicitly extinguish that right, along with the *lex talionis* (the law of retribution) in the Sermon on the Mount? Jesus said, "You have heard that it was said, 'An eye for an eye and a tooth for a tooth.' But I say to you, Do not resist an evildoer."[61] Was Jesus not proscribing a new law of complete nonviolence to supersede the old? To respond we must return to the basic principles of good biblical exegesis, for the New Testament cannot be accurately interpreted out of the context of the Old. Jesus also said, "Do not think that I have come to abolish the law or the prophets; I have come not to abolish but to fulfill"[62]—at the Sermon on the Mount, no less. The God of the Old Testament is very much a warrior and the God of the New Testament cannot be divorced from that image. Christianity views God the warrior, God the just, God the merciful, and God the loving all as the same. Cole writes that God has warlike characteristics *because* he is just, merciful, and loving[63] and nothing in the Old Testament law prohibits the use of force in statecraft or by individuals defending someone else from oppression. Nor was Jesus instructing his followers to eschew the *lex talionis*; rather, he was simply defining the proper time and place for its use, which was not in response to minor insults or injuries such as being struck or coerced for some easily replaceable possession. His admonition "Do not resist evil" was also a command to exercise restraint in advancing one's own cause, but as Thomas Aquinas explains, not to prevent someone from resisting injustice "for the common good, or for the good of those with whom he is fighting."[64]

Whereupon the pacifist makes a good point that must be conceded: The common good must be defined in a discriminating way. Yoder points out, and

Cole agrees, that an intellectually honest just war tradition must reject some wars as *unjust*,[65] for a just war tradition that permits anything is invalid as tautological. That proposition is accepted as true, but so must be the reverse: that an intellectually honest just war tradition must also *permit* some wars. For the pacifists to use the just war criteria to find all wars unjustified is equally dishonest. Paul Ramsey attacks this practice, complaining that the pacifist construes the just war tradition in a way to find *every* war unjust.[66] This is the trap Yoder falls into when he argues that no war has ever met all the criteria, and that no state has ever declined to undertake a war "in a situation of great military and political pressure"[67] after applying them. Yoder's argument is analogous to advocating the repeal of criminal law because it does not deter all crime. The fact that the just war tradition is sometimes honored in its breach is not sufficient cause to do away with it.

The pacifist also points out the ill effects of war, rejoining that the death and suffering of thousands of innocent people, who harbored no ill will toward the belligerent and played no part in the aggressor's design, cannot be an act of love. As H. Richard Niebuhr puts it, "Wars are crucifixions. It is not the mighty, the guides and leaders of nations and churches, who suffer most in them, but the humble, little people."[68] This objection is also well-taken, for it jolts Christian just war theory back to reality. The perfect war (i.e., that in which only the aggressors and their means of aggression are prevented or stopped from doing harm without affecting the lives of anyone else in any way) is just that—*perfect*, and by definition, unachievable in a fallen world. Just as there is a little Crusader in every just warrior, there is a little beast as well, and war unleashes that beast. The atrocities (intentional and unintentional) that are committed by even the best-intentioned parties continually remind us that military force is almost never precise, fraught with unintended, collateral damage. The just warrior must use the same weapons for doing justice as the unjust aggressor uses, and the weapons themselves do not discriminate between good and evil. This is what makes war a drastic solution, to be employed only in response to a drastic problem. The just war trajectory therefore has a number of safeguards, that is, specific, enumerated criteria that must be satisfied, to preclude the resort to force unless it is truly necessary and calculated to achieve a greater good than otherwise. The consequence of prohibiting any just war because it is not perfect is to idolize the mere absence of war, which is an imperfect peace,[69] thereby allowing the immoral trajectory of aggressive realism to prevail and flourish. One may as well abolish all churches because they cannot achieve perfection either.

Finally, the pacifist raises the argument that several resistance movements have succeeded in achieving social change without resorting to violence, to wit, those led by Mahatma Gandhi and Martin Luther King, Jr.[70] Gandhi and

King, however, lived in countries with reasonably scrupulous governments, under which sufficient liberties existed to make their success possible. Neither Gandhi nor King would have stood a chance against Josef Stalin, Idi Amin, Kim Il-Sung, Pol Pot, Saddam Hussein, or Adolf Hitler.[71] The proposition that pure pacifism can overcome the force of an aggressor as hard-hearted as one of the above seems dubious. For every Gandhi and King there are countless would-be activists who are cowed into abject fear, or murdered relentlessly, before their statements are even made.

For the above reasons the just war trajectory is selected over all others as the Christian ideal.

CONCLUSION

It is an historical postulate that especially destructive wars give birth to peace movements; such was the case with the foundation of the Red Cross, after the 1859 battle of Solferino, and the renunciation of war initiative, after World War I, that led to the Pact of Paris.[72] It is easy to imagine, therefore, the fortitude of the peace movement after World War II, the largest and most destructive war in history. Out of the ashes of that global conflagration was born today's peremptory norm of *jus ad bellum*, enshrined in the U.N. Charter, that "All Members shall refrain in their international relations from the threat or use of force against the territorial integrity or political independence of any state, or in any other manner inconsistent with the Purposes of the United Nations."[73]

However lofty the objective of such a blanket prohibition of force may be, it seems as though modern international law, along with *jus ad bellum*, has lost its moral compass. Genuine peace is not merely the absence of conflict, but a state of concord or tranquility of order in which all share in goodness. An order imposed on one side by the other is not truly peace, as Thomas Aquinas pointed out in the thirteenth century.[74] Today's international law is built upon the faulty premise that *peace* is more desirable than *justice*, and it imposes restraints in the name of peace that undermine the other, equally vital, human need for justice. It forecloses any cause that does not satisfy a narrow, strict interpretation of the right of self-defense. The reason modern *jus ad bellum* is faulty is that thousands of years of human history and Judeo-Christian thought show that the need for justice is at least as strong as that of peace. The renunciation of war is a comparatively recent innovation—a most welcome one, for sure, for it was necessary to curb the abuses of the nineteenth century by forcing states to put their grievances in proper perspective. But the norm of pacific relations also assumes that states do not engage in covert or indirect aggression or other end-runs around it. The spread of Communism by force during the Cold War, the rise of state-sponsored terrorism, and the abuses of nuclear nonproliferation agreements by rogue states all show that this assumption amounts to little more than wishful thinking.

All of this stems from a misapplication of the just war tradition as originally conceived. Christianity is the bedrock of Western thought and therefore also the bedrock of Western philosophy of law and governance. Because the Western philosophy of international law and politics has evolved into the global philosophy, the church is well positioned to effect change. It is incumbent on the Christian community to reverse the downward trend of morality in international relations, by reasserting the role of ethics, morality, and justice in the decisions by states to use military force. In doing so, the Christian community can contribute to the return of just war theory to its original design, which was as a mechanism for holding states and their leaders accountable for their follies.

· 3 ·

The Historical Development of Just War Theory

$\mathcal{A}$ comprehensive study of the just war tradition must begin with an overview of its historical context.

JUST WAR THEORY AND ITS CATHOLIC FOUNDATION

To the extent that any concept of war for justice existed in the days of the ancient Israelites, its scriptural foundation could be found in the law of redress for personal injury, the *lex talionis*, or "law of the talon": "If any harm follows, then you shall give life for life, eye for eye, tooth for tooth, hand for hand, foot for foot, burn for burn, wound for wound, stripe for stripe."[1] As primitive, even barbaric, as this law seems today, it does represent an advancement in the concept of justice, as it requires the punishment to be commensurate with the offense. When extended to the causes and goals of war, the *lex talionis* mandates any war with the object of punishing the enemy be undertaken for that purpose *only*, not to inflict greater injury than the offense that gave rise to it. Otherwise the conflict deteriorates from a war of retribution to a war of revenge. This "kindler, gentler" form of retribution (comparatively speaking) is visible in the Deuteronomic law of warfare, which imposes a condition that the enemy be first made an offer of peace (Deuteronomy 20:10). If the enemy complies with Israel's demands, then the people's lives are spared. This tradition is followed in the treatment of Gaza at the hands of Simon as depicted in the first book of Maccabees.[2]

The basis for this trajectory of war is less visible in the New Testament. Although Jesus is not recorded as explicitly approving of war, neither is he recorded as condemning it absolutely,[3] otherwise Jesus would not have resorted

27

to such militaristic imagery as "I did not come to bring peace, but a sword."[4] Not once does he condemn the military profession, not even to the Roman centurion whose subordinate he heals and whose faith he extols over that of his own people (Matthew 8:8–10).[5] John the Baptist expressed the same sentiment when asked by soldiers, "What should we do?"; his reply was not that they should forsake the warrior profession, but rather, "Do not extort money from anyone by threats or false accusation, and be satisfied with your wages."[6] This passage suggests that he found some worth in the military profession, as long as a standard of just and charitable conduct was upheld.

The New Testament shows not only the worth of the military profession to society, but also that some violence, or resistance thereto, may be necessary to achieve justice. One example of this idea is depicted in the cleansing of the Temple. Indignant at the defiling presence of moneychangers and vendors in the Temple courts, Jesus fashions a whip and drives them out by force.[7] This vignette shows that some violence may be necessary to achieve a greater good and that love of one's neighbor also includes love for justice. However, Jesus also teaches temperance in applying the retributive principle of justice, rejecting strict application of the *lex talionis* in favor of a form of justice seeking deterrence and rehabilitation, as exemplified in his treatment of the adulteress.[8] This theme of righteous war (and indirectly, righteous rebellion), undertaken to secure a more comprehensive form of justice, lays the foundation for the just war trajectory in Christian political thought.

While early Christianity was the domain of the lowly and oppressed, it is natural that despite the biblical foundations above, the absolute pacifism of Tertullian and his contemporaries would prevail, at least in the West where the *Pax Romana* made it possible.[9] However, two events facilitated the emergence of a different paradigm for war in Christian thought. The first event was the vision and later conversion of Roman Emperor Constantine. On the eve of battle with a rival to the throne, the then-pagan Constantine had a vision of his inferior army fighting under the Christian banner. He obeyed God's command to have his soldiers mark the cross on their shields and his forces were victorious (Battle of the Milvian Bridge, 312 CE), clearing the way for him to assume full title of Emperor. In gratitude he promulgated the Edict of Milan, granting tolerance to Christians throughout the Empire.[10] Thereafter Christendom had a champion willing to use force to protect it, and Constantine himself is believed to have converted by 324,[11] setting the stage for Emperor Theodosius I to make Christianity the official religion of the Empire in 391 CE. Christendom had moved from a position of martyrdom to one of power.

The other historical event shaping Christian attitudes toward war was the threat to Italy from the Goths. Many Christians of this era came to believe that Isaiah's prophecy of swords beaten into plowshares[12] was being fulfilled in an unintended way: With the conversion of the Roman Empire itself, the Roman army had become a more professional and charitable functionary whose purpose was to protect the people from the onslaught of the barbarians from outside.[13] This threat to Rome, now also a threat to Christendom, forced a reappraisal of the proscription against war. In response, Ambrose, Bishop of Milan (and a public official), merged Christian ethics with the Ciceronian tradition of public and private duties to derive rationales for self-preservation, defense of others, and intervention, finding justice in war that "preserves the country from the barbarians . . . or defends one's neighbors from robbers."[14] This early step paved the way for the works of Augustine.

Augustine's outlook on war was based not on Cicero but on Aristotle, who viewed war as a necessary instrument for achieving peace.[15] The evil of war, writes Augustine, was not the death and destruction that accompanies it, but rather the *love* of these things: "The desire to do harm, cruelty in taking vengeance, . . . the lust of domination . . . these are the things that are rightly blamed in wars."[16] A legitimate war can be prosecuted without passion or hatred, in order to stop sinners from sinning, "[f]or it is the wrongdoing of the opposing party which compels the wise man to wage just wars."[17] The just warrior, in restraining the sinner from committing acts of evil, is actually acting in the best interest of the sinner, an act of charity. Love for one's enemies does not preclude physical punishment for their transgressions and hatred, only the malice in inflicting it.[18] The charitable nature of Augustine's just war theory is in the notion that it would save the sinners' souls. As Roland Bainton puts it, "Killing and love could the more readily be squared by Augustine because in his judgment life in the body is not of extreme importance. What matters is eternal salvation. The destruction of the body may actually be of benefit to the soul of the sinner."[19] War, to Augustine, is a charitable punishment for sin.

After the fall of the western Empire to the Germanic tribes in 476, the church found it much easier to justify war, primarily as a result of its own ascent to political power to fill the void left by the demise of Rome. As such the church had to assume the role of enforcer and defender. Pope Gregory I organized the defense of threatened cities, reluctantly exercising a degree of temporal influence, even on the tactical level. But he also believed in the propriety of force to maintain unity of faith and in the duty of secular rulers to make war at the behest of the church, thus laying the foundation for a Christian doctrine of holy war.

After the Saracen invasion of Italy, the bulk of Christian doctrine on just war was directed toward two issues: (1) Muslim incursions into and conquest of the lands of Christendom, and (2) confronting heretical sects. The *Decretum Gratiani* expounds on just war within a hypothetical case of how best to respond to the lapse of a group of bishops into heresy.[20] Raymond of Peñafort approaches the question from the perspective of distinguishing genuine warriors from brigands and rogues.[21] Hostiensis classifies war into seven categories, but always in the context of the "Roman Empire's," that is, Christendom's, right to make war against foreign infidels, and permissible wars against Christians to uphold authority.[22]

It took a saint, literally, to return the war doctrine of the church to its Augustinian roots. The work of Thomas Aquinas was the first since Isidore of Seville in the seventh century[23] to treat war in its original Augustinian context of punishing sin. In the *Summa Theologica*, Thomas enumerates three specific, now classic, conditions that must be satisfied for a war to be just:

> First, the authority of the sovereign by whose command the war is to be waged. . . .
>
> Secondly, a just cause is required, namely that those who are attacked should be attacked because they deserve it on account of some fault. . . .
>
> Thirdly, it is necessary that the belligerents should have a right intention, so that they intend the advancement of good, or the avoidance of the evil.[24]

But Thomas carries Augustine's concept of war against sin a step further, differentiating the role of the state to protect its people from outside threats from its other role of protecting against the internal threats posed by disorder. The just war, to Thomas, is a Christian response to the sins of sedition and strife, which were both contrary to peace.[25] Thomas's advances in Christian just war theory are evident in the works of his students: Peter of Auvergne is critical of wars of domination in which the domination itself is the end rather than the means to the end;[26] Ptolemy of Lucca regards the maintenance of an army to defend against external aggression, as well as to assist the prince in preserving justice, as a component of good governance;[27] Giles of Rome goes as far as characterizing war as divinely virtuous defense against aggression and preservation of order.[28]

As the Medieval period gave way to the Scholastic period, the most significant advances in just war theory continued to originate from the church. In 1517, the same year that Martin Luther launched the Reformation with his *95 Theses*, and on the heels of European discovery of the New World, the Dominican Cardinal Cajetan was the first to articulate a formal distinction between offensive and defensive wars, within a broader treatment of the Thomist just war criterion of proper authority. A defensive war, that is, to ward off an attack, required no special authority to fight; in contrast, an offensive war was a voluntary action which warranted greater scrutiny.[29] Cajetan focused exclusively on war as a measure of punishment against evildoers.[30] The Spanish Jesuit professor Franciscus de Victoria altered the course of the just war trajectory in two lectures that would go on to be reprinted as *relectiones* ("re-readings") after his death. The first, *De Indis*, framed primarily around the conquest of previously unknown lands and people (i.e. the native peoples of the New World), subjects the Spanish conquest to devastating scrutiny. The second, *De Iure Belli*, is the most comprehensive treatment of war since Thomas Aquinas. In these two works, Victoria considers war not merely as a punishment for wrongdoing, but as an instrument of self-defense, defense of others, recovery of things wrongfully taken, and punishment of evil. He presents all of these facets of war in a single package, together with an exposition of righteous means for accomplishing those goals. Victoria is the first to link just war theory (and along with it the general rules of interaction between sovereign nations) to "divine" or "natural" law, thus providing an important foundation for the formation of modern international law.

The pinnacle of the Catholic contribution to just war theory came in the following century. In 1612, the Spanish Jesuit professor Francisco Suarez published the disputation *De Bello* as a component of a larger work on charity, itself a part of a treatise on the three theological virtues. Like Victoria, Suarez offers a comprehensive treatment of war as an institution of justice, but unlike Victoria he is better able to divorce his treatment of the subject from the events of the day. Thus Suarez's treatment of war is more philosophical, systematic, and dispassionate—the perfect legal treatise, which is how the piece is regarded in international law. Suarez's work completes the conversion of war from an instrument of retributive justice to vindictive justice. In the latter, one state may use force against another by reason of the other state's *fault*, as opposed to the deliberate evil act that Cajetan's formulation supposed. Suarez restores the Thomist criterion of just cause and expands the Thomist criterion of proper authority, continuing Cajetan's distinction between defensive and offensive wars.

At this point, however, Suarez departs from Thomas Aquinas. In contrast to Thomas's third criterion of right intent, focusing on the mental state of the warrior, Suarez introduces a much broader criterion of proper manner (*debitus modus*): "the method of its conduct must be proper, and due proportion must be observed at its beginning, during its prosecution and after victory."[31] In doing so, Suarez not only affirms the three traditional Thomist criteria but also introduces several new ones. One is that the war must be necessary, that is, that the injury giving rise to the war cannot be avenged any other way, which is the forerunner of the criterion of last resort advanced by many denominations today. Another, which Suarez considered more important for offensive wars, is that the likelihood of victory must be balanced against the risk of further loss in the event of failure; this point has evolved into the modern criterion of reasonable prospect of success. Finally, although Victoria is the first of the classical Christian writers to treat the execution of war alongside its justification,[32] it is Suarez who successfully merges the two, linking charitable conduct in warfare with the justice of the war overall,[33] a topic labeled in this book as the criterion of just means. After Thomas Aquinas, the advances of Francisco Suarez are the most significant in Christian just war doctrine and this book will return to his disputation often. Thus, the real father of just war theory in modern Christianity is Suarez, with Aquinas and Augustine as the grandfather and great grandfather, respectively, and Cajetan and Victoria akin to great uncles.

JUST WAR IN THE PROTESTANT TRADITIONS

The Reformation spawned largely from the complaint of corrupt practices in the Catholic Church. Originally conceived as a movement to reform the church from within, it quickly evolved into a large-scale revolt against and exodus from the authority of the Pope. Protestantism itself developed along four major branches. The original branch, Lutheranism, is based on the works of Martin Luther and is the largest Protestant denomination worldwide, though not in the United States. The second branch, the Reformed branch, is derived primarily from the theology of John Calvin. In the U.S. the Reformed branch is represented primarily by the Presbyterian churches (the progeny of the Scottish Calvinist John Knox) and the United Church of Christ.[34] The third branch, Anglicanism, is the result of the withdrawal of the Church of England from the authority of the Pope in 1534, the fallout of a personal dispute between the Pope and King Henry VIII of England.[35] In the United States the Anglican branch is called the Episcopal Church. The Methodist denomination began around 1730 as a movement within the Church of England among followers of the Anglican minister John Wesley, and split from the Church of England after the American Revolution. Methodism is represented in America today primarily by the United Methodist Church and is far more Protestant in character than its parent. The fourth branch, the Radical Reformation branch, evolved largely from the Anabaptist movement founded in present form by Thomas Müntzer. The Radical Reformation branch, which is also comprised of the Quakers, Mennonites, and Amish, is highly decentralized and originally notable for its extreme pacifism and disengagement from political affairs. The Baptist denomination is often sorted into this branch, though it is far too decentralized and diverse in viewpoints to uniformly fit into any one branch of Protestantism. The documents of the Southern Baptist Convention, the largest organization of Baptist churches in the United States, will be treated in this work as representative of the denomination in America.

The range of viewpoints on Christian participation in civil government, and therefore in war and rebellion, is quite broad. In Lutheranism, the state is ordained by God due to the sinful nature of man, and Christians are encouraged to assume political responsibilities, for without leadership the state would collapse. Calvinism is notable for its emphasis on the doctrine of predestination, that is, that all that happens on earth, including sin, does so according to God's will. In Calvinism, like in Lutheranism, the state is ordained because of sin but also to foster righteousness and faith. To the Anabaptists, the coercive power of the state is ordained by God in response to sin and should be administered only by sinners.[36] What all Protestant denominations have in common is their Catholic heritage, complete with sixteen centuries of Catholic just war theory, which most Protestant denominations have accepted, except for the several pacifist denominations within the Anabaptist branch.[37] The works of Augustine and Aquinas, for example, are generally (though not universally) regarded as highly influential, if not outright authoritative.[38] Among the founding fathers of Protestantism in America today, Luther and Calvin are generally regarded as the most doctrinally fundamental to the Reformation movement itself and their works, along with those of the early Presbyterian Church, are the most significant contributors to the Protestant theories of just war and rebellion.

Just War Theory in the Lutheran Church

Martin Luther's political philosophy is favorably disposed toward temporal authority and its role in prosecuting just wars. Luther regards the natural state of human society as Hobbesian, human wickedness being such that the law and the "sword" (government) are essential to the survival of the society or community.[39] After weighing the conflicting biblical trajectories of pacifism and justice, Luther tries to reconcile them with the notion that true Christians (those living in the Kingdom of God) abide by God's law of love and therefore have no need for the law or the sword. In contrast, the Kingdom of the World (everyone else, which practically speaking, is everyone) does need the law as well as the sword, both of which serve to restrain sinners from actualizing their wicked thoughts. Therefore, according to Luther, Christians are encouraged to participate in temporal authority structures, for order and restraint of sin would otherwise fall victim to anarchy and natural human depravity.[40]

Turning to the limits of that temporal authority, Luther focuses on the duty of the sovereign to deal justly with evildoers by inflicting punishment on them without injuring the innocent, and to make war only for public interests, never private interests.[41] Likening war to amputation, whereby a part must be destroyed in order to save the greater whole, Luther concludes that God created the institution of war as a tool for Man to enforce peace and goodness:

> For the very fact that the sword has been instituted by God to punish the evil, protect the good, and preserve peace . . . is powerful and sufficient proof that war and killing along with all the things that accompany wartime and martial law have been instituted by God. What else is war but the punishment of wrong and evil? [Why] does anyone go to war, except because he desires peace and obedience?[42]

The institution is not to be used lightly, however; a sovereign should wage war only when it is forced upon him.[43] Luther rejects the notion of holy war, considering it to lie beyond the sovereign's purview, which is to defend the state, not usurp God's work by trying to save souls.[44] These writings form the basis for the curt, unequivocal endorsement of an Augustinian just war theory by Luther and his followers in their restatements of Lutheran doctrine, in Luther's Large Catechism: "God has delegated His authority to punish evil-doers to the government;"[45] and in the Augsburg Confession: "[I]t is right for Christians to bear civil office, . . . *to engage in just wars*, to serve as soldiers."[46]

Just War Theory in the Reformed Church

The Calvinist branch of Protestantism shares the Lutheran view of civil government as a divine instrument of law and order. Calvin writes, "The Lord has not only testified that the function of the magistrates has his approbation and acceptance, but has eminently commended it to us, by dignifying it with the most honorable titles."[47] Hence Calvin allows for Christians called to civil office to accept it and take up arms if necessary to discharge their official functions.[48] Civil magistrates are in effect ordained by God[49] and their subjects are mandated to accept their authority and obey their lawful commands. But although Lutheran and Calvinist just war and political theories agree in the essentials, they arrive at their common ground from different paths. In contrast to Luther's approach of *preventing* sin, Calvin views the role of authority through the lens of *avenging* it. "The law of the Lord commands, 'Thou shalt not kill,'" he writes, "but that homicide may not be unpunished, the legislator himself puts the sword into the hands of his ministers."[50] It is but a short step to treat war as the means by which a wrong is avenged:

> Now, as it is sometimes necessary for kings and nations to take up arms for the infliction of such public vengeance, the same reason will lead us to infer the lawfulness of wars which are undertaken for this end. For they have been entrusted with power to preserve the tranquility of their own territories, . . . can

they exert this power for a better purpose, than to repel the violence of him who disturbs . . . the general tranquility of the nation? . . . [S]hall they suffer a whole district to be plundered and devastated with impunity?[51]

But like Luther (and Augustine before him), Calvin warns against such punishment undertaken with anger or hatred, as opposed to action "wholly guided by public spirit."[52]

For nearly a century the only foundation of just war in the Presbyterian church specifically was the work of Calvin himself. The Scots Confession of 1560, written by John Knox and others as the founding confessional document of the Scottish kirk (the Old World parent of the American Presbyterian Church) curiously contains no mention of war, nor does the Heidelberg Catechism of 1562, which was influential in the kirk's development.[53] The next major foundation for a just war theory in Presbyterianism was the Westminster Standards, adopted in 1647 to replace the two older documents. Like the Lutheran foundational documents, the Westminster Standards' formula for war is rather curt and unassuming:

> It is lawful for Christians to accept and execute the office of a magistrate, when called thereunto; . . . as they ought especially to maintain piety, justice, and peace, . . . so, for that end, *they may lawfully . . . wage war upon just and necessary occasion.*[54]

> The sins forbidden in the sixth commandment ["Thou shalt not kill"] are taking away the life of ourselves, or of others, except in case of public justice, *lawful war,* or necessary defense.[55]

Mention should also be made of a Calvinist document that was significant in the foundation of the Baptist denomination. The Second London Baptist Confession of 1689 includes a chapter on the civil magistrate, the first two sections of which are nearly identical to the corresponding sections of the Westminster Confession.[56] Interestingly, the two documents cite almost entirely different sources in support of the proposition; the Westminster Confession cites to New Testament scriptures only (Romans 13:1–4, Luke 3:14, Matthew 8:9, and Acts 10:1–2) whereas the London Baptist Confession cites more Old Testament scriptures (2 Samuel 23:3, Psalms 82:3–4, and Luke 3:14). The verse in common, Luke 3:14, is John the Baptist's advice to soldiers on how to fulfill their offices justly.

JUST WAR THEORY IN THE MORMON CHURCH

The Church of Jesus Christ of Latter-day Saints, also known as the Mormon Church, traces its beginning to an 1820 vision of its founder, Joseph Smith, in which God and Jesus appear to Smith and call him to be their prophet. Several years later, according to Mormon tradition, Smith unearthed and translated a collection of gold plates containing a history of the lost tribes of Israel that had relocated to North America several hundred years before the birth of Christ and died out in the fifth century CE. The resulting work is known today as the Book of Mormon, which the LDS Church considers co-canonical with the Bible. The church itself was formally organized in 1830 and it gradually migrated westward over the next decade to flee persecution (Smith was lynched in 1844), settling in Utah in 1847.

The LDS approach to just war theory is derived not from the Bible, but from the Book of Mormon, which chronicles the wars between the righteous Nephites and the unrighteous Lamanites. The book of Alma recounts the intent of the Lamanites, under the leadership of Amalickiah, to unjustly dominate the Nephites—to "destroy their brethren, or to subject them and bring them into bondage that they might establish a kingdom unto themselves over all the land,"[57] a motive for aggression consistent with what could be regarded the root cause of all wars, "murder to get gain."[58] In contrast, the Nephites, under the leadership of Moroni, "were inspired by a better cause, for they were not fighting for monarchy nor power but they were fighting for their homes and their liberties, their wives and their children, and their all, yea, for their rites of worship and their church."[59] The entire LDS war ethic is encapsulated in the following passage:

> [W]hile Amalickiah had thus been obtaining power by fraud and deceit, Moroni, on the other hand, had been preparing the minds of the people to be faithful unto the Lord their God. . . . And thus he was preparing to support their liberty, their lands, their wives, and their children, and their peace, and that they might live unto the Lord their God, and that they might maintain that which was called by their enemies the cause of Christians. And Moroni was a strong and mighty man; . . . a man that did not delight in bloodshed; a man whose soul did joy in the liberty and the freedom of his country, and his brethren from bondage and slavery; . . . and he had sworn with an oath to defend his people, his rights, and his country, and his religion, even to the loss of his blood. Now the Nephites were taught to defend themselves against their enemies . . . and they were also taught never to give an offense, yea, and never to raise the sword except it were against an enemy, except it were to preserve their lives.[60]

Mormon political theory seeks to emulate that of the Nephites, a peaceloving people who never undertake war except when necessary and then only with great reluctance. This point is reinforced in the book of Mormon,[61] in which Mormon resigns his leadership of the Nephites because having successfully defeated the Lamanites, the Nephites follow a path of vengeful aggression.[62] The Lamanites eventually regain their strength, defeat the Nephites, and destroy their civilization.[63] From these two passages the LDS just war tradition legitimizes war against unjustified aggression, but only on the condition that the war is fought with humble and honorable intentions.

Early LDS practice can be observed in the Doctrine and Covenants of the LDS Church.[64] In Doctrine and Covenants 98, Joseph Smith calls upon members of the church to "renounce war and proclaim peace"[65] and to bear many attacks from their enemies and forgive them;[66] "[n]evertheless, thine enemy is in thine hands; and if thou rewardest him according to his works thou art justified."[67] The doctrine suggests that violence in self-defense is permissible but the reward for restraint is far greater. In doing so, it reveals a tension between submission and aggression, while simultaneously revealing the relationship between war and rebellion. While the church is to renounce war as a general policy, offenses against the law must be redressed for justice's sake:

> [F]or the public peace and tranquility all men should step forward and use their ability in bringing offenders against good laws to punishment. . . [68]

> We believe that men should appeal to the civil law for redress of all wrongs and grievances, . . . but we believe that all men are justified in defending themselves, their friends, and property, and the government, from the unlawful assaults and encroachments of all persons in times of exigency.[69]

Rather than renouncing war *in toto*, the Mormon Church renounces *aggression*, declaring its intent to oppose and suppress the same while reserving the right to resort to force when necessary to guard against fundamental injustices.

MODERN DEVELOPMENTS IN CHRISTIAN JUST WAR THEORY

By the time of Suarez, just war theory had already been flirting with secular theories of international law advanced by Pierino Belli, Balthasar Ayala, and Alberico Gentili. After Suarez, the law of nations (and just war theory with it) went secular for good, thanks to the systematic treatise of the Dutch jurist (and Protestant) Hugo Grotius, whose 1625 work *The Law of War and Peace* revolutionized the field. As a result of the confluence of Protestantism winning its independence from the Catholic Church, the rise of Protestant scholars such as Gentili and Grotius, and repudiation of the Catholic Church's sovereignty over other nations, the church itself no longer enjoyed any significant political dominance. In legal treatises, the use of historical illustrations of natural law evolved into the citation of specific events as evidence of the formation of so-called positive law. Thus the system of natural law gradually gave way to a new system of positive law, in which states strived to codify the rules of interaction by which they would consent to be governed. In positive law, states are only bound to a rule of law by their consent; God is left out of it. Consequently positive law is the purview of the secular and it is, ironically, now the secular scholars of international law that influence the church.[70]

The just war tradition changed as well, though whether it changed for the better is a matter for debate. On the positive side, the religious wars that had racked Europe for centuries were largely over (except in Britain, where they took another 40 years to completely subside), and along with the Enlightenment in the eighteenth century came a general revulsion against war for the sake of religion.[71] This development facilitated the emergence of a universal theory of just war that could be applied without reference to religion (a factor which tended to exclude rather than include). On the negative side, which overshadowed the positive, the new system of positive law made it impossible for the just war tradition (a product of natural law) to flourish. Because natural law was no longer regarded as valid, states were free to reject *any* restrictions on their prerogatives to make war that they themselves did not consent to. This development is evident in a comparison of legal treatises in the seventeenth and nineteenth centuries: The just war tradition is a central component in seventeenth century treatments of international law, whereas nineteenth century treatises make little mention of it, usually merely for historical context, and several omit the subject entirely. By the end of the nineteenth century, the right to use military force was no longer regulated by international law. Pacifism did gain sway during this period, but a number of pacifist proposals calling essentially for a collective security system[72] went unheeded, primarily because of states' unwillingness to be bound by them.

Although the churches no longer exerted direct influence on states, they did continue to influence them indirectly, especially in America, where they impressed upon a deeply religious population. In the eighteenth and nineteenth centuries, the American churches could be divided roughly into two spheres: traditionalist (Catholic and Anglican/Episcopal) and revolutionist (Presbyterian and other Calvinist denominations, Baptist, and to a more limited extent the Lutherans and Methodists). The traditionalists tended to view American wars through the lens of rebellion against legitimate authority and the revolutionists had a more crusading spirit, favoring wars that advanced certain values. Hence the Catholics and Anglicans opposed the Revolutionary War and War of 1812; the Presbyterians (and other Calvinists) and Baptists generally favored them. The Methodists generally opposed the Revolutionary

War (primarily because John Wesley did[73]) but favored the War of 1812.[74] During the Civil War, the northern churches generally viewed the war as either a suppression of rebellion (Catholic, Lutheran, Episcopal) or a crusade to abolish slavery (Presbyterians and other Calvinists, Baptists, and Methodists).[75] Similarly, the Presbyterians and other Calvinists, Baptists, and Methodists viewed the Spanish-American War as a crusade to liberate Cuba from Spanish tyranny, whereas the Episcopalians, Lutherans, and Catholics were, in Bainton's words, "more temperate."[76] The American churches were more united in their support of the Allies during World War I in their efforts to protect the world, in their view, from German aggression.[77]

However, as war evolved from limited conflicts between kings and queens to total conflict between nations, and the means of war grew more destructive, movements to regulate the resort to war (or outlaw it altogether) began to gain broader support. Beginning with a *postulata* introduced during the First Vatican Council in 1870, Catholic official doctrine has tended to frown on war due to its destructiveness.[78] The pacifist sentiment was very strong after World War I for the same reason. After the Kellogg-Briand Pact, in which states renounced war as an instrument of international relations,[79] the Anglican Church passed a resolution at the Lambeth Conference of 1930 declaring war "incompatible with the teaching and example of our Lord Jesus Christ"[80] and at the Conventus of Fribourg in 1931, the Catholic Church rejected all justifications for war except self-defense.[81] Consequently, the churches (including American churches), which had generally supported the U.S. position during World War I, were more critical of the Allies' cause in World War II.[82]

It was during the inter-war period that the just war tradition, defunct for nearly two centuries, began to reassert itself. James Turner Johnson attributes its rediscovery to the works of Alfred Vanderpol (who wrote on the Catholic tradition from Augustine to Suarez), James Brown Scott (who argued that Victoria and Suarez, not Grotius were the two fathers of international law), and John Eppstein (who compiled Catholic doctrine on war from Ambrose to the 1930s), as well as the reprinting of many of the classic works of international law.[83] But the pioneering role of actually recovering the tradition Johnson assigns to the American Protestant theologian Reinhold Niebuhr.[84] Niebuhr objects to the prevailing *a priori* assumption that any violence is immoral. "Nothing is intrinsically immoral except ill-will and nothing intrinsically good except goodwill," he writes in 1932,[85] pointing out the error of ascribing all violence to ill will and all nonviolence to good will.[86] Yet Niebuhr encounters what he views as a paradox, due to his belief in the absolutism of Jesus's so-called proscription against any violence.[87] His workaround is his development of the concept of

Christian realism, the notion that, because Jesus's ethic is impossible to achieve in the temporal world, it must occasionally be abandoned:

> I am forced to admit that I am unable to construct an adequate social ethic out of a pure love ethic. I cannot abandon the pure love ideal because anything which falls short of it is less than the ideal. But I cannot use it fully if I want to assume a responsible attitude toward the problems of society.[88]

Niebuhr thus wholeheartedly supports the use of force against the Axis powers as well as against Communism, finding that to do otherwise would allow greater evil to prevail.

After World War II the focus of the newly resurfaced just war tradition was redirected to the problem of nuclear weapons. Niebuhr was an influential member of an American Protestant ecumenical commission of the Federal Council of Churches (now the National Council of Churches) to examine the justifiability of World War II in Christian ethics. The Calhoun Commission, as it came to be called, found war to be just but regrettable, in a document that Charles Raynal describes as the best theological foundation for the use of force in the twentieth century.[89] The Commission's contrition is evident in its second report, in which it condemns the practice of obliteration bombing and the nuclear attacks against Japan. The churches had long been sensitive to war's increasing destructiveness but it was the prospect of nuclear annihilation that galvanized the Catholic Church into action. Pope Pius XII, whose reign encompassed World War II, utterly condemns aggressive war while allowing for self-defense,[90] but his successor, John XXIII, rejects war entirely on the basis of the destructive potential of nuclear warfare. "[I]n an age such as ours which prides itself on its atomic energy," he writes, "it is contrary to reason to hold that war is now a suitable way to restore rights which have been violated."[91] John XXIII's successor Paul VI, in an address to the U.N. General Assembly, repudiates the destructiveness of war, but is unclear as to whether he repudiates war entirely, as opposed to aggression.[92] The dualism of the Vatican during this period reflects the dilemma created by the nuclear standoff between NATO and the Warsaw Pact, a subject that will be explored in greater detail in chapter 13.

The nuclear dilemma was the catalyst for a sea-change in the stature of the just war tradition. In his landmark work, *War and the Christian Conscience*, Paul Ramsey subjects nuclear warfare to the scrutiny of the just war tradition, going all the way back to Augustine in order to resurrect its original design. Ramsey returns just war theory to its roots, finding Christian love of an innocent neighbor as the justification—even obligation—to resort to force if necessary to defend that neighbor from harm or injustice, as well as the love of a guilty neighbor as the source of the obligation to limit force to that which is necessary.[93] Ramsey, however, limits his treatment to the principles of discrimination and proportionality, which are essential to the proper execution of armed conflict, but have little bearing on the decision to resort to it in the first place. This unbalanced approach is continued in the pastoral letters and pamphlets of American churches on nuclear war in the 1980s, which will be introduced shortly.

This failing has been remedied in the numerous works of James Turner Johnson (a student of Ramsey's). If Ramsey gets the credit for returning just war theory to its roots, then Johnson must be credited with returning it to its original function. Johnson parses the two types of justice that a just war is intended to uphold: distributive justice, in which war is visited on the guilty in proportion to their guilt, and vindictive justice, in which war is a tool for righting wrongs.[94] He also frees just war theory from the confining parameters of the nuclear dilemma, applying it to a variety of provocations and situations, from the rise of radical Islam and other forms of ethnic militarism to the U.S. invasion of Iraq.[95] Johnson places great stock in the primacy of some just war criteria over others. He argues, for example, that the criterion of proper authority must always come first, where Thomas Aquinas placed it, because it is a fundamentally definitional attribute of war; that is, a war not waged on the authority of a state is not war but brigandage.[96] In making this point, he exposes the fallacy of subjecting a provocation to a just war analysis in which many criteria are accorded equal weight.

JUST WAR THEORY IN THE MODERN CHURCH

Overview

The modern church generally takes a teleological view of war, considering both what war is intended to, and actually does, accomplish. War is accepted in theory, but only as a means of achieving peace. This mindset explains the duality of the official position on war of the Catholic Church, which has remained fairly consistent over the last five hundred years. The Catechism of the Council of Trent absolved soldiers and civilians alike of sin for killing under specific circumstances:

> [T]he soldier is guiltless who, actuated not by motives of ambition or cruelty, but by a pure desire of serving the interests of his country, takes away the life of an enemy in a just war.[97]
>
> If a man kills another in self-defence, having used every precaution consistent with his own safety to avoid the infliction of death, he evidently does not violate this commandment.[98]

Thus the church, by imposing strict conditions such as "*pure* desire" and "*every* means," expressed its preference for peace over war. This expression is stronger and more direct in the modern catechism:

> Because of the evils and injustices that accompany all war, the Church insistently urges everyone to prayer and to action so that the divine Goodness may free us from the ancient bondage of war. All citizens and all governments are obliged to work for the avoidance of war.[99]

But having said that,

> [A]s long as the danger of war persists and there is no international authority with the necessary competence and power, governments cannot be denied the right of lawful self-defense, once all peace efforts have failed.[100]

> The defense of the common good requires that an unjust aggressor be rendered unable to cause harm. For this reason, those who legitimately hold authority also have the right to use arms to repel aggressors against the civil community entrusted to their responsibility.[101]

This stance places the Catholic Church on the same footing as the Mormon Church, whose official position on resorting to war has not evolved significantly since its founding. At the outbreak of the First World War, the president of the Mormon Church issued a letter expressing the church's preference for peace but asserting the right to self-defense. "War is to be deplored," he wrote, "and steps to prevent it or avert its consequences should be promoted and encouraged, within the bounds of justice and mercy and self-protection."[102] In 1953, the LDS President wrote of conditions for righteous war, placing considerable emphasis on the virtue of *entering into* war, as opposed to initiating it.[103]

In contrast, the Protestant denominations took more militant positions in their nascent periods and over time have gravitated toward pacifism. Older confessions of faith of several Protestant denominations flatly affirmed the duty of civil magistrates to engage in "just wars" when necessary to the interests of the state:

> [I]t is right for Christians to bear civil office, . . . to award just punishments, to engage in just wars, to serve as soldiers. [Lutheran][104]

> It is lawful for Christians to accept and execute the office of magistrate, when called thereunto; . . . they may lawfully . . . wage war upon just and necessary occasions. [Presbyterian][105]

> It is lawful for Christian men, at the commandment of the Magistrate, to wear weapons, and serve in the wars. [Anglican][106]

It is lawful for Christians to accept and execute the office of a magistrate when called there unto; . . . they may lawfully now . . . wage war upon just and necessary occasions. [Baptist][107]

Curiously, the trend of modern Protestant confessions of faith has been to omit entirely the structured discussions of civil authority contained in the older documents. Consequently their treatments of war and civil obedience (or disobedience) is somewhat haphazard. The Presbyterian Confession of Faith of 1967 states only, "God's reconciliation in Jesus Christ is the ground of the peace, justice, and freedom among nations which all powers of government are called to serve and defend,"[108] while containing no mention of the duties regarding resort to war by Christian citizenry or their leaders. The Baptist Faith and Message of the Southern Baptist Convention makes no provision for just war at all, expressing merely a desire for the end of war.[109] The position of the Methodist Church merits close scrutiny:

> We believe war is incompatible with the teachings and example of Christ. We therefore reject war as an instrument of national foreign policy, to be employed only as a last resort in the prevention of such evils as genocide, brutal suppression of human rights, and unprovoked international aggression.[110]

This stance is too extreme; it does provide for war upon a few limited occasions, but denies any possibility of reconciling war with Christian principles. Rather, it codifies the Niebuhrian argument that realism may require Man to deliberately choose to disobey God's law—a surprising position coming from the intellectual progeny of John Wesley! What the Methodist position allows for a just war is too limiting; by specifying *only* self-defense and humanitarian intervention as just causes for any use of force, it forecloses any possibility of a state using a relatively small amount of military force to achieve a relatively small, albeit just and necessary, objective such as a hostage rescue or deposing a criminal regime. What all the modern Protestant confessions have in common is that they express profound regret and contrition that any war be undertaken or even be necessary—a theme that is absent from the more hawkish confessions from the sixteenth and seventeenth centuries. In doing so, the modern confessions attempt to apply the Christian ideal of total peace (i.e., no war, sedition, or strife whatsoever because every actor is perfect) in a place where it cannot be achieved—a fallen world populated by sinners (and many non-Christians, to boot).

A better Christian ideal for the temporal world is to renounce war not absolutely, since war comes in many shapes and sizes, but rather to renounce *aggression*. In response to the overly detailed secular definition of aggression propounded by states in 1974,[111] Christian ethics offers a concept of aggression that is distillable to a simple formula: the use of force in pursuit of an uncharitable objective. In contrast, a just war is fundamentally the use of force in pursuit of a charitable objective, which is to remediate the other side's uncharitable acts. The charitable nature of a just war is most visible in the sacrifices that individuals and nations make when they use force. Individuals in the armed forces put their own lives at risk—and some die or sustain agonizing injuries—to defend the lives, homes, and well-being of their fellow citizens from attack or oppression, or to liberate another citizenry from the same. Nations make vast expenditures of equipment, training, manpower, and ultimately people for these purposes. Just as Christ performed the ultimate act of love in enduring the agony of crucifixion and death in order to save humankind, Christians may love their neighbors by giving themselves in order to protect or liberate others from harm. That is the ultimate act of Christian love.

Modern Church Restatements

It is for this reason that the modern American churches, save a few of the Radical Reformation or Anabaptist posterity, generally continue to admit the possibility of a just war (though some consider it more possible than others). The first modern church restatement of the just war theory was undertaken in 1969 by the Presbyterian Church of the United States (PCUS), the immediate predecessor to the largest American Presbyterian church today, the Presbyterian Church (USA) [PCUSA], adopting verbatim six specific criteria enumerated a year earlier by the Presbyterian author and professor Edward Long.[112] Long's criteria have endured in later writings of the PCUSA.[113]

In the early 1980s a pastoral letter of the Catholic Church in America launched a wave of studies on the moral questions posed by the American nuclear deterrence strategy of "mutually assured destruction." Commissioned by the United States Catholic Conference to study the problem, the National Conference of Catholic Bishops (now the United States Conference of Catholic Bishops) published the pamphlet *The Challenge of Peace* in 1983. This statement set forth specific criteria for a just war and examined the American nuclear deterrence policy in that light. Several other denominations followed suit. In 1986, the United Methodist Council of Bishops published its commissioned report on nuclear deterrence under the title *In Defense of Creation*.[114] In 1987, the Episcopal Diocese of Washington published its own report on nuclear deterrence, *The Nuclear Dilemma*. That same year, the Presbyterian Church in America (PCA, a smaller and more conservative Presbyterian denomination that broke away from the PCUS in 1973) issued a position paper titled *Christian Responsibility in the Nuclear Age*.[115]

In the 1990s and 2000s, several churches have issued other official statements enumerating just war criteria. The new, comprehensive *Catechism of the Catholic Church*, issued by the Vatican in 1992, restates several just war criteria.[116] In 1995, the Evangelical Lutheran Church in America (ELCA), which is the largest American Lutheran church, listed several just war criteria in its social statement *For Peace in God's World*. In 2003, the General Convention of the Episcopal Church officially adopted its own criteria and reprinted them in its latest edition of *Cross Before Flag*. These restatements are valuable as records of official positions of various denominations, but are quite brief and far less detailed than the commissioned studies mentioned above.

For some denominations, the quasi-official statements and publications are more valuable to the development of modern Christian just war theory than the official ones. In 1986, the Lutheran Council in the USA published a collection of essays on nuclear deterrence by prominent theologians of three major American Lutheran denominations.[117] Two of those essayists will be given particular attention in this book, James Childs and Paul Jersild. Both were academic deans of Lutheran seminaries and both were of the Lutheran Church in America, the predecessor to ELCA. Their essays will be treated in this book as representative of the ELCA, with the caveat that the official position is stated in the 1995 document, albeit more vaguely. The Lutheran Church Missouri Synod (LCMS) also has made no official statement; however, an article by John Johnson that appeared in the LCMS magazine *The Lutheran Witness* will also be studied in this work.

The Baptist denomination presents a special problem in identifying official doctrine because the denomination is so decentralized and churches operate independently. For lack of any better authority to represent the Baptist position, this work will look to the statements of the Southern Baptist Convention (SBC), which is the largest organization of Baptist churches in the United States. The SBC has never issued any official restatement of just war theory, but in 1991 the Executive Director to the Christian Life Commission, Dr. Richard Land, published an article in the SBC magazine *Light*, analyzing whether the Persian Gulf War to liberate Kuwait from Iraqi invasion and occupation was a just war according to the traditional criteria.[118] That article will be treated in this work as the best and most current Baptist restatement of just war theory, but with the disclaimer that the SBC does not regard the piece as its official position.

The Mormon Church has also never enumerated modern just war criteria so specifically, at least not officially. The church has never adopted any official statements, resolutions, or other positions setting forth specific criteria that must be met for a war to be just, not even in Robert Wood's article "War and Peace" in the *Encyclopedia of Mormonism*. The most likely reason for this is that writings of church fathers outside of the Mormon tradition are not regarded as authoritative in the Mormon Church. The consequence of this position is that the Latter-day Saints have no Augustine or Aquinas to draw from, and the works of Victoria and Suarez would be regarded as authoritative only in modern, secular international law. Any official Mormon analog to any of the seven just war theory criteria endorsed by other churches would have to be derived from uniquely Mormon scriptures.[119] Nevertheless, a number of modern Mormon writers—pacifist and just war theorist alike—have adopted and applied the same criteria as the Catholic and Protestant branches, occasionally even citing the works of Augustine and Thomas Aquinas, albeit more as works of philosophy or political theory than religion. This growing body of literature includes the works of the Mormon pacifist Edwin Brown Firmage and a collection of essays recently published by Brigham Young University titled *Wielding the Sword.*

Seven Modern Criteria for Just War

The criteria themselves, as articulated by the American churches, are similar but not uniform. To summarize, they are as follows.

(1) Proper Authority. War is an instrument of the state, that is, the lawful government, not private actors. The satisfaction of this criterion is what differentiates noncriminal acts of war (the use of force by a state) from criminal acts of force by marauders and terrorists. The primary differences among denominations is whether the proper authority to execute war comes from the legitimate authority, or the *de facto* authority that holds power regardless of its legitimacy.

(2) Just Cause. For the war to be just, the reason for going to war must also be just. This criterion differentiates war from aggression; the former is legitimate, the latter is not. American denominations differ widely on what constitutes just cause for war; causes range from specific causes such as self-defense or collective defense and defense and protection of human rights, to general purposes such as preserving order and combating evil.

(3) Right Intent. The war must be motivated by charity, not sin, and must be undertaken without hatred or anger, or out of pride, envy, or other sinful desires. Generally speaking the proper goal of war is justice, though some denominations characterize it as peace, or peace with justice.

(4) Proportionality of Cause. Modern churches articulate proportionality in many different ways, synthesized here under this label. Essentially it stands for the proposition that the overall good that the war is calculated to achieve must outweigh the harm that it is likely to inflict. This criterion must not be confused with proportionality in the execution of the war, which speaks to the

means and methods of warfare; that principle is encompassed in the criterion just means (see below).

(5) Reasonable Prospect of Success.   War is a messy business and should be undertaken only when it is calculated to achieve a greater good. If, however, the just objective of the war is futile, then the war should not be undertaken, for it would only cause further damage and suffering. This criterion is not included in the statements of the LCMS, the PCUSA, the PCA, or the Mormon Church. This work is highly critical of this criterion, and would treat it as an extension of proportionality of cause rather than separately.

(6) Last Resort.   Because war is such a messy business, the threshold for its resort must be high. The war must be truly necessary, with no other available solution. Some denominations require that all peaceful alternatives actually be tried; others simply state that they must be exhausted, suggesting that only *reasonable* alternatives be explored. This work is also highly critical of this criterion, as it is based on premises that cannot withstand scrutiny, and further is really a mélange of other criteria already set forth.

(7) Just Means.   This criterion is also stated in many different ways; many denominations have added conditions such as "discrimination" (between combatants and noncombatants) and "proportionality" (in the selection of means) in determining whether the war is just. International law separates the regulation of the decision to go to war (*jus ad bellum*, or law *of* war) from the regulation of its execution (*jus in bello*, or law *in* war), and that separation is appropriate in the Christian just war tradition as well. In this criterion there is substantial agreement among all the denominations.

The next seven chapters are devoted to exploring in detail each of the criteria above, tracing its history and development, exploring its modern application (including in some cases a discussion of its very validity), and assessing the consequences and remedies (if any) for the failure to satisfy it.

II

JUST WAR CRITERIA

Proper Authority

$\mathcal{T}$he criterion of proper authority distinguishes war from crime. Both involve the taking of human life and destruction of property, but while murder and destruction are immoral and unlawful, a properly executed war carries no such consequences or stigma. The need for proper authority to wage war is inherent in its very definition. Following the etymology of the Latin word *bellum*, Gentili defines war as "a just and public contest of arms,"[1] with the word "public" denoting that war be waged between nations, that is, between sovereigns. The use of force between private persons does not qualify as "war" because of their ability to appeal their grievances to a higher authority (the sovereign).[2] The concept of war, to Gentili, can *only* refer to a contest between sovereigns, for lack of any other involuntary forum to adjudicate disputes and enforce its decisions.[3] This criterion thus limits the purview of war to the organs and instrumentalities of the sovereign, that is, the national government.

ORIGIN AND DEVELOPMENT

Augustine writes that "the authority and the decision to undertake war rest with the ruler."[4] Since the sovereign ruler is answerable to none except God, and God works through the sovereign, it follows that a war carried out without proper authority would usurp the role of both. Consequently, reasons Augustine, the authority for executing a decision to make war rests with the officials of the sovereign (the soldiers) exclusively.[5] In his treatise on canon law, Gratian also addresses the question of authority, within the context of executing punishment for sin. Wars could be undertaken only by the command of God or legitimate earthly rulers;[6] those who kill without authority are guilty of murder.[7] Hostiensis follows Gratian's lead,[8] thus solidifying the principle that a war against sinners, conducted without proper authority, is little more than brigandage.

These developments set the stage for the formulation of Thomas Aquinas:

> In order for a war to be just, three things are necessary. First, the authority of the sovereign by whose command the war is to be waged. For it is not the business of a private person to declare war, because he can seek for redress of his rights from the tribunal of his superior. . . . [A]s the care of the common weal is committed to those who are in authority, it is their business to watch over the common weal of the city, kingdom or province subject to them. And just as it is lawful for them to have recourse to the material sword in defending that common weal against internal disturbances, when they punish evil-doers, [here follows a passage from Romans 13:4] . . . so too, it is their business to have recourse to the sword of war in defending the common weal against external enemies.[9]

The most significant aspect of the Thomist iteration is its placement—first.[10] Implicit in his ordering of criteria is the assumption that war is *by definition* an act of state, proclaimed and executed by those who speak and act on the state's behalf.[11] By the twentieth century this criterion was so well settled that significant explorations of proper authority were limited to the lawfulness of war by subordinates against their superiors.[12]

On the national level, American churches have affirmed the need for a public authority to legitimize the resort to war, but in a fairly summary manner, rendering their positions somewhat inconsistent. Compare the following:

> [W]ar must be declared by those with responsibility for public order, not by private groups or individuals. [Catholic][13]

> [A] just war must be declared by a legitimate government. [ELCA][14]

> Since the use of military force is the prerogative of government and not of private individuals, properly constituted procedure for declaring the waging of war must be followed. [LCMS][15]

> A just war must be explicitly declared by a legitimate authority. [PCUSA][16]

> It is the function of the civil government in a fallen world to maintain justice and peace. [PCA][17]

> War must be declared by legitimate authority. [Episcopal][18]

Only duly constituted public authorities may use deadly force or wage war. [Episcopal][19]

A decision for war may be made and declared only by a properly constituted governmental authority. [Methodist][20]

The use of military force is only the prerogative of governments. Consequently, only the duly constituted civil authority can legitimatize military action. . . . [T]he authorizing vehicle is a declaration of war. [SBC][21]

All the churches above legitimize only public wars, never private wars. It is also interesting that most of the statements include a requirement that the war be "declared"; we shall return to this subject shortly.

The differences in the formulations of this criterion are significant. Several characterize proper authority as the "legitimate" government (presumably of a state) and others even go so far as to designate the "properly" or "duly constituted" government or public authority. This formulation forecloses the authority of a government that is recognized by other states (thereby achieving legitimacy on the international plane), but which came to power though extra-constitutional means. This approach ignores the practical necessities of international relations, as many governments fall within this category. In contrast, the Catholic formulation makes no distinction between a legitimate and illegitimate authority, as long as that authority is responsible for maintaining public order. The formula of the LCMS is unusual; its focuses on whether the war has been declared in accordance with that state's law. Paul Jersild of the ELCA has also made this connection.[22]

AUTHORITY TO WAGE WAR
CONSIDERED ON DIFFERENT LEVELS

There are many shades of proper authority to use force. On an individual level, the state's monopoly on force is suspended at the moment the individual is being attacked and has an immediate need to ward off the attacker, pending the arrival of law enforcement. Hence Victoria recognizes that even though only the sovereign can declare war, any private person can defend himself against attack.[23] The individual right to self-defense is not predicated on requesting and being granted express permission to strike back at the aggressor. However, once the self-defense becomes organized on a corporate level, or when the use of force is not defensive against an immediate attack but rather offensive to remedy an injury, the inherent right of self-defense by individuals no longer applies. At that point the use of force must flow from some higher authority.

That authority may be granted on an *ad hoc* basis, such as the formal declaration of hostilities, or pursuant to directives promulgated in advance. The Standing Rules of Engagement for U.S. Forces is an example of the latter. Under these rules, U.S. military forces are authorized to use force in self-defense or collective defense without having to seek specific authorization (as long as an immediate attack exists or is imminent). However, U.S. forces have this authority only because it has been granted to them in advance by the state, that is, those who "speak for" the U.S. government. They do *not* have the independent authority to engage in offensive operations.

Thus the criterion of proper authority serves two purposes. First, it contributes to public order by reaffirming the consolidation of the power of the sword to the state. By prohibiting "private wars," that is, military operations by nonstate actors against the people or governments of other states, it contributes to public order on the global level. Second, it imposes a "cooling off" period, whereby those who wield the power of the sword, and who may otherwise be prone to act rashly, are forced to submit their rationale to higher authority (or a collective one) for evaluation.

However, while the basic premise of the criterion is sound, most Protestant formulations are too narrow. Phrases such as "duly constituted civil authority" denote a regime that has assumed authority in accordance with the regularly constituted means for selecting (and changing) the individual regime elites. A constitutionally elected government is "legitimate" and so, arguably, is a peaceful change of hands within the ruling party of an authoritarian state. It excludes a regime that seizes power in a coup. Nevertheless, such a regime is the *de facto* "civil authority" and as such it bears the responsibility for maintaining public order and protecting the state from outside harm. Such responsibility flows independently of political recognition from other states, and even whether or not the new regime desires it. The PCA's formulation, on the other hand, rightly acknowledges the function of the "civil government" to maintain justice and peace, without further elaboration or judgments of how that regime came to power. A war undertaken by an illegitimate, but *de facto*, government is still a public war, not a private war, and that is the real distinction between a war conducted under proper authority and one that is not. Thus the Catholic formulation, that the war must be conducted by "those with responsibility for public order," may be broader but is actually more precise.

MULTILATERAL AUTHORITY?

In the twenty-first century, we must also consider whether an international organization has the authority to initiate a war, specifically the United Nations

Security Council. All 192 members of the United Nations, including the United States, have agreed to an arrangement by which the Security Council, a body of five permanent members and ten additional members elected from the General Assembly, take up matters that threaten international peace and security. By a majority vote, including concurring votes from all five permanent members,[24] the Security Council can make recommendations as to courses of action under chapter 6 of the U.N. Charter, or even direct states to engage in or refrain from some act under chapter 7. The Security Council has the power to make its provisions mandatory, and enforce them by force if necessary, because the member states of the U.N. have delegated to the Council the authority to do so.[25]

The Security Council goes to war in two ways. The first, most common way is to authorize member states to use force against a specific state for a specific purpose, such as to liberate Kuwait from Iraqi occupation during the Gulf War[26] or to force the restoration of the legitimately elected government of Haiti in 1994.[27] For the purpose of proper authority, however, there is no difference between this scenario and states waging war on their own initiatives. A Security Council authorization does not *mandate* a state to use force, it simply legitimizes it legally and politically. The choice is then left to the states to decide for themselves whether to exercise that authority. Richard Land of the SBC correctly emphasizes this point when he writes, "However helpful a United Nations Security Council vote may be, for Americans the duly constituted authority is the government of the United States."[28]

The second way the Security Council goes to war is through U.N. forces, which states have donated to serve in one of the many ongoing peacekeeping operations today. The U.N. does not often deploy peacekeeping forces without the consent of the host state, but in those rare cases when it does, the Council is effectively committing what would be an act of war if committed by any other state. For example, the Council deployed the United Nations Operation in Somalia (UNOSOM) to that country in 1992, following a cease-fire agreement between the two main rivals for power there, as a chapter 6 "recommendatory" measure.[29] However, the force did not enjoy full consent and cooperation from the local authorities and the Council remanded the operation under chapter 7, giving UNOSOM the power to achieve its mission by force if necessary.[30] Rarer still, but not unheard of, is a decision of the Council to authorize (or order) a U.N. force to engage in offensive operations. This the Council did in 1961 when it authorized the United Nations Operation in the Congo (ONUC; the acronym is derived from the French name), which was already there at the consent of the rival political factions, to use force to stop all military operations and control armed factions in Katanga province.[31] Since Katanga province was controlled by a rebel faction intent on seceding from the Congo, this authorization effectively put the U.N. at war with the secessionist movement. The Council put the U.N. on a war-footing again in 1993 in the former Yugoslavia, where it authorized the United Nations Protection Force (UNPROFOR) to use force to stop Serb shelling of Bosnian Muslim enclaves and obstruction of humanitarian relief.[32] In both of these cases, the U.N. carried out offensive operations as a state would do, but only because member states volunteered their own military forces to carry them out. While the Council may have legal authority to commit the U.N. to war, its real power is only as effective as the forces of states that are willing to enforce its decisions.

THE ROLE OF GOD IN AUTHORITY TO WAGE WAR

The need for proper authority to use force in self-defense in an urgent situation exposes a fault in one aspect of the just war doctrine in the Mormon Church, that God must (and does) intervene in the decision-making process directly and unambiguously. No Mormon scripture or official writing of the church imposes any criterion of proper authority, at least not any earthly authority, on a just war.[33] Before the Mormon community is permitted to engage in war, it must bring its grievances to God, and only upon a specific command from God can the Mormons proceed. Lest this proscription be explained away by distinguishing it from a defensive war, scripture further admonishes Mormons to seek divine approval to resort to war even after multiple injuries.[34] The procedure is not unlike the *jus fetiale* in Roman law, in which the justness of the cause was decided on religious grounds.[35] The Roman *jus fetiale*, however, dispensed with this requirement in cases of self-defense, that is, "a sudden and violent attack was made by a foreign nation, or when that nation had already been committing various acts of open hostility."[36] In contrast, the Mormon *jus fetiale* makes no provision for national self-defense when the urgency of the situation makes it impossible or impractical to suffer four separate attacks. In a nuclear age, it is conceivable that a nation could be rendered defenseless or even destroyed on the first blow. Moreover, it seems unreasonable to force a state to endure *four* attacks, even noncrippling ones; imagine if the U.S. could only strike back at al-Qaida after four 9/11s.

The other problem with the Mormon *jus fetiale* is the same one that is inherent in any divinely commanded defense ethic—it blurs the distinction between holy war and just war. In Roman thought, as long as Rome's cause was superior (as determined by Romans), victory would be assured by the gods.[37] Similarly, the Mormon *jus fetiale* is a petition to God to go to war on their behalf: "And I, the Lord, would fight their battles, and their children's battles, and

their children's children, until they had avenged themselves on all their enemies, to the third and fourth generation."[38] This transforms a defensive war
into a holy war, exposing it to all the excesses and abuses of the holy war trajectory. The reference to the fourth generation furthermore suggests that the
war would effectively never end, even after the genuine threat has long since
subsided. For these reasons, it ought to suffice that the state be the proper authority for waging war.

FORMAL DECLARATION

As noted above, most of the modern churches' restatements of just war criteria require a "declaration" of war, that is, an announcement to the enemy of
the state of hostilities, or at least a public proclamation in a forum accessible
to the enemy. Essentially, it prohibits "secret wars." The PCUSA would require
that the state of hostilities be "explicitly declared" and the LCMS even labels
this criterion "formal declaration," rather than proper or legitimate authority.

This condition did not originate from Thomas Aquinas. Thomas's criterion is not a *declaration* of war from a prince with the authority to make it, but
only the authority itself. Nor did it originate from Augustine, who actually argues against such a condition.[39] The first inclusion of formal declaration as a
condition for a just war appears to be from Isidore of Seville, who in the seventh century defines a just war as "one waged on predication (by an edict)" for
various causes, but which ironically makes no mention of the need for proper
authority to make such a declaration.[40]

The early fathers of international law, both religious and secular, did not
treat the requirement of formal declaration consistently. Victoria and Suarez
both affirm the exclusive prerogative of the sovereign to declare and wage
war.[41] The existence of a declaration is assumed but not explicitly required.
Suarez's introductory summary of the conditions for an "honorable" war includes that "the war must be *undertaken* by a legitimate power," but omits the
word "declare."[42] Gentili quotes a passage from Pomponius that defines the enemy as "those who have officially declared war upon us, or upon whom we
have officially declared war; all others are brigands or pirates," but immediately
rephrases it in terms of who directs the war (the sovereign), not whether it is
formally declared.[43] In contrast, Grotius concludes in his exposition of the
concept of public war that it must be publicly declared, not only to the people of that state, but also communicated to the other side.[44]

The rationale for this added condition of formal declaration is unclear.
Perhaps its proponents had in mind the passage from Deuteronomy that reads,
"When you draw near to a town to fight against it, offer it terms of peace."[45]

This instruction, however, assumes that Israelite forces have already reached the city and surrounded it. God does not instruct them to declare their intent to march upon the city *before* they embark on the journey. The fact that the city's people are subject to enslavement (instead of death) if they do not resist (Deuteronomy 20:11-12) is evidence that the state of war commences even before the Israelite armies begin their march. The Bible mentions no other requirement to declare a state of hostilities before they are carried out. The purpose of the Deuteronomic instruction was not as much to impose a formal code of chivalry on the Israelites as it was to spare the city and its people from the death and destruction that would result if they resisted. This position is reflected in Thomas Aquinas's treatment of ambushes, in which he points out that unless the element of surprise is secured by treachery or perfidy,[46] nothing about ambushes is unjust or unrighteous; as authority for this proposition he quotes Augustine and God's commands to the Israelites to ambush the city of Ai.[47] Indeed, such a requirement is counterproductive. A declaration of war is essentially an announcement to the enemy of the intent to attack it, which gives the enemy the opportunity to prepare by fortifying its defenses and mobilizing its armed forces. The military advantage of surprise, which is a fundamental aspect of good military strategy, is thus lost, making victory more difficult. The element of surprise, like war itself, is no more than a tool of statecraft, which both evil and good wield. Since there is no Biblical basis for a requirement that war be formally declared, there should be no such requirement in Christian just war theory.

There is even less support for the proposition, advanced by the LCMS, that the criterion of proper authority is dependent on a declaration of war made pursuant to a "properly constituted procedure." This position does have support in Jewish law, which requires that an optional (i.e., offensive) war be undertaken only with the approval of the Great Sanhedrin, which is a body of 71 judges.[48] Indeed, it is the preferred practice that the use of force by a state conform to that state's own internal law. However, the consequence of denying proper authority to a state that has undertaken a war in contravention of its own internal procedures is to punish the foot soldiers for the bad decisions of the regime elites. Recall that the rationale for this criterion articulated by Thomas Aquinas was to dichotomize proper authority between the state and the private individual; legitimate acts of war that would be lawful if carried out by order of the state are unlawful (and criminal) if carried out by private individuals with no such authorization. Such authority defines the difference between a lawful combatant, who if captured is repatriated at the end of hostilities, and an unlawful combatant, who may be tried, convicted, and sentenced in a criminal proceeding for the same acts.[49] This dichotomy makes no distinction between decisions to use force that are made in accordance with

the state's internal law and decisions made in violation of it. The duties of ordinary military members to carry out their orders are the same, and so therefore must their treatment be, if captured during hostilities.

FAILURE TO SATISFY THE CRITERION

Christian prudence and the maintenance of order in a fallen world both mandate that war be initiated only by the proper authority, which is the state. But
does the failure of an armed conflict to satisfy this criterion make it unjust?
The answer to this question depends partly on who is asking it. Viewed
through the lens of international law, this criterion makes sense, for only states
have full legal personality and it is the law of nations that immunizes a lawful
combatant from criminal liability for acts that would otherwise be punishable
in criminal law. From the perspective of maintaining international peace and
security, it also makes sense, for the more prospective parties to an armed conflict, the greater the potential for a kind of disorder that is antithetical to God's
design. We do not want armed private actors forcing national governments
into conflicts, nor do we want national policies or strategies to be influenced
by intimidation and coercion. The atrocities by insurgents in Bosnia, Sierra
Leone, Liberia, and Iraq provide ample cause for pessimism about the ability
of such groups to handle weapons responsibly or charitably. However, this answer assumes that the central government acts reasonably charitably itself, that
is, not grossly violating fundamental human rights on a large scale, or otherwise giving the population sufficient cause for revolt. When this assumption is
invalid, the question whether proper authority is always linked to the central
government will be answered differently. This situation will be addressed in
chapters 11 and 12.

Assuming that the lack of proper authority to wage war renders the war
unjust, is such a defect curable? It is possible to convert an unjust war (for
lack of proper authority) into a just war, but only if a state assumes authority over the fighters and adopts their cause as its own. The case of the American hostages in Iran illustrates how this can happen. In 1979, a student
group calling itself the "Muslim Student Followers of the Imam's Policy"
stormed the U.S. embassy and consulates in Iran and took more than 50
Americans hostage. Although the acts of private persons are not normally
imputed to the state, the state does have a duty in international law to diligently prevent and punish wrongdoing by its people that injure other states.[50]
Evidence presented in the International Court of Justice showed that even
though there was no proof that the group was acting as agents or organs of

the Iranian government at the time of the hostage-taking, the central government willingly permitted the incident to happen.[51] In addition, the Iranian head of state, Ayatollah Khomeini, along with his foreign minister, publicly endorsed the hostage-taking and Khomeini further declared his intent to hold the hostages until his demands were met. The Court therefore found the continued detention to be converted to an act of state.[52] Of course, the fact that the hostage-taking was imputed to Iran did not legitimize it, for there was no just cause, but the fact that the government adopted it as its own shifted the responsibility from the hostage takers to the Iranian state itself. If a private group embarks on a war against another state, and the group's own state adopts its cause as its own and commits its own forces to it, then the original lack of proper authority is remedied.

But caution must be exercised in how and when states are held accountable for the acts of private persons. The relation of Afghanistan to the 9/11 attack illustrates this point. In addition to responsibility by endorsement, international law also imposes vicarious responsibility for acts of private persons when the state fails to take measures to prevent or punish them.[53] When al-Qaida perpetrated the 9/11 attack on the United States, it was sheltered and materially supported by the Taliban, a group of extremely conservative Islamist armed fighters that had taken over the government of Afghanistan in 1995. Although only a few states recognized the Taliban as the legitimate government of Afghanistan, the Taliban held *de facto* political power and thus had a duty to fulfill the international obligations of the Afghan state. One of those duties, of course, is not to attack other states, and especially not to commit terrorist attacks against them. Because the *de facto* government of Afghanistan permitted al-Qaida to perpetrate attacks from its territory and continued to shelter them afterward, Afghanistan became responsible for the attack and was subject to the same treatment as if it had carried out the attack itself. After the attack, the United States provided material support for various rebel groups to overthrow the Taliban. The regime elites of the Afghan government today (which *does* enjoy broad recognition) did not perpetrate the attack. For most acts of state this would not matter; a state is not absolved of responsibility simply because of a change of administration (even a forcible one), especially in commercial matters. In this instance, however, it would have been unfair to bomb Kabul, exact reparations from, and impute responsibility to the new government, which disavowed the attack and even the ideology of the former regime. This scenario raises the possibility that proper authority, once achieved, can also be destroyed, if the individual regime elites who perpetrated the attack are ousted from power and the new regime repudiates it and makes a genuine effort to bring the elites of the former regime to justice.

CONCLUSION

The criterion of proper authority speaks to the dichotomy of force by the state and the actions of private persons. This dichotomy distinguishes official acts of war, upon which certain legal statuses and protections are conferred, from criminal acts of brigandage. This criterion should not be confused with, or contaminated by, formal declarations of hostilities or compliance with a state's internal *jus fetiale*, neither of which are relevant to the distinction between state and non-state actors, nor to the consequences of that distinction.

We move now to the second criterion for a just war, just cause, which is submitted as the most fundamentally crucial, after proper authority.

• 5 •

Just Cause

$\mathscr{T}$he criterion of just cause embodies the notion that the use of force must have some rationally moral purpose to be legitimate in law, politics, and ethics. In the Western lexicon, "just cause" refers to the existence of an injury at the hands of another—a wrong to be righted. It should not be confused with the related principle of defining what manner of remedy to that injury is appropriate. That question is addressed separately in chapter 7, on proportionality of cause, which in statecraft defines what injury is sufficient to legitimize the drastic and imprecise solution of war. Instead, this chapter speaks only to what constitutes an injury in statecraft, without regard to proportionality. Viewed from another angle, this chapter addresses the function of military force in statecraft, that is, what purpose legitimate force strives to serve. That question makes the criterion of just cause the most hotly debated.

ORIGIN AND DEVELOPMENT

In Western civilization, the concept of just cause is nearly as old as Western civilization itself. The ancient Greeks considered war the instrument by which peace was obtained and secured,[1] and were the first to trace the root cause of war to an injury at the hands of another state: wrongful enslavement, wrongful conquest, unprovoked raids, and wrongful acquisition of property, to name a few.[2] It was the Romans, however, who introduced the term "just war" (*bellum justum*) to the Western lexicon. The reader has already been introduced to the process by which Rome embarked on an offensive war; one element of the *jus fetiale* was a determination of a *casus belli*, a cause or injury that when sustained was worthy of war, such as hostile territorial incursions, deserting an alliance with Rome, or unjustified violations of the rights of Rome (as determined by Rome).[3] Cicero wrote, "wars are unjust when they are undertaken without proper cause. No just war can be waged except for the sake of punishing or repelling an enemy."[4] As the Romans introduced their legal system to much of Europe and the Mediterranean, including the cradle of Christianity, it stands to reason that, as a component of Roman legal theory, just war theory would find its way into Christendom.

The nature of the injuries providing just cause for Christian war has evolved considerably over time. The first Christian writing to acknowledge the distinction between righteous and unrighteous wars was that of Origen, to whom "battles for the defence of the fatherland" constituted a just cause for war.[5] After the conversion of Emperor Constantine and the legitimization of Christianity within the Roman Empire, Ambrose successfully merged Christian ethics with the Ciceronian tradition of public and private duties to derive rationales for self-preservation, defense of others, and intervention. "Fortitude," he writes, "which in war preserves the country from the barbarians . . . or defends one's neighbours from robbers, is full of justice."[6] Ambrose regards intervention as a charitable duty, relying on the words of King Solomon, "Deliver them that are led to death."[7]

Augustine follows Ambrose's Ciceronian approach, equating a breach of the peace with the commission of an injustice. A just war, to Augustine, is that which redresses an injury. Nine years after the sacking of Rome at the hands of the Goths, Augustine defines just wars as "those which avenge injuries, when the nation or city against which warlike action is to be directed has neglected either to punish wrongs committed by its own citizens or to restore what has been unjustly taken by it."[8] From this definition it may be inferred that a war undertaken with an evil purpose—love of killing or destruction, anger, desire for power, and so forth—is an unjust cause. Conquest for conquest's sake is unjust[9] but defense of one's homeland, people, and property is just.[10]

Although Augustine frames Christian war in terms of combating sin, on the plane of statecraft he is expanding the role of war in maintaining order in the material world, a function that became imperative once Christendom acquired temporal political power and responsibility. In the ninth century, amid internal unrest in the Holy Roman Empire following the death of Charlemagne, church officials seized upon this need and assigned that role to the church. Agobard, Archbishop of Lyon, views the internal dissension as unjust, advocating the forcible pacification of barbarians both within the Empire and on its borders.[11] Hincmar, Archbishop of Reims, favors war to quell strife between Christian rulers and officials within the Empire, which Hincmar saw as unjust and unworthy of Christian leaders.[12] During the Crusades, just war theorists were more focused on defense (especially of Christendom) and recovery,[13] but by the thirteenth century the

Crusading fervor had begun to subside, enabling the theological literature of the church to shift from expositions and analyses of individual rulings to more holistic compilations of Christian philosophy. Thomas Aquinas, along with his immediate predecessors and successors,[14] thus explores war within the broader framework of sins contrary to peace, couching just cause more in terms of maintaining peace and preserving order than of any specific injury.

Thomas phrases the criterion of just cause rather curtly: "namely that those who are attacked should be attacked because they deserve it on account of some fault."[15] In doing so, Thomas, like Augustine, views war through the lens of fraternal correction, as an act of charity that all Christians have a duty to carry out.[16] The sin of strife, which Thomas intends to denote fighting between individuals, is the result of quarrelsomeness, engendered by anger[17] and the *sin* of war (as opposed to the *virtue* of war) is waged for the purpose of self-aggrandizement or cruelty.[18] The commonality of these sins, along with the vices contrary to peace such as schism and sedition,[19] is that they are committed with pride and placement of personal desire over the common good. The Thomist restatement of just cause is worded very simply but the words are packed with meaning.

The Thomist concept of just cause is evident in the work of Victoria, who finds the "avenging of wrongs" a necessary aspect of protection, for "wrongdoers would become readier and bolder for wrongdoing, if they could do wrong with impunity,"[20] thus also affirming the Augustinian concept of force to maintain a just order. Victoria's summation of just cause for an offensive war is similarly curt: "There is a single and only just cause for commencing a war, namely, a wrong received."[21] Victoria's statement, however, lacks the Thomist expression of proportionality; whereas in Thomas's formulation the enemy must "deserve" war because the injury is grave enough to justify it, in Victoria's formulation that limitation is absent.

The formulation of just cause took a more legalistic turn at the hands of Suarez, whose work *De Bello* is regarded as an early text on international law. Unlike Thomas Aquinas, who treats sinful war as an outward expression of sinful pride, Suarez focuses on the earthly ramifications of that pride, specifically the injuries to state by which sinful pride manifests itself, methodically enumerating several types of just causes, and setting the stage for centuries of vigorous debate. We shall return to Suarez momentarily.

MODERN CHURCHES' RESTATEMENTS OF JUST CAUSE

Today the ongoing debate is not whether just cause is a necessary criterion for a just war, but rather how that cause will be defined, that is, what manner of event or injury warrants the drastic and messy solution of war. Consequently, the differences between denominations, and even within them, range from subtle to profound:

> *[F]or legitimate defense by military force* . . . the damage inflicted by the aggressor on the nation or community of nations must be lasting, grave, and certain. [Catholic Catechism][22]

> War is permissible only to confront a 'real and certain danger,' i.e., to protect innocent life, to preserve conditions necessary for decent human existence, and to secure basic human rights. [National Conference of Catholic Bishops][23]

> [O]ne must have a just cause before considering war. The kingdom of God promises not only peace but life, wholeness, equality, harmony, freedom, and joy. [ELCA][24]

> *The cause must be just.* This is usually understood to mean that the nation must defend itself against attack, preserving an order that serves its citizens and preserving the lives of innocent citizens. [ELCA][25]

> The right to self-defense against an aggressor has consistently been regarded as fundamental. Only defensive war is legitimate. [LCMS][26]

> War can be just only if employed to defend a stable order or morally preferable cause against threats of destruction or the rise of injustice. [PCUSA][27]

> A just war is simply war undertaken and conducted in the defense and promotion of the dictates of justice. [PCA][28]

> Force may be used only to correct a grave, public evil, i.e., aggression or massive violation of the basic rights of whole populations. [Episcopal General Convention][29]

> [War must be] employed only . . . in the prevention of such evils as genocide, brutal suppression of human rights, and unprovoked international aggression. [United Methodist Church, *Book of Discipline*][30]

> A decision for war must vindicate justice itself in response to some serious evil, such as an aggressive attack. [United Methodist Council of Bishops][31]

> War is only permissible to resist aggression and defend those victimized by it. Only defensive war is defensible. [SBC][32]

And now the design of the Nephites was to support their lands, and their houses, and their wives, and their children, . . . and also that they might preserve their rights . . . and also their liberty [Book of Mormon][33]

From the statements above, four themes emerge. The first is that nearly all of them expressly affirm the right to self-defense against aggression. The exceptions are the Presbyterian statements; they do not speak to self-defense explicitly but that right is implied under the larger umbrella of defending justice or a "morally preferable cause." Self-defense is the one cause upon which all nonpacifist Christian denominations agree. The doctrine of the Mormon Church in this regard is particularly interesting as a most distinctly American interpretation of self-defense: At the core of what a defensive war is fought to defend is not specifically lives or property, but *liberty*. Two commentators, from the LCMS and the SBC, even take the position that self-defense is the *only* just cause for war, which seems like an overly restrictive position in light of the growing body of cases and arguments for the justifiability of humanitarian intervention.

Humanitarian intervention, the use of force to protect human rights, is the second theme visible in the above statements. In contrast to the more conservative LCMS and SBC, the American Catholic bishops and the Episcopal and Methodist churches expressly support military intervention for the protection of human rights. Mormon doctrine is in flux; original Mormon scripture speaks only to a nation's own liberty, but in 2003, the LDS President, Gordon B. Hinckley, opened the door to reassessing that position. In an address before a General Convention of the LDS Church, he said, "[T]here are times and circumstances when nations are justified, in fact have an obligation, to fight for family, for liberty, and *against tyranny*, threat, and oppression. . . . [W]e are a freedom-loving people, committed to the defense of liberty *wherever* it is in jeopardy."[34] Without using the exact words "humanitarian intervention," Hinckley's statement is an unequivocal announcement of his support for the doctrine.

The third and fourth themes that emerge from the passages above are somewhat more vague: war to preserve order and war to promote a moral cause. Defense, to Jersild, includes "preserving an order that serves its citizens and preserving the lives of innocent citizens." To the PCUSA, it includes defending "a stable order" or "morally preferable cause." The PCUSA statement does not elaborate on the meaning of this broad formulation, but other churches do: The PCA defines it as justice; the Episcopal and Methodist churches as defeating evil; the Mormon Church as defense of rights and liberty. There is something to be said for some vagueness; it is far too easy for mischief-makers to skirt around, or "out-lawyer," overly detailed definitions of right conduct. On the other hand, the ELCA formulation (by Childs) is too vague. Childs juxtaposes just cause for war with life, wholeness, equality, harmony, freedom, and joy, suggesting that the deprivation of any of them could constitute a just cause for war. Equating the lack of joy and harmony with the deprivation of life and liberty would substantially lower the threshold of injury constituting just cause, and violate the criterion of proportionality of cause as well (addressed in chapter 7).

There is thus no majority opinion, much less consensus, as to the range of causes that justify war. In assessing the universe of just cause, therefore, it is necessary to return to its doctrinal roots. The formulation of just cause by Suarez, which is the most methodical up to his time, warrants the most detailed study. Suarez enumerates four types of just causes for war: defense, recovery, enforcement of rights, and vindication of honor.[35] Although this formulation seems outdated by today's standards, it sets the standard by which later treatises may be compared. Each of the four types will now be explored.

DEFENSIVE WAR

Suarez, like all just war theorists before and after him, considers a defensive war to be just; "the right of self-defence is natural and necessary."[36] It is a tendency in any discussion of just causes for war to return to the idea that the war is defensive in character, whether it be defense of one's rights, defense of others, or defense of God. Even the Crusades had defensive elements: the Muslim conquest of the Holy Land and encroachment on the Byzantine Empire and the plight of Christians living within those conquered lands. Gratian, writing during the Crusades, proclaims the righteousness of war to defend Christian lands from attack by non-Christians.[37] In the following century, when Crusade fervor had subsided somewhat, it sufficed to simply affirm a defensive war as just.[38] Although Thomas Aquinas does not specifically mention defense as a just cause, his contemporaries do: Vincent of Beauvais presents war as necessary to preserve liberty and territory[39] and Ptolemy of Lucca deems the maintenance of an army to defend against external aggression and to assist the prince in preserving justice to be a part of good government.[40] In contrast, Giovanni da Legnano's emphasis is on defense of the person, that is, against *bodily* danger.[41] An emphasis on personal defense is also implied by Victoria, who goes out of his way to find a right of self-defense in natural law, even by nonstate entities.[42] From the above, two components of defense are discernable: defense of the person and defense of the nation.

Personal Defense

Catechisms of various denominations, from the sixteenth century to today, have all qualified the commandment "You shall not kill [or murder]" as a proscription against aggression. The Catholic Catechism of the Council of Trent says, "If a man kill another in self-defence, having used every means consistent with his *own safety* to avoid the infliction of death, he evidently does not violate this Commandment."[43] The Catechism of St. Pius X reads, "It is lawful to kill when fighting in a just war; . . . and, finally, in cases of necessary and lawful defense of *one's own life* against an unjust aggressor."[44] The Larger Catechism of the Presbyterian Church includes among the duties required of this commandment, "to preserve the life of ourselves and others . . . by just defense thereof against violence."[45] The Doctrine and Covenants of the Mormon Church also unequivocally supports the right of individual self-defense when necessary[46] and the modern *Catechism of the Catholic Church* does the same: "Someone who defends his life is not guilty of murder even if he is forced to deal his aggressor a lethal blow."[47] In contrast, the catechism of the Lutheran Church makes no provision for defending one's *own* person (as opposed to others), leaving that function to God and government.[48]

The Lutheran approach appears to best exemplify the charitable approach to personal defense. Luther writes, "This commandment aims at this, that no one offend his neighbor on account of any evil deed, even though he have fully deserved it."[49] If the Christian ideal is to defend not oneself, but another, then it is incumbent on Christians to refrain from resisting aggression, instead relying on the aid of those who are legally responsible for safeguarding the lives of the people. But Luther also writes, "under this commandment not only he is guilty who does evil to his neighbor, but he also who can do him good, prevent, resist evil, defend and save him, so that no bodily harm or hurt happen to him, and yet does not do it."[50] Christians who *are* responsible for protecting others, or are able but fail to come to another's aid, have violated their duty to God. The modern Catholic catechism, in contrast, takes a more self-centered position: "Love toward oneself remains a fundamental principle of morality. Therefore it is legitimate to insist on respect for one's own right to life."[51] Perhaps the Catholic Church is simply trying to be practical, acknowledging the power of the survival instinct that is innate in all forms of life. But Christians are called to rise above their primal instincts by loving their neighbors as they love themselves. In the alternative, perhaps the passage is intended to affirm the right—or even duty—to make one's best effort to restrain sin, for "[t]he defense of the common good requires that an unjust aggressor be rendered unable to cause harm"[52] and even Luther admits that restraining sinners is necessary to prevent human depravity.[53] But to construe these points as supporting the virtue of individual self-defense is to read them out of context, for in both instances the real argument being made is for the virtue of the role of the government (civil magistrate) in defending the people.

Although the Lutheran position may be the purest ideologically, the Mormon position achieves the optimum balance between virtue and practicality in a fallen world. Doctrine and Covenants 134:11 reads,

> We believe that men should appeal to the civil law for redress of all wrongs and grievances, where personal abuse is inflicted or the right of property or character infringed, where such laws exist as will protect the same; but we believe that all men are justified in defending themselves, their friends, and property, and the government, from the unlawful assaults and encroachments of all persons in times of exigency, where immediate appeal cannot be made to the laws, and relief afforded.[54]

The Doctrine expresses a preference that the injured person appeal to authority for redress *first*, before taking matters into his own hands. But if redress cannot be had from authority, or if the person needs immediate help and would suffer irreparable harm without it, the right of self-help is affirmed.

So to what extent is defense from bodily harm charitable? For an individual, the most charitable form of defense is intended to prevent or alleviate harm to another. It could also encompass defense of one's home, in order to protect the family, or defense of one's person to avoid the loss of the family's breadwinner. For military forces and police, it encompasses defense of their persons in order to remain capable of carrying out their responsibility to defend others (and we assume a genuine need to carry out that responsibility, otherwise the argument is circular). For a community or nation, charitable self-defense includes all of these things and more, which is the next topic.

National Defense

Only a few denominations offer any substantive position as to what self-defense, considered on a national level, really is. Most seem content to simply affirm the right and move on, for example, the Methodist justification of war to stop "unprovoked international aggression," without further elaboration.[55] "Aggression," however, comes in many forms and is seldom as undisputedly recognizable as Iraq's invasion of Kuwait. It has been established that Christian charity provides for the right of a state to defend its people from bodily harm. But few "unprovoked international aggressions" are executed specifically to inflict bodily harm; a right to national defense so limited would preclude the right to resist an enemy whose object was not to exterminate, but instead enslave or expel, or substitute its own civil authority (which is the most common purpose).

The Catholic, Presbyterian, and Mormon churches offer more comprehensive definitions of national defense, allowing the possibility of a just war to defend freedom and human dignity. This is the root of general support among churches for American participation in World War II against the Nazis, as exemplified by the Presbyterian statement that "the cause which our nation is at war is just and righteous and that our freedom, culture and our historic faith are dependent upon the outcome of this conflict."[56] The Book of Mormon is quite revealing as to the priorities on national defense. The book of Alma recounts the story of the leader of the Nephites, Moroni, whose people are under threat of attack by the Lamanites: "he was preparing to support their liberty, their lands, their wives, and their children, and their peace."[57] Observe that defense of liberty comes first, then territory, then people—a position reiterated by several LDS presidents in the twentieth century.[58] Conspicuously absent is any mention of the Nephite warriors fighting to defend *themselves*.

All of the above writings have rightly seized on the point that national defense does not, and cannot, consist only of saving the nation's people from genocide, mass rape, or wanton plunder. Protecting the lives and property of the state's people from external attacks or threats is the beginning of charitable self-defense, not the end. It is generally legitimate, and within the confines of charity, for a state to prevent its territory from being seized by another state; what it is really defending is the right of the inhabitants to retain their cultural and national identities (which is often linked to their geographic locations). Defense of the state is also necessary to protect the people's liberty—not merely freedom from mass enslavement but also the right to choose their leaders, governments, and national, cultural, and religious identities.

Finally, a state's duty to its people does not end at its borders. States have the responsibility to safeguard the well-being of its nationals abroad as well (within the boundaries of legitimate rights of other states). If the use of force is necessary to rescue its nationals from harm (and the harm is not of their own making), then it may be justified, but only for that specific purpose. Such operations can range from an evacuation operation, in which foreign nationals are offered transportation out of a war or disaster zone, to a hostage rescue operation, in which force is engaged against the hostage takers. Examples of the former category include evacuations during the Liberian civil war of the 1990s; examples of the latter include the Israeli hostage rescue at Entebbe in 1977 and the U.S. attempt to rescue the Teheran hostages in 1980. In each case, the operations had limited objectives, which were to defend the nation's people from harm.

OFFENSIVE WAR

The distinction between proper authority to conduct defensive and offensive wars, articulated by Cajetan and Victoria,[59] lays the groundwork for Suarez to treat them separately with regard to just cause as well. He frames this treatment around the *initiation* of war as a means of redress for an injury; as to the proper grounds for an offensive war, Suarez writes, "just and sufficient for war is the infliction of a grave injustice which cannot be avenged or repaired in any other way."[60] He divides justifications for offensive war into three types: recovery, enforcement of rights, and vindication of honor.[61]

Recovery

This category of just cause, precipitated by the seizure of and refusal to restore property, is traceable to Augustine, who defines a just war as, among other things, "to return something that was wrongfully taken."[62] Later authors interpret Augustine literally, theorizing wars to recover stolen goods (Isidore of Seville, Gratian, and Laurentius Hispanus).[63] The injury suggested by Raymond of Peñafort is more generalized; "recovery of stolen goods" evolves to simply "recovery of property."[64] Thomas Aquinas is not so specific as to just causes for war, though he does quote the passage from Augustine above in support of the criterion overall,[65] as does Victoria.[66] The recovery of property also has the support of pioneers of secular international law such as Grotius and Pufendorf.[67] Indeed, it is Grotius who sets forth the reasoning behind such a cause in the best and simplest terms. Grotius writes,

> I shall not deny that in order to preserve property a robber can even be killed, in case of necessity. For the disparity between property and life is offset by the favourable position of the innocent party and the odious role of the robber. . . . From this it follows, that . . . a thief fleeing with stolen property can be felled with a missile, if the property cannot otherwise be recovered.[68]

All of this, of course, presupposes that the thing to be recovered has been taken unjustly.

But this line of argument draws the objection that a true Christian should not be concerned with the material world: "If someone wants to sue you and take your tunic, let him have your cloak as well" (Matthew 5:40). The response lies in Augustine's concept of charitable force to restrain sin. To love one's neighbor means also to deplore the sinful act, for if the sin is allowed to go unrectified then not only is the sinner emboldened to commit more sin (thus further separating himself from God) but also the potential victims are exposed to greater risk. It is granted that the unjust possession of an object is seldom so great a sin as to warrant forfeiting the sinner's life, and yet the threat of deadly force is a necessary component to the effective functioning of law enforcement—a function that the Sermon on the Mount does not address because it was an exposition on *personal* conduct, not statecraft. In statecraft, absent an available forum for dispute resolution and enforcement between the contenders, states have no option but to resort to self-help to recover things unjustly taken from them.

In further reply, it must be pointed out that the notion of a just war to recover a physical object has little application in the modern world. In Western civilization, the instances of nations embarking on war in response to unjust taking of objects number very few. The closest thing to an exception is the two American wars against the Barbary states in the early 1800s (First Barbary War, 1801–1805; Second Barbary War, aka Algerine War, 1815). Those wars were in response to the scourge of piracy and hostage-taking for ransom along the North African coast, all with the support of Morocco, Algiers, Tunis, and Tripoli, who exacted tribute from the U.S. and other sea-faring states in exchange for safe passage in the Mediterranean. However, the naval operations were motivated more by the desire to protect American sailors than to recover lost goods. Indeed, the world reaction to Iraq's invasion of Kuwait in 1990 suggests that a modern claim to the right of war to recover an object is at best disingenuous, and at worst repudiated. Prior to the invasion, Iraq accused Kuwaiti oil production facilities of slant drilling, a technique by which wells are drilled into the ground at an angle, thereby reaching into reserves in land owned by another. No credible evidence exists to support Iraq's claim, but assuming *arguendo* that the allegation were true, and that no other meaningful remedy were genuinely available to Iraq (also a doubtful proposition), then the manner in which Iraq responded—invading and annexing the entire country instead of only the offending facility, and indiscriminately plundering and raping the Kuwaiti capital—totally belied Iraq's claim of injury.

If the concept of a just war to recover goods has no real-world application, why did it remain part of church doctrine for so long? A possible answer to this question is that Augustine's work reflects the strong influence of pre-Christian Roman and especially Greek philosophy and the wrongful acquisition of property was mentioned by the Greeks as a just cause for war.[69] As Augustine is widely revered even today as the first major figure in Christian just war theory, it is only natural that later Christian scholarship should build on such a premise.

Augustine's restatement of just cause, however, is more general than recovery of physical objects. His phraseology "return something that was wrongfully taken" is not specific as to what that something would be. Although later fathers restate the just cause as recovery of *property*, that is, chattel, Augustine's choice of words suggests another interpretation, that just causes for war include the recovery of *territory* wrongfully taken. The idea of a just war to recover territory *does* have significant real-world application. In contrast to a defensive war to prevent territory from being taken over by another state, a recovery action seeks restoration of territory that was already wrongfully taken from its rightful ruler. If such a cause of action were not available, then aggressors could invade and assume authority over a piece of territory of another state before that other state had time to react, then present the other state (and the world) with a *fait accompli* and deny any further basis for defense because the territory then belonged to the aggressor, that is, there is nothing left to defend. Such an absurd result cannot be permitted.

Finally, Augustine's wording of the objective as the return of something wrongfully taken suggests the possibility of encompassing persons. It would apply most directly to cases in which persons are kidnapped and taken across the border (the root cause of the 2006 war between Israel and Hezbollah forces in Lebanon), but could conceivably apply also to recovering persons who were already in another state but have been wrongfully detained, notably hostage rescue cases. The use of force by states to protect their nationals from harm has already been covered above.

Enforcement of Rights

Suarez's second type of just cause for an offensive war, denial of "common rights of nations" without good cause, is traceable to the Pentateuch. The Israelites requested safe passage through the Amorite kingdom on their way to the Promised Land, pledging not even to eat from the fields or drink from the wells. The Amorite king refused and marched against Israel, whereupon the Israelites destroyed the Amorite kingdom and appropriated its land.[70] Augustine finds the war by Israel to be just, based on the Amorites' refusal to grant Israel its "divine right" of innocent passage.[71] This stance is memorialized in the *Decretum Gratiani*[72] and even finds its way into some secular works.[73] It is curious that few scholars from Augustine to Grotius mention the Amorite episode, yet none of them are willing to refute Augustine's position entirely. The work of Balthazar Ayala is interesting in this regard; Ayala was the Spanish Judge Advocate General and although his 1582 work is more secular in its analysis and authorities than most written in that era, it nevertheless reflects the same Catholic influence as his predecessors. Ayala derives his just causes for war primarily from the right of defense inherent in natural law, but finds defense to also encompass the enforcement or "defense" of rights: "Another just cause of war is to take vengeance for some wrong which has been unjustifiably inflicted,"[74] illustrating his point with biblical examples (including the Israelite war against the Amorites).

This brings us back to Suarez, who defines the second of his three types of just causes for offensive wars as "denial, without reasonable cause, of the common rights of nations, such as the right of transit over highways, trading in common, &c."[75] Did Suarez have in mind the Israelite cause against the Amorites? Suarez does not refer to these rights as "divine" as Augustine does, nor does he mention the Amorite case by name, but his mention of a right of transit is too glaringly close to ignore the association. Perhaps Suarez omitted the citation intentionally, knowing how little open support it had.

In addition to its obvious holy war implications, the "divine right" theory is problematic for another reason. If Suarez really did have the Amorite case in mind, then to hold the enforcement of a divine right of nations as a just cause is to assert that transit and trade are rights of nations in divine or natural law, as opposed to manmade or positive law. Contemporary events would seem to refute this assertion. For example, no reasonable person would consider the United States to have a cause of action against Turkey for its refusal to permit its forces to invade Iraq from Turkish soil in the run-up to the Iraq war, nor would the refusal of one state to engage in trade with another be regarded as a reasonable basis for war. Indeed, the reverse is true—the U.N. Security Council has occasionally authorized the use of force to enforce trade embargoes against various states.[76] We are also faced with the problem of defining which rights of nations are divine. As pointed out in chapter 2, Suarez and Victoria both regard the propagation of Christianity as a right, the denial of which is sufficient to justify conquest of non-Christian peoples.[77] Today however, that position has the support neither of international law nor of the church, which suggests that Victoria and Suarez may have been overreaching. The alternative, that God changed his mind between then and now, violates the eternal nature of God (see Hebrews 13:8). If something as important as saving the souls of nonbelievers (as Victoria and Suarez would put it) cannot justify war, then surely something as comparatively trivial as the right of innocent passage cannot either. A just cause for war to enforce positive rights, based on the one-time case of the Israelites' divine quest to reach the Promised Land, is unworkable by today's legal standards and ethics.

The history of the nineteenth century offers further testimony to why such a formula is unworkable. Georg Friedrich von Martens, whose 1789 treatise on international law was influential in the United States, equates just cause with the "violation of a perfect right."[78] After Martens, most European and virtually all American treatises speak of just wars in terms of preserving the rights of the warring state.[79] The history of European imperialism in the nineteenth century suggests that the kinds of "rights" that were contemplated included the so-called right to conquer. Spain had justified its colonial expansion in the Americas on the basis of the right to preach the Gospel, as preached by Victoria and Suarez; European imperialism in the 1800s was an expanded version of the same. Great Britain solidified its hold on India, France took control of Indo-China, Russia expanded into southwest Asia, and Africa was carved up by five powers. All of this took place under the auspices of the so-called "white man's burden" to spread Western, that is, Christian, civilization. Nor was the United States immune to such temptations; in expanding westward to the Pacific, the U.S. displaced Native Americans from their ancestral lands and contrived a war with Mexico (Mexican War, 1846–1848), all under the mantra of "Manifest Destiny," suggesting some manner of divine right, not unlike the Israelites' claim to the Promised Land. The United States also initiated a war against Spain (Spanish-American War, 1898), ostensibly to liberate Cuba from Spanish oppression, but it also forced Spain to cede Puerto Rico, Guam, and the Philippines.[80] This one element of the just war tradition took on a life of its own, growing into a Leviathan that swallowed up the tradition itself. There being no restraint on the nature of states' "rights," there was no restraint on war.

Enforcement of Rights, Recast as Redress of Injury

A formula of just cause based on enforcement of rights can be made workable, despite the poor illustration that the Amorite case offers, if it is recast as punishing an injury. The reason the Amorite case is a bad example is that God interfered with the outcome by hardening the heart of the Amorite king,[81] thereby creating the very "injury" that the Israelites were meant to avenge. In addition, the two biblical accounts are ambiguous as to which side was the first to march against the other; the Numbers version says it was the Amorites but in the Deuteronomy version God issued his command before the battle takes place. A better biblical example of a war to enforce rights is the case of King David's war against the Ammonites, as cited by Ayala in his treatment of just cause.[82] Upon the death of Nahash, the king of the Ammonites, David sends a delegation to express his sympathy to Nahash's son Hanun. Instead of receiving the delegation, Hanun seizes and humiliates them, then hires an army in anticipation of David's wrath. David responds by destroying the Ammonite kingdom.[83] In contrast to the Amorite case, this case consists of not merely a denial of diplomatic rights, but also an injury to their persons, and by extension an injury to the Israelite kingdom itself. The war against the Ammonites was thus not merely a war to enforce the rights of ambassadors, but also to punish the Ammonites for inflicting a clear, meaningful injury on the Israelite state.

The development of international law from the Roman Empire to today softened the original biblical concept of war to enforce a divine right into war to punish wrongs committed by one state against another. It is Augustine's famous formulation in *Quaestiones in Heptateuchum*, that a just war "avenge[s] injuries,"[84] that carries far greater weight than the Amorite case, and that is the passage that Thomas Aquinas chooses to quote in his articulation of just cause.[85] In turn, the Thomist formula is repeated or cited many times in the works of Cajetan, Victoria, and Molina.[86] The Catholic fathers are in turn cited by secular scholars such as Belli, Gentili, Pufendorf, Wolff, and the father of international law, Hugo Grotius.[87]

The Augustinian concept of *justa bella ulciscuntur injurias*—just war to avenge injuries—does remain relevant and applicable in the modern world. The use of the word *ulciscuntur* is unfortunate, for the modern English translation of the word is burdened with an uncharitable connotation that is incompatible with the Christian duty to love one's neighbors and enemies alike. To dismiss the concept on this basis is to misconstrue what Augustine was trying to convey; far from calling for "revenge," Augustine advocates the use of force for retributive justice. The difference is articulated quite well by Daryl Charles:

> At its base the moral outrage expressed through retributive justice is first and foremost rooted in moral principle, not mere emotional outrage and hatred. . . . *[I]t is virtuous and not vicious to feel anger at moral evil.* . . . Whereas revenge strikes out at real or perceived injury, retribution speaks to an objective wrong. Whereas revenge is wild, insatiable and not subject to limitations, retribution has both upper and lower limits. . . . Vengeance, by its nature, has a thirst for injury and delights in bringing further evil upon the offending party. . . . Retribution has as its goal a greater social good and takes no pleasure in punishment.[88]

Just as punishing children for their infraction is a necessary but unpleasant function of parenting, law-abiding nations must sometimes carry out the equivalent action against lawless nations. In such a case, provided that all other criteria for a just war are met, the Christian duties of love and charity mandate that the possibility of going to war be given its due consideration.

Vindication of Honor

Suarez's third category of just cause for offensive wars is "any grave injury to one's reputation or honour."[89] This passage must not be misunderstood. Suarez is not suggesting that Christian princes should go to war to add to what honor and prestige they may already have; rather, he refers to the restoration of honor lost due to some insult or affront to the prince (and by extension, the state) or to the state's subjects. That Suarez would adopt this position is puzzling; he cites no writings, ecclesiastical or otherwise, in support of this thesis and no major Christian works on just war theory prior to Suarez even proposes it.[90]

To find such a precedent in Western philosophy one must go all the way back to Cicero, who in true Roman fashion writes that "a war is never undertaken by the ideal State, except in defence of its honour or its safety."[91] The Roman concept of a just war includes a variety of causes more akin to diplomatic insult than injury (e.g., deserting an alliance with Rome, refusing to receive an ambassador, or refusing to extradite a person[92]) and even those broad criteria apply only to another equal, sovereign, organized state. They considered any other kind of community, such as a nonindependent state or a band of "savages" (by Roman standards), as free for the conquering.[93] Surely Suarez did not have the Romans in mind in professing the vindication of honor to be a just cause for war. What he did have in mind we will never know; not even James Brown Scott's detailed studies of Suarez contain any discussion of it, nor do they offer any explanation for it.[94]

In natural law, Suarez's proposition does not appear to have been influential. Of the various classical writers on the law of nations according to natural law, only one, Jean-Jacques Burlamaqui, makes any mention of war to vindicate honor, listing as one of the just causes of war "defending ourselves against an insult."[95] Burlamaqui's work, however, is relatively obscure compared to the giants (both naturalist and positivist) who preceded and followed him, such as Gentili, Grotius, Pufendorf, Wolff, Vattel, and Martens, none of whom mention this as a possible just cause for war. The differences in this area between Suarez and Victoria, and Burlamaqui and Vattel, underscore the depth of disagreement on this point among the naturalists, which stretched across sectarian lines—Suarez and Victoria were both Spanish Jesuits and Burlamaqui and Vattel were both Swiss Protestants.

In positive law, however, the notion of a just war to vindicate honor did eventually gain a following. The 1680 work of Johann Wolfgang Textor reduces the concept of just cause for war to redressing a serious grievance, one type of which is a grievance to reputation, that is, by gross outrage or insult.[96] In 1803, Gérard de Rayneval includes as a just cause the reparation of an injury, including any injustice against the nation or offense against the honor and dignity of its head.[97] Wheaton's repudiation of a legal requirement of just cause altogether[98] clears the way for defense of honor to appear as a cause for war in quite a few treatises, including those of the Europeans Heffter, Creasy, and Bluntschli, and the Americans Woolsey and Davis.[99] In view of the rationalization of conquest by the major powers in the nineteenth century, the flimsy excuse of vindication of honor undoubtedly contributed to the demise of the just war tradition during that period.

That Suarez's restatement of just war theory would include vindication of honor as a just cause for war is all the more troubling given its incompatibility with other Christian principles. In the Augustinian concept of the charitable war against sin, charity flows in two directions: toward the benefit of the innocent victims, by preventing or relieving their suffering; and toward the benefit of the sinner, by preventing the sin or punishing it, leading to repentance, forgiveness, and redemption. A war to avenge an insult accomplishes neither of these things. A mere insult or slight does not kill or physically hurt anyone; it does not damage or destroy property; it does not threaten the safety or security of the state, its government, or its people. There is no "injury" to punish (if there were, the war might be justifiable on other grounds), save that to the personal pride of the sovereign, the institutional pride of the government, or the national pride of the people. A war to avenge an insult, far from being an instrument of charity, is an act of pride or vainglory, which Thomas Aquinas denounces as the root of sins that are contrary to peace,[100] and which breeds the vices of schism, strife, sedition, and war (i.e., aggression).[101]

Christianity extols a different kind of honor—for God, who prioritizes faithfulness and subservience to pride and dignity. As Martin Luther puts it in an essay directed to Christian soldiers, "it is better for God to call you loyal and honorable than for the world to call you loyal and honorable."[102] Heavenly honor for obeying God's law far outweighs any earthly scorn for not observing the expected norms of behavior, and as King David found out upon the delivery of the Ark of the Covenant to Jerusalem (2 Samuel 6:21–22), honor from God and the lowly masses is far more gratifying than the elitist honor that emanates from earthly dignity and pride. This priority of honor is further exemplified in the New Testament, which recounts that Jesus does not actively seek honor for himself (he declines political imperium[103]), but does graciously allow others to honor him. Jesus accepts the role of guest of honor at a dinner in Bethany, and allows Mary to honor him by anointing his feet with perfume and wiping them with her hair.[104] These episodes reflect an understanding and appreciation of the good that personal honor is capable of accomplishing. The path to genuine, lasting personal honor is the glorification of God; the so-called "honor" gained by glorifying oneself is meaningless by contrast (John 8:54).

In statecraft, the path to Christian honor begins with glorifying God by doing good, that is, governing well and fairly, with the object of bettering the lives of the general population rather than the select few. It also means protecting or increasing the well-being of other states, or their people. In matters of war, doing good means resorting to force when necessary to achieve these aims, but *only* when necessary, and fighting well, with charitable motives and means. All of these things gain honor from God, which in Christendom is the only kind of honor that matters. In contrast, going to war over an insult is nothing more than defense of the sovereign's (or the state's) earthly pride, and is antithetical to the Christian ideal motive for the use of force, which is defending others.

The notion of the use of force to vindicate a nation's honor is not some anachronistic holdout from a bygone age of chivalry; it has real application to several armed conflicts that took place in the 1990s. The first was the U.S. missile strike against Iraq in 1993, conducted in response to a foiled Iraqi plot to assassinate former President George H.W. Bush. Bush had been the chief architect of the Gulf War, in which Kuwait was liberated from invasion and annexation by Iraq. Not only were the Iraqi forces badly defeated, but Iraq itself was humiliated, forced to submit to no-fly zones covering over two-thirds of its territory, international inspections of its weapons of mass destruction (WMD) programs, and devastating economic sanctions. True to revanchist form, the Iraqi intelligence service attempted to assassinate Bush with a car bomb while he was visiting Kuwait. In response, the U.S. struck the agency's headquarters with guided missiles. The U.S. Defense Secretary justified the strike on the basis that "[t]his crime was committed against the United States, and we elected to respond and to exercise our right of self defense."[105] The application of the right of self-defense in this case is debatable. Iraq's actions, while certainly not justifiable, were not carried out with the intent of killing innocent people or in large numbers, but rather were directed against a specific person who played a discernable role in Iraq's defeat. The attempt on Bush's life was not a political act of terrorism to intimidate an enemy into doing Iraq's will (and which under certain circumstances could trigger the right of self-defense), but instead was a criminal act of assassination solely for the purpose of revenge. Furthermore, even if innocent people had been killed (a likelihood, given the weapon of choice), the assassination attempt did not even take place in the United States and therefore posed no threat to the American infrastructure, culture, property, territorial integrity, or political independence. In contrast to the American response to this plot, the bombing of an American jetliner over Lockerbie, Scotland, was treated as a criminal case (with Scotland taking the lead role), even though the death and destruction far exceeded that which would have ensued from a car bomb.[106] Despite the provocation, the 1993 missile strike against Iraq is best characterized as an act of vindication of the U.S.'s national honor, which cannot suffice as a just cause for the use of force.

The U.S. air strikes against Iraq in 1998 lie on similarly shaky ground. As a condition for cessation of hostilities after the Gulf War, Iraq had an obligation to dismantle its WMD programs and submit to inspections to monitor and verify its compliance.[107] However, as the Director of the IAEA put it, Iraq "chose to follow a course of denial, concealment and obstruction"[108] against the inspectors, leaving them with no confidence whatsoever that Iraq had actually destroyed its WMDs and was not seeking to reconstitute its programs. After a long series of broken promises and assurances, the United States and

Great Britain conducted four days of air strikes on Iraq in December 1998 (Operation Desert Fox).[109] A variety of legal arguments have been made as to whether the air strikes were justified, usually focusing on whether explicit Security Council authorization was required or they were already authorized inherently based on the law of truce; I have argued in favor of legal justification, on the basis that Iraq's failure to comply with its obligation to dismantle its WMD programs posed a threat to its neighbors and to the U.S., given Iraq's past record of aggression and revanchism.[110] But although I approved of the decision to resort to force, the half-hearted manner in which the operation was executed was sufficient to cast doubt on the legitimacy of the U.S.'s stated motivation. Even though the U.S. was easily capable of continuing the air strikes for months, the strikes were halted after only four days, far short of the time necessary to coerce Iraq into cooperating with the inspections. The inspections themselves, which were the *raison d'être* for the operation, did not resume for another four *years*, during which time Iraq had ample opportunity to reconstitute its WMD programs and conceal them extremely well. Worse still, a former weapons inspector claims that the U.S. did not strike the weapons facilities themselves, nor the military units involved in their concealment, but instead targeted little more than empty buildings.[111] This claim, if true, supports the argument that the U.S. was not genuinely committed to the cause of dismantling Iraq's WMD programs, but instead was motivated primarily by vindicating its credibility. Having in the past threatened air strikes and called them off after Iraq backed down,[112] the U.S. could not fail to carry out its threat in the event that Iraq stood its ground. To do so would have meant a loss of face—and at the worst possible time for President Clinton, who was undergoing impeachment proceedings.

The credibility argument also came up in the NATO air campaign against the Serbs in the Bosnian Civil War. In 1994, only two months after NATO shot down four aircraft violating the Bosnian no-fly zone,[113] the U.S. secretary of state argued for the need to "escalate bombing in Bosnia partly to boost its own [i.e., the United States'] credibility. . . . Stronger military action is needed . . . to 'vindicate United States leadership.'"[114] It is granted that the secretary made this argument in order to persuade a skeptical Congress. However, he was essentially characterizing the conflict as a war of wills, or a war of face. In effect, he was saying that the U.S. should escalate the war otherwise it will be dismissed as a global wimp. The real basis for going to war in Bosnia was to stop the humanitarian disaster of ethnic cleansing that was unfolding. The basis for NATO's involvement in that war was the presence of an internationalized civil war taking place in close proximity to its members, thereby threatening their security, and the basis for U.S. involvement was its long-standing and extensive commitment to the security of western Europe. Furthermore, the prospect of NATO intervention already had legal and political cover from the U.N. Security Council. In sum, the U.S. had excellent reasons for going to war in Bosnia, but boosting its credibility was not one of them.

FAILURE TO SATISFY CRITERION

Does the failure of a war to have a just cause render the war unjust, even if all other criteria are met? The answer to this question is a resounding yes. If a righteous war is to be regarded as a remedy for sin or a bulwark against evil, then some evil or sin must exist before the war is commenced, otherwise the war itself *is* the evil. Mere belief in the justice of one's cause is insufficient to support the drastic measure of war, nor is a genuine but mistaken belief of a just cause sufficient to convert an unjust war into a just one. For the war to be just, it must be for an objectively just reason from its inception and must be prosecuted with an objectively just goal.

The lack of just cause is a curable defect only in one extremely limited and highly unlikely way: The original victim gives the original aggressor a new, genuinely just cause. For example, if the aggressor pursues an unjust war against the victim, and the victim responds using highly disproportionate means, then the original aggressor may then have a just cause for continuing the war, though not for the original cause or with the original objective. Suppose that Iraq's war against Kuwait in 1990 had been limited to destroying the Kuwaiti oil wells along the border. Iraq had pressed the claim that Kuwait was slant-drilling (drilling its oil wells at an angle instead of straight down), thus illegally tapping into Iraqi oil reserves. Let us assume Iraq's claim to still be disingenuous. Instead of invading Kuwait, Iraq launches Scud missiles across the border to destroy the oil wells—and that is the extent of Iraq's aggression. Suppose Kuwait responds by firebombing Baghdad, deliberately killing thousands of Iraqi civilians. Iraq had no just cause against Kuwait before but it does now, for Kuwait has given Iraq just cause to destroy Kuwait's ability to wage war and exact reparations for Kuwait's damage to Baghdad. However, Iraq remains responsible to Kuwait for the damage to the oil wells—it does not get a free pass for its originally unjust war. As was said before, this is a highly unusual and severely limited exception to the general rule that lack of just cause is not curable; even this exception is predicated on events that are beyond the control of the state with the originally defective cause.

CONCLUSION

The criterion of just cause speaks to the legitimacy of the rationale for going to war, which must be based on some injury sustained at the hands of the party against which the war is directed. Just cause, as treated in this work, refers only to the injury itself, which must be of a nature that necessitates the charitable use of force in pursuit of a remedy. The Thomist formulation of just cause embeds the additional criterion of proportionality of cause, which will be treated separately. Subject to the very narrow exception described above, just cause is the *sine qua non* of Christian just war theory. The cause must be just *ab initio* or else the war is unjust; even the limited exception above can only bestow a different just cause on the original aggressor; it cannot convert an originally unjust cause into a just one.

Even if an injury exists, the use of force in response must still be carried out with a charitable design and purpose, which is the topic of the next chapter.

· 6 ·

Right Intent

If just cause was foremost on the minds of the first Christians to reconcile war with the teachings of Christ, then the principle of right intent, first given its name by Thomas Aquinas, was a close second. Here we move out of the legal and political realms of just war theory and into the spiritual realm, for Thomas argues that the belligerent's internal motivation is just as relevant to the legitimacy of war as the external justification claimed. However honorable the outward, legal cause for war may be, if it serves as merely a pretext for fulfilling an inwardly sinful motive, such as lust, greed, pride, or revenge, then the war is unjust in the eyes of God.

Of the three Thomist just war criteria, *recta intentio* is the most difficult to judge. One can never truly know another person's motives for going to war, nor can one simply defer to the motives expressly stated, as Saddam Hussein's bogus justification for invading Kuwait reminds us. The outwardly stated motive must be scrutinized, along with whether the state's actions comport with its words.

ORIGIN AND DEVELOPMENT

The roots of this criterion, more than any other, are traceable directly to the New Testament. John the Baptist advised his soldier followers, "Do not extort money from anyone by threats or false accusation, and be satisfied with your wages,"[1] in effect charging them to conduct themselves professionally and charitably. Jesus teaches his followers to "Love your enemies," and in some manuscripts also to "do good to those who hate you."[2] The

Apostle Paul applies the law of love directly to military force in Romans, chapter 12:

> Hate what is evil, hold fast to what is good.[3]
> Do not repay anyone evil for evil.[4]
> Never avenge yourselves, but leave room for the wrath of God; for it is written, "Vengeance is mine, I will repay, says the Lord."[5]
> Do not be overcome by evil, but overcome evil with good.[6]

In other words, defeat evil with good, including loving punishment if necessary; do not inflict punishment with a vengeful spirit but with a loving spirit; hate *what* is evil, that is, the evil act, not the person who commits it.

Viewed in this light, Augustine's overall theme of just war as a righteous frame of mind is easy to grasp. To Augustine, war is a lamentable human tragedy, instituted as a result of sin:

> The desire to do harm, cruelty in taking vengeance, a mind that is without peace and incapable of peace, fierceness in rebellion, the lust for domination, and anything else of the sort—these are the things that are rightly blamed in wars.[7]

> For it is the wrongdoing of the opposing party which compels the wise man to wage just wars; and this wrongdoing, even though it gave rise to no war, would still be matter of grief to Man because it is Man's wrongdoing. Let everyone, then, who thinks with pain on all these great evils . . . acknowledge that this is misery.[8]

The sin must be ended by the just warrior serving as God's instrument of justice:

> When you are arming yourself for battle, think first that even your bodily strength is a gift of God.[9]

We thus return to a theme from chapter 1, that war, like money, is not evil in itself, but rather it is the *love* of war that is evil. A righteous warrior fights not for the love of war, but for the love of doing justice and preventing sin, remaining soberly cognizant of war's tragedies and not giving in to his passions. Augustinian love for one's enemies does not prohibit punishment, only hatred and malice.[10]

To Thomas Aquinas, aggressive war is a vice comparable to schism, strife, and sedition—a just war is the opposite of those things. Thomas remains grounded in the Augustinian tradition but focuses on a different aspect of it: "Augustine says: . . . 'True religion does not look upon as sinful those wars that are waged not for motives of aggrandizement, or cruelty, but with the *object* of securing peace, of punishing evil-doers, and of uplifting the good."[11] Thus Thomas redirects the focus from the punishment itself to the mental state of those who administer it: "[T]he belligerents should have a right intention, so that *they intend* the advancement of good, or the avoidance of evil."[12] That focus, the *intent* of the warrior (and by extension the regime elites who initiate the war), is what won the day at the Council of Trent, whose namesake catechism states, "the soldier is guiltless who, actuated not by motives of ambition or cruelty, but by a pure desire of serving the interests of his country, takes away the life of an enemy in a just war."[13]

The criterion of right intent thus has two facets. The first, *fraternal correction*, posits that a just war prevents sin or alleviates its harm, and in doing so motivates the sinner to repent and seek salvation. The second facet, *charitable motives*, mandates that war be prosecuted not as an act of hatred or vengeance, but as an act of love for those who would otherwise be victimized.

Tension between these two facets is evident in Reformation era writings, especially from Luther and his vehement critic, Victoria. Victoria systematically reviews what specific actions may be rightfully accomplished in a just war, such as reclaiming lost property, securing oneself from attack, and punishing the enemy for its transgressions.[14] "[E]ven after victory has been won and redress obtained and peace and safety been secured," he writes, "it is lawful to avenge the wrong received from the enemy, and to take measures against him and exact punishment from him for the wrongs he has done."[15] Luther, on the other hand, focuses almost exclusively on charitable motives:

> [W]e must distinguish between an occupation and the man who holds it, between a work and the man who does it. An occupation or a work can be good and right in itself and yet be bad and wrong if the man who does the work is evil or wrong or does not do his work properly.[16]

> I say that [going to war], even though it is godly and right, can nevertheless become evil and unjust if the person engaged in it is evil and unjust.[17]

> No war is just . . . unless one has such a good reason for fighting and such a good conscience that he can say, "My neighbor compels and forces me to fight, though I would rather avoid it."[18]

Luther also adds the condition that even a just war be prosecuted with the utmost humility toward God, devoid of any arrogant presumption of victory, for "such confidence may result in your defeat—even though you have a just cause for fighting the war—for God cannot endure such pride and confidence except in a man who humbles himself before him and fears him."[19]

To reconcile these two positions, we return again to the wisdom of Suarez, who successfully melds them thusly:

> [O]ne may deny that war is opposed to an honourable peace; rather, it is opposed to an unjust peace, for it is more truly a means of attaining peace that is true and secure. Similarly, war is not opposed to the love of one's enemies; for whoever wages war honourably hates, not individuals, but actions which he justly punishes.[20]

Prosecuted with that mindset, war becomes the instrument by which the enemy's course of sin is stopped and the enemy is brought closer to salvation, and the injustice or other suffering by the victim is remedied. The two facets of fraternal correction and charitable motives are not in conflict after all; rather, each flows from proper application of the other. The various restatements of right intent by modern churches generally reflect this. The restatements on each of the two facets will now be considered separately.

FRATERNAL CORRECTION

The criterion of right intent is the mechanism for defining the *telos*, the ultimate goal or objective to be achieved, of any just war (as opposed to a specific goal such as self-defense or enforcement of human rights). In this respect the modern American churches are quite diverse in their positions:

> It is praiseworthy to impose restitution "to correct vices and maintain justice." [Catholic Catechism, quoting Thomas Aquinas][21]

> [W]ar can be legitimately intended only for the reasons set forth . . . as a just cause. [National Conference of Catholic Bishops][22]

> War must be carried out to secure a just peace, not for territorial conquest, economic gain, or ideological supremacy. [LCMS][23]

> Love is not inconsistent with the infliction of punishment for wrong. . . . [W]hen we view the demand of love in its broader proportions, the demand of love and the demand of justice are really one. . . . [W]ar in the protection or vindication of justice . . . never contradicts the love of our enemies. [PCA][24]

> Even in the midst of conflict, the aim of political and military leaders must be peace with justice. [Episcopal][25]

The ends sought in a decision for war must include the restoration of peace with justice. [Methodist][26]

The only acceptable motive must be to secure justice for all involved. [SBC][27]

And [Moroni] also knowing that it was the only desire of the Nephites to preserve their lands, and their liberty, and their church, therefore he thought it no sin that he should defend them. [Book of Mormon][28]

The Mormon Church characterizes the *telos* in terms of self-preservation, but it seems that with the resurgence of humanitarian intervention, the *telos* of just war should be broader. The Catholic, PCA, and SBC positions characterize the *telos* as "justice," without further qualification. This seems too broad, for not every injustice is sufficiently grave to justify resorting to the blunt instrument of war as a remedy. The rest of the statements frame war as an instrument to secure not merely peace and not merely justice, but a "just peace" or "peace *with* justice." This mutual qualification better captures the essence of fraternal correction—an equilibrium of peace (the absence of war) and justice (the absence of injustice) that the *telos* of war strives to achieve.

Perspicuous in the Catholic and PCA formulations, and inherent in the others, is the idea that one legitimate objective of war is to *punish* a transgressor (Augustine's "just war to avenge injuries"). This is one of the ill-considered objections of the pacifists to the just war trajectory, that war is little more than an un-Christian act of revenge, an objection fueled by the unfortunate tendency of classical just war theorists to use a Latin word that often translates into English as "vengeance." However, the difference between war as an instrument of revenge and an instrument of punishment is as easily distinguishable as that between a lawful criminal punishment and a lynching. The latter is an impulse of anger whereas the former is a carefully considered act of justice.[29] Just as the prospect of retributive punishment acts as a deterrent against crime, it does so also against aggression.

That retribution can, and often does, result in greater damage to the aggressor than the aggressor originally inflicted on the victim. For example, during World War II the United States ultimately inflicted greater damage on Japan than Japan inflicted on the United States (not even counting the nuclear strikes, which we shall set aside for now). During the Gulf War, which was fought with the objective of liberating Kuwait from Iraqi invasion and annexation, the coalition inflicted more damage to Iraq's military forces and infrastructure than the Iraqis inflicted on Kuwait's. The mere fact that a just war causes more damage than that which provided just cause is not, by itself, an indicator of wrong intent.

If, on the other hand, the remedy *grossly* exceeds the injury, or does not appear calculated to further the right intent of the war, then it could render the war unjust. The cases of Uganda and Cambodia in the late 1970s are instructive. In October 1978 Uganda, then controlled by the murderous Idi Amin, invaded and briefly annexed a small portion of the territory of neighboring Tanzania, the Kagera Salient. After pursuing a "scorched-earth" policy on the Salient, essentially plundering or destroying everything of value, Ugandan forces withdrew and Amin renounced any further claim on the territory. Three months later, Tanzanian forces launched a full-scale invasion of Uganda, deposed Idi Amin, and supervised the formation of a provisional, less aggressive government. Only a month before the ouster of Amin, Vietnamese forces invaded Cambodia, then ruled by the equally murderous Khmer Rouge, after a year-long series of Cambodian incursions into Vietnamese territory. The Khmer Rouge was quickly ousted and Vietnam set up a new government. Both Tanzania and Vietnam had arguable, if weak, claims of self-defense, based on their neighbors demonstrated propensities for territorial aggression.[30] Neither country claimed a right of humanitarian intervention (the doctrine in its modern form was still in its infancy) but in both cases the ouster of the regime was warranted. However, what distinguishes Tanzania's right intent from Vietnam's wrong intent is what the two countries did after winning their respective military engagements. Tanzania helped established a provisional government and withdrew its forces in 1981, after elections had been held. In contrast, Vietnam installed and maintained a puppet government, without elections, and its forces remained in Cambodia until 1990. Although a good argument has been made that Vietnamese forces had to remain in order to prevent the Khmer Rouge from regaining power,[31] the fact that Vietnam replaced one dictatorship with another to its liking suggests that Vietnam's true objective was not as much to eliminate a border threat as to exercise, or extend, its hegemony.

The lesson we may derive from these examples is that the intent of the belligerent will be judged by whether its actions further any legitimate objectives that the war may have, even the unspoken ones. A state that uses a just cause as a pretext for initiating war with an unjust *telos* will invariably betray its sinister intent by its actions. Its outward claims of justice will eventually be proven disingenuous, even if the injuries giving rise to those claims were genuine. However, a state that goes to war with the genuine objective of fraternal correction, whether in response to aggression or to protect others from harm, should ultimately see its actions validated in the long term.

CHARITABLE MOTIVES

Notwithstanding the above, it remains possible for a state to have a just cause for war and *telos* of fraternal correction, and still be motivated primarily by anger, hatred, revenge, or greed, thereby failing to satisfy right intent. This stance has broad support among the modern churches:

> To desire vengeance in order to do evil to someone who should be punished is illicit. [Catholic Catechism, quoting Thomas Aquinas][32]

> [R]ight intention means pursuit of peace and reconciliation, including avoiding unnecessarily destructive acts or imposing unreasonable conditions. [National Conference of Catholic Bishops][33]

> *There must be right intention or attitude.* . . . [O]ne ought not enter into war with a spirit of hatred or vindictiveness. [ELCA][34]

> Since the purpose of a just war must ultimately be peace, unconditional surrender or the complete obliteration of the social or political institutions of a nation is unwarranted. [LCMS][35]

> The sword is never intrinsically, and should never be in practice, the instrument of vindictive and malicious hate. . . . [W]ar in the protection of vindication of justice is not prompted by hate but by the love of justice, and such love never contradicts the love of our enemies. [PCA][36]

> Force may be used only in a truly just cause and *solely* for that purpose. . . . [A]cts of vengeance and indiscriminate violence . . . are forbidden. [Episcopal][37]

> The ends sought in a decision for war . . . must not seek self-aggrandizement or the total devastation of another nation. [Methodist][38]

> Revenge, conquest, and economic benefit are insufficient, illegitimate, and unacceptable motives. [SBC][39]

> And now, because of this great thing which my people, the Nephites, had done, they began to boast in their own strength, and began to swear before the heavens that they would avenge themselves of the blood of their brethren who had been slain by their enemies. . . . And it came to pass that I, Mormon, did utterly refuse from this time forth to be a commander and a leader of this people, because of their wickedness and abomination. [Book of Mormon][40]

A common theme in all of the above declarations, inherent in the proscription against vengeance and hatred, is that a war prosecuted with right intent seeks to accomplish its just *telos* without totally destroying the enemy, that is, killing all the people and wiping out the nation, but instead destroying the enemy's ability to commit the injustices that precipitated the war. This is one of the distinctions between the just war and holy war trajectories; the conquest of Canaan by the Israelites, the Roman destruction of Carthage, and the radical Islamist *jihad* against modern Israel all have (or had) the design of obliterating the enemy completely. In contrast, a just war seeks only to destroy the enemy's ability to fight, reverse its wrongful acts, and prevent and deter further wrongful acts. Such restraint is impossible when the primary motivation for the war is hatred or vengeance.

This is how the Serbian army ran afoul of just war criteria in dealing with the separatist movement in Kosovo in 1998 and 1999. Kosovo is a province in southern Serbia adjoining Albania, with a majority Albanian population that was systematically discriminated against by the Serbs. Under Tito the province enjoyed a degree of autonomy from the central government but that autonomy was reduced in 1990 in the same wave of Serb nationalism that brought Slobodan Milosevic to power. In Kosovo itself, the majority Albanian and minority Serb communities had a long history of antipathy and even a little fighting, which flared up when a guerilla/terrorist movement, known as the Kosovo Liberation Army (KLA), began to attack Serbian police and army units in 1995. The attacks and counterattacks escalated and in 1998 and 1999 the Serb army conducted all-out offensives against the KLA. However, the Serbs, who had already gained notoriety in Bosnia for their "ethnic cleansing" atrocities against Bosnian Muslims, attacked entire towns indiscriminately and drove nearly a million Albanians from their homes. Serb military and paramilitary forces systematically robbed and plundered their persons and homes, and shelled or burned homes, farms, businesses, and entire towns. They also destroyed their identity papers and personal records in an effort to deprive them of their identities, and in so doing make it impossible for them to return to their homes.

Ironically, despite a number of legitimate grievances against the central government, it was the KLA who had precipitated the Serb offensive due to their terrorist attacks. However, media statements, such as Milosevic's wife's infamous quip that it was not possible to rape an Albanian, indicate that the Serbs' primary motivation was little more than ethnic hatred. Even if the Serbs had a just cause for putting down the KLA, their atrocities displayed an uncharitable intent (hatred). Hence the perpetrators of the Serb campaign are likely to be convicted of war crimes in the International Criminal Tribunal for Yugoslavia, whereas the commander of the KLA was acquitted of all charges in the same court.[41]

The treatment of Zerahemnah in Mormon scripture illustrates the ideal outward manifestation of genuinely charitable motives for war. Zerahemnah is the commander of the Lamanites, who have been continually at war with the Nephites, who is captured by Moroni, commander of the Nephite forces. Rather than succumbing to the temptation to kill the architect and orchestrator of Lamanite aggression, Moroni offers to spare his life if he will end the conflict, saying "I command you by all the desires which ye have for life, that ye deliver up your weapons of war unto us, and we will seek not your blood, but we will spare your lives, if ye will go your way and come not again to war against us."[42] Zerahemnah rejects the offer, renews the war, and quickly finds his forces defeated again. Once again holding Zerahemnah's life in his hands, Moroni once again spares it, offering the same covenant as before (this time it is accepted).[43] This episode exemplifies the ideal charitable motives in fighting wars.

However, subsequent events in the Book of Mormon challenge the ability to put Moroni's purest form of charity into practice in the real world. Despite the Lamanites' truce with the Nephites under Zerahemnah, the Lamanites continue to make war against the Nephites over the next several hundred years and eventually defeat and utterly destroy them.[44] It could be argued that the Nephites are destroyed because they become iniquitous and no longer fight with charitable motives; indeed, Mormon says as much in his narrative,[45] but the claim that the Nephites deserved what they got overlooks two other aspects of the story. First, the Lamanites are no more righteous than the Nephites, and often far less, and have embarked on a course of almost continuous aggression against the Nephites for about eight centuries. Second, had Moroni and the Nephites, in more pious and blessed times, destroyed the Lamanites four centuries earlier, the Lamanites would no longer be around to slaughter the Nephites by the tens of thousands in Mormon's time.

The demise of the Nephites thus illustrates a practical limitation to the unfettered, selfless charity that Moroni displayed toward Zerahemnah. It may not be possible to show mercy to an unrelenting, indefatigable foe without assuming a substantial risk of defeat when that foe resumes his wickedness. This is the primary failing of statements of the Catholic, LCMS, and Methodist churches that forbid the imposition of "unreasonable conditions," which may include unconditional surrender or "total devastation" of the enemy. In those rare cases in which no amount of fraternal correction will induce the enemy to change its aggressive ways, the enemy must be eradicated utterly and completely. Michael Walzer argues this point persuasively, in his book *Just and Unjust Wars*, with respect to the Nazis. Recognizing that a policy of unconditional surrender represents the "outer limit" to a reasonable *telos* of war, Walzer nevertheless accepts a right of total conquest "in cases where the criminality of the aggressor state threatens those deep values . . . in the international order, and when the threat . . . is inherent in the very nature of the regime."[46] Jean Bethke Elshtain's exposition of radical Islamist militarism in her book *Just War Against Terror* leads to a similar conclusion; that such an ideology, like that of the Nazis, must be subdued and/or destroyed without any possibility of negotiation or appeasement.[47] But one must also be careful to define the enemy as that which compels a nation to commit *acts* of aggression, rather than the nation itself. Not every German was a Nazi and not every Muslim is a radical militant; to hold every member of the group accountable by association is hardly a charitable way to defeat the ideology that fuels the aggression. This is not to say that adherents to the aggressive ideology cannot be targeted and killed and their facilities destroyed, but even if destroying an ideology requires considerable physical destruction, it does not follow that the entire nation, including the innocents, must be razed to the last building and the very ground made uninhabitable, as the Romans did to Carthage.

FAILURE TO SATISFY THE CRITERION

The criterion of right intent is satisfied when the war is fought with the objective of securing a just peace (fraternal correction) and with an attitude of love instead of hatred, lust, or greed (charitable motives). A war fought with charitable motives but without the *telos* of peace with justice is pointless, for it inflicts greater damage and injury without the possibility that any good can flow from it—like breaking eggs to make an omelet but then throwing them away and having a bagel instead. A war to punish an injury but fought with hatred or other sinful motives eventually results in the kinds of atrocities that marred the Vietnam War and threaten to do the same with the Iraq War. In such situations, any injury conferring just cause is but a pretext for acting on darker ambitions. *Both* elements must be met for the criterion of right intent to be satisfied.

But does the lack of this criterion truly convert an otherwise just war into an unjust war? An examination of the Gulf War reveals an answer. The coalition effort to liberate Kuwait from Iraq, and subsequent U.S. operations against the Ba'ath regime in Iraq culminating in the Iraq War, have been decried in some circles as a "war for oil"; its proponents advance the claim that all U.S. operations in or against Iraq from 1990 to the present have been primarily motivated by the American thirst for Middle Eastern oil. It is difficult to deny that a major factor in the decision of the United States to lead the coalition to liberate Kuwait was the fact that Kuwait is a major world oil producer; a British parliamentarian once reminded us of the uncomfortable truth that "if Kuwait had been famous for its carrots, the United States would not have lifted its proverbial finger" to save it.[48] However attractive this charge may be to those already predisposed to oppose the United States, the Bush administration, the military, and/or any use of force, the charge does not withstand closer scrutiny. To condemn the Gulf War as an unjust war on this basis is to ignore the fact that Kuwait had indeed been the victim of a terrible injustice, that Kuwait did have a right to self-defense and to request other states to assist it, and that other states had a right to act on that request and restore Kuwait's sovereignty and territorial integrity. Even if the primary motive for the liberation of Kuwait had been the desire for Kuwaiti oil (a doubtful supposition in itself), Kuwait did not forfeit its right of self-defense or its national identity on that basis. The Gulf War resulted in a considerable amount of good, independently of the intent of the coalition, for a gross injustice was reversed, the norm that protects states from invasion and annexation by other states was affirmed, and the violator of that norm was held accountable for its transgressions.

The example of the Gulf War illustrates how a war could be illegitimate to God but legitimate to Man. International law permitted the liberation of Kuwait regardless of the motives of the liberators, and even the Gulf War's detractors cannot deny that Kuwait's sovereignty, political independence, and national dignity were in fact restored, in contrast to the result of Vietnam's invasion of Cambodia to oust the Khmer Rouge. If the Gulf War were not fought with right intent, thereby rendering it sinful to God, should it therefore not have been fought at all? Inaction would have resulted in rewarding Saddam Hussein for his hateful avarice, and permanently subjected the Kuwaiti people to the atrocities committed regularly by Iraqi occupying forces. In the temporal world, the greater good may be accomplished by allowing a war with a just cause but wrong intent to proceed (as long as it is also well executed). The war will be regarded as just in the temporal world and its architects will ultimately answer to God for their personal motives, which only they and God truly know. When, however, the lack of right intent is manifested in earthly consequences, the war is rendered unjust in both worlds.

Whether the lack of right intent is curable depends on whether a war that is unjust solely because of unrighteous intent can be converted into a just war if the precipitator has a "change of heart" or "sees the light." If the unrighteous intent has not resulted in outwardly unrighteous acts, then it would seem to not matter temporally. Spiritually, that "change of heart" probably does convert an unrighteous war into a righteous one, in the same manner that repentance of sin pleases God. If, however, the previously wrong intent has led the warrior to commit an outwardly evil act, then the warrior will still have to answer both to God and to human law for it. Nevertheless, a genuine change of heart would seem likely to infuse justice into a war that lacked it originally.

CONCLUSION

It is therefore submitted that the criterion of right intent has spiritual, but not temporal application. It is a valid condition for theological purposes but the Kuwait hypothetical above shows the practical pitfalls of delegitimizing military force undertaken for other than completely unselfish movies. Were such a ban actually enforced, it seems likely that the reign of terror of Idi Amin would have lasted much longer, the Khmer people would be virtually extinct, and it is further possible that Kosovo would today be homogenously Serb and Saddam Hussein would still be having his way with Kuwait. Thus, while right intent remains a valid theoretical criterion, its practical application is limiting. However, I submit that the limitation itself has little impact, for the use of force undertaken with malevolent intent is likely to lead to violations of other criteria, especially proportionality of cause, which we turn to next.

· 7 ·

Proportionality of Cause

$\mathcal{W}$e now venture beyond the three classic just war criteria articulated by Thomas Aquinas into other criteria that modern churches have retained in various forms. We begin with the principle of proportionality, which mandates that the benefit of going to war outweighs the cost. The Christian duties of charity and love, as described by Augustine, may conceive of force to stop sin, but it is hardly charitable if the force causes more suffering than is justified by the good that the force is intended to bring about.

This principle lies at the point of transition from the Thomist criteria to the non-Thomist criteria. Proportionality did not emerge as a separate criterion until after the *Summa*, but it is noticeably embedded in Thomas's criterion of just cause, in which "those who are attacked should be attacked because they deserve it *on account of some fault*." In this chapter the phrase is considered with a different emphasis: that "those who are attacked should be attacked *because they deserve it* on account of some fault," that is, that the fault must be grave enough to warrant the drastic and messy solution of war.

However, the elegant brevity of the Thomist formula belies the complexities and nuances of the calculus with which the gravity of the fault must be measured. For example, is evil to be equated with *any* harm, or only harm unjustly inflicted? What types of harm are graver than others? Is the harm to be considered on the spiritual or temporal planes, or both? This chapter will explore some of those complexities, categorizing various sinful and virtuous causes of war and ranking them from most sinful (least virtuous) to most virtuous (least sinful). In doing so this chapter offers a methodology for evaluating whether the war's foreseeable good outweighs its foreseeable harm.

It is, however, first necessary to distinguish between two varieties of proportionality in the just war tradition. Several churches, including the LCMS and PCUSA, view the concept only as a limitation on the means and methods of war.[1] The rule of proportionality, to them, limits the weaponry and amount of force used to that which is calculated to secure a just peace; it governs the *execution* of warfare, or put another way, the *remedy* that the injured state exacts from the injuring state. That is proportionality of *means*, which will be addressed in chapter 10 on just means. This chapter is devoted to proportionality of *cause*, as a criterion for the decision to initiate war, independent of the manner by which it is executed.

ORIGIN AND DEVELOPMENT

The Christian concept of proportionality is older than Christianity itself. It begins with the *lex talionis* (law of the talon) stated in the Pentateuch: "If any harm follows, then you shall give life for life, eye for eye, tooth for tooth, hand for hand, foot for foot, burn for burn, wound for wound, stripe for stripe."[2] This passage is commonly misunderstood as a law of retribution, possibly due to the way Jesus refers to it in the Sermon on the Mount: "You have heard that it was said, 'an eye for an eye and a tooth for a tooth.' But I say to you, Do not resist an evil doer."[3] But the *lex talionis* is also a law of proportionality, as evident when the passage is read in reverse: "for an eye, an eye; for a tooth, a tooth." This is a prescription for justice, imposing on the offender the punishment deserved, but no more than that.

Sometimes, however, the law of love mandates that the offender be given *less* punishment than deserved, as suggested in a passage on criminal sentencing from Deuteronomy:

> If the one in the wrong deserves to be flogged, the judge shall make that person lie down and be beaten in his presence with the number of lashes proportionate to the offense, forty lashes may be given but no more; if more lashes than these are given, your neighbor will be degraded in your sight.[4]

The more retribution heaped on the offender, however justified it may be, the less likely the offender will choose to surrender to God's command; punishment is hardly charitable when calculated to harden the offender's heart instead of inducing him to repent and rehabilitate.

Although the foregoing passages are most immediately relevant to the criminal and tort settings, they are readily adaptable to just war theory. So applied, they permit a state to exact a remedy in response to an injury from another state, by force if necessary, but only if the injury warrants it. A massively destructive war in response to a slight injury would fail this principle. The limitation on just punishments in Deuteronomy reminds us that the *lex talionis* can go too far, and be inhumane even if it is deserved. This is the reason, for example, that torture and execution of enemy prisoners of war is not permitted in international law, even if the enemy has committed similar atrocities.

The first hint of a rule of proportionality in Christian *jus ad bellum* is from the hand of Augustine, who in *The City of God* writes, "[T]o carry on war and extend a kingdom over wholly subdued nations seems to bad men to be felicity, to good men necessity. But because it would be worse that the injurious should rule over those who are more righteous, therefore even that is not unsuitably called felicity."[5] Augustine effectively weighs what he regards as the "evil" of establishing dominion over another people through war against the "evil" of allowing injustice to prevail. To him, the necessity of preventing the unjust from dominating the just outweighs the unpleasant prospect of unleashing war against another people.[6]

After the holy-war zeal of the Crusades, Thomas Aquinas reintroduced proportionality into the just war calculus, in the *Summa Theologica* quoted above, though it was subtly integrated within the more essential and fundamental criterion of just cause, instead of standing on its own. Still, to Thomas, an evaluation of proportionality is properly directed toward the gravity of the cause.

That focus began to shift during the Reformation. In a work intended for the young King Charles I of Spain (later Holy Roman Emperor Charles V), Desiderius Erasmus offers a different balancing test, focusing on the sovereign's responsibility to safeguard the people:

> [I]f [the prince's rights] are established beyond doubt, he must ask himself whether they have to be vindicated to the great detriment of the whole world. Wise men prefer sometimes to lose a case rather than pursue it, because they see that it will cost less to do so. . . . Let the prince pursue his rights by all means, if it is to the state's advantage, so long as his rights do not cost his subjects too dear.[7]

Thus Erasmus redirects the debate on the proportionality of war away from the injury that precipitates it and toward the foreseeable consequences to the warring state itself. The consequences of war to the world community also merit consideration, to the extent that harm to the community of states translates into harm to the individual state.

After Erasmus, the Catholic founders of international law gave proportionality a dual focus. Victoria, with whom King Charles actually consulted, proceeds from the Deuteronomic tradition of the *lex talionis*,[8] and yet he also counsels against war, even when the injury justifies it, if the remedy is too costly:

> [I]t is admitted that one may be entitled to recapture a city or a province and yet that, because of some scandal, this may become quite unlawful. . . . if some one city can not be recaptured without greater evils befalling the

State, such as the devastation of many cities, great slaughter of human beings, provocation of princes, occasions for new wars . . . it is indubitable that
the prince is bound rather to give up his own rights and abstain from war.[9]

In this vein the two antagonists Victoria and Luther are actually in agreement.
Luther counsels princes to temper the need for justice with the need for wisdom and prudence, pointing out that "He is a mighty poor Christian who for
the sake of a single castle would put the whole land in jeopardy . . . here must
go by the proverb, 'He cannot govern who cannot wink at faults.'"[10]

Suarez travels the same path, limiting war to the severest causes but also
likening it to a scenario in which a physician administers a medicine that heals
a disease at the cost of causing a more serious one. Suarez writes:

> [I]t is not every cause that is sufficient to justify war, but only causes which
> are serious and commensurate with the losses that the war would occasion.
> For it would be contrary to reason to inflict very grave harm because of a
> slight injustice. In like manner, a judge can punish, not all offences what-
> soever, but only those which are opposed to the common peace and to the
> welfare of the realm.[11]

> [I]f one prince begins a war upon another, even with just cause, while ex-
> posing his own realm to disproportionate loss and peril, then he will be sin-
> ning not only against charity, but also against the justice due to his own
> state.[12]

Thus from Christian thought, spanning Thomas Aquinas through Suarez,
emerge three distinct balancing tests. First, the foreseeable good must outweigh the foreseeable harm to the adversary. This is the logical conclusion of
Thomas's condition that the enemy "deserve[s] it on account of some fault."
Second, the foreseeable good should outweigh the foreseeable harm to one's
own state. Bankrupting the state, exhausting its military capacity, or incurring
the wrath of much greater power is hardly in the interest of the people for
whose well-being the sovereign is responsible, unless the state already has
nothing to lose. Finally, the foreseeable good should outweigh the foreseeable
harm to the community of states. Victoria applies this test in suggesting that a
just war should not be undertaken if it causes greater harm and loss to the
Christian community as a whole, citing a hypothetical war that so weakens
Europe that the Ottomans are able to expand their territorial holdings of
Christian lands.[13] This test recognizes that the disturbance of war to the common tranquility and order damages the entire community to some extent. A
successful war to remedy an injury may serve the short-term interests of the
injured state, but may also create a more unstable political environment in the
long term.

As with the other criteria, the contribution of the church to the development of early modern just war theory ends with Suarez. The task of formulating the criterion of proportionality in a more comprehensive way fell to the secular founders of international law. Grotius fuses the three tests into a single maxim that the overall good to be achieved in war must outweigh the overall harm,[14] effectively reducing the criterion to a test of the best interest of others. This breakthrough paved the way for the other major proponent of natural law, Samuel Pufendorf, to condense it even further: "[P]rudence and humanity persuade us not to resort to arms, if more harm than good will result for us and ours from the avenging of our wrongs."[15] Put another way, war must be limited to achieving a *greater good*.

PROPORTIONALITY IN THE MODERN CHURCHES

This Pufendorfian conception of proportionality as seeking the greater good is what the modern American churches endorse today (at least, those that explore proportionality of *cause* rather than *means*). Compare the following:

[T]he use of arms must not produce evils and disorders graver than the evil to be eliminated. [Catholic Catechism][16]

[T]he damage to be inflicted and the costs incurred by war must be proportionate to the good expected by taking up arms. [National Conference of Catholic Bishops][17]

Proportionality has taught us that the good to be obtained by war must outweigh the suffering it causes. [ELCA][18]

The good likely to be achieved by victory must outweigh the possible evil effects. . . . Even if a nation believes its prospects for winning the war are good, the cost in terms of loss of life and massive destruction may not warrant the conflict. [ELCA][19]

[T]he means be proportionate to the end; . . . the harm done must be commensurate with the values being defended and maintained. [PCA, citing Exodus 21:23–25][20]

The overall destruction expected from the use of force must be outweighed by the good to be achieved. [Episcopal Church][21]

[T]he value of the objective sought must outweigh the harm done in seeking it. [Episcopal Diocese of Washington][22]

The war's harm must not exceed the war's good. [Methodist][23]

Will the human cost of the armed conflict to both sides be proportionate to the stated objectives and goals? Does the good gained by resort to armed conflict justify the cost of lives lost and bodies maimed? [SBC][24]

[The Nephites] were sorry to take up arms against the Lamanites, . . . Nevertheless, they could not suffer to lay down their lives, that their wives and their children should be massacred by the barbarous cruelty of those who were once their brethren. [Book of Mormon][25]

[War was permissible] if it were likely that a better peace would emerge if force were used than if restrained. [Firmage, of LDS][26]

The statement of Edwin Firmage is particularly interesting; the requirement is that the war achieve a *better peace*, which can be equated to a *greater good*. It may also be construed to require that the war have a reasonable prospect of success, since an indecisive conflict does not achieve a *better* peace than if it had never been fought. We shall return to reasonable prospect in the next chapter.

Some churches compare the good achieved to the *evil* inflicted, as opposed to the *harm* inflicted. This variation appears to reflect a difference of opinion as to what equates to evil. Is any and all harm evil, regardless of the intent of the inflictor? Or can some harm be good? If the latter, then the motivation behind the harm, as opposed to the harm itself, renders it evil. In Augustinian theory, if the harm is inflicted only as a necessary aspect of eradicating sin and inducing sinners to repent, and inflicted with charitable motives, then the harm is good. However, if the harm is unnecessary, or without charitable purpose, or inflicted with uncharitable motives, then it is evil. The proportionality calculus becomes one in which the good that is reasonably expected to result from inflicting the harm outweighs the suffering that some guilty or innocent persons will have to bear.

If, on the other hand, all harm is evil regardless of justification, then the proportionality calculus measures the evil of harm inflicted justly against whatever evil would be allowed to continue otherwise. Instead of a greater good, war becomes a lesser evil. Although an element of proportionality is still factored into the decision to go to war, the outcome of the decision itself is still evil. Under this analysis, no Christian state could ever go to war, regardless of cause, or even defend itself from attack. Such an absolute ethic invites the aggressor to inflict even further evil. This absurdity reinforces the reason that pacifism in international relations cannot stand as the ideal Christian politic.

We are thus left with the calculus that the good must outweigh the *harm*. On the temporal plane, harm includes the deaths, injuries, destruction and damage, and suffering to the state that committed the injury giving rise to a just war, and also to the injured state (by virtue of the foreseeable attacks on it as the conflict escalates, as well as the drain on its own finances). It must be emphasized that the focus of this criterion is on the suffering that is *foreseeable*, assuming all other criteria being met, rather than the actual body count (which is known only in hindsight). For example, the Crimean War (1853-1856) was initiated by an alliance of Great Britain, France, Austria, and Sardinia against Russia in response to its invasion of the then-Ottoman provinces of Wallachia and Moldavia (part of present-day Romania), under the pretext of protecting the rights of Orthodox Christians against abuses at the hands of the Turks.[27] Even if Russia's plea of charity toward its religious confrères had been genuine, its military invasion, compounded with a series of other successful military engagements against the Turks, had upset the balance of power carefully crafted by the Concert of Europe to maintain the peace in Europe. The Crimean War is notable in history for its excessive number of casualties, brought on mostly by poor and incompetent execution of the war on both sides. However, the high casualties are known only in hindsight. Assuming for the sake of argument that the alliance's cause was just, and that the war was a proportionate response to Russia's greed, then the Crimean War would have been a just war in its initiation. The lesson from the Crimean War is not to confuse the legitimacy of the decision to undertake war with the legitimacy of execution.

As the American Catholic Bishops remind us, the calculus of harm also takes place on the spiritual plane.[28] If charity is the motivation to selflessly promote the well-being of others, then it must also encompass the motivation to counter the opposing motivation to selfishly deny the well-being of others. Weighing only the temporal harm, out of the context of its motivation, causes the result of the calculus to be misleading; spiritual good and harm must also be considered against their temporal counterparts and each other. Acts of force may entail immediate temporal harm but a greater spiritual good overall. It is equally conceivable that the use of force entails spiritual good but be outweighed by its temporal harm; similarly, refraining from force may entail immediate temporal good but be outweighed by the spiritual harm resulting from restraint. A Christian calculus of the proportionality of war as a response to a just cause must, in the end, strive to achieve the greatest good, which is the totality of the temporal and spiritual good balanced against the temporal and spiritual harm to both sides of the conflict.

We now turn to the specific methodology of the proportionality calculus itself.

MEASURING SPIRITUAL GOOD AND HARM

The proportionality calculus begins with the premise that spiritual good is attained by countering an opposing spiritual harm. The key aspect in measuring harm in the spiritual plane is the motivation behind the infliction of harm. A war in opposition of sin has a degree of virtue in proportion to the gravity of the sin against which it is directed. For example, because murder is a more grievous sin than gluttony, a war to stop genocide is more virtuous than a war to stop another state's hypothetical "war for oil." The latter would be again more virtuous than a hypothetical war in which the purpose were simply to check another state's national pride. It is thus appropriate to evaluate the comparative sinfulness and virtues of each side in a given war. In evaluating this aspect it is useful to draw from the Catholic Church's taxonomy of sin and virtue.

The Catholic Catechism divides sin into several categories. The worst kind of sin, mortal sin, is defined as "sin whose object is [a] grave matter and which is also committed with full knowledge and deliberate consent."[29] The phrase "grave matter" means direct violations of the Ten Commandments, specifically murder, theft, adultery, false witness, fraud, and defiance of authority.[30] Within this subset, sins still have varying levels of gravity, for example murder being graver than theft.[31]

Mortally Sinful Wars

In the above taxonomy, the most sinful kind of war has the specific object of murder, for example, genocide. Two prime examples include the Holocaust and the genocide in Rwanda in 1994. Slightly less severe, but not by much, would be a war whose object is to perpetrate *crimes against humanity*, defined in international law as killings, maimings, displacements, and so forth directed against a racial, ethnic, or religious groups which falls short of genocide.[32] The "ethnic cleansing" that took place during the Bosnian Civil War of 1992-1995 is a modern example of such a war. The next tier of mortally sinful war is that in which the object is to kill people indiscriminately, but not on the scale of crimes against humanity. Most terrorist attacks would fit this category. In all of these cases, the purpose of the aggression is to kill noncombatants, either because of their identity or to avenge a perceived transgression. The war may have a definite political objective, such as influencing a state to change a policy, but its immediate *telos* is to deliberately kill those who are least likely to have taken part in setting the policy upon which the aggressor's grievance is based. On a higher level, the invasion and purported annexation of a state without a valid legal claim to it, such as the Iraqi invasion of Kuwait in 1990, is tantamount to the "murder" of state, even if its object and purpose is not necessarily the death of its people. Next in severity would be a war to take control of *part* (not all) of another state and incorporate it into the aggressor state.

On the next lower tier of sinful motive for war is a war of robbery, in which the object is to take something unjustly. As noted in chapter 5, the early church fathers contemplated just wars with the object of recovering physical objects unjustly taken, but a just cause could also include recovering hostages or a dependent territory. Since the worst thing that can be taken from people (besides life and limb, already addressed above) is their freedom, a war perpetrated for the specific purpose of enslaving an entire population, or on a state level, reducing a previously independent state to a vassal status, would fall into this category. Abducting individuals would be the next gravest; the North Korean practice of abducting Japanese nationals to take back to North Korea, admitted by Kim Jong Il in 2003, falls into this category. An equivalent would be a war to take a dependent territory of another state without a valid legal claim to it. A modern example of such a war is the brief invasion and annexation of the Kagera Salient in Tanzania by Uganda in 1978. The next lower tier would be a war to unjustly take a physical object, but otherwise leaving the other state fully intact and independent. At that point the gravity of the sin must be evaluated using the more temporal factor of the value of the object taken, measured either in currency or in the degree to which it is venerated as a national treasure. For example, the theft of the Ark of the Covenant from the Israelites by the Philistines[33] was an extremely grave matter, not because it was worth so much money that its loss would impoverish the Israelite nation, but because it was the single most holy relic to the Hebrews; one could say that its loss left the Israelites spiritually impoverished. In modern times, a war in which the object is to extract a resource would fit into this tier of sinful wars, but only if the aggressor state physically extracted the resource from the other state for its own use, without permission or compensation, and there were no genuine dispute over the rightful ownership of the territory in question.

Venially Sinful Wars

In contrast to the mortal sins described above, the Catholic Catechism classifies other sins, called *venial* sins, into a lower tier of gravity. A venial sin is defined as (1) a transgression less serious than those enumerated above (murder, theft, etc.) even if the perpetrator is fully knowing and willing or (2) a "grave" matter "but without full knowledge or without complete consent."[34] Consequently the next lower tier of sinful wars consists of those motivated by a sin other than those enumerated in the Ten Commandments as shown above.

Here it is useful to draw from the seven deadly, or capital, sins as a model: lust, gluttony, greed, sloth, wrath (or anger or hatred), envy (or jealousy), and pride.[35] Six of these are easily translatable to sinful motives for war, and are here addressed in order of gravity.

Wrath. A war of wrath, motivated by hatred or anger, is the most grave due to its enormous potential to escalate into the mortally sinful war of murder. Indeed, Jesus equated anger to murder[36] and the catechisms of several churches affirm this association.[37] A war of revenge for an unjust injury, real or perceived, exemplifies this category, for revenge is usually disproportionate to the original injury. One example is the Anglo-Spanish War of 1655–1659, in which Great Britain attacked and plundered Spanish colonies in the New World, out of revenge for Spain's refusal to grant trade concessions to Britain. Another is the Polish Rebellion of 1830–1831, in which the kingdom of Poland made a bid for independence from Russia. Russia responded by dissolving the kingdom entirely and incorporating the territory into Russia itself as a province, in an effort to destroy the Polish national identity. The U.S. invasion of Panama in December 1989 could also reasonably be argued to be a war of wrath. That invasion took place only two days after Manuel Noriega's junta declared war on the United States, and only one day after Panamanian forces deliberately shot and killed an unarmed U.S. Marine stationed there. Although the ouster of Noriega may have been justifiable for other reasons (the criminal drug smuggling activities of the Noriega regime), the timing of the invasion creates the appearance of the U.S. unleashing war in retaliation for the death of a single person—not unlike Austria-Hungary's reaction to the assassination of the Archduke Franz Ferdinand in 1914.

Lust. A war of lust is motivated by the desire for physical or bodily pleasure, including sexual gratification, to be distinguished from material wealth or power. The Trojan War in Greek mythology stands out as an illustration of a national war precipitated over competing desires for the extremely beautiful Helen of Troy. On a group or individual scale, participation in armed conflict motivated by the opportunity to commit rape is a form of war for lust, for example, the establishment of rape camps by Bosnian Serb militias during the Bosnian Civil War. Another variety of war for lust is motivated by the desire for creature comforts. This type of war was prevalent at the dawn of civilization. Early city-states were continually harassed by marauders seeking "the good life." A hypothetical invasion by the inhabitants of a harsh climate seeking a more temperate one also serves as an example of such a war; perhaps the discomfort of Mongolian winters was a factor that motivated the expansion of the Mongol Empire in the thirteenth century.

Greed. The next most venially sinful war is motivated by greed, that is, the desire for material wealth, power, or control. On an individual scale, greed leads to robbery and theft; on a national scale, it leads to conquest and unjust exploitation. The most sinful type of war of greed is motivated by personal greed, that is, the desire of a single person for power and wealth. One can hardly count the number of rebellions and civil wars, past and present, that have been precipitated by one or a few people so hungry for the power of governance that they resort to any means, however immoral, to get it. History is also replete with aggressive wars of kings, emperors, and dictators who, not being content to rule their own nations, succumb to the desire to rule over others as well. A small sampling of such wars include the War of Devolution of 1667–1668, sparked by a dubious claim to the Spanish Netherlands by King Louis XIV of France; the Napoleonic Wars, sparked by self-styled French emperor Napoleon Bonaparte's territorial designs on Europe; and the Guatemalan War of 1885, in which the Guatemalan president waged an unsuccessful military campaign to unite all of Central America with himself as president. Wars of greed are not limited to absolute monarchs. In the nineteenth century, major world powers carved up much of Africa, Asia, and the Pacific among themselves; the usual legal form was to make a show of force to an undeveloped people and thus coerce them into signing a treaty of protection. It was also a common practice to use force to wrest colonial claims from other, weaker powers. This practice often crossed the line from a venially sinful war of greed to a mortally sinful war of robbery, for example, the Sino-French War of 1883–1885 in which France forced China to cede its hegemony over Vietnam[38] and the Franco-Siamese War of 1893 in which France forced Siam to cede Laos.[39] An example of forcible coercion driven by greed that does not rise to the level of a war of robbery is the case of China in the late nineteenth and early twentieth centuries. The central government was so weak that the major powers were able to virtually partition the country into "spheres of influence"; it took a general uprising against foreigners and their interests (the Boxer Rebellion, 1899–1901) for those powers to pull back from these policies. Wars of greed may also be directed toward the exploitation of resources. For example, the discovery of valuable nitrate deposits in the Atacama desert, of which rightful ownership had not been definitively established, led to a three-way war between Peru, Bolivia, and Chile (War of the Pacific, 1879–1884); and Mali and Burkina Faso fought two wars in the 1970s and 1980s over the (genuinely) disputed and mineral-rich Agacher strip.

Envy. The next tier of venially sinful war is motivated by envy, jealousy, or *schadenfreude.* What differentiates it from a war of greed is that whereas the instigator of a war of greed seeks to appropriate for itself an asset that belongs to another state without compensation, the objective of a war of envy is simply to deprive another state of an asset, not necessarily to take it for oneself, and not necessarily without compensation. Some early examples include the dozen or so wars between major trading powers in the seventeenth century. The Dutch East India Company and British East India Company had both been chartered to break up the Portuguese monopoly on trade in the East Indies. The Dutch waged a 40-year war to drive Portuguese trade out of the Spice Islands (Dutch War, 1601–1641). The English did the same to Portuguese trading interests in India (Anglo-Portuguese War of 1612–1630), reducing the Portuguese presence there to a few enclaves. In the eighteenth century, the cycle repeated itself, this time with the formation of the French East India Company, which sought to establish a French empire in India to counter the British monopoly. Aggressions on both sides escalated into the three Carnatic Wars in the eighteenth century. A modern example of a war of envy is the damage Iraq inflicted on the Kuwaiti oil intrastructure in the final days of the Gulf War. Retreating Iraqi forces deliberately set fire to hundreds of oil wells and deployed land mines around them to impede access by fire suppression crews. The oil fires burned for eight months before fire crews could put them out, consuming over a billion barrels of crude oil and 20 billion cubic meters of natural gas and doing vast—and pointless—economic damage to Kuwait.

A lower tier of the war of envy is the Mexican War of 1846–1848. Diplomatic relations between the U.S. and Mexico had been at an all-time low due to the U.S. annexation of the breakaway Mexican province of Texas. Despite the animosity, the U.S. sent an envoy to negotiate the purchase of Mexico's California and New Mexico territories but Mexico had no interest in the proposal. After a series of skirmishes provoked by the U.S., the U.S. declared war. American forces handily defeated the Mexican army and forced Mexico to sell those provinces—almost half its territory—for less than the envoy's original price.[40] The Spanish-American War of 1898 had a similar result, albeit a different objective. That war was motivated primarily by the desire to intervene in Cuba against what the American public viewed as a Spanish campaign of atrocities against the Cuban independence movement, but also secondarily to test American military might against a world power. U.S. forces easily defeated the Spanish, thereby guaranteeing Cuba's continued independence and security from Spain. However, the U.S. forced Spain to cede Puerto Rico and Guam and sell the Philippines.[41] In these cases the sinfulness was mitigated somewhat by the fact that the United States paid a reasonable amount of compensation for the territory. They were not wars of robbery or *schadenfreude* but they were motivated in full or in part by American envy for those territories.

Gluttony.   The next lower tier of venially sinful war is the war of gluttony, that is, to satisfy a state's over-consumption of a commodity. Here again, such a war is distinguishable from a war of greed or robbery in that its object is not the accumulation of wealth or the desire to take something belonging to another state (with or without reasonable compensation). Rather, the purpose of a war of gluttony is to ensure the state's continued ability to *buy* a consumable product from another state at a fair price. An example of such a situation is the Opium Wars between Great Britain and China (1834–1843, 1856–1860). Britain was a major consumer of tea, spices, porcelain, and other commodities from China but had no commodities to exchange except silver. As the trade imbalance and strain on Britain's finances compounded, Britain sought permission to import opium, a drug whose importation and trade China had long since prohibited. In the face of Chinese disapproval, Britain proceeded to import the drug anyway. When Chinese officials destroyed three million pounds of it in 1840, the British responded by attacking Chinese government installations and securing an indemnity for the loss.[42] The opium trade continued, engendering another crisis the following decade, when Chinese authorities seized a British ship. In the resulting Second Opium War, Britain forced China to legalize the opium trade.[43] The Opium Wars were not for the purpose of securing Britain's access to opium for its own consumption, but to continue the opium trade that facilitated Britain's continued consumption of other Chinese goods. For this reason, both wars may be characterized as wars of gluttony.

Pride. The final category of venially sinful war is that in which the object is to increase the precipitator's esteem (of itself and/or from others), sometimes by avenging a prior injury to that esteem, such as a perceived insult or offense against the precipitator's honor. The worst kind of war of pride is initiated solely to advance the state's esteem, or its leader's personal esteem, without regard to anything the other state has done. An example would be a hypothetical war for nonmaterial tribute or accolades. Suppose the fictional state of Aramaea demands that all officials of the fictional state of Babylonia bow to all Aramaean officials, and Aramaea launches a war against Babylonia when Babylonia does not comply. There is no demand of material tribute, vassalage, or other subordination, or involvement in Babylonia's affairs, that is, no effect on Babylonia's political independence, which differentiates it from a war of robbery or conquest. It is, however, a war of pride. Another type of war of pride was introduced in chapter 5, the "war of credibility," in which a state is motivated more by making good on a threat (to avoid a loss of face) than actually enforcing its demands.

The next worst kind of war of pride seeks to punish another state for an act or omission that is absolutely within that state's rights. Within this category, wars of nationalism are the worst offenders. In the presently unfathomable case in which it does not reach the severity of a war of murder or robbery, a war of nationalism punishes another state or people simply for being of another nationality. The next worst type is a war to maintain hegemony, that is, to punish another state for "disrespecting" it. An example is the Sino-Vietnamese War of 1979, in which China invaded Vietnam in response to Vietnam strengthening its ties with the Soviet Union, expelling Chinese living in Vietnam, and encroaching upon China's regional hegemony by invading Cambodia and Laos.[44]

After that, the next worst type is a war to punish an act which the instigator unreasonably perceives as an insult. A modern example would be al-Qaida's so-called war against the United States, which according to Osama bin Laden himself, was originally motivated by the presence of American military forces in Saudi Arabia (during and after the Gulf War), which the group regards as the heartland of Islam.[45] To bin Laden, the mere presence of an instrumentality of the infidels on what he regards as hallowed ground constituted a grave offense against Islam. However, the American forces were in Saudi Arabia at the invitation and with the approval of the legitimate government of Saudi Arabia, which has the absolute right to take necessary measures to secure and defend its country from attack, including seeking outside assistance. Next on the scale of sinfulness is a war to avenge an act which is reasonably regarded as insulting on both sides, but which the other state has the right to commit. For example, the Third Anglo-Burmese War of 1885 began as a military response to Burma's diplomatic snubbing of Britain in favor of France.[46] Britain may have had ample cause to be insulted but it was Burma's right (however imprudent) to commit the insult. Finally, a war initiated in response to a relatively minor injury may also be properly characterized as a war of pride; we have already seen such an example, in chapter 5, with the U.S. air strikes on Iraq in 1993 after Iraq's attempt to assassinate former President Bush. In this type of war, at least, there is a genuine injury that warrants redress; however, without trivializing what would be a great personal tragedy for an individual, a full-scale war would have been disproportionate to the injury.

War to Enforce Virtue

This section explores the other, more problematic type of "virtuous" war, which is war to enforce a virtue. The Catholic Catechism enumerates three theological virtues: faith, hope, and charity;[47] a war to advance one of these is tantamount to holy war. The Catechism also enumerates four cardinal virtues: justice, temperance, prudence, and fortitude.[48] A war for justice is virtuous by definition, as the *raison d'être* of just war theory. A war of justice must be preceded by an actual or threatened *injustice*, and the good achieved by the war is in reversing the injustice; this is the calculus described above. A war to enforce any of the other three cardinal virtues is not provoked by an injury or injustice and therefore lies outside the just war trajectory. Such motivation may have some virtue at the heart of whatever act has provoked it, but the offending state has satisfied its sinful desires through means that do no injury to others.

Temperance.   A war for temperance imposes a policy of moderation or self-restraint on another state, in response to its excesses and self-indulgence (greed and gluttony). However, in this case the excess is accomplished by means that are peaceful and/or lawful, such as consumption of a commodity bought without coercion for its fair market value. The War of Spanish Succession (1701–1714) illustrates the pitfalls of a war for temperance. In 1701, the last surviving member of the Spanish Hapsburg dynasty, King Charles II, died without an heir. Before his death he named as his successor Philip, Duke of Anjou, who was also the grandson of King Louis XIV of France and third in line to the French throne, raising the prospect of a union between France and Spain. Such a union would have severely upset the balance of power that had kept the peace in Europe despite Louis XIV's aggressive expansionism. Alarmed by this prospect, Britain, Holland, and Austria went to war against France. The war dragged on until the ascension of the other major contender for the Spanish throne to the throne of Austria as Holy Roman Emperor Charles VI (in 1711) made negotiations possible. The outcome was the Peace of Utrecht, in which Philip was confirmed as King of Spain (as Philip V) but renounced his claim to succeed to the French throne. Although the war did achieve some good in preserving the balance of power, it plunged western Europe into a long war fought on many fronts,[49] despite neither Charles II nor his chosen successor having done anything untoward to bring about the prospect of a Spanish-French union. Philip had a reasonably good claim in his own right, being the son of Charles's half-sister, and Charles had the right to name his successor since he himself had no children. The fear of a united France and Spain was largely the product of the prior record of Louis XIV, who was aggressive in expanding his hegemony in Europe. The objective of the war was essentially to counter what the other powers perceived as the Sun King's avarice, even though it was by no means certain that Philip, as king of France, would continue the aggressive policies of his grandfather. Unlike the wars of greed described above, the prospect of the Spanish-French union was brought about, not by unjust territorial conquest, but by peaceful political maneuvering. Applying the modern Christian criteria, the War of Spanish Succession would not have been a just war because France and Spain had committed no injury.

Prudence.   A war for prudence is undertaken to impose a policy on another state that is in its own best interest, that is, a war against imprudence. This type of war presupposes that the imprudent policy does not arise from a mortal or venial sin and does not lead the state to commit unlawful acts, otherwise it would be treated as a war against sin on that basis. A historical example of such a case is the forcible procurement of the first modern treaty between the West and Japan. Before the 1850s, only one Japanese port was open to foreigners for limited trade. In 1852, in response to Japanese ill treatment of shipwrecked American crews, the United States dispatched an American naval squadron to make a show of force and secure a treaty of amity.[50] Japan had not injured the United States in a way that provided just cause for war, the mistreatment of a few shipwrecked crews not being a sufficiently grave injury to justify war (and even if it had been, the treaty of amity provided for no compensation for their treatment). The primary motive for the threat of force was to change an imprudent Japanese policy. It is conceded that despite the minor injury to Japan in the short term, in the long term Japan benefited greatly from it; it compelled Japan to reverse its isolationist policies and it set in motion Japan's emergence as a world power. But for that threat, Japan would have remained isolated and undeveloped, a peril poignantly illustrated by the economic situations of North Korea today and Cambodia under Pol Pot. However, Japan had committed no injury sufficient to warrant the prospect of considerable destruction for acts which, unfortunately for the shipwrecked sailors, were within Japan's right to commit. Although the forcible opening of Japan did benefit Japan, it also benefited the West, which raises the possibility of a war for prudence being motivated more by the benefit to the aggressor than the victim. It is arrogant for a state to presume that what is good for *it* must also be good for other states.

Fortitude.   A war to enforce fortitude is initiated to impose or maintain a hardship on another state in order to make it stronger from the experience. The motivation must be genuinely charitable, otherwise fortitude becomes a pretext for some other sinful, uncharitable purpose, thus violating the criterion of right intent. The best example of such a situation is the enforcement of economic sanctions. In the 1990s, the U.N. Security Council imposed a series of sanctions on Iraq, Yugoslavia, and Haiti, which virtually halted trade between those countries and the outside world. A major motivation behind their imposition was to make daily life so intolerable for the general population that it would rise up and overthrow its local regime; the plight of the local populations led in part to the downfall of Raoul Cédras in Haiti in 1994 and Slobodan Milosevic in Yugoslavia in 2000. However, total sanctions are often devastating to a state's economy and in many cases it is the population that is hit hardest, not the leaders. The positive results in Haiti and Yugoslavia are overshadowed by the counter-examples of Iraq and Bosnia. Total sanctions on Iraq in the 1990s only increased the misery of the Iraqi people because the sanctions enabled Saddam Hussein and his associates to consolidate control of the black market for their personal enrichment. The arms embargo on the former Yugoslavia during the Bosnian Civil War[51] immediately placed the Bosnian

Muslims at a military disadvantage against the well-armed and well-organized Bosnian Serbs, who had the support of the central government in Serbia. The embargo forced the Bosnian Muslims, whose territory consisted of enclaves that were already difficult to defend, to persevere through several painful years in order to hang on to their territories, their lives, and their national identity. In both cases the sanctions were not only ineffective, but life-threatening to an already brutalized population.

Thus, upon examining the wars for virtue described above, we find that they do not satisfy the test of spiritual proportionality presented in this chapter because the good expected to be achieved does not outweigh the harm that is foreseeable for both sides. Those wars were carried out, not for the purpose of suppressing sin, but to impose a virtue on other states. As such, they stand in contradiction to God's intent that Man be free to choose righteousness over sin. For example, if my neighbor chooses to act on his sinful gluttony and lust by drinking himself silly and watching porn flicks in the privacy of his own home (and poses no disturbance to others), I cannot break into his house and destroy his video player and pour his whiskey down the drain. By the same token, states should not force other states into choosing virtue over sin when they cause no significant harm to others. In the wars described above, the foreseeable good is quite insignificant compared to the foreseeable harm.

MEASURING TEMPORAL GOOD AND HARM

As seen in the treatment of war for virtue above, a war based solely on suppressing sin is not sufficiently just absent an injury. Were a sinful desire sufficient to justify force, every nation would find itself in constant war with every other. The just war tradition is an earthly institution, conceived to counter earthly transgressions and establish earthly justice. The consequences of sin must be ascertainable as earthly injuries to warrant the remedy of war; this section explores those categories of earthly injuries, in order of gravity.

Gravity of Injury

Prerequisite to ranking temporal injuries is an understanding of the hierarchy of needs of a state, or more fundamentally, a well-defined community. An adaptation of Maslow's hierarchy of needs will serve this purpose. In 1943, the psychologist Abraham Maslow theorized that human beings must meet certain basic needs before they can aspire to higher ones. The most fundamental needs are physiological, that is, necessary for the body to survive. After survival, the most fundamental need is for safety, that is, protection from physical harm and security of resources and property. Next in importance are social needs, specifically love, belonging, and self-respect. Only after the first three tiers of needs are met can human beings address the highest tier, the need for self-actualization—to be the best persons they can be.

States have hierarchies of needs as well, the most fundamental of which is survival. For a state to survive it must have a population, a territory, and independence; these needs are so fundamental that a state deprived of any of them ceases to exist.[53] Just as the gravest sin one person can commit against another is murder, the gravest injuries that a state can commit against another are annexation (directed against the territorial integrity and political independence of the other) and genocide and/or mass expulsion (to deprive the other state of its population). These actions effectively constitute the murder of another state.

The next tier of need for a state is security. The more fundamental type is from physical attack. Because territory and population are both essential elements to the very existence of the state, the need for security from attack is second only to pure survival. This need also encompasses security of assets and resources, attacks upon which are intended to deprive the state of these things. Examples include a war to destroy without purpose (induced by wrath or envy) or to rob a state of a commodity such as oil deposits or the central gold supply (induced by greed). Either could potentially so impoverish a state that it is unable to procure goods and services necessary for the survival of the population. This is an example of a sinful cause that is less grave on the spiritual plane having graver temporal consequences.

A related need is the ability to procure basic goods and services necessary to meet the fundamental needs of the people, through trade. A blockade against another state violates this need and could potentially threaten its survival. For this reason classical texts of international law have often characterized a blockade as an act of war. Indeed, the blockade of Israel's only southern port was one of the several hostile acts against Israel that sparked the Six-Day War in 1967.

Once the first two tiers of needs are met, the state can then begin to address higher tiers. The third tier of need is for prosperity, the ability to acquire more than just the basic needs but also to acquire finer and more luxurious goods. For a population this is tantamount to greater personal wealth for a large portion of it; for a state this means the ability to improve the infrastructure beyond the essentials and to implement discretionary programs. The characterization of prosperity as a "need" is a misnomer; it is derived from Maslow's terminology of love and esteem as human "needs" for growth. In actuality, prosperity is a want, not a need, and as such the use of force to protect a state's prosperity must be scrutinized more carefully. The highest tier on the hierarchy, leadership among states, is a greater want and the use of force in furtherance of it warrants even greater scrutiny.

Measuring Good Against Gravity of Injury

The gravity of the temporal injury is linked to the position of the affected need on the hierarchy. An injury to a state that threatens its survival is the gravest temporal harm that can be committed against it, therefore preventing or stopping the injury is the highest form of temporal good achievable in war. An injury that deprives a state of security, that is, an armed attack against a state that does not rise to the level of genocide, invasion, or annexation, is also grave and warrants the use of force against the attacker. Within this tier, however, gradations of just objectives vary widely, according to the number of people targeted, the amount and value of the territory being conquered, and so forth. For example, an invasion of the U.S. with the object of annexing one of the 50 states is not likely to threaten the survival of the United States as a whole, but would warrant a vast expenditure of resources, blood, and considerable firepower against the aggressor to recover the lost state. However, the conquest of a small, remote, mineral poor, strategically insignificant island, while still meriting a military response, is probably not worth the same suffering that recovering one of the 50 states would cause to both sides. This principle is illustrated by the fact that during the Falklands War, during which British forces liberated the British dependency from invasion and annexation by Argentina, the British limited their military operations to the Falklands and South Georgia Islands, rather than taking the war to the Argentine mainland. On the other hand, during the Gulf War in which a U.S.-led coalition liberated Kuwait from complete annexation, the first offensive operations by the coalition were against targets in Iraq. The more fundamental the deprived need, the greater the good achieved by a war that restores it, and consequently the greater the suffering justifiable to both sides.

In contrast, since prosperity and leadership are not so much needs as wants, their deprivation is not so grave. Indeed, absent an injury by another state, a war to protect a state's prosperity or leadership status among states is simply a war of greed, gluttony, or pride.[54] For this reason, the use of force cannot be permissible to *achieve* or *build* upon a state's prosperity or leadership, only to restore prosperity lost due to an injury by another state. Note the use of the word *permissible*, rather than permitted, for not every such injury is grave enough to justify force, even if committed out of greed, gluttony, envy, or pride. For example, no serious discussion of force ensued after the OPEC cartel increased the price of crude oil in the 1970s, because a state's right to control its own resources was (and is) well recognized in international law.

However, if one member threatened (or used) force to coerce the rest into raising the price, a military response by OPEC's major customers might be justified. The gravity of such an injury being comparatively low, there would be a low threshold of tolerance for casualties and destruction in the response.

This hypothetical brings to light an additional principle: The suffering inflicted in and by a just war must have a nexus to its objective. In the OPEC scenario above, retaliating by leveling the aggressor's capital city and occupying the entire country would probably not be a proportionate response. If the threat were directed against other states' oil producing facilities, then the proportionate response may be the amount of force necessary to prevent those attacks, but no more. Only if the aggressor's actions escalate into actual and major attacks would total subjugation of the aggressor become a reasonable objective.

Because scenarios like this entail many complexities and nuances, it is not possible to formulate a "bright-line" test for force to protect prosperity or leadership. However, no state should be permitted to benefit from a policy of aggression and/or intimidation against other states. Rogue states must be dissuaded from indulging their sinful desires in ways that harm other well-behaved and well-meaning states. The international law of state responsibility prohibits force in response to wrongful acts in which force is not used,[55] but when wrongful acts are procured by force, proportional counter-force must be a legitimate option for securing a remedy and restoring justice.

FAILURE TO SATISFY THE CRITERION

Assessing proportionality of cause as a necessary condition for a just war is a similar exercise to assessing right intent. Ideally, the foreseeable good would outweigh the foreseeable harm on both the temporal and spiritual planes. In the spiritual calculus, the initiator's adversary must have committed a sinful act, which makes opposing that act a virtue, all other criteria being satisfied. If the war to oppose the sinful act is itself motivated by a sinful desire, then the war could still be legitimate to Man, but not necessarily to God. For example, if the Gulf War had been motivated primarily by securing access to Kuwaiti oil, then proportionality would still be satisfied temporally because the virtue of opposing the sin of Iraq's invasion and annexation of Kuwait would outweigh the sin of the West's gluttony for Kuwait's oil. If the roles had been reversed and the West had used force to coerce Kuwait into selling oil to the West instead of to Iraq, Iraq's response of annexing Kuwait would still be unjust because Iraq's murderous motive would outweigh the motive of the West.

But the calculus does not end there, for the sinful act must result in a temporal injury to another state. The spiritual calculus now yields to the temporal one. A war to liberate another state from an unjust invasion would not be just if, for example, the liberating state intended to annex that state for itself. Similarly, a war to oppose another state's conquest of a small piece of mineral-rich territory would not be just if the victim's true object were to completely and utterly destroy the conquering state and dismember it. Finally, a war to oppose a relatively minor injury cannot meet the test of proportionality if it is likely to result in unnecessarily excessive military or civilian casualties.

A defect of proportionality of cause is not curable, except in a narrow, rare circumstance similar to the hypothetical case presented at the end of chapter 5. The victim of the disproportionate war would have to itself escalate the conflict beyond a proportional response to the aggressor. We return to the hypothetical war of pride launched by Aramaea against Babylonia, in order to force Babylonian officials to bow to Aramaean officials. If Babylonia responds by annexing a province of Aramaea (a war of greed), Babylonia's response is disproportionate. However, if Aramaea then responds with a war of genocide, then Babylonia's full-scale invasion becomes proportionate to the injury. However, restoring justice to both sides would require not only compensation by Aramaea for the Babylonian lives claimed by the genocide but also the return of Aramaea's lost province and an affirmation that Babylonian officials have a duty to bow to Aramaean officials. Essentially, the *status quo ante* would be restored with each side responsible to the other for the damage caused by it in escalating the conflict.

CONCLUSION

The criterion of proportionality of cause is the hidden fourth Thomist condition that must be met to justify the use of force. Its application is admittedly complex, for the total foreseeable good of using force must outweigh the total foreseeable harm resulting from it. Among the many factors to be considered are the good and harm to both sides (along with third parties and the community of states as a whole), the gravity of sins and virtues at stake on both the spiritual and temporal planes, the gravity of injuries committed on the temporal plane, and a careful separation of the *prospects* of good and harm at the time that the decision to use force is made from the *actual* good and harm known only in hindsight. These factors make proportionality of cause the most difficult criterion to apply.

Fortunately this problem is mitigated by the likelihood that defects in proportionality will also put stress on the other criteria. For example, proportionality of cause is related to just cause because it is derived from Thomas

Aquinas's original formula that the attacked party must have deserved its attack on account of some fault. A question as to whether the victim deserved war may also raise doubts about the initiator's cause, or it may be a symptom of an uncharitable motive, thus affecting right intent.

A specialized form of this criterion will now be taken up, which is reasonable prospect of success.

· 8 ·

Reasonable Prospect of Success

$\mathcal{I}$n this chapter, as in the last, the calculus in which the foreseeable good is weighed against the foreseeable harm takes on a different tone. The previous chapter assumed that the war could actually achieve some good, that is, that the objective was not futile. In this chapter that assumption is removed in order to test how the lack of an attainable goal, or the lack of a reasonable prospect of success, changes the outcome. The criterion of reasonable prospect of success embodies the proposition that it is unjust to inflict the suffering of war when the effort is unlikely to succeed. This proposition lies at the heart of the tension between the Christian duties to oppose and suppress sin and the duty to love one's neighbors, and addresses the fundamental question that the proportionality of cause calculus cannot resolve: How much good, if any, is there in *opposing* sin without *suppressing* it? Assuming there is some, and surely there must be, how much suffering is worth the futile cause?

ORIGIN AND DEVELOPMENT

This criterion is not one of the original Thomist just war conditions, nor can it be derived from any of them. Rather, it originates in the basic principles of military strategy and doctrine, which dictate that it is better to conserve one's resources to fight a winnable battle than to squander them in a hopeless cause. This principle has found its way into classics of military doctrine as ancient and diverse as the works of Sun Tzu and Kautilya.[1] As a principle of military doctrine, it is visible in the Old Testament as well; when the Philistines invaded Israel and captured the Ark of the Covenant, the Israelites' most sacred relic, the Israelites did not immediately attempt to recover the Ark because they lacked the military capacity to do so.[2]

This criterion is not mentioned in the majority of founding texts on international law. Its first appearance in Christian doctrine is a passage from Cajetan's commentary on the *Summa Theologica*, in which he suggests that a judge should not attempt to arrest a criminal without sufficient force to prevent the arrestors from being overpowered.[3] Building upon that foundation, it is once again the trailblazing Suarez who introduces the concept that a just war must be "morally certain" to succeed. Specifically, "A prince . . . is, indeed, bound to attain the maximum certitude possible regarding victory. Furthermore, he ought to balance the expectation of victory against the risk of loss, and ascertain whether, all things being carefully considered, expectation [of victory] is preponderant."[4] To Suarez, the question merits careful deliberation and forethought, in order to assure that the criteria of just cause and right intent are objectively met. This thread of reasoning was adopted by Grotius, who warns against undertaking war rashly, but only when opportune:

> A second occasion to engage in war is when . . . the war is found to be in accordance with right, and at the same time—which is of the highest importance—the necessary resources are available. . . . [W]ar ought not to be undertaken save when the hope of gain was shown to be greater than the fear of loss.[5]

Grotius, like Suarez, sets the degree of certainty of victory at preponderance, that is, more likely than not that the effort will succeed.

Interest in this criterion was rekindled during the resurgence of interest in just war theory generally, thanks to Paul Ramsey's and others' theological treatments of American nuclear deterrence doctrine and its emphasis on mutually assured destruction (the threat of total annihilation of both sides if one of them commits a certain *casus belli*). Even then, however, the criterion was, and is, not universally embraced by the American churches:

> [T]here must be serious prospects of success. [Catholic Catechism][6]

> [I]ts purpose is to prevent irrational resort to force or hopeless resistance when the outcome of either will clearly be disproportionate or futile. [National Conference of Catholic Bishops][7]

> *There must be a reasonable hope of success.* It is irresponsible to go to war if there is no realistic prospect of a nation's successfully defending itself. [Jersild, of ELCA][8]

Arms may not be used in a futile cause. [Episcopal Church][9]

A decision for war must be based on a prudent expectation that the ends sought can be achieved. It is hardly an act of justice to plunge one's people into the suffering and sacrifice of a suicidal conflict. [United Methodist Council of Bishops][10]

[U]nless one's survival or liberty are imperiled, it is not acceptable to resort to war unless the goals are achievable. [SBC][11]

[War was permissible] if it were likely that a better peace would emerge if force were used than if restrained. [LDS][12]

The criterion is not mentioned in the positions of the LCMS, PCUSA, or PCA, or in any official position of the Mormon Church.

As noted in the previous chapter, Firmage's iteration is worthy of further exploration, as it is a hybrid of proportionality of cause and reasonable prospect of success. As a condition of proportionality, it means that the war must be calculated to achieve a greater good than would exist if the war did not take place, by overcoming the results of a terrible sin and by alleviating a severe injury in the temporal world. As a restatement of reasonable prospect, Firmage's criterion stands for the proposition that, if the war cannot be calculated to produce a *better* peace, it should not be undertaken. A war that would inflict great suffering on either side without producing a desirable outcome does not produce a better peace, only a different peace, or a worse one.

A comparison of the restatements above yields two noticeable commonalities. One is that they focus almost exclusively on the suffering likely to be incurred on one's own side; this may be a consequence of viewing just war theory through the lens of the potential for nuclear annihilation. The other common trait is that all the restatements except one (Firmage's) fail to define the degree of certainty of success that will be required.

CERTAINTY OF SUCCESS

In the abstract, neither a proportionality test nor a just cause test should distinguish between offensive and defensive wars; both are undertaken because of an injury committed by the enemy, which for defensive wars is the attack itself. Similarly, the reasonable prospect test should not distinguish between them either. However, this does not mean that the threshold of certainty of success is the same for all conflicts. Suarez recognizes that fact, even though he too is a prisoner to the archaic distinction between offensive and defensive wars. Suarez writes,

> [I]f the expectation of victory is less apt to be realized than the chance of defeat, and the war is offensive in character, then in almost every case that war should be avoided. If . . . the war is defensive, it should be attempted; for in that case it is a matter of necessity, whereas the offensive war is a matter of choice.[13]

Suarez is making the point that the certainty of success depends on the necessity of fighting the war; the greater the necessity, the lower the certainty required.

The degree to which a war is "necessary" may be measured using the same method presented in the previous chapter. In the spiritual calculus, the necessity of fighting the war, and therefore the certainty of success required, is linked to the magnitude of the sin that must be opposed and suppressed. As James Childress puts it, "Success could include witnessing to values as well as achieving goals."[14] The Catholic bishops also appear to have recognized this correlation, pointing out that "The determination includes a recognition that at times defense of key values, even against great odds, may be a 'proportionate' witness."[15] When those "key values" consist of stopping genocide or the total conquest of another state, then the required certainty of success is low. For a weak state to offer no resistance at all to what is tantamount to its "murder" is to invite further aggression with impunity. On the other hand, a war to counter a lesser sin, for example, gluttony or pride, would need a greater prospect of success to be worth the effort. A war to enforce a virtue (which the previous chapter established is already not a just war) would need an extremely high threshold of certainty of success. We thus see that the "one size fits all" chance of success propounded by Suarez is not an appropriate measure of reasonable prospect. When an extremely grave sin is at issue, even the attempt to oppose it is a worthy, honorable, and charitable venture, even if the chance of failure is greater than the chance of success. Somewhere in the middle of this scale lies a point at which the certainty of success is a preponderance (more likely than not); the debate ought to be where that point is.

Whereas the Catholic bishops make their point in spiritual terms, Land of the Southern Baptist Convention introduces a temporal element to the calculus. Recall his iteration, "unless one's survival or liberty are imperiled, it is not acceptable to resort to war unless the goals are achievable." Thus the would-be victim of the aggressor's "murderous" acts has every right to resist, regardless of the likelihood of success; indeed, a state that is fighting for its very survival has little else to lose at that point. In contrast, a war to secure a remedy from a minor injury must have a very high chance of success; otherwise the expenditure of military manpower, resources, and lives, along with the injuries and destruction on both sides, makes the remedy hardly worth the effort.

FAILURE TO SATISFY THE CRITERION

The major problem in assessing whether the failure to satisfy this criterion truly renders a war unjust is that the prospect of success is highly subjective and almost undiscoverable until after the outcome, as illustrated by the well-known biblical account of David and Goliath, during the ancient Israelites' encounter with the Philistines at Elah.[16] Each side was to select a champion to fight the other to the death, and the entire confrontation would be settled by the outcome of that duel, with the losing side becoming the subjects of the winning side. The Philistine's champion was the nine-foot-tall giant Goliath, undefeatable in battle (at least, on Goliath's terms). Leaving aside the role of faith in God in deciding the outcome (which we must do, otherwise we venture into holy war territory), the prospect of success was seemingly negligible to King Saul and his military advisors, as evidenced by their being terrorized into inaction for 40 days. It is only known in hindsight that David did not consider the duel to be hopeless; quite aside from his belief that God would work through him, he knew objectively that he could kill Goliath because he had killed stronger opponents than himself before (a lion and a bear). The outcome is well-known: David did defeat Goliath, using a slingshot to propel a stone into his opponent's forehead. The modern state of Israel faced a different kind of Goliath in its formative weeks: A multinational Arab army, three times the size of its own hurriedly established force, whose mission was to exterminate Israel. Yet the Arab states were unable to do so even after numerous attempts. These cases reinforce the proposition that when fundamental values such as survival and liberty are at stake, a condition of reasonable prospect of success is rendered virtually meaningless.

A point made by Luther should be reiterated here: Even a genuine belief in God does not by itself convert a temporally unreasonable prospect of success into a reasonable one,[17] the history of the ancient Israelites notwithstanding. As a counter-example to David one may cite the Crusades, which were instigated by genuine believers in Christ but were only marginally successful in achieving their objective of restoring Christianity to the Holy Land. For adherents to the Mormon faith, a counter-example is also plainly visible in Mormon scripture, in which God occasionally warns the Nephites to flee into the wilderness rather than fight.[18] It is thus not surprising that reasonable prospect of success is not among the just war criteria articulated by most Mormon writers. Although faith in God may create conditions beneficial to *achieving* a reasonable prospect of success, from a temporal perspective, it does not itself create that prospect.

As to whether the lack of reasonable prospect of success actually renders the use of force unjust, the answer is the same for proportionality of cause, for it depends on the values that using force seeks to promote. A war to counter an extremely grave injury resulting from an extremely grave sin warrants much less certainty of success than a war over a relatively minor injury. In his own somewhat crude way, Suarez is correct to require a higher certainty for an offensive war than a defensive one. A lack of certainty of success, if required to legitimize the use of force, is curable, if the force is actually successful in the end; the premise behind this condition is to avoid suffering in furtherance of a futile mission. But if the mission is actually accomplished without disproportionate suffering, then whether its proponents were reasonably certain of success when they made the decision to undertake it no longer matters. The criterion is rendered moot.

CONCLUSION

The reasonable prospect of success calculus is no more than a calculus of proportionality of cause with a zero value, which makes it redundant. As a result of viewing reasonable prospect for what it is, we now begin to better appreciate the elegance of Firmage's proposition that the use of force be more likely to produce a better peace than if no force be used. Such a calculus involves considering all the same factors as proportionality of cause: the types of injuries, gravity of sinful motives, effect on both sides, and so forth. Compared to other statements presented, Firmage's formula has the benefit of forcing one to be more dispassionate about the merits of the cause, to avoid being too quick to act on anger or indignation. In doing so, it also strengthens the right intent of the decision maker. Whether the conventional calculus or Firmage's formula is used, the outcome is that certain values essential for the well-being of civilization itself must be defended, regardless of certainty of success. In such a case, even an unreasonable prospect of success is preferable to the alternative of not trying at all—which has *no* prospect of success.

· 9 ·

Last Resort

The last remaining principle of *jus ad bellum* to address is that of last resort, which demands that war be employed only when it is the last remaining alternative that will remedy an injustice. This criterion did not originate within the church, but is evident in the works of Cicero, who divides conflict into the two categories of debate and force, "and since the former is characteristic of man, the latter of the brute," he writes, "we must resort to force only in case we may not avail ourselves of discussion."[1] This outlook is inherent in the reluctant warrior mindset of Augustine, though it is not expressly stated.

ORIGIN AND DEVELOPMENT

Prior to the twentieth century, this criterion garnered relatively little attention from the church compared to the Thomist criteria. The concept of war as a last resort does not appear in its present form until the twelfth century, with the gloss of William of Rennes.[2] In its early development two themes emerge, the first of which is articulated by William: that war is not the preferred method for settling disputes between nations. William opines that peaceful adjudication of a dispute should be attempted if possible and the parties may resort to war only if the adjudication fails to resolve the dispute, or if neither party offers suitable satisfaction to the other. Cajetan builds upon this theme, concluding that an aggrieved party must accept an offer of just satisfaction instead of resorting to war.[3] Suarez's line of reasoning follows the same thread, finding arbitration of disputes to be "the best means of decision"[4] and agrees with Cajetan on the sovereign's duty to accept restitution if offered.[5] The secular naturalists Gentili and Pufendorf follow the church's lead.[6]

The second theme that emerges from the early development of this criterion is the concept that princes should resort to war only when it is necessary. It is first articulated by Thomas Aquinas, but limited to the question of whether waging war on holy days is sinful (he concludes that it is not, if necessity demands it).[7] The early Protestant fathers were the first to apply this concept generally. Martin Luther returns to the Augustinian roots of just war theory, declaring that "no war is just . . . unless one has such a good reason for fighting and such a good conscience that he can say, 'My neighbor compels and forces me to fight, though I would rather avoid it.'"[8] Like Augustine, he recognizes the distinction between wars of desire, which are "of the devil," and wars of necessity, which are more akin to human tragedies.[9] John Calvin draws a parallel between necessity and prudence. "[I]f arms are to be resorted against an enemy," he writes, "they ought not to seize a trivial occasion, nor even to take it when presented, unless they are driven to it by extreme necessity."[10] In this way Calvin challenges the Ciceronian outlook of war as a means of procuring peace, seeking instead the moral high-ground of assuring that the war be truly necessary: "[C]ertainly we ought to make every other attempt before we have recourse to the decision of arms."[11]

From these two trajectories of last resort (peaceful dispute settlement and necessity) emerges a third: that war should be a last resort because of a general presumption against its use. Perhaps the best rationale for such a presumption comes from Erasmus, who writes, "other actions have their different disadvantages, but war always brings about the wreck of everything that is good, and the tide of war overflows with everything that is worst."[12] By this reasoning, war must be presumed undesirable until the presumption is overcome by a compelling need. Victoria alludes to this concept in designating the first canon of warfare as avoiding it,[13] as does Suarez when he writes that "princes are bound to avoid war in so far as is possible, and by upright means."[14] Among the secular fathers of international law, Grotius warns against undertaking even a just war rashly and that "often a right should be given up in order to avoid war. . . . It frequently happens that it is more upright and just to abandon one's right."[15]

The coalescence of these three themes into a unified criterion of last resort is chiefly attributable to the early fathers of positive, international law. During the Age of Reason, Emmerich de Vattel writes,

> If men were always reasonable they would settle their quarrels by an appeal to reason; justice and equity would be their rule of decision, their judge. The method of settling disputes by force is a sad and unfortunate expedient to be used against those who despise justice and refuse to listen to reason; but, after all, it is a method which must be adopted when all others fail. A wise and just Nation, a good ruler, will only use it as a last resort.[16]

It is, ironically, not to the historical church but to the authorities of secular law that modern churches owe their expressions of this criterion.

The Mormon Church is the exception. In LDS scripture, the Nephites are taught "never to raise the sword . . . except it were to preserve their lives"[17] and modern Mormons to endure several attacks before rising up to defend themselves.[18] The LDS Church exercises restraint in resorting to war not because of any secular or enlightened presumption against war, but because God and the President of the Church (whom Mormons regard as the prophet of God) have both dictated it.

These three themes of last resort (dispute settlement, necessity, presumption against war) are visible in the statements of modern American churches, in varying degrees:

[A]ll other means of putting an end to it [i.e., the damage inflicted by the aggressor] must have been shown to be impractical or ineffective. [Catholic Catechism][19]

[A]ll peaceful alternatives must have been exhausted. [National Conference of Catholic Bishops][20]

A just war must be the last resort after all other avenues have been thoroughly explored and tried. [ELCA][21]

Every peaceful means of resolving international problems must be vigorously pursued. [ELCA][22]

War may be waged only when all negotiations and compromise have been attempted and have failed. [LCMS].[23]

All other means to the morally just solution of a conflict must be exhausted before resort to arms can be regarded as legitimate. [PCUSA][24]

Force may be used only after all peaceful alternatives have been seriously tried and exhausted. [Episcopal][25]

Every possibility of peaceful settlement of a conflict must be tried before war is begun. [Methodist][26]

Resort to arms can only be morally legitimate when all other avenues of conflict resolution have been rebuffed or have demonstrably failed. [SBC][27]

A just war is characterized by: . . . war as a last resort engaged only when negotiation, arbitration, compromise, and all other peaceable paths fail. [LDS][28]

THE INVALIDITY OF LAST RESORT
AS A CONDITION OF JUST WAR

The most noteworthy feature of the above statements is that they nearly all treat war exclusively in the context of dispute settlement. Herein lies the first problem: such treatment inappropriately characterizes aggression, invasion, annexation, and hateful destruction as a mere "dispute." It further neglects instances in which humanitarian intervention (the use of force to protect a people from large-scale violations of human rights) may be a legitimate cause for going to war; these are also not appropriately labeled "disputes." Rather, this mindset is a relic from the eighteenth and nineteenth centuries, in which the use of force to settle trade or commercial disputes or exact damages for small-scale injuries, was a commonly recognized state practice.

Another noteworthy feature of several modern statements is the condition that all peaceful alternatives at settling the "dispute" not only have failed but also have been tried. This condition does not appear in any of the classical writings presented above, and is unworkable for three reasons. First, it does not qualify the possibilities of peaceful resolution with reasonableness. Most of the positions above maintain that *all* peaceful alternatives must be attempted, regardless of likelihood of success. This requirement only plays into the hand of the aggressor state, giving it time to solidify its military position and inflict further damage, making it more difficult to reverse the unjust act. This is one of the failures of the United Nations system in dealing with the nuclear weapons development programs of Kim Jong Il and Saddam Hussein. By stretching out the course of pointless diplomatic efforts to convince them to halt their programs over a period of years, the international community gave them time to harden their facilities, disperse and conceal their nefarious products, or in the case of Iraq, bury the evidence in a very deep hole or spirit it out of the country altogether.

Second, the condition that all possibilities of peaceful settlement be tried is unworkable because the possibilities themselves are infinite. Even if one alternative of peaceful settlement fails, there is always the *possibility*, however remote, that the aggressor will recant and restore the *status quo*. This subjects the dispute to an endless cycle of appeasement and disappointment, as the Allied powers of the Second World War discovered to their detriment in the 1930s.

Third, the only peaceful alternatives may be morally unacceptable themselves, such as accepting the forcible annexation of another state as a *fait accompli*, or paying a large sum of money to the aggressor state or its leader(s) in exchange for a promise to restore the *status quo*. The former does not procure justice and defeats the whole purpose of the just war tradition; the latter is extortion and simply invites the aggressor to commit more of it. Thus the problems in implementing a requirement that *all* possibilities of peaceful settlement be exhausted are "formidable," as the American Catholic bishops admit.[29] A more realistic and workable criterion has been articulated by the Vatican itself. The Catholic Catechism excuses diplomats from the absurdities imposed by an absolute requirement to actively try every remote possibility. It does not excuse them from diligently *exploring* all peaceful alternatives, but does permit them to show that all peaceful alternatives are impractical or ineffective, without having to actually try them all.

FAILURE TO SATISFY THE CRITERION

The failure to satisfy the criterion of last resort does not render the war unjust, for none of the three supporting arguments can withstand close scrutiny. The notion that all disputes should be settled peacefully is generally desirable, even admirable, as a measure of military economy and also as a manifestation of loving one's neighbor. Indeed, many genuine disputes between states are not worth war. But this is the calculus of proportionality of cause weighing the foreseeable good against the foreseeable harm. As noted above, however, many just causes for using force are not *bona fide* disputes and should be appropriate for negotiation.

The maxim that war should be undertaken only when necessary also does not support a condition of last resort. If this maxim is true (and this work accepts it as true), then the reverse applies as well: War *should* be undertaken when it *is* necessary. Darrell Cole goes even further, suggesting that when the criteria for a just war are met, Christians have not only a right but a moral *duty* to fight.[30] When such a situation presents itself, not even the arrival of a holy day negates it, as Thomas Aquinas pointed out. Martin Luther's just warrior's lament that "My neighbor compels and forces me to fight though I would rather avoid it" further underscores the principle that when a war cannot be avoided, it must be fought. Objectors will point out that William of Rennes, Cardinal Cajetan, and Francisco Suarez all embrace the proposition that if the injuring state offers full satisfaction for the injury, the injured party must accept it and may not resort to war, for the war would no longer be necessary. This proposition implies (and Suarez states outright) that the injured party must first make a demand for satisfaction, rather than plunge headlong into a destructive conflict. All of these points are granted but none of them prove that war must be the *last* resort, only that it is not usually an appropriate *first* resort. Indeed, the fact that a demand for satisfaction may be made at all is an outward manifestation of right intent. It is the first step of fraternal correction, giving the enemy the opportunity to recognize its sin and repent, and also a sign of charitable motives, displaying reluctance to inflict the suffering of war unless truly necessary.

Finally, a condition of last resort cannot stand on the foundation of a presumption against war, because the presumption itself is an illusion. As Daryl Charles has pointed out,[31] the classic just war tradition has no presumption against *war*, only against *injustice*. The mutation of the latter into the former is probably attributable to the return of the just war tradition amid a politico-moral environment in which explosives, chemicals, toxins, and nuclear reactions are all potential weapons. Erasmus's maxim of war "wrecking everything" refers to the potential for war to release a beast that is difficult to control once freed, despite the most just and charitable of causes and motives. However, what Erasmus and modern proponents of the so-called "presumption against war" fail to appreciate is that the *potential* for great harm does not equate to its inevitability, as evidenced by the relatively few casualties and little destruction caused in the liberation of Kuwait from Iraqi occupation (most of the destruction was committed, needlessly, by Iraq—the aggressor).

James Childress, however, makes an excellent point, that "because it is *prima facie* wrong to injure or kill others, such acts demand justification. There is a presumption against their justification."[32] On an individual level this makes sense but it certainly does not preclude the right of an individual to use force in self-defense, or the propriety of a surgeon cutting into a patient in order to save the person's life, notwithstanding the fact that the procedure entails a temporary injury. Surgeons do not sacrifice the greater good of healing the patient in order to avoid inflicting great, but short-term, suffering.

On the level of statecraft, some just causes must also entail great suffering. If only the undesirable effects of war were considered, it would be quite natural to presume against war and set a high threshold for overcoming that presumption. But a calculus based only on the foreseeable *effects* of war is incomplete without considering its *purpose*. For Christians, earthly life is not an end unto itself, only an intermediate state preceding life in heaven. Christians are expected to use this intermediate state for doing good works on earth; works that elevate love and righteousness over material comfort are more pleasing to God than the reverse. Sparing a murderous dictator because an air strike on his palace would also destroy an innocent person's home is precisely the type of calculus that elevates material comfort over spiritual love and righteousness. It serves the short-term interest of the innocent person's physical well-being, but at the cost of the greater long-term interest of restoring justice and good governance to an entire nation. It is this spiritual dimension of doing good that the so-called presumption against war ignores.

Christian teleology holds that, in God's larger plan, the material aspects of earthly life, and even earthly life itself, are less important than spiritual development through adversity. This is the premise that prompted Martin Luther to liken Muslim incursions into Christendom to God's punishing "rod."[33] Perhaps Luther was hyperbolizing to be provocative but his basic point of God's design as a challenge and opportunity for spiritual development is sound. All other criteria for a just war being met (especially right intent), the adverse effects of war warrant less weight than the so-called presumption against war would require.

When attention is redirected toward the *purpose* of a just war, a different outcome emerges, which is most visible if the ill effects of war are removed from consideration by imagining the "perfect" war. In the perfect war, only the guilty are killed or injured; only the guilty's homes are destroyed; the only property destroyed or damaged is strictly dedicated to the guilty's war effort or some other sinful agenda. No member of the armed forces of the just belligerent is harmed in any way, nor is any innocent member of the unjust belligerent's armed forces, that is, those who are not willing, supportive, and sympathetic participants in setting or executing the belligerent's unjust policies. Furthermore, not a single innocent person is harmed, displaced, or inconvenienced in any way. In this hypothetical war, the foreseeable good far outweighs the foreseeable harm because there *is* no harm. There is no longer any basis for a presumption against war.

CONCLUSION

The foregoing exercise demonstrates that last resort is rooted not in the so-called presumption against war but in proportionality. The presumption against war assumes that the foreseeable harm will always cancel out a significant portion of the foreseeable good. This is nothing more than a proportionality of cause test in disguise. To use a presumption against war as a foundation for last resort is to mix proportionality of cause with right intent, thereby giving more weight to both than they should have. Upon closer scrutiny, last resort is found to be a stew of otherwise valid principles of just war theory, all derived from other criteria. When the contaminants are filtered out, no good reason remains for retaining last resort as a criterion for just war.

• *10* •

Just Means

*T*he first six criteria explored in this book are devoted to whether the *decision* to use force is consistent with the tenets of the Christian faith. The final criterion, just means, speaks to whether the *execution* of that decision is consistent. Up to this point, a strict separation of *jus ad bellum* (law *of* war) and *jus in bello* (law *in* war) has been maintained; now the latter topic is explored in order to discover whether it is possible for an otherwise just war to be executed so badly or unjustly that the war itself is delegitimized.

The Christian church has historically parsed *jus in bello* into two basic principles. In the first, *discrimination*, the use of force must be directed only against the wrongdoers and no one else. In the modern law of armed conflict, this principle is realized through the distinction between combatants (defined loosely as organized forces who wear uniforms or other identifiers and carry their arms openly) and noncombatants (everyone else). The second principle, *proportionality*, condemns greater force, and consequently greater suffering, than is necessary to accomplish an otherwise just objective. This principle, proportionality of *means*, is different from proportionality of *cause*, in that the latter calculates whether the cause of the war is sufficient to justify the damage that is foreseeably necessary.

ORIGIN AND DEVELOPMENT

The concept of mercy toward noncombatants, as well as that of the "fair fight," is common to many cultures of the world, past and present. In ancient India, the *Mahabharata* (a Sanskrit epic) prohibited killing women, children, and the elderly[1] and the *Code of Manu* proscribed types of weaponry such as barbs, poison, and fire.[2] The Japanese Code of Bushido forbade wanton execution of prisoners of war.[3] The ancient Greeks regarded temples and priests as inviolable and condemned treacherous stratagems of warfare,[4] and Plato wrote of the need for proportionality of force.[5] The ancient Romans similarly deplored treachery and indiscriminate slaughter.[6] The concept of honorable warfare was also adopted in Islamic warfare under Caliph Abu Bakr[7] and memorialized in the classic Islamic treatise on the law of nations.[8]

The Christian tradition of moderation of means of warfare begins in the Old Testament, which contains passages on sparing women and children (noncombatants)[9] and prisoners of war.[10] Indeed, King Solomon points out the expediency of treating the enemy with kindness: "If your enemies are hungry, give them bread to eat; if they are thirsty, give them water to drink; for you will heap coals of fire on their heads, and the Lord will reward you."[11] The New Testament encapsulates the entire Christian ethic toward the enemy in the simple phrase: "Love your enemies."[12]

This passage implies the very principle that the entire *jus in bello* seeks to codify: that the enemy must be treated with kindness and compassion, with force directed only against targets that are militarily necessary with due consideration for the well-being of the innocent, inflicting suffering only when necessary (and never when unnecessary). These two principles, discrimination and proportionality, are visible in the medieval development of the criterion of just means in the Christian faith. For example, the *Pax Dei* [*Peace of God*], of the tenth century was the result of an effort to immunize the church from the ill effects of warfare, along with the peasantry. To attack the peasantry was to attack the agrarian economy, the damage from which was more widespread than from an attack merely on enemy combatants.[13]

It is Raymond of Peñafort, through the commentary of William of Rennes, who first articulates the norms of charitable conduct in warfare in terms that are recognizable to modern soldiery. In the spirit of Augustinian charity for the wrongdoing nation, a just war can be waged only against offenders (*nocentes*), and not the innocent (*innocentes*).[14] Also in the spirit of charity, legitimate self-defense required that only an amount of force necessary to repel an attack be used, otherwise the defender would be liable for the excess damage.[15] Thomas Aquinas arrives at the same conclusion but in a different way, by examining the intent of the defender (in keeping with his third criterion, just intent). If defense is carried out in moderation, with the sole intent of repelling the injury, then whatever results from it is not sinful. If, however, the defense is inspired by vengeance or hatred and exceeds the limits of moderation, the defender commits a venial sin. If the defender is motivated by a premeditated desire to kill the assailant, the defender commits a mortal sin.[16]

Thomas's more enduring contribution to the just means criterion is his introduction of the concept of *double effect*, the genesis of which is to counter the objection that even the Augustinian mode of self-defense does not allow the defender to kill the aggressor. Thomas's repost is reproduced here at length:[17]

> Nothing hinders one act from having two effects, only one of which is *intended*, while the other is *beside the intention*. . . . Accordingly the act of self-defense may have two effects, one is the saving of one's life, the other is the slaying of the aggressor. Therefore this act, since one's intention is to save one's own life, is not unlawful, seeing that it is natural to everything to keep itself in "being," as far as possible. And yet, though proceeding from a good intention, an act may be rendered unlawful, if it be out of proportion to the end.

> Wherefore if a man, in self-defense, uses more than necessary violence, it will be unlawful: whereas if he repel force with moderation his defense will be lawful. . . . But as it is unlawful to take a man's life, except for the public authority acting for the common good, . . . it is not lawful for a man to *intend* killing a man in self-defense, except for such as have public authority, who while intending to kill a man in self-defense, refer this to the public good.[17]

Thomas applies the concept of double effect to proportionality but Victoria applies it to discrimination as well. Having reiterated the unlawfulness of *deliberately* killing innocent persons, Victoria cites the principle of double effect to excuse the *accidental* or *collateral* (even if foreseeable) deaths that occur in the execution of necessary military operations. "Sometimes it is right, in virtue of collateral circumstances, to slay the innocent even knowingly."[18] However, he also tempers this statement with an immediate infusion of proportionality of cause: "Great attention, however, must be paid . . . to see that greater evils do not arise out of the war than the war would avert."[19] As noted below, Victoria's major advance in *jus in bello* is his calculus of how much force is permitted to accomplish the objective.

The primary contribution of Suarez is to introduce just means as a full-fledged condition of just war, through his over-arching criterion of proper manner (*debitus modus*). He does make one interesting statement which must not be misconstrued: "[I]f the end is permissible, the necessary means to that end are also permissible."[20] In contrast to the amoral proposition purporting that the end justifies the means, Suarez does not advocate the use of *any* means to achieve the desired (just) outcome, only all *necessary* means. Intrinsic in this qualification is the principle of discrimination, which Suarez is careful to reaffirm. Thus tempered, Suarez is comfortable in affirming Victoria's proposition that all means necessary to defeat the unjust adversary are permitted: "[I]t is just to visit upon the enemy all losses which may seem necessary either for obtaining satisfaction or for securing victory."[21] Suarez also reaffirms the principle of double effect.[22]

After Suarez, *jus in bello* went secular along with the rest of the law of nations, though the traditional rules of fair conduct of warfare remained in effect among European nations. Modern *jus in bello* is well documented in a long series of international conventions, which the church had no significant or direct role in developing. However, the development of positive *jus in bello* is attributable to Christendom. The founder of the Red Cross movement, Henri Dunant (1828-1910), was a Geneva businessman (and devout Christian) who had witnessed the bloody Battle of Solferino in 1859, in which there were nearly 40,000 casualties. Distressed at the carnage and lack of medical care, Dunant and four other prominent Genevans formed a commission that eventually became the International Committee of the Red Cross, one of whose early accomplishments was hosting an international convention that resulted in the first Geneva Convention in 1864.[23] Whereas the Hague has become known as the epicenter for regulations of weaponry and other methods and means of warfare between combatants (Hague law),[24] Geneva is known as the epicenter for mitigating the ill effects of war on noncombatants (Geneva law).[25]

Given the attention that Geneva law commands today, it should not be surprising that the modern American churches generally include principles of *jus in bello* in their articulations of the just war criteria, though with varying degrees of separation from just war theory (*jus ad bellum*). The two principles of *jus in bello* will now be taken up individually.

DISCRIMINATION

Just response to aggression must be discriminate; it must be directed against unjust aggressors, not against innocent people caught up in a war not of their own making. [Catholic][26]

The right means must be employed in the conduct of war. . . . A nation is responsible for avoiding acts that show a wanton disregard for life. [ELCA][27]

Since war is an official act of government, noncombatants and civilians should be immune from attack. [LCMS][28]

The just war theory has also entailed selective immunity for certain parts of the population, particularly noncombatants. [PCUSA][29]

Civilians may not be the objects of direct attack, and military personnel must take due care to avoid and minimize indirect harm to civilians. [Episcopal][30]

Justice . . . requires respect for the rights of enemy peoples, especially for the immunity of noncombatants from direct attack. [Methodist][31]

If the purpose is peace, then annihilation of the enemy or total destruction of his civilization is not acceptable. [SBC][32]

[War was permissible] if weapons used and military strategy allowed a distinction between combatant and noncombatant. [LDS][33]

With one minor exception (the *non sequitur* in the LCMS statement)[34] all of the above statements are accurate reflections of positive international law, the differences being only in the aspects of the principle of discrimination that each denomination chooses to highlight. The statement of the American Catholic bishops is noteworthy as the best expression for the rationale of applying discrimination to the just war trajectory. To paraphrase Thomas Aquinas, a just war is waged against those who have done something to warrant it. The civilian population, taken as a whole, does not commit aggression against other states and to purposely direct the military response against it is not justice. The rank–and–file soldiery has no say in the decision to resort to force, yet they are responsible for its execution, and as such are legitimate objects of attack. Modern international law is cognizant of this dichotomy; it is the rationale for humane treatment of enemy combatants.

What, then, about the problem of aerial bombing and other means of warfare that cause extensive collateral damage? What holds true in Thomas Aquinas's concept of double effect also holds true in the modern law of war. Military forces are not *strictly* liable for attacks on civilians or other noncombatants; they are only liable for *deliberate* attacks. Often it is to a state's greater advantage to attack a target by aerial bombing. It must be granted that sometimes bombing such a target will cause unintended, collateral damage or civilian casualties, especially if the target is in a densely populated area or if that target is being deliberately shielded with noncombatants or protected sites. That being the case, if attacking the target is necessary to secure a military advantage in a just war, then the fact that some civilian deaths may occur does not *per se* render the attack unjust. Indeed, if the enemy has abused the protections of noncombatants by using them to shield lawful targets, then the responsibility for their deaths and injuries rests with the enemy. The PCA, whose statement on discrimination is too lengthy to reproduce here, articulates this principle very well, distinguishing between deliberately targeting noncombatants and killing them as a foreseeable, collateral (but unintentional) consequence of attacking a lawful target.[35]

PROPORTIONALITY OF MEANS

The principle of double effect, however, does not negate the responsibility to minimize collateral damage to the greatest extent that is reasonable. To assess that responsibility we now move into the realm of proportionality of means, articulated by the modern churches as follows:

> When confronting choices among specific military options, the question asked by proportionality is: once we take into account not only the military advantages that will be achieved by using this means but also the harms reasonably expected to follow from using it, can its use still be justified? [Catholic][36]

> Proportionality has taught us that the good to be obtained by war must outweigh the suffering it causes. . . . [T]he quality of the means will affect the quality of the ends. [ELCA][37]

> The weaponry and force used should be limited to what is needed to secure a just peace and attain better conditions after the conflict than existed prior to it. [LCMS][38]

> A just war may be conducted only by military means that promise a reasonable attainment of the moral and political objectives being sought. [PCUSA][39]

> [E]fforts must be made to attain military objectives with no more force than is militarily necessary and to avoid disproportionate collateral damage to civilian life and property. [Episcopal][40]

> The amount of damage inflicted must be strictly proportionate to the ends sought. Small-scale injuries should not be avenged by massive suffering, death, and devastation. [Methodist][41]

> If the purpose is peace, then annihilation of the enemy or total destruction of his civilization is not acceptable. "Total war" is beyond the pale. [SBC][42]

> [War was permissible] if a rough proportionality existed between weapons used (damage done) and the nature of the hostilities. [LDS][43]

Slaughter and destruction of an enemy's civilization are forbidden.
[LDS][44]

Again, all of the above statements are consistent with modern international law, and the statement of the American Catholic bishops articulates the principle most accurately. The just warrior must weigh the military advantage gained by incapacitating the target against the death, injury, and damage (the suffering) that is reasonably expected to result when the target is attacked with the intended weapon. If the collateral damage outweighs the necessity, then the just warrior is left with a choice: either attack the target with a weapon that does less collateral damage, or do not attack it at all. The presence of human shields or protected sites deliberately placed there by the enemy does figure into this calculus, but it does not weigh against striking the target as much as their innocent presence would. For example, a central command post is such an important target that it would take a great amount of foreseeable collateral damage to weigh against striking it but an antiaircraft battery situated on top of a hospital, and which does not impede the operations of combat aircraft (i.e., they can easily go around it) is probably not worth attacking from the air. The principle of proportionality thus tempers the use of the double effect as a justification for the incidental, though regrettable, killing in warfare.

Proportionality, however, must not be confused with being "sporting." Here we return to an aspect of Victoria's work that is especially practical, his calculus of how much force may be necessary to accomplish a military objective. "[A] prince may go even further in a just war and do whatever is necessary in order to obtain peace and security from the enemy"; a relatively noncontroversial proposition, but he continues, "for example, destroy an enemy's fortress and even build one on enemy soil, if this be necessary in order to avert a dangerous attack of the enemy."[45] In Victoria's analysis, the defender should be allowed to use *greater* force than the aggressor. He makes two crucial points, the first being that the belligerents need not be evenly matched. Gone, even in Victoria's day, is the outmoded chivalric code in which knights can only honorably defeat other knights on equal footing.[46] Victoria is being realistic, seeing no dishonor in using overwhelming force to achieve an objective so long as it does no disproportionate harm and violates no other tenet of just warfare. The aggressive swordsman of Indiana Jones lore may be justly shot; the munitions factory may be destroyed with cannon shot or a two-ton bomb.

The second point Victoria makes is that proportionality of means does not impose any nexus between those persons and facilities whose actions give just cause for war and the persons and facilities that are targeted in response. If the overall war is just, it may be justified to pull down the enemy fortress that posed a threat, even if it was never used in the attack, just as it is perfectly justified to drive Iraqi occupation forces out of Kuwait by attacking targets in and invading Iraq. It must be reiterated, however, that an attack on any person or facility must further the overall object and purpose of the war, which is to reverse or repair the injury that the other state has committed.

FAILURE TO SATISFY THE CRITERION

In evaluating whether the failure to justly execute an armed conflict renders unjust an otherwise just cause, two scenarios must be considered: unjust acts committed by individuals without official authorization, and unjust acts committed in furtherance of a corporate or national *policy*.

The first scenario essentially consists of the commission of war crimes by a few rogue persons acting outside of the law. The actions of those individuals are unjust (indeed, criminal) but they should not be allowed to detract from the otherwise good cause for which the state is fighting. Otherwise a just war would become a practical impossibility, since a large number of adrenaline-pumped soldiers inevitably includes a few bad actors. To impose a requirement that *every* act by *every* participant be *absolutely* charitable is unreasonable. As long as the crimes are not condoned, but duly investigated and punished when possible, then sporadic lapses of just means at a lower level should not affect the justice of the cause overall.

The second scenario consists of the unjust execution of a war as a policy. In this case, the central government is complicit in the unjust acts and the military forces' uncharitable conduct is part of a systematic, centralized campaign orchestrated at the national level. The argument for negating the otherwise just cause of an unjustly executed war is stronger in this instance, since the unjust execution of the war gives rise to new, legitimate grievances of the original party against whom the just war was directed. A hypothetical, if far-fetched, example of such a scenario would be as follows: Aramaea advances an illegitimate claim to part of Babylonia's territory, and launches a ground invasion for the purpose of annexing it. Aramaea's military forces follow the law of armed conflict scrupulously—although its cause is unjust, its means are just. Babylonia responds to the invasion by launching aerial raids that deliberately target open, undefended cities that have no strategic value to the war effort. Whereas Aramaea targets only places with military value, Babylonia targets civilians. Babylonia has clearly acted unjustly, but if its conduct negates its just cause of repelling the invasion, Aramaea is allowed to keep the territory it has unjustly seized. Furthermore, a strict legalistic calculus would grant Aramaea a new, just cause against Babylonia, which is to stop Babylonia from attacking its civilian population. The problem with allowing Aramaea a just cause for war is that the conflict was of

Aramaea's making; were it not for Aramaea's unjust invasion, Babylonia would have had no just cause for using force against Aramaea at all.

The way out of this quandary is to reevaluate the true motives of Babylonia. A just cause for war exists on behalf of Babylonia against Aramaea, namely repelling the invasion, restoring its sovereignty over the territory, and degrading Aramaea's ability to invade Babylonia again. However, Babylonia's conduct is evidence that it has embraced a *different* cause, hatred and extermination of the Aramaean people. That is not the just cause that Aramaea's injury gives rise to. In such a scenario, a just peace would restore Babylonia's sovereignty over the territory and provide for Aramaean reparations to Babylonia for·the damage caused in its invasion, but it would also provide for Babylonian reparations to Aramaea for the attacks on Aramaean civilians. The conclusion drawn from this scenario is that a just cause for war is not cancelled out by that war's unjust execution, even though the unjust execution can be the source of a legitimate grievance. The party whose unjust injury started the war does not get a free pass.

CONCLUSION

The foregoing hypothetical illustrates the need to keep *jus ad bellum* and *jus in bello* strictly separated. While violations of both components of the law of war entail similar legal, moral, and political responsibilities, to link the legitimacy of the cause with the legitimacy of the execution would create some odd results, as shown above. An execution of war that violates discrimination or proportionality of means may introduce a new just cause for war that did not exist before, but should not affect the right of the original victim to a remedy for the original injury.

The next three chapters are devoted to several contemporary challenges that Christendom faces today in applying the just war tradition.

III

MODERN CHALLENGES TO THE CHRISTIAN JUST WAR TRADITION

• *11* •

Just Rebellion

$\mathscr{U}$p to this point, we have been engaged almost exclusively in an exploration of the tradition of the just *war*. Now we address the just war's neglected cousin, just *rebellion*. The tendency to treat war and rebellion separately has persisted throughout Christian (and Western) philosophy, law, and political theory. For example, to Thomas Aquinas, war is only one of several vices contrary to peace, the others being discord, contention, schism, and strife;[1] tangential to this spectrum of vices is sedition.[2] However, a more holistic assessment of the use of force in political theory (and statecraft) requires that *all* use of force, whether interstate or intrastate, be taken into consideration. Since an important component of American foreign policy historically has been promoting freedom, no study of the American war ethic would be complete without an understanding of the values that drive populations to make war against authority.

The states of war, rebellion, and intervention are all ultimately part of a larger entity that comprises all uses of force to impose one community's will upon another. Even though Thomas set sedition apart from war, the placement of his discourse of the topic under the heading of vices contrary to the peace indicates some connection between war and rebellion. Suarez also recognized a connection, applying the three classic Thomist just war criteria to rebellion.[3] In the modern age, a precursory examination of the Western lexicon also reveals a relationship; Anglophones (along with their Latin and continental counterparts) cannot avoid using the word "war" to describe internal conflicts, from the Peasant *War* that plagued Germany during the time of Martin Luther, to the U.S. Civil *War* between the Union and Confederacy, to the ongoing Iraq *War* between ethnic and political factions there. Several twentieth century authors have also noted the connection, from the *Catholic Encyclopedia*[4] to America's own Paul Ramsey, who observed that legitimate causes for the use of force between states are easily adaptable in evaluating just causes for rebellion[5] (as well as the external interventions that support them, which are addressed in the next chapter).

The notion of any Christian involvement in temporal political affairs at all is somewhat counterintuitive, for Jesus turned down every opportunity for political office.[6] His counsel to renounce the use of force in interpersonal relations would also seem to preclude, at first glance, the possibility of any Christian governance in the temporal world, for no civil authority can function without the ability to use force to uphold the law when necessary. In the temporal world, God has instituted government for the benefit of Man, as shown in several passages of the Old Testament[7] that Jesus never refutes. Since civil government must be able to use force to carry out its functions in the temporal world, that force must also be ordained by God, as Paul points in his letter to the Romans:

> For rulers are not a terror to good conduct, but to bad. Do you wish to have no fear of the authority? Then do what is good, and you will receive its approval; for it is God's servant for your good. But if you do what is wrong, you should be afraid, for the authority does not bear the sword in vain! It is the servant of God to execute wrath on the wrongdoer.[8]

Thus the "power of the sword" helps Christians fulfill their already existing charitable duty to obey and submit to the civil authority, by giving them a temporal incentive to do so (or alternatively, a disincentive for not doing so). Fear, according to Augustine, is a powerful check on the evil of Man.[9]

But this leaves us with a conundrum. The duty to obey and submit to authority is a fundamental precept of Judeo-Christian behavior ("Honor your father and your mother"),[10] yet the Bible, particularly the book of Judges, also recounts numerous instances in which God allows his people to revolt against authority. In recent history, civil authorities have inflicted terrible atrocities on the people in Uganda, Cambodia, Iraq, Rwanda, and Darfur, and Christian thought surely cannot legitimize them by endorsing submission to such regimes. This conundrum is as old as that of war, and indeed both the problems and solutions are fundamentally the same. This chapter explores the intrastate variant of just war trajectory, the theory of just rebellion.

ORIGIN AND DEVELOPMENT

Scriptural Basis for Rebellion and Intervention

The foundation of Judeo-Christian political theory consists of two passages from the Pentateuch. The first, referenced above, is the Decalogue's admonition to "Honor your father and your mother." The other is a section from the book of Deuteronomy concerning the duties of kings, here reproduced in full:

> When you have come into the land that the Lord your God is giving you, and have taken possession of it and settled in it, and you say, "I will set a king over me, like all nations that are around me," you may indeed set over you a king whom the Lord your God will choose. One of your own community you may set as king over you; you are not permitted to put a foreigner over you, who is not of your own community. Even so, he must not acquire many horses for himself, or return the people to Egypt in order to acquire more horses, since the Lord has said to you, "You must never return that way again." And he must not acquire many wives for himself, or else his heart will turn away; also silver and gold he must not acquire in great quantity for himself.

> When he has taken the throne of his kingdom, he shall have a copy of this law written for him in the presence of the Levitical priests. It shall remain with him and he shall read in it all the days of his life, so that he may learn to fear the Lord his God, diligently observing all the words of this law and these statutes, neither exalting himself above other members of the community nor turning aside from the commandment, either to the right or to the left, so that he and his descendants may reign long over his kingdom in Israel.[11]

From the above, several basic responsibilities of the civil authority may be derived. First and foremost, to never forget that its authority is temporal not spiritual, that is, to never deify itself. Second, to be of the same nation as that over which the authority rules. Third, to be the person whom God chooses to place in a position of authority. Fourth, to not be greedy, lustful, or proud. These responsibilities lie at the heart of good governance; a violation of any of them is the root of what in Western parlance is known as tyranny. These duties are also the underpinnings of the concepts of *tyrannus in titula* (tyranny by usurpation) and *tyrannus in regimine* (tyranny by oppression). The first, usurpation, is precisely that—seizure of political power by someone not entitled to it, either by unjustly assuming dominion over a foreign nation or unjustly deposing the legitimate sovereign. The second, oppression, is the outward manifestation of inward corruption. A fundamental duty of the civil magistrate is to obey the law and the uncontrolled, corrupt desires that lead to excessive wealth or physical pleasure result in the breakdown of law.

In contrast to the absolutism of the norm of self-rule depicted in Deuteronomy, Jesus takes a more holistic view of submission to authority, linking its legitimacy not to its national identity, but to that authority's adherence to the will of God. In the book of Mark, the Pharisees attempt to entrap Jesus with a question about the lawfulness of paying taxes to Rome in

Jewish law. Holding up a coin bearing the emperor's image, he responds, "Give to the emperor [Caesar] the things that are the emperor's, and to God the things that are God's,"[12] suggesting that as long as the Romans exercise temporal authority over Israel the Jews owe them their allegiance in temporal matters. At no time does Jesus ever encourage his followers to rise up against the Roman occupation. Indeed, his prophecy of the destruction of the Temple[13] would seem to suggest the opposite. Paul expounds further on Jesus's political theory thus:

> Let every person be subject to the governing authorities; for there is no authority except from God, and those authorities that exist have been instituted by God. Therefore whoever resists authority resists what God has appointed, and those who resist will incur judgment. . . . [The one in authority] is God's servant. . . . Pay to all what is due them—taxes to whom taxes are due, revenue to whom revenue is due, respect to whom respect is due, honor to whom honor is due.[14]

And yet in the same passage, Paul equates submission to freedom, in this case freedom from fear (see Romans 13:3-4 above). Freedom requires submission; the tension between them is especially visible in an excerpt from the first book of Peter:

> For the Lord's sake accept the authority of every human institution, whether of the emperor as supreme, or of governors, as sent by him to punish those who do wrong and to praise those who do right. . . . As servants of God, *live as free people*, yet do not use your freedom as a pretext for evil. Honor everyone. Love the family of believers. Fear God. Honor the emperor.[15]

This seemingly contradictory passage instructs Jesus's followers to pay the ultimate (temporal) price for their faith, and yet also to live free. According to the Pauline passage above, even the tyrant is God's servant and holds an office that is God's institution, yet he governs in a manner totally contrary to God's law. Therein lies the conundrum.

The way out of it is to take note of what Jesus and Paul do *not* say. Jesus does not teach his followers to render to Caesar what is God's, nor does Paul teach the Romans to pay taxes, respect or honor to those to whom they are *not* owed. Christians do not owe allegiance to temporal authorities in *all* matters, nor even all temporal matters. The ruler is owed allegiance and obedience, except when they conflict with the duty of allegiance and obedience to God, upon which Christians must obey God's law instead.[16] Two biblical vignettes illustrate the limitations of submission to authority. In the book of John, the Pharisees bring an adulteress to Jesus and challenge him to affirm the law of Moses, which prescribes stoning to death for such an offense, but Jesus does not allow the stoning.[17] In another chapter from John, Jesus fashions a whip and drives the money-changers and vendors from the Temple.[18] In this instance, Jesus is clearly flouting civil authority, for their function is to supply the half-shekels used to pay the Temple tax and to supply the oxen, sheep, and birds that worshippers sacrifice at the altar; the rabbinic law of the day specifically permitted their presence there.[19] From the above, there may be inferred a point at which the duty to submit to authority yields to the duty to God to promote justice and morality; Christians are to be slow to revolt against tyranny but are expected to act when necessary to prevent or remediate a supreme injustice.

Pre-Reformation Practice

In Western political theory, just war and just rebellion are rooted in the same concept, introduced by Ambrose[20] and Augustine, of the power of the sword to *correct* sin, as opposed to condemning it. Augustine's concept of force as a measure of charitable correction of sin is visible in his treatment of law enforcement, whereby the righteous magistrate loves the criminal but hates the crime. "Therefore if you take action against the crime in order to liberate the human being, you bind yourself to him in a fellowship of humanity rather than injustice."[21] And further, "[s]ometimes indeed it is mercy that prompts punishment, and cruelty that prompts leniency."[22] Augustine's theory of using force makes no distinction between a war to correct the sins of another state and intrastate force to correct the sins of individual criminals. Meanwhile, in the East, where Christian political theory had more robust beginnings, John Chrysostom recognizes that God commands not obedience to *any* authority, but only to *God's*, through the institutes of government. Whereupon Chrysostom rephrases Paul thusly:

> I am not talking about each ruler individually, but about the institution of government. That there should be structures of government, that some should govern and others be governed, that things should not drift haphazard and at random. . . . That is why the text does not say, "there is no *ruler* except from God," but, speaking of the institution: "there is no *authority* except from God, and those that exist have been instituted by God.[23]

This distinction would become important in later works dealing with tyranny, especially in the founding texts of Protestantism.

Speaking of tyranny, an often overlooked development took place in the twelfth century with the work of the English scholar and theologian John of Salisbury. Deriving his logic from Christ's maxim that he who takes up the sword shall die by the sword, John defines tyranny as abuse of power, or rule outside the law. "[H]e is understood to take up the sword," he writes, "who usurps it by his own temerity and who does not receive the power of using it from God."[24] John ascribes tyranny as the root cause of war:

> For if iniquity and injustice, banishing charity, had not brought about tyranny, firm concord and perpetual peace would have possessed the peoples of the earth forever, and no one would think of enlarging his boundaries. Then kingdoms would be as friendly and peaceful . . . and would enjoy as undisturbed repose, as the separate families in a well-ordered state.[25]

To John, tyranny is the worst crime imaginable, "not merely a public crime, but, if there could be such a thing, a crime more than public."[26] The penalty for this most terrible of crimes is also the remedy: "To kill a tyrant is not merely lawful, but right and just."[27] Thus was born the concept of *tyrannicide*, which by virtue of the word's etymology ("killing a tyrant") would distract the church for centuries.

Whereas John of Salisbury forges the link between tyranny and war, Thomas Aquinas forges a methodical approach for dealing with tyranny within the larger framework of Christian political theory. Thomas regards human law as an institution ordained by God for the common good.[28] "[L]aw is nothing else," he writes, "but a dictate of practical reason emanating from the ruler who governs a perfect community"[29] Being a path toward virtue, it must have virtue as its end.[30] Thomas then places tyranny outside the law-as-virtue paradigm:

> A tyrannical law, through not being according to reason, is not a law, absolutely speaking, but rather a perversion of law. . . . For all it has in the nature of a law consists in its being an ordinance made by a superior to his subjects, and aims at being obeyed by them, which is to make them good, not simply, but with respect to that particular government.[31]

Tyrannical law not being true law, the duty of Christian subjects to obey it is negated:

> Laws framed by man are either just or unjust. If they be just, they have the power of binding in conscience. . . . [L]aws may be unjust . . . by being contrary to human good . . . as when an authority imposes on his subjects burdensome laws, conducive, not to the common good, but rather to his own cupidity or vainglory. . . . Wherefore such laws *do not bind in conscience*.[32]

This point sets the stage for Thomas's later treatment of the sin of sedition, to which he makes an exception for deposing a tyrant:

A tyrannical government is not just, because it is directed, not to the common good, but to the private good of the ruler [citing Aristotle]. Consequently there is no sedition in disturbing a government of this kind. . . . Indeed it is the tyrant rather that is guilty of sedition, since he encourages discord and sedition among his subjects [referring to the effect of the tyrant's deeds], that he may lord over them more securely [now referring to the tyrant's objective in those deeds]; for this is tyranny, since it is ordered to the private good of the ruler and to the injury of the multitude.[33]

It is thus apparent that Thomas Aquinas supports the right to revolt against tyranny.

To Thomas, the threshold of iniquity to warrant killing a usurper is quite low.[34] Having never been rightfully under the usurper's authority, he reasons, no private would-be assassin owes allegiance to him, rendering private assassination no different from killing in self-defense. However, an oppressive ruler with legitimate title is another matter; drawing from Peter ("For it is a credit to you if, being aware of God, you endure pain while suffering unjustly"[35]), and pointing out the triumph of the faith even over the Roman emperors who persecuted the earliest Christians, Thomas advocates seeking recourse from a higher earthly authority, or if there is none, from God, who will deal with oppressors as he has done with King Nebuchadnezzar (by converting him, in Daniel 4) and the Egyptian Pharaoh (by drowning his army, in Exodus 14).[36]

In 1407, an unremarkable political assassination in France became the center of a controversy that would shift the church's position on tyrannicide. The Duke of Orléans, brother of the mad King Charles VI, was murdered by assassins in the pay of the Duke of Burgundy. Orléans had ruled in the stead of his brother, and his misrule had imposed heavy burdens on the people. Called to account for himself at the royal court in 1408, Burgundy (who, having opposed Orléans' abuses, was popular with the masses) relied on the professor and theologian Jean "Petit" Parvus to defend him. Parvus delivered an impassioned plea in which he advanced the proposition that *any* tyrant, even a legitimate ruler whose rule is oppressive, is guilty of high treason and deserves to be punished with death, and that natural law permits *any* subject to carry out the sentence.[37] This is a significant departure from the canon that distinguishes a usurper from a lawful oppressor, and the church rejected the proposition at the Council of Constance in 1415.[38] Indeed, the proposition was so controversial that the church wound up migrating to the other extreme, that *no* tyrant, not even the usurper, is a legitimate target for assassination.[39]

But in the political environment of the day, the idea of tyrannicide refused to die. In 1472, Thomas Basin, Bishop of Lisieux, defended the many plots against the life of King Louis XI of France, portraying the king as a threat to both the church and the lay nobility and finding it justifiable to depose and kill a tyrant when necessary for the survival of the state.[40] Meanwhile, the church itself had a credibility problem. The Council of Constance had set out to discredit what the church regarded as the heresies of John Wyclif and Jan Hus, as well as to reform some of its more odious practices. The Council failed in both objectives; their reforms had no teeth and by trying and executing Hus for heresy (having enticed him to Constance with a promise of safe passage) they elevated him to martyrdom. Furthermore, only six years after Basin's work, the Archbishop of Pisa was a conspirator in the notorious attack on Lorenzo de Medici in Florence (in the cathedral on Easter Sunday, no less) and was immediately killed by the outraged citizenry; the church responded by excommunicating Lorenzo (the target of the attack) and placing Florence under interdict for lynching the archbishop.[41] Challenges to the church's central authority mounted, with the church itself now cast as the tyrant. The culmination of these challenges, the publication of Martin Luther's *Ninety-Five Theses* in 1517, plunged western Christianity into its own rebellion.

The Reformation

Notwithstanding Luther's role in spearheading the revolt against Rome, his writings reveal him to be reluctant to endorse active resistance against civil authority, for it exercises its role of restraining sin as a consequence of God's will.[42] However, Luther acknowledges that no law should ever preclude exceptions, for rigid absolutism is itself unjust,[43] hence the subjects are not bound to obey a ruler whom they know to be wrong.[44] When the tyrant makes war on the subjects, Luther argues that true Christians will be passive, leaving God to punish the tyrant by having others rise up and depose or kill him.[45] These early teachings, however, were misinterpreted by the precipitators of the Peasant War of 1524–1525, who equated Luther's railings against papal authority with a call for attacking the social hierarchy as well. When the rebels sacked castles and monasteries, Luther turned against them. But Luther maintains his even-handedness: By placing suppression of rebellion within the context of the sovereign's responsibility to the populace, he warns Christian rulers to suppress revolts in a Christian manner, that is, by acting humbly and offering peace before resorting to force.[46]

In defining the purview of Christians to resist tyranny, Calvinism departs from Lutheranism in several key areas. First, in contrast to Luther's view of the state as the temporal extension of God's authority, Calvin rejects the so-called "divine right of kings"—but also rejects the notion, epitomized by his Anabaptist contemporaries, that any institutionalized civil order is unnecessary for Christians, who should exclude themselves from any such order.[47] In this respect Calvin takes a more moderate position, making him quicker than Luther to call for resistance to tyranny. After first concluding that tyranny is God's punishment for the people's iniquity,[48] he then reminds us that what God giveth the tyrant he also taketh away:

> [S]ometimes he raises up some of his servants as public avengers, and arms them with his commission to punish unrighteous domination, and to deliver from their distressing calamities a people who have been unjustly oppressed: sometimes he accomplishes this end by the fury of men who meditate and attempt something altogether different.[49]

Calvin, ever the predestinarian, attributes revolt against tyranny to God's will rather than the people's free choice. Significantly (and this is the second difference from Lutheranism), this passage of Calvin's raises the possibility that God deposes tyrants by calling up his *own* servants, in contrast to the assertion that God would not commit his true followers to such an unsavory enterprise (in Luther's view).

In another respect, however, Calvinism takes a more extreme position. The third point in which Lutheranism and Calvinism diverge is that, in Calvinist political theory, the civil government is responsible not only for the people but also the moral fabric of society. Since magistrates hold their offices in accordance with divine law and are ordained with God's wisdom,[50] the first duty of civil authority is to uphold God's law.[51]

This form of militarism made the Calvinist branch more prone to kill. Calvin's version of the responsibility of civil magistrates includes defending the faith against heresy, a concept borne out notoriously in 1553 with the execution of Michael Servetus for criticizing the doctrine of the Trinity.[52] The primary founder of the Scottish Protestant kirk, John Knox, was also prone to endorse forcible resistance against heretical rule. Already notable (or notorious) for his hyperbole and misogyny, Knox equates tyranny with not only usurpation and misrule, but also rule by a Catholic, in his tractate against Mary Queen of Scots.[53] While Mary did persecute Protestants during her reign, Knox's constant references to Mary as "Jezebel," coupled with evocations of Phineas and Jehu, are tantamount to calling for her death, as opposed to removal. In a later discourse at the General Assembly of the kirk, Knox makes his views toward idolatrous rulers plainer: "Idolatry ought not [only] to be suppressed, but the idolater ought to die the death . . . [b]y the people of God"[54]—an invective directed toward non-Protestants. Knox also looks to Protestant temporal authorities for protection from what he regards as the tyranny of the Catholic Church: In a piece protesting his trial and sentence for heresy *in absentia* by Catholic clergy, he writes,

> [I]t is lawful for the servants of God to call for the help of the civil magistrate against the sentence of death if it be unjust . . . and also that the civil

sword hath power to repress the fury of the priests and to absolve whom they have condemned.[55]

Essentially he calls upon the Scottish nobility to disobey a higher temporal authority when that authority has transgressed God's law (or at least the Reformist version of it). Knox goes on to call them to fulfill what he regards as a divinely mandated function of civil authority:

> to promote the glory of God, to provide that your subjects be rightly instructed in His true religion, that they be defended from all oppression and tyranny [here referring to oppression by the Catholic Church against Protestant reformers]. . . . And to the performance of every one of these do your offices and names . . . bind and oblige you.[56]

The works of John Knox represent an extreme view that is toned down considerably in the modern text of the Westminster Confession and other foundational documents of the Presbyterian Church.

Post-Reformation and Counter-Reformation Practice

With such vitriolic rhetoric flying around, along with the willingness of many Catholics to preserve unity of faith by force, the battle lines between Catholics and Protestants formed quickly, with many European wars taking on a religious character. Amid the bloodshed, it is somewhat surprising that official church documents of the day do not speak to the right of active rebellion, let alone tyrannicide. To the extent that they addressed disobedience of civil authority at all, they counseled only disobedience of *unlawful* commands:

> The same [entitlement to obedience] is to regulate our conduct toward princes and magistrates, and others to whose authority we are subject. . . . But should they issue a wicked or unjust mandate, they are on no account to be obeyed. [Catholic][57]

> If he will not do it [i.e., obey the civil government] in love, but despises and resists (authority) or rebels, . . . he shall have no favor nor blessing. [Lutheran][58]

> Christians are necessarily bound to obey their own magistrates and laws save only when commanded to sin; for then they ought to obey God rather than men. [Lutheran][59]

> We hold that any men who conspire to rebel or overturn the civil powers, as duly established, are not merely enemies to humanity but rebels against God's will. [Scottish Reformed][60]

What does God require in the fifth commandment ["Honor thy father and mother"]? That I show honor, love, and faithfulness to . . . all who are set in authority over me; that I submit myself with respectful obedience to all their careful instruction and discipline. [German Reformed][61]

[L]et [the subjects] honor and reverence the magistrate as the minister of God . . . and let them obey all his just and fair commands. [Swiss-German Reformed][62]

[Princes] should rule all estates and degrees committed to their charge by God, whether they be Ecclesiastical or Temporal, and restrain with the civil sword the stubborn and evil-doers. [Anglican][63]

In formulating their official positions, churches were more apt to affirm the civil authority of their respective followers who were in power than to advocate revolt by those who were not.

Given the above, it is equally surprising that so many influential theologians challenged the official stances of their churches by favoring a right of rebellion and tyrannicide. The work of John Knox has already been mentioned. Knox's fellow exile in Geneva, Christopher Goodman, also published a tractate calling for resistance to and punishment of "ungodly" magistrates as if they were private persons, that is, stripped of their civil authority.[64] John Calvin's deputy Theodore Beza argued the right to resist tyranny in terms of the classical distinction between usurpation of authority (along with foreign occupation) and oppression by lawful authority, and cautiously came out in favor of it.[65] Among Catholics, the Dominican professor Domingo Bañez wrote in favor of rebellion against tyrants *in regimine* in extreme situations, when no other recourse was available.[66] His work was quickly followed by that of the Jesuit Juan de Mariana, whose 1599 work *On the King and the Training of the King* advanced the theory that tyranny breeds rebellion and tyrannicide as a matter of course and that tyrannicide was an act of defending the state against the ill effects of kingly abuses.[67] Mariana's failure to toe the Catholic line and condemn tyrannicide resonates all the more for his work having been commissioned by the arch-defender of Catholicism of the day— King Philip II of Spain.

Since Mariana's work was disavowed by the Jesuit order,[68] the task of refining the Catholic doctrine of revolt against tyranny fell to his fellow Jesuit and Spaniard, Suarez, who devoted a chapter of his tractate *Defensio Fidei* to the overreaching of James I of England/James VI of Scotland. But Suarez, too, challenged the Council of Constance's unqualified condemnation of tyrannicide, foreseeing the possibility that a lawful sovereign may be lawfully deposed and slain by his subjects, but only in limited circumstances and within the boundaries of law.[69] It is his emphasis on *process* that brought the Catholic stance on tyranny back to moderation.

Two Protestant political works must also be mentioned, since they are both rooted in the religious divisions of their day. The first, *Vindiciae contra Tyrannos*, was published anonymously in 1579 in response to the St. Bartholomew's Day Massacre in 1572, in which thousands (perhaps tens of thousands) of French Huguenots (Protestants) were murdered with the tacit support of the royal court.[70] Also in 1579 was published *De Jure Regni apud Scotos*, the political opus of George Buchanan. It was written in response to the forced abdication of Mary Queen of Scots, a Catholic, descended from (as well as married into) the Guise family of France (which had precipitated the Wars of Religion), and whose morals in private life and heavy-handed rule in Scotland had grossly antagonized the increasingly militant Presbyterian majority in that country.[71] In contrast to the restraint of the *Vindiciae*, Buchanan argued in favor of the right of the people to overthrow a tyrant, who was the "enemy of all humanity" and against whom a war was "the most just of all."[72] This work was especially influential during the formative years of the United States.[73]

The proponents of rebellion eventually won out; the conflict between the Catholic Church and Protestant movements came to a head in 1618, when Austrian Emperor Ferdinand II (a Hapsburg and Catholic) went to war against Bohemia in response to the Bohemians having passed him over for their throne and elected a Protestant instead. This was the spark that ignited the Thirty Years War (1618-1648), in which a Catholic alliance of Austria, Spain, and Catholic Germany sought to dominate Europe, but was checked by German Protestant princes, France, Sweden, Denmark, the Netherlands, and England. The ideological components of the conflict were manifold: Tolerance of Protestantism versus hard-line Catholic attempts to eradicate it, pluralistic tolerance versus arbitrary imposition of faith, and centralized authority of sovereigns versus rising independent principalities, especially in Germany. The war is best characterized, however, as Protestantism's "War of Independence" from the central authority of the Roman Catholic Church.

The Peace of Westphalia, which ended the war in 1648, changed the entire Western political system. The immediate results were that German principalities gained autonomy and Dutch independence as the United Provinces was finally recognized, thus also ending the Eighty Years War.[74] The long-term ramifications of the Peace were that Catholic and Protestant states within the Holy Roman Empire were granted equal status, legitimizing both Lutheranism and Calvinism. The Protestant rebellion against what it regarded as the tyranny of the Roman Catholic Church was successful, thus solidifying the right of rebellion in Western Christianity.

Rebellion in the Mormon Church

The Mormon political theory of the divinely ordained government is similar to that of the older Protestant confessions,[75] holding submission to lawful authority in high regard. Article of Faith 12 reads: "We believe in being subject to kings, presidents, rulers, and magistrates, in obeying, honoring, and sustaining the law." However, LDS scripture reflects a deep tension between submission to authority and assertion of fundamental rights. On one hand, the LDS Church places high value on individual liberties; in Mormon theology the freedom of choice, which the church calls "agency," is essential to Man's existence and progression.[76] On the other hand, LDS doctrine also upholds respect for and obedience of civil authority:

> We believe that all men are bound to sustain and uphold the respective governments in which they reside, while protected in their inherent and inalienable rights by the laws of such governments; and that sedition and rebellion are unbecoming every citizen thus protected, and should be punished accordingly; and that all governments have a right to enact such laws as in their own judgments are best calculated to secure the public interest; at the same time, however, holding sacred the freedom of conscience.[77]

Note the last phrase of the passage, imposing a limit to the legitimacy of the government's authority. Freedom, however, is to be tempered by rule of law.[78] The example of coercing obedience to legitimate authority is illustrated in the book of Alma. The leader of the Lamanites, Amalickiah, aspires to replace Moroni as leader of the Nephites and stirs dissent among them. Moroni gathers up the people to stand against the dissenters and Amalickiah's forces find themselves outnumbered and flee. Not wishing the Amalickiahites to join the Lamanites, Moroni's army pursues them and leads most of them back to Nephi. Those who "would not enter into a covenant to support the cause of freedom" are put to death.[79]

On the other, other hand, the case of the Anti-Nephi-Lehies shows how obedience to authority may give way to self-defense. The Anti-Nephi-Lehies are a group of Lamanites who accept Christ, secede from the Lamanites, and renounce all use of the sword, even in self-defense.[80] When the Lamanites attack them, it is considered righteous that they should be defended.[81] The Doctrine and Covenants do not bar the use of force in defense when it becomes necessary, in spite of or even against authority:

> We believe that men should appeal to the civil law for redress of all wrongs and grievances, where personal abuse is inflicted or the right of property or character infringed, where such laws exist as will protect the same; but we

believe that all men are justified in defending themselves, their friends, and property, and the government, from the unlawful assaults and encroachments of all persons in times of exigency, where immediate appeal cannot be made to the laws, and relief afforded.[82]

Tyranny, however, does not constitute lawful authority: "That which breaketh a law, and abideth not by law, but seeketh to become a law unto itself, and willeth to abide in sin, and altogether abideth in sin, cannot be sanctified by law, neither by mercy, justice, nor judgment."[83] It follows that "assaults and encroachments" by a tyrannical civil government would also give rise to self-defense.

On the other, other, other hand, the book of Mosiah warns that revolt against tyranny is a very painful, destructive, and bloody affair:

> And behold, now I say unto you, ye cannot dethrone an iniquitous king save it be through much contention, and the shedding of much blood. For behold, he has his friends in iniquity, and he keepeth his guards about him; and he teareth up the laws of those who have reigned in righteousness before him . . . And he enacteth laws, and sendeth them forth among his people, yea, laws after the manner of his own wickedness; and whosoever doth not obey his laws he causeth to be destroyed.[84]

It is precisely this danger that prompted Joseph Smith, having gathered a Mormon army and dispatched it to Missouri and found that he could not win a military confrontation, to counsel restraint against the persecutors of Mormons in Missouri in 1834.[85] The Mormons took a similar stance during the so-called Utah War of 1857–1858, when federal troops moved into Utah to displace Brigham Young as governor of the territory. Other than a few guerrilla attacks on supplies, the Mormons offered little resistance and soon allowed the federal government to reassert its authority.

JUST REBELLION IN THE MODERN CHURCHES

Modern church doctrines on just rebellion vary widely. Some contemplate the possibility of active resistance to an unjust authority or overthrowing it altogether:

> The citizen is obliged in conscience not to follow the directives of civil authorities when they are contrary to the demands of the moral, to the fundamental rights of persons or the teachings of the Gospel. *Refusing obedience* to civil authorities, when their demands are contrary to those of an upright conscience, finds its justification in the distinction between serving God and serving the political community. . . . Armed *resistance* to oppression by po-

litical authority is not legitimate, unless all the following conditions are met: [here follow five enumerated conditions]. [Catholic][86]

For the sake of a greater good or for reasons of conscience, citizens may need to oppose a prevailing understanding or practice of national identity and interest. Citizens may even need to resist oppressive government. [ELCA][87]

The honor which inferiors owe to their superiors is: . . . willing obedience to their lawful commands and counsels. . . . The sins of inferiors against their superiors are: . . . rebellion against their persons. . . . The sins of superiors are . . . commanding things unlawful, . . . *provoking them to wrath,* . . . or lessening their authority, by an unjust, indiscreet, rigorous, or remiss behavior. [PCUSA][88]

The Methodist Church accepts the legitimacy of resistance only grudgingly:

Some of us believe that war, and other acts of violence, are never acceptable to Christians. We also acknowledge that many Christians believe that . . . the force of arms may regretfully be preferable to unchecked aggression, *tyranny* and genocide. [Methodist][89]

This canon makes no distinction between interstate and intrastate conflict. The Methodist Church and SBC appear to favor passive resistance to or civil disobedience of unjust laws:

It is the duty of all Christians . . . to observe and obey the laws and commands of the governing or supreme authority [of their countries] and to use all laudable means to encourage and enjoin obedience to the powers that be. [Methodist][90]

Citizens have a duty to abide by laws duly adopted by orderly and just process of government. . . . [W]e recognize the right of individuals to dissent when acting under the constraint of conscience and, after having exhausted all legal recourse, to resist or disobey laws that they deem to be unjust. [Methodist][91]

Civil government being ordained of God, it is the duty of Christians to render loyal obedience thereto in all things not contrary to the revealed will of God. [SBC][92]

The Episcopal doctrine stands out for its emphasis on the *legitimacy* of the civil authority, rather than on the manner of its rule. Note the absence of any express condition of lawfulness of the authority's commands:

[W]e hold it to be the duty of all men who are professors of the Gospel, to pay respectful obedience to the Civil Authority, regularly and legitimately constituted. [Episcopal][93]

The Mormon position is already stated above.

The modern just war criteria will now be applied systematically to rebellion against tyranny.

Proper Authority

As with war, evaluating the legitimacy of rebellion begins with defining its rightful authority. The idea that *any* person may have temporal "authority" to revolt, or even a right to disobey lawful authority, is counterintuitive, for no lawgiver, democratic or authoritarian, would ever admit to a "right" of its subjects to disobey it, much less depose it by force. Indeed, to do so would undermine one of the fundamental tenets of democracy, which is the orderly and peaceful transfer of power from one regime to another.

Even though "proper authority" to revolt against the government appears impossible to legitimately acquire, it is still a necessary component for just rebellion. In interstate conflict, the distinction between a hostile act carried out by a public authority or a private entity is the difference between a legitimate act of war and an act of brigandage; the latter is a crime and the former is not. In intrastate conflict, an attack by a public actor is construed as an act of rebellion whereas an attack by a private actor is regarded as terrorism or murder. Both are crimes in the state's domestic law but not all crimes are universally legitimate. Viewed through the lens of public opinion, a public actor or authority is just that: public, and therefore more likely to gain the acquiescence of the public and eventually legitimacy. Private actors will be regarded as little more than mobs. Indeed, only the latter "crimes," terrorism and murder, are recognized as such outside the state in which they are committed.

History offers several examples of how proper authority to remove a government by force may be created. In the English Civil Wars of 1642–1651, Parliament itself revolted against, deposed, and executed King Charles I. The French Revolution had the support of the Third Estate, an official body within the legislature of the *ancien régime* that represented the interests of the commoners. The American Revolution began as a popular tax revolt against London, led by wealthy landowners, statesmen, and other prominent persons. In the U.S. Civil War, state governments themselves voted to secede from the Union. In the twentieth century, many military coups were undertaken by military officers or other, self-made military leaders with a following, in the mold of a modern leader like Idi Amin. The military coup in Thailand in 2006, in which the prime minister was overthrown, had the support of none other than the king. In many cases the new governments are recognized, thus legitimized, by other states. Temporal proper authority to lead a revolt appears to be conferred simply by virtue of leading it—for a leader must by definition have followers.

What confers proper authority spiritually is less clear. The authority to depose a civil government and replace it with another must ultimately come from God; the mystery is in defining how that authority is revealed and exercised. In this respect classical writings, both Protestant and Catholic, diverge widely. At one extreme, that of unrestrained popular revolt, is the work of Buchanan, who reasons that since kings must rule in accordance with the law,[94] those who go outside the law place themselves "beyond the bounds of civilized society" and in doing so "forfeit their rights to be treated as human beings."[95] Buchanan regards the authority from God as inherent. At the other extreme, that of complete restraint absent an explicit authorization, is the Doctrine and Covenants of the Mormon Church, which prohibit force even in self-defense prior to suffering three times at the hands of the enemy and then requesting and receiving a specific mandate from God, as communicated through the prophet (who is also the president of the church). A modest step removed from this extreme is the contention of Suarez in *Defensio Fidei* that the pope, by virtue of his "coercive power" over wicked, heretical, and disobedient princes,[96] has the power to authorize and legitimize a rebellion against the king.[97] The problem with the two latter approaches is that they arrogate to a single person the authority to speak on behalf of God, which other churches do not recognize. As a practical matter, Suarez's theory could not be implemented today, as the Vatican's temporal power over other states is long since defunct. The suggestions of Luther and Calvin that God deposes tyrants by working through others, while theoretically sound, are similarly dissatisfying; not only do they leave open the question of specifically who will act on God's behalf but also they cannot distinguish those with truly divine authority from those who merely claim it.

A sound middle-ground position can be forged from Mariana, the *Vindiciae*, and the other major point of Suarez's *Defensio Fidei*. All three authors agree that the state, in one form or another, retains the power to revoke the authority of the sovereign to rule over it. The *Vindiciae* provides for resisting tyranny on a corporate level, organized by "duly appointed" authorities who represent the people, and fought much like resistance to an outside invasion. Inherent in this requirement is a measure of active support from persons with some degree of political authority, thus distinguishing a genuine rebellion from the anarchy of a peasant revolt. Mariana recognizes the need for even the absolute monarch to consult with and retain the support of the aristocracy (the simple reality being that provoking those with the means of defeating the ruler invites them to do exactly that), thus implying that a sovereign who cannot govern other elites cannot legitimately govern the state either. Suarez's emphasis on the *process* by which a sovereign is lawfully deposed, tried, and sentenced for crimes against the state implies a requirement of some form of public authority with superior jurisdiction over the sovereign. In addition to the pope, that public authority is the state itself, taken as a whole, acting "in accordance with the public and general deliberations of its communities and leading men."[98] In Suarez's view, the sovereign can be deposed and slain lawfully by his or her own subjects, but only in an orderly, public, and corporate fashion. This, to Suarez, is the surest path to legitimacy, or proper authority, of the rebellion. James Brown Scott offers the English Revolution and execution of Charles I as a case study of legitimate tyrannicide according to the Suarezian model.[99]

In one respect, however, the Suarezian model is too permissive. Suarez agrees that even a revolt to depose a usurper must act under color of public authority. Suarez considers such authority to be implied, since the usurper has no lawful jurisdiction over the people.[100] In view of the Christian predilection for order and restraint, such a premise would seem to invite anarchy; the experiences of Somalia since 1992 and the Iraq War today poignantly illustrate the danger of removing a civil authority without another to take its place, one that has the popular support and ability to maintain order afterward. Otherwise, the field is open for any individual to claim the office of sovereign, which is a recipe for civil war.

Just Cause

Classical Christian political theory calls for two different standards of misrule to justify rebellion, depending on the legitimacy of the sovereign's claim of authority. In the case of the illegitimate usurper, *tyrannus in titula*, just cause to revolt is inherent—the usurping authority can be deposed and killed simply by virtue of not being the lawful claimant to the office. In the case of the legitimate sovereign whose rule is tyrannical, *tyrannus in regimine*, the degree of misrule must be substantial.

This distinction, however, confuses legitimacy with justice, and in doing so, overlooks the possibility that a usurping, illegitimate sovereign could rule *more* justly than the previous, legitimate one. In such a case, the greater benefit to the state is preserving the more just regime. The classical distinction also does not provide for the possibility that an illegitimate usurpation can be legitimized by the consent of the people. If it is true that the population (or the state, taken as a whole) ultimately retains its collective authority over the sovereign, then this must be the case. The consent must be genuine, given freely and not coerced by fear or intimidation. If the usurpation works to the overall benefit of the state, then perhaps the state should accept it for the sake of maintaining peace and order. The mere absence of proper authority to govern *per se* may no longer be sufficient cause for rebellion.

What, then, is sufficient cause? A common theme throughout of the Bible and other sources is that those who hold political power must govern for the collective benefit of their subjects, not the private benefit of themselves. Mariana writes, "One can conceive of no graver pestilence than a king who serves his personal inclinations, or governs the public and private affairs of his subjects on the sole basis of his own judgment or that of his courtiers."[101] Corruption, he continues, is the root of that evil which we call tyranny.[102] But it is not merely the corruption that makes tyranny so insidious; rather, it is the unjust violence on the subjects that a tyrant's corrupt greed motivates. "The tyrant, . . ." reiterates Mariana, "afflicts his subjects with a grievous power which—in many cases—has been seized by violence; or else, even if this power be sound in its origin, it lapses into vice, and particularly, into avarice, lust and cruelty."[103] A tyrant, to Suarez, "either turns all things to his private advantage, neglecting the common advantage, or else unjustly oppresses his subjects by plunder, slaughter, corruption, or the unjust perpetration of other similar deeds, with public effect and on numerous occasions."[104] The just cause for violent rebellion is not the corruption *per se*, but the violence that flows from it.

In contrast, Buchanan's concept of just cause for rebellion is too broad. Buchanan finds "disgust with ambition, disorder, murders, and civil war" to justify deposing a tyrannical ruler.[105] In Buchanan's politic, however, it is not the ambition, disorder, murders and war *themselves* which justify rebellion, but public outrage from them. This formulation does not account for public opposition to the government based on a mistake of fact, or worse, opposition to a policy that the government has the prerogative to implement. For example, there is considerable "public disgust" with the Iraq War (rightly or wrongly), but no reasonable person seriously entertains any idea of deposing the Bush administration by force. Even worse than that, Buchanan's formulation does not account for the *lack* of public outrage at acts of state that are objectively criminal (except outrage from the victims), a situation to which ultranationalist ideologies have been prone.

Instead, the tyrannical acts must be "public and manifest," as Suarez puts it.[106] Only defense of one's own life justifies a subject killing his sovereign,[107] though Suarez does acknowledge the possibility of extending that right to defense of the state as a whole, when "the king is actually attacking the state, with the unjust intention of destroying it and slaughtering the citizens."[108] Just as it is reasonable to resort to violence to prevent oneself from being unjustly abducted, enslaved, or tortured, it may be inferred that a government that "attacks" its people in such a manner invites just rebellion against it. However, Suarez also emphasizes that defense must be legitimate; if a wicked king "is not inflicting actual violence upon the state subject to him, so long as he does not begin an unjust war against it . . . no occasion for defence is offered."[109]

The articulation of just cause for rebellion offered by Suarez is visible in the criteria for just rebellion advanced by the Vatican today. The Catholic Catechism requires that for armed resistance to an oppressive government to be legitimate, there must be a "certain, grave, and prolonged violation of fundamental rights."[110] Otherwise citizens are bound to submit to and cooperate with the civil authority. However, the political obligations are mutual; the catechism also states that "[p]olitical authorities are obliged to respect the fundamental rights of the human person. They will dispense justice humanely by respecting the rights of everyone."[111] In more basic terms, the duty of the citizenry to submit to authority is predicated on the authority's duty to safeguard and improve the lives of the citizenry. When the authority fails to discharge that duty, and in doing so inflicts injury on the citizenry, just cause for rebellion is created.

Right Intent

Recall the thread of argument, first advanced by Ambrose of Milan and John Chrysostom and perfected by Augustine, that the power of the sword is virtuous when employed for the correction of sinners. Chapter 6 concluded that the use of force between sovereign states is just if carried out with charitable motives and with the objective of fraternal correction. That argument is extrapolated from the divinely ordained power of the civil government to use force against its subjects for the same purpose, that is, for law enforcement.

In just rebellion, right intent addresses whether the reverse is true: Does the citizenry of a state, or state taken as a whole, have the right to use force against civil authority in order to stop *it* from committing sin? If the sovereign is subject to the collective jurisdiction of the people and governs only with their consent, as the early modern writers propound, then the answer must be yes—provided, of course, that all other criteria are satisfied as well. Once this right is established, then whether any given rebellion is actually a collective act of the people will be determined by the facts. The *Vindiciae* rightly points out that a just rebellion must be organized, as opposed to the random acts of a fringe element. How well organized the rebellion is, as well as the level of support among the general public, indicates the degree to which the prospect of rebellion has been deliberated by the public, a process which helps ensure that the rebellion is engineered for the collective good of many, rather than for the private gain of a few. Suarez makes this point in showing that the execution of a tyrant must further the common good, not private advantage. As in interstate war, the conduct of the fighters is likely to reveal their true motives; their inward intent will be observable by whether their outward actions stop the oppression, or aggrandize themselves. The orderliness of the treatment of the deposed leaders is also revealing, which is why a lengthy, well-deliberated criminal trial and sentence (e.g., Charles I) commands greater legitimacy than a two-hour proceeding followed by a mob-style execution (e.g., Nicolae Ceausescu of Romania).

Proportionality of Cause

Just as a righteous war must be calculated to achieve a greater good (or in Firmage's formula, a better peace), so must it also be with rebellion; the foreseeable good must outweigh the foreseeable harm. This proviso is traceable to Thomas Aquinas, who points out that the rebellion should inflict no greater harm than that which the people are already suffering.[112] Suarez also propounds this condition in his treatment of tyrannicide; slaying the tyrant must not be likely to bring about the same or greater ills as before.[113] The modern Catholic Church provides for righteous resistance to authority if "such resistance will not provoke worse disorders."[114]

The same type of analysis offered in chapter 7 may be adopted to evaluate what nature of cause is worth the drastic remedy of rebellion. On the spiritual plane, the justness of revolting against authority is linked to the severity of the sin that motivates the oppression. Oppression resulting from the mortal sin of murder, or the venial sin of wrath, may be a more serious matter than that which results from pride or gluttony.

On the temporal plane, the severity of the injury to the population caused by the oppression can be judged according to another adaptation of Maslow's hierarchy of needs. The most fundamental need of a community is survival, which equates to freedom from genocide on a societal level and from being killed arbitrarily on an individual level, in a campaign of ethnic cleansing, or for trumped-up, political, or petty offenses. The next fundamental need is security, that is, protection from injury and/or confinement. This need encompasses freedoms from torture and rape, arbitrary detention, and slavery, as well as freedom from a justifiable fear of these tragedies, which can be instilled in a large society merely by well publicizing the infliction of such injuries on a few. Injuries to these two fundamental human needs are probably grave enough to satisfy proportionality of cause. In contrast, injuries to the next two tiers of fulfillment and leadership probably are not severe enough to justify the harm that insurgency and civil war often inflict on a state.

Reasonable Prospect of Success

The modern Catholic Church imposes a condition on just rebellion that there be a "well-founded hope of success,"[115] analogous to the similar condition for just war. In chapter 8 this criterion was reevaluated as an extension of proportionality of cause, finding that the greater the injury, the lower the certainty of success needed to be to legitimize the war. The same is true for rebellion; when the oppression threatens the survival or security of the population, resistance should be justified even when more likely to fail than succeed. On the other hand, an attempt to depose a regime for a relatively minor injury (even assuming it satisfies proportionality of cause) should not be undertaken unless the probability of success is extremely high.

Last Resort

Catholic thought on rebellion has also adopted an analog to the criterion of last resort in just war theory. Suarez maintains that tyrannicide is justifiable only absent recourse to any authority over the tyrant.[116] Aside from the definitionally obvious, that the sovereign has no temporal superior authority, Suarez also implies that the legal machinery of the state (the law itself is superior even to the sovereign) is unable to provide a remedy. Modern Catholic doctrine articulates two conditions of just rebellion, which may both be classified under this heading: that "all other means of redress have been exhausted" and that "it is impossible reasonably to foresee any better solution."[117]

The objections to last resort set forth in chapter 9 apply to just rebellion as well, with one modification. It is incumbent upon Christians to do as little harm to their neighbors as is reasonable, and if rebellion is not necessary to overcome tyranny then it would be uncharitable to resort to it. If some peaceful means is genuinely available for redress of the would-be rebels' grievances, then they should avail themselves of it in good faith before taking up arms. Such means could consist of the state's own courts (assuming judicial independence, impartiality, and enforcement powers). For political grievances, peaceful means of resolution could consist of mediation or arbitration. This only works, however, if all sides are confident that the others will act in good faith and comply with any adverse decisions or rulings. When that confidence is breached, then this avenue of peaceful resolution is not reasonably available and the rebels need not resort to it. Thus the Catholic Catechism's criterion above, that no better solution than armed rebellion can reasonably be foreseen, may be a workable condition of just rebellion.

Just Means

That any Christian-based armed resistance to authority must adhere to the same norms of armed conflict as for international conflicts is so obvious that it almost needs no mention. Much of the world's distaste for civil war today results from atrocities against noncombatants of and by both sides. Modern international law affirms the principle of noncombatant immunity even in domestic armed conflicts. The Genocide Convention makes no distinction between civil and international wars and Common Article 3 of the 1949 Geneva Conventions prohibits combatants from committing violent acts against noncombatants and taking hostages, among other things. The Second Additional Protocol to the Geneva Conventions expressly extends the law of armed conflict to civil wars. The definitions of genocide, crimes against humanity, and war crimes set forth in the Rome Statute of the International Criminal Court also make no distinction between international and civil wars. Acts of rebel forces in violation of these proscriptions must not be regarded as legitimate, even if the original cause for rebellion were just.

CONCLUSION

In keeping with the premise that war, intervention, and rebellion are all part of the same political phenomenon, this chapter has examined the theory of just rebellion and finds it to closely parallel that of just war. It must be undertaken by some public actor that enjoys popular support. It must be provoked by some injury to the people, grave enough to warrant revoking the social contract between the governing and the governed, such that the foreseeable good of an armed rebellion outweighs the foreseeable harm. The rebellion further must be motivated by charity for the common good as opposed to the private benefit of the rebels. Unlike for just war, the criterion of last resort has some application for just rebellion, if only by virtue of the aggrieved population nominally having a higher temporal authority from which to seek relief. Finally, modern *jus in bello* clearly applies to intrastate conflicts as well as interstate.

This chapter has focused only on the question of internal rebellion, assuming no outside involvement or assistance. This assumption frequently does not hold in modern state practice; the next chapter will therefore address the prosecution of just rebellion by another state on the aggrieved population's behalf.

· *12* ·

Humanitarian Intervention

*H*umanitarian intervention is the use of force by states to prevent or stop gross violations of fundamental human rights on a large scale in other states. The term has also been used, inaccurately, to describe hostage rescue or evacuation operations (usually from war or civil unrest),[1] or interventions to keep in power or install a democratic government in the absence of any significant humanitarian crises (prodemocratic intervention). In contrast, "humanitarian intervention" is a military response to atrocities committed against persons numbering in the thousands or millions, or a substantial risk thereof, by the civil authorities or by an armed rebel or other paramilitary group.

A right of humanitarian intervention is inextricably conjoined with the right of a population to revolt against civil authority. A regime's abuse of its people usually does not do significant harm to other states. For a humanitarian intervention to be legitimate, the state conducting it cannot act on behalf of itself, for it has sustained no injury to warrant the use of force. Rather, the intervening state acts on the behalf of the aggrieved population of the other state. The right of a state to remove another state's government from power can *only* be derived from the right of the latter state's own population to rebel against and depose its government.

ORIGIN AND DEVELOPMENT

In Theory

Biblical examples of humanitarian intervention, whether historical or philosophical, are quite limited. In the Old Testament, such examples include the passage "rescu[e] those who are taken away to death" in Proverbs[2] and "Deliver from the hand of the oppressor anyone who has been robbed" in Jeremiah.[3] The New Testament contains no overt mandates, only that which is implied in the commandment that Christians love their neighbors as themselves—a willingness to put oneself at risk for self-defense mandates a willingness to put oneself at risk to defend others. Historically the church has applied this principle to the duties of civil authorities and the military to defend the general population from attack, the former from criminals and the latter from other states. But nothing in the Bible or in church doctrines precludes a state from giving of itself, that is, expenditures and military forces, to defend the populations of *other* states from attack, whether from their own governments or from outside. Indeed, this would seem to be an even higher moral calling than defending one's own state.

The church also has said very little about the right of one regime to depose another for mistreating its subjects. In the first few centuries of Christianity, this is not so surprising, given the confluence of the Pauline admonition to submit to authority, the pacifist influence of Tertullian, and the *Pax Romana*. After Augustine, who had treated the use of the sword to correct sinners domestically and internationally as the same, the dearth of church doctrine on such a cause for war is surprising, especially after John of Salisbury and Thomas Aquinas supported the right to revolt against tyranny. Perhaps the lack of ecclesiastical discourse during the Middle Ages reflects a lack of state practice—before the Reformation there are no cases in Western history of one sovereign going to war against another for such a purpose.

In this area, like all others, the Reformation changed everything. The heavy-handedness by which religious partisans on both sides pursued their causes brought just rebellion to the political forefront. With entire states and whole communities taking sides, the political atmosphere was ripe for states supporting oppressed populations in other states. Thus Catholic and Protestant theologians alike now had something to say on the subject, though key differences ensued. Luther interprets Christ's words as forbidding Christians from wielding the sword on their *own* behalf but instead obligating them to wield it "to restrain wickedness;"[4] having done so, he points out that "God has still another way to punish rulers. . . . He can raise up foreign rulers. . . . Thus there is vengeance, punishment, and danger enough hanging over tyrants and rulers, and God does not allow them to be wicked and have peace and joy."[5] Calvin, drawing from Old Testament scriptures extolling defense of others, is not so explicit about inviting foreign interventions but compensates by unabashedly affirming the righteousness of protecting the innocent:

But as [magistrates] cannot do this [i.e., protect the public], unless they defend good men from the injuries of the wicked, and aid the oppressed by their relief and protection, they are likewise armed with power for the suppression of crimes, and the severe punishment of malefactors, whose wickedness disturbs the public peace.[6]

For if [kings and nations] have been intrusted with power to preserve the tranquility of their own territories, . . . can they exert this power for a better purpose than to repel the violence of him who disturbs . . . the general tranquility of the nation, who . . . perpetrates acts of oppression, cruelty, and every species of crime?[7]

In contrast, the Catholics continued to frame intervention around retention of the faith. Victoria supports the right of the Spaniards to conquer the native peoples of the New World if necessary to protect the right of new converts there to remain Christian,[8] in addition to protecting the innocent from being killed in pagan sacrificial rituals.[9] Suarez, however, assigns such authority to the church; in supporting Pope Innocent III's authority to strip King John of England of his "kingly dignity,"[10] that is, his spiritual power over his subjects, he concludes that "[I]t is a function of the papal office to defend the subjects of an heretical or perverse prince, and to free them from that evident peril."[11] Recall that Suarez includes defense of the state as a whole against the tyrant as part of the right of self-defense;[12] as well as the right to defend others; "Therefore," he writes, "the killing of a tyrant on this ground is permitted not only to the members of a state, *but also to foreigners*, in either case and with respect to either kind of tyrant."[13] Suarez thus supports the right to humanitarian intervention.

Suarez was writing during the twilight of the Catholic Church's influence on political affairs; it remained to secular (and overwhelmingly Protestant) theorists in the natural law tradition to develop the concept further. The French jurist Jean Bodin propounds that all sovereigns are subject to natural law[14] but, like Luther, Bodin disavows the right of the populace to rebel against a legitimate ruler, even a tyrant; because of this restriction, foreign sovereigns are empowered to act on the people's behalf.[15] The author of the *Vindiciae* goes further, finding not merely a right but a moral *duty* to intervene.[16] After the *Vindiciae*, the development of humanitarian intervention in natural law goes secular, treated in the works of Gentili, Grotius, and Pufendorf.[17]

In Practice

Despite the lack of attention from the church, modern state practice in humanitarian intervention has its genesis in charity for the plight of oppressed

Christian nationalities. In the early nineteenth century, the work of the Concert of Europe—through the Holy Alliance—in preserving the *status quo* against revolutionary movements[18] effectively foreclosed the possibility of interventions to support rebellions against tyranny within the Concert itself. The situation of eastern Christians was another matter, however; the decline of the Ottoman Empire enabled the major powers to intervene on behalf of oppressed Christian nations in Ottoman-controlled lands. Christian suzerainty to a non-Christian empire was the source of considerable discomfort in some circles, for on one hand, the Holy Alliance was dedicated to maintaining the rule of law by preserving Turkish rule over those lands but on the other hand was also dedicated to preserving what it regarded as "Christian principles." Russia was particularly interested in the affairs of southeastern Europe, for much of the population was Orthodox Christian, and Russia had by the eighteenth century become the epicenter of eastern Christendom and the self-proclaimed champion of oppressed Orthodox Christians in the Ottoman Empire.[19] Russia exercised this power in 1810, and again in 1815, on behalf of the Serbs, who had been reduced to near slavery in their own homeland, forcing Turkey to grant Serb autonomy. Horrified by Ottoman atrocities committed against the Greeks, the other European powers forced the Ottomans to grant it independence.[20] Collective interest in the condition of eastern Christians was borne out again in 1860 with the French intervention in Lebanon. In May 1860 heavy fighting broke out between the various religious factions and 11,000 Christians were massacred and 100,000 displaced. By agreement with the rest of the Concert, France intervened to restore order.[21] Although Turkey consented to the intervention, it did so reluctantly and its consent was more akin to acquiescence to Western firepower. In 1876, the rebellion of Christians in Ottoman-held Bosnia and Herzegovina led to the Russo-Turkish War of 1877-1878 and the Treaty of Berlin, which forced the Porte to grant independence or autonomy to most of the Balkans and to affirm their religious rights.[22]

Thus humanitarian intervention was born under Christian auspices and owes its heritage to Christian charity, albeit veiled by the expediency of the power politics of the day. Whatever the inward motivations of the statesmen may have been, they were also prompted by a desire to liberate nations from a foreign rule that was neither desired nor benign. These cases are distinguishable from the Crusades, for the Crusaders' presence was not particularly desirable to eastern Christians and the general population among the Byzantines preferred Turkish rule to Latin. In the nineteenth century, the interventions were more welcome. Even the legal commentaries of the day, which were otherwise dismissive of the legal regulation of the use of force, justified these cases (and Greece in particular) using charitable language such as "stopping the effusion of blood"[23] and principles of humanity.[24] The doctrine had enough support in the United States that one of the primary causes of the Spanish-American War was public outcry against Spanish brutalities in Cuba, in which over 100,000 people were said to have perished.[25] In what may be called the first modern humanitarian intervention without an overtly religious component, the United States forced Spain to recognize Cuban independence.[26] By the end of World War II, however, the doctrine of humanitarian intervention had come to be regarded as defunct. The League of Nations Covenant, the Kellogg-Briand Pact, and the U.N. Charter all omit any specific reference to the right of humanitarian intervention. All of those instruments, however, were written at a time when human rights were not considered to be matters of international concern, but remained exclusively domestic affairs. The drafters of these instruments, however, did not anticipate the blossoming of human rights law and the emergence of human rights as a fundamental norm in international law and politics. With that norm now firmly entrenched in modern statecraft, it is again possible for humanitarian intervention to enjoy political, legal, and moral legitimacy, provided that the humanitarian situation truly warrants it.

In modern statecraft, the label "humanitarian intervention" is commonly affixed to several specific conflicts. In 1971 India invaded East Pakistan in response to the atrocities committed by the (West) Pakistani army against the civilian population; East Pakistan emerged from the conflict as the independent state of Bangladesh. In 1979 a wave of interventions took place in quick succession; Vietnam invaded Cambodia and deposed the Khmer Rouge, Tanzania invaded Uganda to oust the regime of Idi Amin, and France supported a coup to depose the self-styled Emperor Bokassa in the Central African Republic. In all three cases, the prior regimes had committed major human rights violations, including torture and executions. After the Gulf War, the United States and several coalition partners began enforcing no-fly zones in Iraq; the northern zone to protect the Kurdish minority and the southern zone to protect the Shi'ite majority. Both groups had been the victims of atrocities at the hands of Saddam Hussein's regime, dominated by the Sunni minority. In 1999 NATO allies conducted air strikes in Yugoslavia to induce the central government to stop the ethnic cleansing of Kosovo; Serb military and paramilitary forces had displaced nearly one million ethnic Albanians and were systematically destroying their homes and villages, leaving them with no place to return. Finally, this author has argued that humanitarian intervention should play a significant role in the debate over the justification of the U.S. invasion of Iraq in 2003 to depose Saddam Hussein, whose regime was at least as bad as that of Idi Amin.[27]

In addition to the above cases, several multilateral interventions conducted with the consent or acquiescence of the Security Council should be mentioned. In 1990 a joint military force of the Economic Community of West African States (ECOWAS) intervened to stop a civil war in Liberia, in which both sides had committed numerous atrocities against civilians.[28] In 1993 the U.N. Security Council authorized a multilateral intervention in Bosnia, in order to stop the atrocities and "ethnic cleansing" perpetrated primarily by the Serbs against the Muslims, and to a lesser extent by the Croats and Muslims against the Serbs and each other.[29] In 1997, ECOWAS invaded Sierra Leone to restore the elected government to power after it had been deposed in a coup led by factions that had been notorious for their atrocities against civilians.[30] Legally these interventions do not have to be justified as "humanitarian interventions," because they were authorized by the Security Council (thereby resolving any doubts about their legality). However, the motivation of the U.N. in authorizing them provides further evidence that humanitarian intervention is reemerging as a legal—and moral—justification for war.

HUMANITARIAN INTERVENTION
AND THE MODERN CHURCHES

When the positions of the modern denominations on humanitarian intervention are measured against their positions on violent rebellion, the relationship between the two is quite revealing. The Grotian approach to humanitarian intervention links its right to the right of the people suffering under the oppressive regime;[31] that correlation is plainly visible in how the modern churches responded to the Kosovo crises of 1998-1999. The Catholic Church, PCUSA, and the Mormon Church all affirm the right of an oppressed population to revolt against civil authority if necessary to defend their lives[32] and their positions on humanitarian intervention are consistent:

> *The international community as a whole has the moral obligation to intervene on behalf of those groups whose very survival is threatened or whose basic human rights are seriously violated.* . . . States cannot remain indifferent; on the contrary, if all other available means should prove ineffective, it is "legitimate and even obligatory to take concrete measures to disarm the aggressor." [Catholic][33]

> [The Assembly affirms] the following criteria as guidance in just peace decision making concerning military intervention for humanitarian purposes in situations of massive suffering and/or major violations of human rights [here follow seven criteria, to which we shall return]. [PCUSA][34]

[T]here are times and circumstances when nations are justified, in fact have an obligation, to fight for family, for liberty, and against tyranny, threat, and oppression. . . . [W]e are a freedom-loving people, committed to the defense of liberty wherever it is in jeopardy. [LDS][35]

The grudging manner in which the Methodist Church accepts the legitimacy of rebellion is also reflected in its iteration of the just causes of war:

We believe war is incompatible with the teachings and example of Christ. We therefore reject war as an instrument of national foreign policy, to be employed *only . . . in the prevention of such evils as genocide, brutal suppression of human rights,* and unprovoked international aggression. [Methodist][36]

The ELCA's position is also somewhat grudging:

Helping the neighbor in need may require protecting innocent people from injustice and aggression. While we support the use of nonviolent measures, there may be no other way to offer protection in some circumstances than by restraining forcibly those harming the innocent. We do not, then—for the sake of the neighbor—rule out possible support for the use of military force. [ELCA][37]

The other denominations, not being enthusiastic about legitimizing a right to rebellion, do not express positions in favor of humanitarian intervention either.

The PCUSA's formulation is the only one that expresses specific criteria that the intervention must satisfy to be legitimate.[38] The criteria themselves correspond roughly to the modern criteria of just war. They are:

1. Intervention must respond to a real and genuine need that cannot be met by other means [last resort].
2. Intervention must have a reasonable chance of alleviating the conditions it seeks to overcome [reasonable prospect of success].
3. Intervention must constitute humanitarian rescue and not cloak the pursuit of the economic or narrow security interests of the intervening powers [just cause and right intent].
4. Intervention, whenever possible, should have international auspices in order to achieve the greatest presumption of legitimacy [proper authority].
5. Intervention should advance the general welfare of the inhabitants of the region in question and not become a means by which powerful elites further cement their power [just cause and right intent].
6. Intervention should involve the minimum degree of coercion necessary to achieve the purposes of the action [proportionality of means].

7. Intervention in the forms of punitive sanctions should be targeted against those in authority rather than against broad population groups [discrimination].

Not surprisingly, proportionality of cause is absent since that criterion has not been adopted in the PCUSA's just war criteria generally.

Having affirmed such a right in the abstract, however, many modern churches flinched when presented with real-world, concrete crises, as reflected in their reactions to the situation in Kosovo in 1998 and 1999. Observe these samples of straightforward wishy-washiness:

> The NATO bombing campaign poses difficult moral and policy questions on which persons of good will may disagree. It seems clear to us that the humanitarian objective . . . is a legitimate one. What is less clear are the consequences of the use of force. . . . What is the likelihood of bombing achieving its aims, and what is likely to follow if bombing does not succeed? [Catholic][39]

> Like most Americans, I have been distressed by the reports of the evolving crisis in the Balkans. The tragic suffering of the Kosovo Albanians, caused by armed attacks and other forms of violence—including "ethnic cleansing"—conducted by Yugoslav security forces, compels the international community to respond. I regret that military action has largely replaced diplomacy. [Goes on to quote "For Peace in God's World," without elaboration.] [ELCA][40]

> I am personally torn by this decision of NATO because its purpose is noble while the means are so violent. Christ calls us into relationship and the present course leads us to further alienation from one another. Yet for us to stand by and allow the genocide to continue is also intolerable. [Episcopal][41]

Only the PCUSA unequivocally affirmed the right of humanitarian intervention during the Kosovo crisis, and even then it punted on the question of legitimacy of any specific operation, deferring to the Security Council's judgment.[42]

APPLICATION OF JUST WAR CRITERIA
TO HUMANITARIAN INTERVENTION

Although the PCUSA's list of criteria above serves as a useful point of departure, it is flawed for several reasons. First, instead of stating just cause and right intent one time each, the criteria contain two items that are hybrids of the two (the third and fifth). Second, there is no condition of proportionality of cause, which in itself is not surprising since the PCUSA's criteria for a just war generally do not include it. Most importantly, the criteria are not presented in a straightforward, logical manner as they are for just war generally; they are jumbled and appear to be mere articulations of the premises behind the conditions rather than a presentation of the conditions themselves. A better approach would be to apply methodically each criterion to humanitarian intervention.

Proper Authority

Like any other use of force, humanitarian intervention is only recognized as an act of state if it is carried out *by* a state. A private group trying to depose the government of another state cannot claim legitimacy, regardless of the conduct of that other government. Indeed, such an endeavor is ill-advised, as it is likely to invite a counterattack on the state in which that private group operates.

Some suggest that a humanitarian intervention has greater legitimacy if it is multilateral rather than unilateral. The PCUSA especially endorses this viewpoint in its suggestion that an intervention "should" be carried out under "international auspices." This premise is not supported by the record of states' reactions to such interventions in the past. The unilateral invasion of Cambodia and multilateral Kosovo War were both strongly condemned in the U.N., whereas the unilateral invasion of Uganda and multilateral intervention in Liberia were not. State practice suggests that support or condemnation of individual humanitarian interventions is driven far more by geopolitics than multilateralism.

It has also been suggested that humanitarian interventions should be legitimate only if they are authorized by the U.N. Security Council. The PCUSA's formulation is a veiled suggestion to that effect, and the Vatican declares that "[t]he measures adopted must be carried out in full respect of international law and the fundamental principle of equality among States."[43] As a strict measure of legitimacy, however, such a condition is misguided. The first reason for this is that if a humanitarian intervention must be approved by the Security Council, then the doctrine itself is rendered unnecessary. Once a use of force has been authorized (or legitimized afterward) by the Security Council, the inquiry into its legal (and therefore its political) validity ends. The Council can authorize the use of force in any situation that it considers a threat to international peace and security,[44] that is, for whatever reason it wants; consequently it needs no particular rationale for authorizing force. No use of force would ever be justified as humanitarian intervention because it would be justified under Security Council authority instead. The doctrine would then fall into disuse and disappear from the legal landscape, just as it did in the interwar period and during the first two decades of the U.N. The desuetude of the doctrine would remove a powerful disincentive for tyrants to oppress their populations; they need only sow enough dissension in the Security Council to keep an authorization from passing, a dishearteningly simple task.

The second reason such a requirement is not feasible is that it places more faith in Security Council politics, and indeed U.N. politics in general, than their past records justify. The ouster of the Khmer Rouge from power in Cambodia was not well-received in the General Assembly or the Security Council, primarily as a consequence of Cold War politics. The U.S., still licking its wounds from the loss of South Vietnam to the Communist north, was alarmed at further prospects of Communist expansion in southeast Asia, and the other members of the Association of South East Asian Nations (ASEAN) also feared Vietnamese hegemony. The Credentials Committee of the General Assembly even recommended that the Khmer Rouge delegation be accredited, despite that fact that the Vietnamese-backed government, then in *de facto* power, had also put forth a delegation.[45] In the Kosovo War, the tables were turned; NATO countries claimed a moral justification for the bombing of Yugoslavia, with some members even going so far as to assert a *legal* right.[46] Russia and China, however, opposed the intervention, as did many other states. Russia even propounded a draft Security Council resolution condemning the intervention, which got favorable votes only from three members including itself.[47] No resolution authorizing the Kosovo War could have passed, thus rendering it unlawful according to the strict letter of the U.N. Charter. Therefore the legitimacy of these interventions in international law is quite far removed from their moral legitimacy. Nicholas Wheeler has referred to the Cambodian situation as the "triumph of realism over common humanity"[48] and the Independent International Commission on Kosovo concluded that the Kosovo War was illegal but legitimate.[49] The ugly truth about these two cases is that, had the strict proponents of Security Council authorization had their way, Kosovo today would be homogenously Serb and the Khmer people would be nearly extinct. Indeed, the genocide perpetrated on the Tutsis by the Hutus in Rwanda in 1994 serves as a stark reminder of the consequences of inaction. These cases expose the pitfall of requiring approval from a political body that cannot be relied on to achieve a morally sound result.

Just Cause

A just cause for war is an injury caused by a state's breach of its obligations. Humanitarian intervention is governed by this principle just like any other form of war. The difficulty with applying it, however, is that the injury that major human rights violators inflict on other states is either minimal or intangible. Large-scale human rights violations do have the potential of sending large numbers of refugees into other states, for example, the Darfur Sudanese into Chad, but states themselves are often able to control their borders so as to prevent this (Cambodia, Uganda, Iraq, Kosovo). The influx of refugees, however vigorously touted as a justification for humanitarian intervention (East Pakistan, Sierra Leone), may sometimes be little more than a "cost of doing business" for states. Italy's claim, for example, that the influx of Albanian refugees in 1997 impacted its security seemed disingenuous coming from one of the seven major industrial powers.

Ultimately the just cause for humanitarian intervention cannot be traced to the injury of another state. It must instead be traced to the aggrieved population. As the human rights–violating government is effectively making war on the population, the population must at some point acquire the right to fight back in self-defense, that is, to resort to armed rebellion, as covered in the previous chapter. Furthermore, the injured party must be a *population*, not a few selected individuals. That population can be an oppressed minority or community, or the populace of a state at large.

An examination of the core cases of humanitarian intervention in modern statecraft reveals human rights situations in those countries that did significant injury to a minority group or an entire population. In each case the injury was just cause for a rebellion against authority, and therefore just cause for a humanitarian intervention as well. The injuries fall into two basic categories: oppression by the government in peacetime and atrocities committed in armed conflict.

The first category consists of wholesale violations of human rights for the purpose of consolidating power, enriching the elite, and/or terrorizing the population into submission by a legitimate or *de facto* government. The prime examples of this category are the abuses of the Amin regime in Uganda, the Bokassa regime in the Central African Republic, the Khmer Rouge regime in Cambodia, and the Ba'ath regime in Iraq. The Bokassa regime serves as a benchmark for the minimum degree of injury that gives rise to humanitarian intervention. In 1976 the president of that country, Jean-Bedel Bokassa, himself brought to power in a military coup, declared himself "emperor" of the country. As his rule grew increasingly erratic, his crackdowns on political opposition grew more brutal. What probably induced French forces to intervene and depose him was his alleged direct involvement in the beating deaths of 100–200 schoolchildren who had protested against purchasing school uniforms.

The Uganda case is far more severe. In 1971, a rebel force led by Idi Amin seized power in Uganda in a coup and began its reign of terror almost immediately. Government forces openly killed many members of the Lango tribe (to which the previous president had belonged) and summarily expelled thousands of citizens and long-time residents of Asian descent, leaving them with nothing. Amin gave his security forces broad powers of arrest without warrant and indefinite detention without charge. Armed with such authority and accountable to no law except Amin's whim, army officers and soldiers carried out hundreds of thousands of arbitrary arrests and killings, sometimes in order to possess the victims' wives or property, and sometimes for no reason at all. By 1978, corrupt agents of Amin's elite apparatus, the State Research Center, were arresting any Ugandan with the slightest appearance of affluence and making them sign away their bank accounts, killing them when the funds ran out. Amin's forces abducted and raped women with impunity. Torture at detention centers was routine, whether the detainees had been tried or not. After publicly complaining that the six percent Muslim minority in Uganda was coercing Christians to convert to Islam, Archbishop Luwum was murdered and Amin's persecution of Christians of the Lango and Acholi tribes escalated. The death toll during Amin's tyranny is estimated at 300,000.

The barbarity in Uganda was surpassed only by the killing fields of Cambodia under the Khmer Rouge. In 1975, the Khmer Rouge, an indigenous Communist insurgency, seized power from the U.S.-allied government in a coup. The following year, the leader of the Khmer Rouge, Pol Pot, embarked on a course of turning Cambodian society upside down, relocating entire villages, eliminating all property, eradicating all religion, evacuating millions of city dwellers to collective farms, and exterminating ethnic and religious minorities. In the newly reorganized society, the lowest class, known as "depositees," had no rights whatsoever, not even to food. For the masses, punishment for the slightest offense, even tardiness to work, usually meant torture and death for the offender and his or her entire family as well, including children. After the growing and harvesting seasons, thousands of farm workers were killed simply because they were no longer needed. Out of population of six and one-half million, between one and three million people died from the mass evacuations, slave conditions, starvation, disease, and executions.

The human rights situation in Iraq under Saddam Hussein was analogous to that in Uganda under Idi Amin. The Ba'ath regime arrested and executed thousands for political crimes, "insult" crimes (e.g., insulting the president), vaguely defined crimes such as subversion, and nonviolent crimes recast as "security offenses," including economic crimes such as violating currency regulations, forgery, and smuggling (except, of course, for Saddam's inner circle). Torture, including sexual violence, was routine for both political offenses and as a means of interrogation or intimidation. Saddam and his inner circle were extremely corrupt, having personal financial interests in all aspects of smuggling, heavy industry, and even the grocery business; they assessed fines and appropriated property at will. Saddam's son, Uday, was notorious for his propensity to commit rape and murder with virtual impunity.[50] Kenneth Pollack estimates the death toll under the regime to be 200,000 by 2002, with hundreds of thousands more survivors of torture.[51] Essentially, Saddam Hussein and his associates ruled Iraq by whim, treating the country as their own personal fiefdom, bank, and harem.

The other category of injury, atrocities committed in armed conflict, is itself divisible into two types. The first type stems from the conduct of the government in responding to civil unrest or low-level conflict. One example of such a case is that of East Pakistan when it was still part of Pakistan. With the center of government, politics, and commerce in the western half, West Pakistan came to dominate the culturally and linguistically different East Pakistan in nearly all sectors of life. In 1970, the Awami League, an East Pakistani political party whose platform was based on autonomy for the east, won virtually every Eastern seat in the Pakistani parliament. Perceiving this political development as a threat to the territorial integrity of Pakistan, the Pakistani president refused to summon parliament, resulting in massive unrest in the east. The central government responded with military force to quell what it regarded as a rebellion, but the army's tactics were designed to terrorize the population into submission and destroy Bengali-Hindu affinities by ridding East Pakistan of its Hindu population. The army killed civilians indiscriminately, tortured and killed political activists, and raped, looted, and burned, sending millions of refugees into India.

Another case is that of the Iraqi no-fly zones established in 1991. Following Iraq's defeat in the Gulf War, the Shi'ite population in the south, long persecuted by Saddam Hussein's regime, began to revolt. For more than a year, Iraq indiscriminately killed noncombatants, shelled villages, and bombed them from the air. Iraq also responded with mass arrests, executions, and destroying their homeland by draining and burning the marshes in order to desertify the region. At the same time that Iraqi Shi'ites in the south were fomenting unrest, the Kurds in the north were in open rebellion. Iraq's military response against the Kurds was as brutal and indiscriminate as it was against the Shi'ites, and over 800,000 Kurdish refugees massed along the border with Turkey. Indeed, Iraq had already garnered a record of atrocities against the Kurdish population in 1988 with its Anfal campaign, in which Iraqi forces destroyed hundreds of Kurdish villages, killed 50,000–100,000, displaced a million more, and used chemical weapons against Kurdish civilians.

A third case is the Kosovo situation, which had its origins in resentment of the Serb policy of *apartheid* against ethnic Albanians under the Serb nationalist regime. Under Slobodan Milosevic, the Yugoslav central government rescinded the 1974 constitution granting autonomy to Kosovo, dismissed Albanians from public posts and school systems, dissolved the Kosovo regional government, and revoked the official status of the Albanian language. In response, the so-called Kosovo Liberation Army (KLA) launched a campaign of terror bombings against Serb targets in Kosovo. By 1998, the KLA had progressed from covert operations to overt ones. The Yugoslav army and Serb security forces responded with excessive force, shelling villages and indiscriminately killing noncombatants. Over the summer, Serb forces burned 300 villages, destroyed mosques, and drove about 400,000 Albanians from their homes. European frustration with Serbia reached the boiling point in the spring of 1999, when peace talks broke down and Serb forces renewed their ethnic cleansing in Kosovo. NATO commenced air strikes on Serb targets and the Serbs responded by intensifying their campaign, displacing or expelling nearly one-and-a-half million ethnic Albanians. Looting, pillaging, extortion, and rape were all widespread.

The second type of injury (within the category of wartime atrocities) is mass atrocities committed by belligerents in open rebellion or other armed conflict. The First Liberian Civil War was notorious for indiscriminate killing, rape, and burning by both the government and rebel forces. Over 200,000 people were killed, with up to a million more displaced. The main rebel faction in the Sierra Leonean Civil War, the Revolutionary United Front, also committed mass atrocities on noncombatants, abducting children to serve as soldiers or prostitutes, forcing children to murder their parents, and cutting off limbs. When Bosnia and Herzegovina declared its independence from Yugoslavia in 1992, the Serbs captured 70 percent of the territory by force and launched a campaign of ethnic cleansing of enclaves of Bosnian Muslims and Croats, displacing thousands and destroying their homes, and systematically killing the men and raping the women.

In this latter type of humanitarian intervention, the so-called "right of rebellion" against authority is different conceptually from the right that flows from a civil authority's abuse of its power. It denotes not necessarily a right against a long-standing government that is recognized by the international community of states, but rather the right of the general population to reestablish civil order, in view of the government's failure to do so. Such a right would not exist under normal circumstances but when the civil authority becomes unable to discharge its primary function of maintaining order then there must be some provision for the people to take matters into their own hands.

Right Intent

For this criterion to be satisfied, the use of force must be undertaken for fraternal correction and with charitable motives. Fraternal correction mandates that the *telos* of the intervention be calculated to stop the human rights violations. When the violator is the government acting against the entire population, such as Cambodia, Uganda, the Central African Republic, and Iraq, achieving that *telos* is likely to necessitate removing the offending regime from power altogether. However, when the violations are directed against only one or more identifiable groups, then it may suffice to simply remove that group from the control of the offending regime and induce it to stop the oppression. This was the result achieved in the East Pakistan, Iraq no-fly zone, and Kosovo cases. In civil wars, the *telos* is to secure a peace with some amount of justice acceptable to the aggrieved. A belligerent that has committed mass atrocities such as those perpetrated by the rebels in Sierra Leone cannot be permitted to govern, for then it would have realized a benefit from its evil acts. On the other hand, if the population, taken as a whole, supports granting amnesty to certain belligerents in order to make peace possible, then that decision should be respected, for implementing justice is the right of the host state, not the intervening state (the remedy for an injury to the population belongs only to the population).

The intervention must also be conducted consistent with a charitable motive. Since the primary purpose of the intervention is to restore the human rights, actions that appear to be calculated more to increase the intervener's own power are not legitimate, as the PCUSA's criterion states. On the basis of this condition, the so-called "humanitarian" interventions perpetrated by the Axis powers in the 1930s and the Soviet Union during the Cold War are rejected. The justifications propounded by Japan for its invasion of Manchuria, Germany of the Sudetenland, and the USSR of Hungary and Czechoslovakia were all transparent pretexts for aggression, all the more disingenuous given the human rights records of the Gestapo, Soviet secret police, and the Japanese military regime. Indeed, it is the potential for abuse that leads some prominent legal scholars to denounce all humanitarian intervention as illegitimate, because of the danger that powerful states will abuse it in furtherance of their own hegemonic designs.[52]

However, as a practical matter, a condition that strictly forbids a state's own interest as *any* factor in the decision to intervene, no matter how insignificant, goes too far toward the other extreme to be workable. While a lack of apparent sinister motives may prop up the political legitimacy of an intervention, to impose a condition that the intervening state have nothing but completely altruistic and unselfish motives is far too naïve for the real world.

No responsible government would ever invest the time, effort, expense, political goodwill, and the lives of its armed forces in a military undertaking in which it has no national interest. It is granted that in most of the cases above, the intervening state was hostile to the host state, but it must also be granted that in most cases the human rights situations were creating security concerns to the surrounding states, primarily in the form of refugees or the risk of widening an internal armed conflict. In the Cambodia case, Khmer Rouge forces had actually made armed incursions into Vietnam itself, giving Vietnam a legitimate right to use force to stop the incursions. It is similarly illogical to condemn all cases of humanitarian intervention on the basis that states choose to oust some tyrannies but leave others in place. The doctrine can *only* be selectively applied, for only a state willing and able to undertake such an operation will ever do so.[53] Liberating some populations from tyranny is better than none.

The application of right intent to humanitarian intervention reinforces the theory that this criterion is better suited to God than to Man. Whatever nefarious motives India may have harbored in securing Bangladesh's independence from Pakistan, or Vietnam in establishing hegemony over Cambodia, one cannot reasonably deny that the general populations of both countries were much more secure, and lived with much less fear, than before the invasions took place. While the architects of those interventions will ultimately have to answer to God for their internalized motives, they did much greater good in the temporal world than if they had chosen not to intervene.

Proportionality of Cause

For a humanitarian intervention to be legitimate it must strive to achieve the greatest good, that is, the goodness or value of the cause must outweigh the death, destruction, and suffering that both sides are likely to sustain. The greatest good is measured by the totality of the spiritual and temporal good that the intervention will foreseeably achieve. The method for such a calculus offered in chapter 7 is easily applied to humanitarian intervention, and further helps to distinguish the validity of humanitarian intervention from that of its cousin, prodemocratic intervention.

In the spiritual plane, the greater the sin to be countered, the greater the good that military force achieves. When a government commits the mortal sin of murder,[54] especially in large numbers, then the good achieved in opposing it is high. Consequently, a war to stop large-scale killings is one of the highest possible purposes of war. Similarly, the sin of wrath, actuated on a large scale, results in mass deaths, imprisonments, torture, and other unjustifiable violence to persons, as well as forced deportations or migrations, that is, crimes against humanity. Stopping these crimes must also be a strong cause for humanitarian intervention. Also high on the scale of justifications should be state-supported robbery (the mortal sin of theft) and rape (the venial sin of lust).

On a lower tier of justifications for humanitarian intervention lie the sins that are the root of government corruption (greed, envy, etc.). Many corrupt regimes are also violent, but the two are intertwined only when the violence is perpetrated in furtherance of the corruption. It is possible for a regime's leadership to be excessively violent but not excessively corrupt, for example, the Khmer Rouge, or to be excessively corrupt but not excessively violent on a large scale, for example, Turkmenistan under Niyazov. Despite the fact that Niyazov instituted a personality cult and amassed a large personal fortune while much of the country remained poor, his regime did not attain the same level of notoriety for arbitrary violence as the Amin and Saddam regimes, and Turkmenistan was never a serious candidate for humanitarian intervention.

An intervention justified by the sin of pride occupies the lowest tier of valid justifications. In this case, the ruling regime is neither excessively violent nor excessively corrupt, but it is authoritarian and suppresses political opposition in order to keep itself in power. A good example of such a case is Singapore. The country is generally respectful of basic human rights but the ruling party has become known for using defamation suits and other intimidation in order to suppress political opposition. Other than in this area, the legal and economic systems are transparent and the lives and security for ordinary residents of Singapore are quite good, as long as they stay out of opposition politics.

The proportionality of cause calculus requires measuring the foreseeable good on the temporal plane as well. This calculus is based on the adaptation of Maslow's hierarchy presented in the last chapter. An intervention to protect a citizenry's right to life, that is, to stop genocide, mass murder and executions, and/or starvation, achieves the highest order of good. An intervention to protect a citizenry's right to security, that is, to stop mass enslavement, imprisonment, torture, and other violence to persons, achieves a good that is almost as high. On this basis, all of the cases of humanitarian intervention presented earlier in this chapter were justifiable, as would be the case for Rwanda and Darfur had such interventions actually occurred. Because the calculus on the temporal plane is based on temporal events, one factor in the calculus must be the scale of the human rights violations. The torture and/or enslavement of hundreds of thousands is a far more grave matter than the torture and murder of a few hundred. For this reason, the benefit of ousting Idi Amin is not widely questioned, whereas the ouster of Jean-Bedel Bokassa of the Central African Republic, while justifiable given his crimes, met only the minimum threshold of validity.

The difficult case is that in which the human needs of survival and security are generally met, but the human need of fulfillment is not. The case of South Africa in its *apartheid* days serves as a good example of such a situation. Unable to claim citizenship, employ whites, own land, get an education, or secure basic amenities such as running water, South African blacks were effectively barred from making their lives better or even from changing government policy. Similarly, in Turkmenistan under Niyazov, the average citizenry had little hope of ascending to rule (in a system of governance based on a personality cult, only the leader and his selected comrades have that right), nor did they have any genuine prospects of bettering their lives, for the corruption was so rife as to discourage any significant economic activity. However, there is little evidence that the economic plight of that country posed a significant risk to the peoples' security or lives (at least, for those who refrained from challenging the authority). This factor distinguishes Turkmenistan from North Korea, where the corruption and lack of economic incentives have put the general population at risk of starvation. I submit that, barring any significant deprivation of the human needs of safety and security, denying the human need of fulfillment probably does not justify military intervention to depose another state's government, any more than its deprivation would justify violent rebellion by the population. However, such situations must be weighed on a case-by-case basis, for those that entail excessive violence or involve extreme deprivations may justify intervention on the basis of another, more fundamental unmet human need.

The lowest tier of validity for intervention is that in which only the human need of leadership is not met (all others being satisfied). This is actually an easier case, for this need is so far from being fundamental that it weighs against justifying military force to attain it. Here we draw the distinction between *humanitarian* intervention, whose object is to protect fundamental human rights, and *prodemocratic* intervention, whose object is to protect the right to democracy (a human right to most people but not "fundamental" in the same way as freedom from torture). While it is true that all of the major human rights violators of the world are or were authoritarian, the Singapore case shows that the reverse is not necessarily true. In such a case, it seems likely that the foreseeable good of putting an opposition party in power does not outweigh the foreseeable damage that inflicting war would do.

If the foreseeable good in using force to uphold democracy is relatively low, then the U.S. interventions in Grenada and Panama are more difficult to justify than the ousters of tyrants like Amin, Pol Pot, and Saddam. That being the case, an intervention to install or restore a totalitarian regime (the opposite of prodemocratic intervention) definitely cannot be justifiable, since hardly any good can flow from imposing tyranny. However, the next section will show that the comparatively lower good can be compensated by a comparatively lower foreseeable harm, combined with a very high likelihood of success.

Reasonable Prospect of Success

Chapter 8 showed that this criterion is little more than proportionality of cause. For the use of force to be justified, the foreseeable good must outweigh the foreseeable harm; the less likely that the desired good is achievable at all, the less likely that the proportionality of cause test can be met. If the desired good is not likely to be achievable, then a very important value must be at stake, that is, an extremely serious sin must be opposed, for the good to outweigh the harm. Chapter 8 showed how a fundamentally vital cause such as fighting for the very survival of a nation can justify even a futile war. The same is true for humanitarian intervention. If genocide is the worst crime imaginable, then the use of force to oppose it achieves good even if the effort is unsuccessful. To find otherwise is to condemn a population to suffer and die, for even an intervention believed to be futile has a greater chance of success than an intervention not even attempted.

The case of the Pol Pot regime in Cambodia underscores this point. Under the Khmer Rouge, the people had no reasonable prospect of successfully revolting against authority, since those with the arms (the Khmer Rouge) acted without any legal or moral boundaries whatsoever. Those who challenged authority died, but those who submitted to authority were destined to die anyway, as evidenced by the staggering death toll. If a requirement of reasonable prospect were applied to rebellion in such a case, then the Khmer people would have had no right to it, and consequently neither would Vietnam, acting on their behalf. Such a mindset rewards the oppressor by giving it an incentive to totally subdue the oppressed as quickly as possible, then present the world with a *fait accompli*, thus foreclosing the possibility of a successful intervention and rendering invalid even the attempt. Such an argument is morally unacceptable.

However, when the human rights at stake, that is, the human needs deprived, are less fundamental, the desired good is not as great. In that situation, a higher certainty of success must compensate for the reduced good, otherwise the harm done in opposing the sin and meeting the human need will outweigh the foreseeable good. For humanitarian intervention, this means that the human rights situation in another state must be truly dire if the prospect for success is not high. For prodemocratic intervention, it means that the authoritarian regime must be very likely to crumble without offering more than token resistance, otherwise the foreseeable harm outweighs the foreseeable good.

Last Resort

Of the three trajectories of last resort, two can be disposed of quickly. Humanitarian intervention is not the use of force to resolve a dispute; rather, its purpose is to stop criminal acts. Furthermore, just as the so-called "presumption against war" is debunked, so should any "presumption against intervention."

The third trajectory, necessity, resonates more with this type of war than with others, because it is linked to the theory of just rebellion. The PCUSA rightly takes the position that "Intervention must respond to a real and genuine need that cannot be met by other means." If aggrieved persons have some remedy other than violence that is genuinely available to them, then they have no genuine need to revolt and therefore no genuine need for intervention. If a state has a reasonably independent and unbiased judiciary, the likelihood of a need to resort to violence to remedy a human rights grievance is remote. If, however, no judicial remedy is reasonably available, the population must be able to resort to other remedies; indeed, the lack of genuinely available judicial remedies facilitated the deteriorations of the situations in Uganda, Cambodia, Iraq, and Kosovo.

Just Means

The principles of *jus in bello* apply the same way to humanitarian intervention as they do in war; that is, force must only be directed against the bad actors, not the innocents, and the necessity of striking a particular target must outweigh the suffering that is likely to result from doing so. The only difference is that the objective is not so much to destroy the enemy's ability to fight as to stop the human rights violations. With that minor difference, the principles of *jus in bello* apply to humanitarian intervention *mutatis mutandis*.

CONCLUSION

In view of the role of the church in championing human rights and justice, the reluctance of many denominations to support real-world cases of humanitarian intervention is surprising, at least, until it is remembered that it is now secular developments of international law that influence the development of religion, instead of vice versa.[55] In a world polity in which authoritarian and/or corrupt regimes outnumber democratic and/or charitable regimes, the norms of international law and politics are shaped in a way that enables and even encourages tyrants, corrupt leaders, and other global miscreants to continue their unacceptable ways virtually unchecked. The norm of noninterference, along with the prioritization in the U.N. Charter of peace over justice, assumes that states will be selfless, well-behaved actors in the world community. However, the emergence of powerful norms of human rights and good governance strongly suggests the need to reevaluate the norm of noninterference in the internal affairs of other states, especially in light of the horrors perpetrated by such selfless, well-behaved statesmen as Idi Amin, Pol Pot, and Saddam Hussein. It is incumbent on the universal church to take the initiative and advocate a change in attitude. As Michael Walzer puts it, "Whenever the filthy work can be stopped, it should be stopped. And if not by us, the supposed decent people of this world, then by whom?"[56]

· 13 ·

Nuclear Weapons

$\mathcal{U}$p to this point the conceptual separation of *jus ad bellum* and *jus in bello* has been strictly maintained. The former assumes the latter, that is, that the just war is fought in such a way that minimizes the suffering (especially of non-combatants) to the greatest extent that is reasonable. Nuclear weapons, however, stress that assumption to its breaking point, because of the magnitude of devastation that even a single atomic explosion causes. Only in rare cases is it possible to avoid large-scale death and destruction in a nuclear attack; there is no such thing as a "surgical strike" with nuclear weapons. It is easily foresee-able, and even assumed, that a nuclear attack on any land-based target, how-ever lawful and necessary that target may be, will cause a great many more civilian casualties than military. Indeed, it is possible for a large-scale nuclear war to destroy nearly all human life on earth—and that prospect overshadows all other considerations.

Yet the simple solution to ban nuclear weapons is hardly more satisfactory than the unpleasant alternative. It was the threat of nuclear annihilation or mu-tually assured destruction (MAD) that halted Soviet expansion into western Europe after World War II. Nothing else was able to check the superior So-viet ground forces and, had the Soviets been able to successfully invade west-ern Europe, all of Europe would have fallen under tyranny. Their political phi-losophy being aggressively expansionist (and atheist), the Soviets had no moral compunction against using their vast arsenals against those who stood in their way; they were deterred only by the threat of inviting a nuclear attack upon themselves. The West was, essentially, forced to hold hostage the Soviet civil-ian population. In order to achieve the moral result of stopping the spread of tyranny, the West had to threaten a decidedly immoral response and signal its willingness to actually carry out that threat if necessary. The threat of the immoral result was successful in containing the Soviet military result, thus achieving a moral result.

Had it been necessary to act on that threat, however, the moral victory would have been Pyrrhic. In Christian political theory, civil government has the responsibility to protect the state from harm. Retaliating against the Soviets with nuclear weapons would have invited Soviet reprisals, doing at least as much damage to the West as to the Soviets. On the other hand, a morally superior response, that is, the West renouncing its willingness to use nuclear weapons under any circumstances, would have made it impossible to make the threat credible, allowing Soviet tyranny to continue spreading unchecked. What a perfectly vicious circle.

Since the advent of nuclear weapons is relatively recent, Christian thought and church doctrine in this area may not have had enough time to fully mature. The just war tradition has had over sixteen centuries to develop and the Thomist criteria have had nearly eight centuries. In contrast, the Bomb has been around for only sixty years. A Christian theoretical approach to its use is raw and unweathered, stiff and uncomfortable; it does not, nor can it purport to, offer a totally satisfactory solution to the dilemma—and this work does not presume to offer one.

DEVELOPMENT OF CHURCH DOCTRINE

The first major ecclesiastical reflection on the effects of nuclear warfare actually predated the bomb. In 1944, Fr. John Ford published "The Morality of Obliteration Bombing," criticizing the Allied practice of massive bombing raids on large population centers. Without denying the possibility of a just war (Ford agrees that the Allies' cause in World War II was just),[1] he rejects the Allied powers' practice of targeting entire cities, in furtherance of a strategy to cripple Germany's war industry and undermine German morale, on the ground that it immorally entails the direct intent to target civilians.[2]

The first major development of church doctrine on nuclear warfare itself was a multidenominational document, drawn up by the Second Calhoun Commission of the Federal Council of Churches in 1946, only eight months after the end of World War II. The commission expressed its deep penitence "for the irresponsible use already made of the atomic bomb"[3] but was divided on the permissibility of *any* use of nuclear weapons whatsoever. Some members desired to leave open the possibility of a just means for using them, or as a last-resort deterrent, that is, "the only effective restraint upon would-be aggressors."[4] Others refused to admit the justifiability of obliteration bombing under any circumstances, however extreme the circumstances. Still others sought to showcase Hiroshima and Nagasaki as the reasons for repudiating just war theory altogether—and, indeed, the pacifist trajectory has gained new life since the end of World War II. What all members could agree on was to urge a national policy of no first use of nuclear weapons.[5]

However, when viewed against the Cold War (still in the Calhoun Commission's future), the quandary of a no-first-use policy becomes evident. Left with no other effective means of overcoming the superior conventional forces of the Soviet Union, the United States had no choice but to declare its intent to respond to a Soviet invasion of western Europe with nuclear weapons. Such a threat is a deterrent only when the state making it is willing to actually carry it out; a no-first-use policy would negate that threat. The Dun Commission, formed in 1950 to revisit the nuclear question after the Soviets had developed a nuclear capability for themselves, recognized that quandary and was thus willing to defer to the ugly reality of the situation. That Commission concluded,

> As long as the existing situation holds, for the United States to abandon its atomic weapons, or to give the impression that they would not be used, would leave the non-Communist world with totally inadequate defense. For Christians to advocate such a policy would be for them to share responsibility for the world-wide tyranny that might result.[6]

But unlike the Calhoun Commission reports, the Dun Commission report was not a completely balanced reflection of the American Protestant leadership as a whole; most of the pacifist contingent from the Calhoun Commissions did not participate in the Dun Commission, nor was the report unanimous even among the remaining members.[7]

This deference to the reality of extreme necessity provides the foundation for Paul Ramsey's contribution to the discourse. In "The Limits of Nuclear War," his approach is to divorce the actual use of nuclear weapons from the mere threat of it, thus also the intended effect of their use from the foreseeable effect. Their actual use would be legitimate only when directed toward military forces, never against the civilian population—in his words, "counter-forces" warfare as opposed to "counter-people" warfare. Drawing from the principle of double effect, Ramsey further finds the threat of counter-forces nuclear attacks to be legitimate, notwithstanding the likely massive civilian casualties. The prospect of this unintended consequence would be sufficient deterrent.[8]

It was the nuclear dilemma, along with a general feeling among the mainstream American churches that Paul Ramsey's position was too permissive, that spurred several churches to craft their own detailed positions, beginning with the pastoral letter of the American Catholic Bishops, *The Challenge of Peace*.

Beginning with the premise, introduced in a 1954 papal statement and again at the Second Vatican Council, that deliberately targeting the innocent is a crime against God,[9] the letter finds no possibility that initiating a nuclear war, or escalating a nonnuclear war into a nuclear one, can be justified due to the inability of the combatants to limit their effects.[10] However effective the deterrence strategy may be in preventing the chain of events that would lead to nuclear war, the pastoral letter maintains that this lesser evil can only be justified as a stopgap measure, in order to buy time to forge a lasting peace and disarmament.[11]

The Catholic document was the benchmark by which the Lutheran, Methodist, Episcopal, and Presbyterian churches laid out their positions, publishing statements and pamphlets of varying depth and quality of reasoning.[12] All agree that the first use of nuclear weapons is not morally defensible, with the Lutheran Church going as far as to label nuclear war a crime against humanity.[13] Underneath that thin veneer of unity lies a broad range of opinion on the question of nuclear retaliation, that is, *second* use. The Methodist document rejects *any* use of nuclear weapons, not just first use;[14] the PCUSA document declares that nuclear war cannot satisfy the criteria for a just war,[15] implying that using a nuclear weapon is unjust even in retaliation. The Lutheran document rejects a "retaliatory strike solely for the purpose of revenge"[16] but is silent as to a strike for other purposes that satisfy the criteria of right intent, for example, stopping aggression. The Episcopal document does not take a position on second use, acknowledging that its authors are divided on the question.[17]

On the subject of the nuclear deterrence strategy, three denominations find themselves reluctantly compelled to accept its necessity in the short term. The Episcopal document acquiesces to its moral acceptability only because it sees no better alternative to countering Soviet aggression, while at the same time acknowledging the serious "moral ambiguities"[18] that flow from its position. The PCUSA document mirrors the Catholic approach, reaffirming its stance from 1971, in which it declares the deterrence strategy indefensible except to give the belligerents time to work toward a peaceful alternative.[19] The Methodist document, however, refuses to compromise; it rejects deterrence policy outright on the ground that instead of allowing the belligerents to work toward a peaceful solution, it enables them to harden their positions.[20] The Methodist document at least is internally consistent, though this present work argues that it is consistent in the wrong way.

DISPELLING MYTHS

Why does the issue of nuclear warfare still vex Christians, even though the church has roundly condemned it? It seems self-evident that using nuclear weapons in the manner foreseen today cannot satisfy the criterion of proportionality of means due to the extremely high collateral damage. The likelihood of massive civilian casualties also raises the threshold of proportionality of cause very high; it would take a supreme evil for the foreseeable good of stopping that evil to outweigh the foreseeable harm resulting from using nuclear weapons against it. The extremely high civilian casualties also calls into question whether right intent is satisfied, that is, whether the nuclear belligerent is motivated in part by an uncharitable motive of hatred or revenge. If these points are so obvious, then why does the justifiability of using nuclear weapons even remain debatable? Is it possible that the massive civilian casualties and the memories of Hiroshima and Nagasaki actually impede a rational assessment of all aspects of the problem? Perhaps, in this area, just war theorists suffer from an inability to see the forest for the trees.

Addressing the problem begins by appreciating the premise that provides so much counterweight to the massive casualties: that nuclear warfare might be the only means available to prevent an aggressor state from triumphing over other, peaceful states. The Mormon Church, whose scripture chronicles the utter defeat and massacres of the good Nephites at the hands of the evil Lamanites, understands this point all too well. For clarity's sake, it behooves us also to correct a number of premises that modern churches have sometimes accepted as true, but which do not withstand closer scrutiny. This section is therefore devoted to dispelling the following myths: (1) in matters of national security the judgment of the people overrides the judgment of the lawful government; (2) the threat to use nuclear weapons in armed conflict is less morally repugnant than their actual use; (3) the party using nuclear weapons is responsible only for the intended damage, not collateral damage; and (4) the two sides of the Cold War were morally equivalent to each other. For all of these propositions, the opposite is true.

State's Judgment versus People's Judgment

One key difference distinguishes the Nephite-Lamanite conflict in Mormon scriptures from the Cold War. The Lamanites' objective was to deprive the Nephites of their *lives*, whereas the Soviet expansion sought to deprive the West of its *freedom*. Using the hypothetical states of Aramaea and Babylonia, we raise one of the two moral questions that so complicate the nuclear dilemma: When may the Babylonian state (here defined as the government and the population at large) take the life of the Aramaean state (same definition) in order to preserve Babylonia's human dignity? In earlier chapters on force to stop evils such as slavery, the discussion was limited to forcing the aggressive regime to sacrifice *its* life as the price for its assault on the victims' human dignity. In this hypothetical,

Babylonia imposes that sacrifice on a large segment of Aramaea's population, in order to preserve its human dignity (we assume that Babylonia's only defense to Aramaea's aggression is a nuclear counterattack). A large part of the discomfort with this situation is that Aramaea is governed by a tyrannical regime and its population neither takes part in formulating its government's policy of aggression nor supports that policy. Babylonia's people are the innocent victims of Aramaea's aggression, but Aramaea's people are the innocent victims of Babylonia's defense; Babylonia is sacrificing *their* lives for *its* freedom.

The second question that must be addressed is: When is it permissible for the Babylonian state to sacrifice its *own* life to preserve the human dignity of its own people (and possibly others, should Aramaea's aggression not be checked)? In making good its threat to reduce Aramaea to a wasteland, Babylonia would virtually guarantee that Aramaea would reciprocate. Perhaps a large swath of the Babylonian population would rather have died in a free society than lived under tyranny ("Better dead than red"), but it seems likely that an equally large swath of the population would rather live under Aramaean tyranny than die. In resorting to nuclear warfare, the Babylonian government effectively imposes its own judgment upon its people. Such a sacrifice is voluntary for some, but not for all.

These, however, are choices that the divine institution of civil government must be able to make in discharging its function. A state must wield the power of life and death over its people (otherwise it could have no effective means of law enforcement) and consequently it must have the prerogative to assign value to the lives of its people. Such a calculation is inherent in many policy decisions of a state: how long a violent criminal should spend in jail; whether or not to ban the possession of handguns, or how many parts per million of insect larvae is acceptable in peanut butter. Any policy decision that initiates, or responds to, force by another state or nonstate entity also includes such a calculation of human value: how many, if any, enemy combatants in its custody to exchange for a hostage; whether or not to participate in a peacekeeping operation; whether or not to invade a country to depose a major violator of human rights; whether or not to support insurgent movements in other states; whether or not to embark on an unjust war of conquest. In each case the state judges the value of the lives for which it is responsible, as it has both the right and duty to do. The point at which it is morally preferable for a state to sacrifice itself for the greater good is a judgment that *only* the lawful government of a state can be allowed to make.

Similarly, in any armed conflict the state is forced to judge the value of the people of another state, relative to the value of its interests and/or the interests of its people. Specifically, how many of the enemy's lives must be lost before the foreseeable good of pursuing its just cause no longer outweighs the harm? Similarly, how many innocent lives are worth preserving a state's right to its independence and sovereignty, or even its right to exist? These judgments must remain the purview of the civil authority.

Threat versus Use

The morality of threatening to use nuclear weapons cannot be divorced from the morality of their actual use, at least not as easily as Paul Ramsey would have us do. No threat can be effective unless (1) the threatened party would sustain harm if the threat is carried out (not a problem here), and (2) the threatened party believes that the threatening party has the will to carry out the action threatened. To satisfy the second condition, the threatening party must say or do something to induce the belief that the threat is sincere, not a bluff. In an open, democratic society, however, public policy is often debated openly, even within governmental circles, and public opinion often influences the government's decisions. Such a society cannot bluff effectively because it cannot keep its true intent a secret long enough to maintain the deterrence value of its threat. This situation is very different from bluffing in a poker game, in which a player misleads the other players as to what he *has*, as opposed to what he intends to *do*. If the threatening party wants others to believe that its threat to use nuclear weapons is genuine, it *must* intend to actually carry it out.

Ramsey and other proponents of his theory, to their credit, do not turn a totally blind eye to the moral "ambiguity" of the threat; the Episcopal Diocese of Washington says as much in its treatment of nuclear deterrence.[21] But referring to the situation as an "ambiguity" is to deliberately overlook the nature of sin. Sin is not merely the bad act *pro se*, but also the separation from God induced by the *intent* to commit the bad act. Jesus taught that not only murder, but also anger (when it threatens murder) is sinful; so is the case with adultery and the mere thought of it.[22] The ELCA document reiterates an uncomfortable but inescapable truth: "What it would be wrong actually to do, it is also wrong to intend or threaten."[23] There is nothing ambiguous about the threat at all; if the use of nuclear weapons is sinful, then so is the threat, however much the latter may be preferred to the former. Any analysis of the morality of using these weapons must assume their actual use, not merely threatened use.

Intent versus Foreseeability

Separating the *intended* effect of using nuclear weapons from its *foreseeable* effect is a fiction. As Ford noted in his piece on obliteration bombing, a total disjunction of the intended from the foreseeable takes Thomas Aquinas's principle of double effect too far.[24] Thomas introduces the principle in the context of individual self-defense, arguing that the intent to preserve one's being may necessarily entail the unintended consequence of slaying the aggressor.[25] It is the charitable motive in killing the attacker that avoids the sin, not whether the defender knows that he is forced to kill in self-defense. In conventional warfare, the principle of double effect regulates the amount of force used against a target, thus affecting the norms of discrimination and proportionality of means. Recall Victoria's statement introduced in chapter 10:

> "Sometimes it is right, in virtue of collateral circumstances, to slay the innocent even knowingly. . . . Great attention, however, must be paid . . . to see that greater evils do not arise out of the war than the war would avert."[26]

The purpose of that regulation is to reduce collateral damage (the unintended damage to innocent persons and their property). Victoria's point is that it is possible for combatants operating with right intent and reasonable care to be excused not only from the collateral damage that is *un*foreseeable, but even from that which is foreseeable, as long as the collateral damage is outweighed by the good that will be achieved in causing it. It thus follows that the greater the foreseeable collateral damage, the greater the military necessity required to justify it. Nevertheless, the damage is foreseeable, and therefore it is *intended*, even if collateral.

The absurdity of separating intent from foreseeability becomes apparent when the above is applied to nuclear weapons. Even a nuclear blast in a rural area must be foreseen to inflict considerable damage and casualties—and many legitimate military targets are located in urban areas. The knowledge that using a nuclear weapon *will* cause considerable collateral damage is unavoidable, and therefore cannot be ignored. As the Episcopal document says, "If one knows that terrible and long-lasting destruction *will* occur *unavoidably*, and accepts that, then 'unintendedness' has no meaning."[27] To sequester that knowledge on the theory that the collateral damage is not the intended purpose of the attack is intellectually dishonest, even Orwellian.

Right versus Wrong

It is also incumbent on the church to restore intellectual honesty to the difference between good and evil in statecraft, and not harbor any illusions of moral equivalency to aggressive or authoritarian regimes. The Methodist document's failure in this regard is spectacular—it places the United States' failure to give diplomatic recognition to the Soviet Union, failure to join the League of Nations, refusal to lend the Soviets billions of dollars for reconstruction, and sending of spy planes into Soviet airspace on the same moral plane as the Soviets' closure of access to Berlin, engineering of Communist coups in eastern Europe, and invasions of Hungary, Czechoslovakia, and Afghanistan.[28] There is no legitimate comparison between the two. The first three items on the U.S. side were not required in the first place and the overflights amounted to a minor breach of world public order. In contrast, the denial of land access to Berlin put millions of lives at immediate risk and the coups and invasions were major breaches of the peace. Brand of the ELCA is also guilty of this, attributing U.S.-Soviet antagonism to "a genuine diversity of interests and in differing ideological commitments and geopolitical drives."[29] To grant moral equivalency to the USSR is to legitimize the fallacy that the Communist, authoritarian system of governance, with its long history of disregard for the norms of human rights and peaceful coexistence, is a morally valid alternative to the democratic system.

That fallacy is exposed in three ways. First, the populations, taken as a whole, do not choose to live under those systems and are often prevented from leaving their countries. Second, rather than releasing the masses from the "capitalist and imperialist tyranny," as the Communist cause professes, it simply imposes a new tyranny on them. Third, the Communist ideology propagates itself by force. No state's population would (or did) elect a Communist national government, so the Soviets had to fund, equip, and arm rebel movements to take power by military coup. Brand's attribution of U.S.-Soviet antagonism to legitimate ideological differences is therefore nonsense; the cause of the antagonism was the self-aggrandizement of the Soviet regime (hardly the epitome of charity) at the expense of the well-being of everyone else, which is the object of any dictatorship and the classic Niebuhrian definition of evil.[30] For this reason, Jersild's complaint that the U.S. strategy of deterrence assumes the worst motives and actions of the USSR[31] is similarly inappropriate; it offers no explanation as to why such an assumption is unreasonable. Ironically, the Methodist listing of the transgressions of the USSR proves why such an assumption is perfectly reasonable.

THE PRICE OF AGGRESSION

World War II

Dispelling the above myths clears the air for a proper reevaluation of the morality of using weapons of mass destruction, beginning with the objection to obliteration bombing during World War II. As a preliminary matter, though hardly dispositive, it must be noted that the Axis powers, not the Allies, were the first to resort to this tactic, a point that even the Second Calhoun Commission conceded.[32] Moreover, the Allies must not be judged by hindsight knowledge of the outcome of the war. The British government made the decision to target German cities in late 1940, after Germany's blitzes on London and Coventry.[33] In 1940 and 1941, notes Michael Walzer, the outcome of the war was not known or even predictable. Nazi Germany had been enormously successful militarily and it appeared to many that Germany would win the war.[34] At the time, aerial bombardment appeared to be the only means available of degrading Germany's ability and will to prosecute the war.[35] It was, in effect, an act of desperation to repel an unrelenting aggressor.

The Allied bombing campaign must also be judged by the standard of accuracy in the 1940s, not of today's "smart bomb" technology. In 2008, the ability to strike a target with pinpoint accuracy with a missile launched from miles away is taken for granted. In the 1940s, an aerial bombing run, in which half the bombs struck within a quarter-mile of their target, was considered well-executed. Such bombs were unreliable for attacking specific targets. Walzer notes, for example, the commonly held belief today that concentrating air power against strategic targets such as oil refineries might have induced Germany to surrender sooner.[36] The only way to reach such targets at all was by air; yet the bombs launched from the air had only a slim chance of actually hitting any given structure, forcing the aircraft to deliver many bombs (only half of which would land within a quarter mile of their target). Thus a considerable amount of collateral damage was predictable, but the bombings' effectiveness against their targets was not predictable. From a strategic, economy-of-force perspective, the most effective use of aerial bombing was, regrettably, obliteration bombing of very large targets, for example, cities. To the objection that those industrial facilities (and lawful targets) should not have been targeted at all, one may counter that to *not* do so would allow the German war machine to continue production at a time when Germany had both military superiority and remarkable military success. In the early 1940s, that would have been a recipe for defeat. One may also raise the question, however, whether obliteration bombing of German cities had the same utility in 1944 and 1945, by which time other military options had become feasible, but that is a debate for another book.

By the end of war, the military advantage achieved by obliteration bombing was not so much strategic as psychological. The Allies were fighting in order to defeat not only the Axis military forces, but also the Nazi ideology and its militarist analog in Japan, which had a great many adherents and supporters in their respective countries. The Allies could not afford to make the same mistake they made in 1918, allowing the Germans to lose the war with their heads held high. Germany and Japan had to be defeated totally, and the ideologies of Nazism, Fascism, and Japanese militarism crushed. It had to be shown that an ideology that inflicts so much aggression on other states would invite great destruction on itself, leading to its utter repudiation for the greater good of civilization. Ford argues that such logic is fallacious, on the ground that the early German strategy of bombing English cities failed because instead of degrading the civilian morale, it stiffened their resolve.[37] He misses the larger point, however, that the German population should have known that their country was fighting for an unjust cause. He further offers no evidence of the result of the Allies' demoralization strategy, but simply (and invalidly) assumes that because Germany's strategy failed, the Allies' strategy must also.

The final point about obliteration bombing, distinguishable from the "they did it first" argument, is that the conventional obliteration bombing, as well as the nuclear attacks that followed, were calculated to win a war *that was of the Axis powers' making*. But for the popular support of the Nazi party, its election to power, its political philosophy of entitlement to conquer and subjugate all other peoples, its numerous unprovoked invasions and conquests, and the ghastly nature of the tyranny that Nazi Germany threatened to impose on the world, the war in Europe and obliteration bombing on both sides would never have occurred. Similarly, but for the rise of Japanese militarism, Japan's invasion of Manchuria, China, and Indochina, and the unprovoked attack on Pearl Harbor (Japanese history books notwithstanding), the war in the Pacific and the obliteration attacks on Tokyo, Hiroshima, and Nagasaki need not have taken place either. Nor was the conduct of the Nazi or Japanese uniformed forces any more upstanding; these were the forces that implemented the Holocaust and the Rape of Nanking. In sum, the Second World War was precipitated by regimes that had no regard or respect for human dignity, rule of law, or peaceful coexistence; rather, they sought to impose their rule on other states out of a misguided belief that their nationalities and military strength gave them the right to do so (recall the place of such motivation on the double-continuum introduced in chapter 2). Such regimes must bear the largest share of responsibility for the civilian deaths that resulted ultimately from their own clearly unjust acts of aggression, at a very minimum.

An analog can be made to the use of human shields in armed conflict. The law of armed conflict forbids belligerents from deliberately putting non-combatants between the enemy and its own lawful targets, thereby forcing the enemy to choose between attacking the target and sparing the lives of the innocent persons put there. The conventional assumption is that the adversary is compassionate and will either refrain from attacking the target or hand the belligerent a propaganda victory. However, the law of armed conflict does not prohibit attacking a lawful target, even if human shields must also be killed in the process, as long as the military advantage to be gained outweighs the cost in additional casualties. If the target is attacked, and the human shields killed, the responsibility for their deaths goes not to the state that attacked the target, but to the state that deployed the human shields.

Yet when an authoritarian regime goes to war for an unjust cause, that is precisely what the regime is doing to its population—putting it at risk of harm from the collateral damage that the regime knows its adversary will have to inflict in response. It is conceivable for the defending state to be reduced to such desperation that it reasonably believes that the only way to stop the aggressor is to deal a mortal blow to not just the aggressive regime, but to the aggressor state itself, that is, the totality of the government and its people. Paul Ramsey conceives of this possibility as the one scenario in which he could find targeting civilians to be licit:

> Now, in mortal combat between nations, when to repel injury it is judged necessary and highly important for the civilized life of mankind to have recourse to arms, it may be that life is pitted against life, one cause or nation against another, in such direct engagement and with so forced a decision between them that practical wisdom and the ends of justice may require that the traditional immunity of the enemy's civilian population from direct attack be ignored.[38]

In other words, the defending state's very survival must be at stake. In such a scenario, to hold the defending state *more* responsible than the aggressor state for civilian casualties is to reward the aggressor for using the defender's compassion against it. Thus Walzer's implication of a double-standard in the Allies holding Axis officials responsible for war crimes, when its own officials were responsible for obliteration bombing and nuclear attacks,[39] is inequitable and unfair given which side started the war and why.

The use of nuclear weapons is simply a greater degree of obliteration bombing and for this reason its introduction into the equation does not alter the equation itself. It does, however, raise the threshold of the urgency necessary to justify it. Walzer gives that threshold a name, "supreme emergency," which he defines as "those rare moments when the negative value that we assign . . . to the disaster that looms before us devalues morality itself and leaves us free to do whatever is militarily necessary to avoid the disaster, so long as what we do doesn't produce an even worst disaster."[40] If a "supreme emergency" is necessary to legitimize the targeting of cities with conventional weapons, then it must take a uniquely colossal emergency to legitimize targeting them with the destructive power of nuclear weapons. If the nuclear attacks on Japan did fall short of being fully justified, this is where the shortfall occurred. The conventional argument in favor of the attacks—that the attacks

were calculated to bring the war in the Pacific to a quick end, which it did—
is compelling. Japan's militarist ideology had to be defeated ignominiously, requiring not only liberating countries from Japanese occupation, but also a
complete conquest and occupation of Japan itself.

By 1945 Japan's defeat was inevitable, but not, according to Walzer, without resistance from two *million* soldiers prepared to resist an Allied invasion (the
capture of Okinawa alone had taken two months and cost 200,000 casualties on
both sides).[41] In invading the Japanese heartland, the Allies faced the prospect of
the war being prolonged for years, with *millions* more casualties. Yet a negotiated
settlement was not a reasonable option, given how such a settlement enabled
Germany to rearm after the First World War.[42] From a strictly mathematical
standpoint, a nuclear attack calculated to kill 200,000–300,000 civilians was better than the alternative of trying to occupy Japan with conventional weapons. In
a cruel way, the attacks did Japan more good than harm, for the end of the war
spared the inevitable attacks on Kitakyushu, Osaka, Kobe, Nagoya, and Tokyo.
But regardless of the strength of that utilitarian (if cold-blooded) analysis, the
bombings of Hiroshima and Nagasaki did fall short ethically in one respect: the
failure to first threaten Japan with the attacks and give it an opportunity to surrender unconditionally before carrying them out. This could have been carried
out with very little risk, either to the aircraft carrying out the attack or to the
strategic effectiveness of the attack itself. A nuclear warhead could even have
been detonated offshore at a safe distance to ensure the threat's credibility. The
threat alone might have been enough to induce Japan to surrender unconditionally; that there is no record of it even being tried is troubling.

Cold War

The above thought experiment is readily adaptable to the prospect of nuclear
war to contain Soviet aggression. In 1949, the Soviet Union was an ally of the
U.S. and Britain in name only; its political and economic ideologies were diametrically opposed to those of capitalism and democracy. The Soviets had
troops in eastern Europe as well as Germany itself, installed Communist dic-
tatorships in Poland, Czechoslovakia, Hungary, and Romania, and sealed off
the Russian zone of occupation in Germany, effectively breaking it away from
the other zones. In the 1950s and 1960s, Communist insurgent movements
abounded in all regions of the world. Popular uprisings against Soviet-backed
regimes were crushed with military force. All of this leads to the reasonable
conclusion that the Communists were attempting to suppress democracy and
impose themselves by force.

A strain of thought claims that the Soviets had genuine defensive interests in occupying eastern Europe and that the real source of tension was the

United States' overly aggressive advancement of its own commercial and economic interests. The USSR, the argument goes, was very weak after the Second World War, especially considering that it had no nuclear weapons to balance those of the U.S., and therefore needed a "buffer zone" between it and the West in order to avoid encirclement. This argument is misleading. While the Soviets' air and strategic forces were inferior to those of the U.S., their ground forces were strong—as amply proven by their ability to hold eastern Europe and force the West to abandon any hope of recovering those countries by force. The Communists' rush to "protect" themselves from the West was driven not by need, but the same fear harbored by any dictatorship, which is losing its power and source of aggrandizement. In the end, all that mattered to the unelected Soviet leadership was maintaining its own power. The Cold War was not a struggle between economic or political systems; it was a struggle of the governments of the free world to keep their people free from having tyranny imposed on them by a growing cabal of power-grabbers more interested in their own well-being than in governing their respective countries justly. Such an enemy may not have been quite as insidious as that of World War II, but the danger of succumbing to such tyranny was no less real.

Two aspects of the Soviet Union made the prospect of nuclear war with it more ambiguous morally than nuclear war with the Nazis. First, the threat was not as much the ideology of Communism itself as the ideology of the Soviet leadership, who perverted Communism into a ideological cover for their own aspirations to power. Second, the Communist ideology did not have the support of the general population, who for the most part merely paid lip service to it under duress. The West did not need to utterly crush the ideology of Communism because comparatively few people really believed in it. Thus Paul Ramsey's qualification for permitting counter-people warfare is inappropriately applied against the Soviets. Ramsey theorizes the possibility that the distinction between military personnel and civilians may have to be ignored when two states are in "mortal combat," but he defines the term "mortal combat" as a situation in which the *entire population* of the enemy state has challenged the peace, not merely the governmental organs of the state, a difficult condition to satisfy.[43] Ramsey's qualification is too limiting for practical utility. He also briefly entertains the possibility that the right to life could be trumped by some other right:

> Should we not weigh, not life against life, or right against right, but the actual probability of saving life against the right of those we would deprive of life, and act on the basis of a notably greater probability of saving for millions a decent order of life for years to come by means of area bombing now?[44]

But Ramsey rejects that possibility because the necessary conditions, that the innocents will soon die anyway and that killing them is certain to save other lives, do not hold true in wartime.[45] Again, Ramsey's condition is too limiting for practical use.

Ramsey, however, was too hard on himself. Both of these premises, that the right to life is not supreme and that the principle of discrimination breaks down upon mortal combat between states, are sound and workable within the tenets of Christian charity. The preservation of physical life, while an important consideration in defining charity and justice, is not the ultimate object for Christians, for Jesus said, "My kingdom is not from this world."[46] It is the spiritual life or afterlife, not physical life, that is of paramount concern in Christian teleology. The Catholic document is inconsistent in this regard; it affirms that "all of the Church's work in pursuit of both justice and peace is designed to protect and promote the *dignity* of every person" and yet in the same paragraph also affirms that "each human life is sacred."[47] The preservation of life *qua* life (referring to physical life), while important, does not advance the greater good unless it is balanced against the preservation of dignity and justice.[48] Charitable pursuit of those attributes leads Christians toward a greater quality of spiritual life; physical life is less important in comparison. We have already seen the calculus that supports sacrificing one's own life in pursuit of justice, as well as the aggressors' lives; a different question now presents itself: At what point does Christian charity favor justice and human dignity at the expense of *innocent* lives?

In response, we turn to Ramsey's premise of the mortal combat between states, which Ramsey characterizes as two states fighting to the death. It is, however, better characterized as a situation in which a state fights for its life. Examples of such situations in recent history include the Israeli War of Independence, the Korean War, and the Gulf War. Had the aggressors been successful, the three defenders would have ceased to exist. But the "life" of a state is not merely its existence; a state must also have a permanent population and sovereign government. A war to kill all the people of another state, that is, a war of genocide, forces the other state into a "fight for its life." A war to install a tyrannical regime in another state is tantamount to a war against its sovereignty. It may still be another state in name but in practice it is reduced to a province or vassal of another. This is what the Soviet Union did to eastern Europe; it installed, by force, authoritarian regimes that were not permitted to deviate from the Kremlin, with the states themselves not free to choose a different form of government. It is also what the Soviet Union would have done to western Europe and eventually the world if allowed to proceed unchecked. In fighting for its freedom, that is, its political independence, the West was in effect fighting for its life.

None of this, by itself, excuses either party from the duty to fight in such a way that minimizes the suffering of the innocent population to the greatest extent that is reasonable (i.e., fighting in a way that still makes it possible to win). If the defender can defeat the aggressor without deliberately targeting noncombatants, then the defender has a duty to not resort to those tactics. But what if the aggressor cannot be defeated except by such tactics? This is the scenario that presented itself to the West during the Cold War. The Soviets' conventional forces were superior to the West's; a favorable outcome in a conventional war was far from certain. Only the Kremlin's unwillingness to invite nuclear strikes on its own imperium kept the Iron Curtain from expanding westward.

Thus the freedom, justice, and human dignity of one innocent population (the would-be victims of an unjust conquest and tyranny) must be considered against the life of another innocent population (the aggressor state's civilian population, which had no part in the aggression). For the former to prevail, the latter's right to life must be valued less than the former's right to freedom. This can happen in two ways. The first is by sheer force of numbers; an act of aggression by a tyranny to increase its power puts at risk not only the object of that specific act of aggression but all other states because the aggressor grows more powerful with each successful conquest (as anyone who has played the game of Risk knows). At some point the value of the freedom of all other states is greater than the lives of even the innocent population of the aggressor; as a Star Trek aficionado would say, "the needs of the many outweigh the needs of the few." The second way is when the aggressor state itself devalues the lives of its own population, by inviting an attack on itself. A regime that is willing to risk such devastation toward its own people for no other purpose than its own aggrandizement evidently puts very little value on the well-being of its people, and cannot be assumed to put any greater value on anything else. It must be stopped, even at a supremely tragic cost to both sides. This is hardly an easy decision to make, but as stated at the beginning of this chapter, this problem has no easy answers.

CONCLUSION

The nuclear dilemma is at best an anomaly and at worst a distraction. It is an anomaly in that it stresses the criterion of just means in an extreme way and is replete with moral paradoxes. It is a distraction in that it strengthened the detractors of the just war tradition, who wrongly assume that *every* war henceforth will cause massive destruction and casualties. Even Ford objected to such broad generalizations. Indeed, post-Cold War experience shows that despite the existence of nuclear arsenals, major wars can be fought by major powers without them (though whether major powers can fight each other with such restraint still remains to be tested). Furthermore, if nuclear weapons are taken out of the equation altogether, it may be easily concluded that Nazi and Japanese aggression was unjust and the Allies' cause was just, and Soviet aggression was unjust and defense against it was just. Despite the existence of nuclear weapons, the foundation of the just war trajectory remains firm.

• *14* •

Conclusion

$\mathcal{A}$nd so we return to the question of my dinner host on that fateful evening, "Does God take sides in war?" In reply, the Calhoun Commission document states relatively concisely many of the points I have been making throughout this work: that even though God leaves the decision to go to war to Man, he nevertheless favors the good and abhors the evil. "God is a not a combatant, nor a neutral onlooker, nor a helpless victim. . . . He is, in war as in peace, the Creator and Sovereign whose power sustains and governs, but does not annul, the activities of nature and of men."[1] The teleology of a Christian just war is further reflected in the image of Jesus at the end of time; the book of Revelation depicts Jesus as a warrior on a white horse. "In righteousness he judges and makes war."[2]

This work has explored the origins and development of the Christian just war tradition over 2,000 years and applied it to the needs of the twenty-first century. The moral trajectory of the just war is still relevant to modern statecraft, though it requires an interpretation of international law that goes beyond the four corners of the U. N. Charter and other documents that view the use of force exclusively within the aggressor-defender model. In actuality, modern just war theory, based primarily on Christian principles, is far more complex and nuanced. This book challenges some of the basic assumptions upon which American churches have crafted their positions on using force in statecraft. Some of these falsified assumptions include: that all war is evil (or a "lesser evil"); that any war is a disproportionate response to whatever provoked it; that aggression is defined as the first use of force regardless of cause, motive, or intent; and that *any* peace, no matter how bad, is preferable to war. In making these challenges, this book strives to forge a comprehensive just war theory, based on time-honored Christian traditions, but modernized to suit the requirements of the twenty-first century, and to restore the traditional prioritization of justice over peace. This book advocates a new way of defining when the use of force is legitimate, steering away from arbitrary indicia such as who fired the first shot or who invaded whom, seeking instead a higher morality of achieving the greater good.

The American Catholic and Protestant churches have all rightly built their just war theories on the foundations of the Augustinian concept of just war to redress injuries and the three classic Thomist criteria (proper authority, just cause, right intent). To those criteria the modern churches have added several others: proportionality, reasonable prospect of success, last resort, and just means, some of which are affirmed as valid. From a legal perspective, the criterion of proper authority must occupy the place of primacy, because war by definition must be an act of state to be called "war."[3] From both the legal and moral perspectives, the criterion of just cause is a *sine qua non* to any use of force in Christian statecraft. It must be caused by an injury, or in Christian terms, a sin. I have argued for an additional essential condition, that the prospective good that the use of force is intended to bring about outweighs the harm that is foreseen in remedying the injury. This balancing test has been offered under the title proportionality of cause, to be distinguished both from proportionality of means and from the specific injury that confers just cause (for an injury must cross a certain threshold of severity to warrant the drastic response of war). In addition, discrimination and proportionality of means remain essential requirements to the conduct of the war once initiated.

Several other criteria, on the other hand, are found wanting. The criterion of right intent, while necessary to justify the use of force in the eyes of God, cannot be permitted to temporally delegitimize a war that achieves a temporally good result, provided that it satisfies the other criteria and is well-executed. A wrong intent, however, is likely to manifest itself in wrongful acts that themselves will provide an independent basis for delegitimizing the war. The criterion of reasonable prospect of success is rejected as redundant to proportionality of cause; both follow the premise that the good must outweigh the harm and this criterion simply assumes the impossibility of achieving any good by fighting—itself a doubtful proposition in some extreme cases. The criterion of last resort cannot withstand scrutiny because it is based on invalid premises, such as the notion that an invasion or genocide is a "dispute" to be negotiated and the so-called "presumption against war" that assumes the inevitability of great human suffering.

This book applied the above criteria to several modern problems. Rebellion and humanitarian intervention are both found to be justifiable if the injuries to the population are severe enough. As to the use of nuclear weapons and the strategy of mutually assured destruction specifically, this book finds it possible to justify both in an extreme case of self-defense, though with much reluctance and contrition.

I shall close with several recommendations directed primarily to the clergy and governing bodies of the various American churches. First, Christians must not dissociate themselves from temporal affairs, for if they do they find themselves in a poor position to discharge their duties to render help to those in society who need it. Similarly, if Christians eschew entirely the power of the sword to do justice, they deprive themselves of an effective means for securing justice and mercy from oppression for their neighbors at a time when they need it the most. The Christian church as a whole cannot afford to be pacifist, nor must individual members be discouraged from wielding political power, including the power of the sword. The church's best role in this regard is to instill those values that make for good statecraft. In this vein, laments James Turner Johnson, the church could do a much better job in reaching both the governing elites and the general public.[4]

Second, the preservation of earthly life, while a very important factor in the just war calculus, must not be regarded as the only factor. The elevation of earthly life to such absolute sanctity is not always compatible with the teleology of Christian living, which is to do good. Refraining to depose a genocidal dictator, for example, on the basis that some undeserving people will die or suffer harm, can itself produce greater harm than good. The preservation of human life must be balanced with the preservation of human dignity and justice.

Third, the distinction between *jus ad bellum* and *jus in bello* must continue to be maintained. The former is the law *of* war, that is, that which regulates the decisions of states to resort to force. The latter is the law *in* war, which regulates the means and methods of the actual fighting. Though linked at the hip, they are not the same. It is conceivable that a state could initiate a war for an unjust cause and yet scrupulously abide by the law of armed conflict. Iraq, for example, could have invaded and occupied Kuwait without committing the atrocities it did, yet the war to liberate Kuwait would still have been justified. Conversely, it is possible that a war advancing a just cause could be conducted with so little regard for the civilian population that the just cause itself is called into question; several atrocities of the Vietnam and Iraq Wars have given their detractors a powerful argument indeed. It is a mistake for churches to presume that *all* wars inflict widespread and terrible suffering; even some modern wars have disproved that supposition, for example, Tanzania in Uganda, the coalition in Kuwait, NATO in the former Yugoslavia.

Fourth, it is a worthwhile venture for the church to draw from outside resources in continuing to develop the just war tradition, when those resources offer a way of thinking that is compatible with its basic principles. Regardless of the theological differences between the Catholic and Protestant branches on one side and the Mormon branch on the other, it would behoove the Catholic and Protestant churches to take heed of Mormon just war theory, for it has the potential to make a worthy contribution to the just war tradition overall. On the other hand, if the Mormon Church desires to contribute to a more universal just war theory in any meaningful way, it must begin drawing from sources other the Book of Mormon, which is not considered authentic in any other branch, much less canonical. Just as early church fathers borrowed from the pre-Christian Greeks, Romans, and Jews, Mormon political theory could gain much from pre-Mormon sources such as Augustine, Aquinas, Luther, and Suarez.

Finally, the church must adhere to a broader view of peace. Peace is not merely the absence of war but, as conceptualized by the American Catholic bishops, "must be constructed on the basis of central human values: truth, justice, freedom, and love."[5] George Weigel has equated peace with the "tranquility of order," which is comprised of justice and security.[6] Without these things, the absence of war is not peace but submission to evil. The church must avoid the mistake that the drafters of the U.N. Charter made in prioritizing the absence of war over the procurement of justice. One cannot thrive without the other. A better mantra for Christendom in a fallen world would be, "Peace on earth, *but first*, good will toward men."

Appendix

Chronology of Major Events

c. 30 CE—Jesus preaches the Sermon on the Mount

c. 57—Paul writes his letter to the Romans

197–211—Major writings of Tertullian

312—On the eve of the Battle of Milvian Bridge, soon-to-be Emperor Constantine has a vision of a cross of fire and orders his soldiers to mark crosses on their shields; his victory ultimately leads to his conversion and the reconciliation of war with Christianity

376–410—The Visigoth threat to the Roman Empire, culminating in the sack of Rome in 410, further contributes to the reconciliation of war with Christianity

398–419—Major writings of Augustine

476—The western Roman Empire falls, leaving a power vacuum that is filled by the church

800—With the coronation of Charlemagne as the first Holy Roman Emperor, the church and the state become unified in purpose

827–902—The Saracen occupation of Sicily, along with invasions of the Italian peninsula, especially the looting of St. Peter's Basilica in 846, prompts Christian doctrine on war to turn to the problem of defense against non-Christians, culminating in the holy war ethos

989—The *Pax Dei* [Peace of God] is proclaimed

1027—The *Treuga Dei* [Truce of God] is proclaimed

1095—At the Council of Clermont, Pope Urban II proclaims the *Treuga Dei* to all Christianity, and also proclaims the First Crusade against the Muslims

1095–1291—The Crusades

c. 1140—The *Decretum Gratiani* is completed, solidifying the place of war in canon law

1202–1221—The disastrous Fourth and Fifth Crusades split the Holy Roman Empire and the church, and the church's influence over political matters begins to decline

1234–1253—Major writings of Raymond of Peñafort and Hostiensis

1273—Thomas Aquinas completes the *Summa Theologica*; his three classic criteria for a just war form the foundation for all future ecclesiastical discourse on the use of force

1492–1541—The Spanish conquest of much of the New World and treatment of the natives prompts Franciscus de Victoria to write *De Indis*, the first major work in modern international law

1507–1522—Major works of Cardinal Cajetan

1517–1528—Major writings of Martin Luther launch the Reformation and the Lutheran branch of Protestantism is founded

1536—John Calvin publishes *Institutes of the Christian Religion* and the Reformed branch of Protestantism is founded

1550–1600—Several writings during the Counter-Reformation form the basis for a modern doctrine of just rebellion in the church

1557—Victoria's *De Indis* and *De Iure Belli* are published

1590–1613—Major works of Francisco Suarez

1625—Hugo Grotius publishes *De Jure Belli ac Pacis*, which modern legal scholars regard as the first major treatise on international law

1648—The Peace of Westphalia ends the Thirty Years War, secures Protestantism's independence from and recognition by the Catholic Church, and creates the modern state system; the church no longer wields significant influence in statecraft

1758—The publication of Emmerich de Vattel's treatise on international law marks the transition from natural law to positive international law, which is completed by 1815

1775–1783—The American Revolution culminates in the independence of the United States from Great Britain, inspiring other independence movements throughout the Western world

1815–1918—The period from the Congress of Vienna to the Treaty of Versailles is notable for the demise of the just war tradition in Western statecraft, resulting in a lack of restraint on Western states' propensities to use force

1830—The Book of Mormon is published and the Mormon Church is organized

1896—With admission of Utah into the Union, the Mormon Church enters the mainstream of American society

1932–1959—Major works of Reinhold Niebuhr

1939–1945—The Second World War is fought against Naziism and its ideological allies, culminating in the first use of nuclear weapons and the renewal of public interest in the just war tradition

1945—The United Nations Charter enters into force and the general prohibition of force emerges as a fundamental norm of modern statecraft

1946–1950—The Calhoun and Dun Commissions publish the first major ecclesiastical articulations of the just war tradition since Suarez

1947–1991—The Cold War between the United States and Soviet Union raises the possibility of mutual destruction by nuclear warfare and the resurgence of the just war tradition is framed around this problem

1948—The Universal Declaration of Human Rights and the Genocide Convention kick off the emergence of respect for human rights as a fundamental norm of statecraft, thus posing a challenge to the other fundamental norm of nonintervention

1961–1968—Major works on war of Paul Ramsey

1983–1987—Several American denominations publish documents articulating their positions on the just war tradition

1999—The Kosovo War thrusts humanitarian intervention into the center of the ongoing debate on the justice of war; American churches respond with considerable uncertainty

2001—The September 11th terrorist attack on the United States solidifies the change of focus of just war scholarship to the problem of ethnic and religious conflict

Notes

CHAPTER 1

1. Thomas Aquinas, *Summa Theologica*, in *Great Books of the Western World*, vols. 19–20: *Thomas Aquinas* (Chicago: Encyclopaedia Britannica, 1952), ii–ii, q. 40, art. 1, r.o. 3.

2. Francisco Suarez, *De Bello*, in *Selections from Three Works of Francisco Suárez, S.J.* (Oxford: Clarendon Press, 1944), i, 3.

3. Martin Luther, *Whether Soldiers, Too, Can Be Saved*, in *Luther: Selected Political Writings*, ed. J.M. Porter (Philadelphia: Fortress Press, 1974), 102.

4. Alma 48:10.

5. The one glaring exception, that of the ancient Israelites, will be dealt with in the section of chapter 2 that introduces the moral trajectory of holy war.

6. Luther, *Whether Soldiers*, 101.

7. Carl von Clausewitz, *On War* (New York: Alfred A. Knopf, 1993), i, 1, 2.

8. 1 Timothy 6:10. All biblical quotations in this work are taken from *The New Oxford Annotated Bible, New Revised Standard Version*.

9. Augustine, *Answer to Faustus* (Hyde Park, NY: New City Press, 1990), xxii, 74.

10. Aquinas, *Summa Theologica* ii–ii, qq. 37 and 41, respectively.

11. Edith Hamilton, *Mythology* (New York: Little, Brown & Company, 1942), 29.

12. Homer, *The Iliad*, in *Great Books of the Western World*, vol. 4: *The Iliad of Homer and the Odyssey* (Chicago: Encyclopaedia Britannica, 1952), book v.

13. In pre-Christian Roman thought, the distinction between good and bad wars was diminished, saved from extinction only by the role of *bellum justum* (just war) in the *jus fetiale*, a formal procedure governing when the Republic could legally enter into hostilities with another state. For a detailed description of the *jus fetiale*, see chapter 4, note 35.

14. Suarez, *De Bello*, 1, 6.

15. *Military and Paramilitary Activities In and Against Nicaragua* (Nicaragua v. United States), Merits, Judgment, (para. 15), 1986 I.C.J. 14, 18 (June 27); *Legality of Use of Force*

(Serbia and Montenegro v. Belgium), Preliminary Objections, Judgment, (para. 1), 2004 I.C.J. 279, 282 (December 15) [similar actions were filed against most other members of NATO]; *Oil Platforms* (Iran v. United States), Merits, Judgment, (para. 1), 2003 I.C.J. 161, 166 (November 6).

16. Alexander F.C. Webster and Darrell Cole, *The Virtue of War* (Salisbury, MA: Regina Orthodox Press, 2004), 138.

17. Daryl Charles, *Between Pacifism and Jihad* (Downers Grove, IL: InterVarsity Press, 2005), 102; see also R.J. Rummel, *Death by Government* (New Brunswick, NJ: Transaction Publishers, 2007), 3 (arguing that eight authoritarian governments killed 128 million people in the twentieth century).

18. See Independent International Commission on Kosovo, *The Kosovo Report* (Oxford: Oxford University Press, 2000), especially chap. 6.

19. Quincy Wright, *A Study of War*, 2d ed. (Chicago: University of Chicago Press, 1965), 155.

20. Samuel P. Huntington, "The Clash of Civilizations," *Foreign Affairs* 72, no. 3 (1993): 22–49.

21. Barry Rubin, "Religion in International Affairs," in *Religion, the Missing Dimension of Statecraft*, eds. Douglas Johnston and Cynthia Sampson (New York: Oxford University Press, 1994), 20.

22. John Howard Yoder, *The Politics of Jesus*, 2d ed. (Grand Rapids, MI: William B. Eerdmans Publishing Company, 1994), 144–58 passim.

23. Webster and Cole, *The Virtue of War*, 52.

24. Matthew 22:39; Mark 12:31; Luke 10:27.

25. Charles, *Between Pacifism and Jihad*, 122.

26. James Turner Johnson, *Just War Tradition and the Restraint of War* (Princeton, NJ: Princeton University Press, 1981), 111–12.

27. Johnson, *Just War Tradition*, 114.

28. Johnson, *Just War Tradition*, 329.

29. James Turner Johnson, *The War to Oust Saddam Hussein* (Lanham, MD: Rowman & Littlefield Publishers, 2005), 16.

30. Johnson, *Just War Tradition*, 330.

31. Central Intelligence Agency, *The World Factbook*, "United States," www.cia.gov/library/publications/the-world-factbook/geos/us.html (accessed January 10, 2008). The breakdown is as follows: Protestant 52 percent, Catholic 24 percent, and Mormon 2 percent, Judaism 1 percent, Islam 1 percent, unidentified 10 percent, and 10 percent with no religious affiliation. The Orthodox branch of Christianity is not specifically mentioned.

32. Rodney Stark, *The Victory of Reason* (New York: Random House, 2005), 211 (citing *Yearbook of American and Canadian Churches*, 2001). In 2000, 409 out of every 1,000 U.S. residents, to be precise. Of those, the Catholic Church claimed 222, the Southern Baptist Convention 56, the United Methodist Church 30, the Evangelical Lutheran Church in America 18, the Mormon Church 18, the Presbyterian Church (USA) 13, and the Episcopal Church 8.

33. The terms *LDS* (Latter-day Saints) and *Mormon* are used interchangeably in this work to designate the Church of Jesus Christ of Latter-day Saints and its members.

CHAPTER 2

1. Reinhold Niebuhr, *The Children of Light and the Children of Darkness* (New York: Charles Scribner's Sons, 1944), 9.

2. Alexander F.C. Webster, "Justifiable War as a 'Lesser Good' in Eastern Orthodox Moral Tradition," *St. Vladimir's Theological Quarterly* 47 (2003): 8; see also Alexander F.C. Webster, *The Pacifist Option* (San Francisco: International Scholars Publications, 1998). I prefer this term over "moralities" of war, as "trajectory" reflects that each of the war ethics described herein is a chosen *course* of morality, and each of the axes in the diagram flows in a separate *direction*.

3. Edward LeRoy Long, Jr., *A Survey of Christian Ethics* (New York: Oxford University Press, 1967), 245.

4. Genesis 17:6–8.

5. Deuteronomy 7:1–5, 24–25; Deuteronomy 20:16–17.

6. Frederick H. Russell, *The Just War in the Middle Ages* (Cambridge: Cambridge University Press, 1975), 28.

7. Pope Urban II, "Appeal for the First Crusade at the Council of Clermont," in *Fontes Historiae Iuris Gentium*, vol. 1, edited by Wilhelm G. Grewe (Berlin: Walter de Gruyter, 1995), 242–43.

8. Edward LeRoy Long, Jr., *War and Conscience in America* (Philadelphia: Westminster Press, 1968), 33–41.

9. John H. Yoder, *When War Is Unjust* (Minneapolis: Augsburg Publishing House, 1984), 27.

10. 1 Nephi 2:20; see also 2 Nephi 10:11 preamble (describing the Promised Land, i.e., America, as a "land of liberty").

11. Doctrine and Covenants 101:77, 80.

12. Brigham Young, "Letter" (July 7, 1846), in *Messages of the First Presidency*, vol. 1, edited by James R. Clark (Salt Lake City: Bookcraft, 1965), 294. The Mormons furnished a battalion to the U.S. during the Mexican War. Although the writings of Brigham Young during the Civil War do not reflect any great love for the central government, neither did the Mormon Church oppose it. See also Brigham Young, "Human Intelligence and Freedom" (February 10, 1861), in *Journal of Discourses*, vol. 8, edited by G.D. Watt (Salt Lake City: Deseret Books, 1974), 319.

13. Wilford Woodruff, George Q. Cannon, and Joseph F. Smith, "Letter from the First Presidency to Heber M. Wells, Governor of Utah" (April 28, 1898), in *Messages of the First Presidency*, vol. 3, 298 (expressing the intent to satisfy the governor's call of 500 soldiers to serve in the Spanish–American War).

14. J. Reuben Clark, "America's Divine Destiny" (1940), in *Messages of the First Presidency*, vol. 6, 96.

15. Ezra Taft Benson, "The Lord's Base of Operations," *The Improvement Era* 65, no. 6 (June 1962): 454–56. The text is an address to the 132nd Annual General Conference on April 8, 1962.

16. Yoder, *When War Is Unjust*, 33.

17. Catechism of the Council of Trent, On the Fifth Commandment, 280 (declaring that "the soldier is guiltless who, actuated not by motives of ambition or cruelty, but

by a pure desire of serving the interests of his country, takes away the life of an enemy in a just war").

18. Isaiah 9:6.

19. Matthew 5:44.

20. Matthew 5:39.

21. Matthew 5:9–10.

22. C. John Cadoux, *The Early Christian Attitude to War* (New York: Seabury Press, 1982).

23. Tertullian, *Apologeticus*, sec. 37, in Cadoux, *Early Christian Attitude*, 79; Tertullian, *De Corona Militis*, sec. 11, in John Eppstein, *The Catholic Tradition of the Law of Nations* (London: Burns Oates & Washbourne, 1935), 36.

24. Tertullian, *De Patienta*, sec. 3, in Cadoux, *Early Christian Attitude*, 51.

25. Tertullian, *De Corona Militis*, sec. 11, Eppstein, *Catholic Tradition*, 36; see also Cadoux, *Early Christian Attitude*, 113–114. This stance may have been prompted as much by the Christian proscription of idolatry as by that of war. See Tertullian, *De Idolatria*, chap. 19, in Eppstein, *Catholic Tradition*, 36.

26. Tertullian, *De Idolotria*, chap. 19, in Eppstein, *Catholic Tradition*, 37.

27. Reinhold Niebuhr, *Christianity and Power Politics* (New York: Charles Scribner's Sons, 1940), 10.

28. Alexander F.C. Webster and Darrell Cole, *The Virtue of War* (Salisbury, MA: Regina Orthodox Press, 2004), 174–75.

29. Reinhold Niebuhr, *The Nature and Destiny of Man*, vol. 1 (Louisville, KY: Westminster John Knox Press, 1996), 283.

30. John H. Yoder, *The Politics of Jesus*, 2d ed. (Grand Rapids, MI: William B. Eerdmans Publishing Company, 1994), 196.

31. Roland H. Bainton, *Christian Attitudes Toward War and Peace* (Nashville: Abingdon Press, 1960), 61.

32. Augustine, *Answer to Faustus* (Hyde Park, NY: New City Press, 1990), xxii, 76.

33. James 4:17.

34. See James Turner Johnson, *Morality and Contemporary Warfare* (New Haven, CT: Yale University Press, 1999), 75–76 (writing of an obligation to defend one's neighbor); Daryl Charles, *Between Pacifism and Jihad* (Downers Grove, IL: InterVarsity Press, 2005), 97 (on the duties of the magistrate to "protect and defend the common good"); Darrell Cole, *When God Says War Is Right* (Colorado Springs: WaterBrook Press, 2002), 78 (on the *duty* to fight when all just war criteria are met); George Weigel, "The Development of Just War Thinking in the Post-Cold War World: an American Perspective," in *The Price of Peace*, eds. Charles Reed and David Ryall (Cambridge: Cambridge University Press, 1987), 23 (envisioning a moral imperative of the responsible statesman to stop evil, defend the innocent, and promote minimal world order).

35. Paul Ramsey, *The Just War* (Lanham, MD: Rowman & Littlefield Publishers, 2002), 143.

36. Michael Walzer, *Arguing About War* (New Haven, CT: Yale University Press, 2004), 14.

37. *Decretum Gratiani* ii, causa 23, q. iii, cc. 7 and 11, in Eppstein, *Catholic Tradition*, 82.

38. *Catechism of the Catholic Church*, sec. 2265.

39. The [Westminster] Larger Catechism, q. 135, in *Book of Confessions*, (Louisville, KY: Office of the General Assembly [PCUSA], 2002), sec. 7.245. In the Presbyterian Church and most other American denominations, the commandment "Thou shalt not kill" is the sixth commandment; in the Catholic and some Lutheran churches it is the fifth.

40. The [Lutheran] Large Catechism, sec. 189, in *Book of Concord*, www.lcms.org/graphics/assets/media/LCMS/TrigBOC.pdf (accessed January 11, 2008).

41. In Matthew 8:5–13; Luke 7:1–10.

42. In Luke 22:36.

43. Romans 13:3. See also Titus 3:1 ("Remind [the people] to be subject to rulers and authorities, to be obedient, to be ready for every good work"); 1 Peter 2:13–14 ("For the Lord's sake accept the authority of every human institution, whether of the emperor as supreme, or of governors, as sent by him to punish those who do wrong and to praise those who do right").

44. Ephesians 6:13–17.

45. 2 Timothy 2:3.

46. Romans 12:17.

47. Romans 12:19–21, citing Deuteronomy 32:35 and Proverbs 25:21–22.

48. Romans 12:9.

49. In Matthew 5:39.

50. Lisa Sowle Cahill, *Love Your Enemies: Discipleship, Pacifism, and Just War Theory* (Minneapolis: Fortress Press, 1994), 32.

51. Romans 12:18 (emphasis added).

52. Yoder, *The Politics of Jesus*, 198.

53. Romans 12:6–8 (emphasis added).

54. Augustine, *The City of God*, in *Great Books of the Western World*, vol. 18: *Augustine* (Chicago: Encyclopaedia Britannica, 1952), i, 21.

55. Matthew 26:52.

56. Yoder, *The Politics of Jesus*, 98.

57. Matthew 26:53–54. Jesus had already made clear to his disciples his intent to suffer and die (Matthew 16:21; Mark 8:31). See also Luke 18:31 ("See, we are going up to Jerusalem, and everything that is written about the Son of Man by the prophets will be accomplished").

58. Bainton, *Christian Attitudes*, 97; see Augustine, *Answer to Faustus*, xxii, 70, 75; see also Thomas Aquinas, *Summa Theologica*, in *Great Books of the Western World*, vols. 19–20: *Thomas Aquinas* (Chicago: Encyclopaedia Britannica, 1952), ii–ii, q. 40, art. 1, r.o. 1

59. Romans 13:4.

60. See James Turner Johnson, *The War to Oust Saddam Hussein* (Lanham, MD: Rowman & Littlefield Publishers, 2005), 18.

61. Matthew 5:38–39.

62. Matthew 5:17

63. Cole, *When God Says War Is Right*, 35 (emphasis in original).

64. Thomas Aquinas, *Summa Theologica*, ii–ii, q. 40, art. 1, r.o. 2.

65. Yoder, *When War Is Unjust*, 22; Webster and Cole, *The Virtue of War*, 174–75.

66. Paul Ramsey, "Can a Pacifist Tell a Just War," in Ramsey, *The Just War*, 259–78.

67. Yoder, *When War Is Unjust*, 20.

68. H. Richard Niebuhr, "War as the Judgment of God," in *War in the Twentieth Century*, ed. Richard B. Miller (Louisville, KY: Westminster John Knox Press, 1992), 51.

69. Charles, *Between Pacifism and Jihad*, 26. See also Reinhold Niebuhr, *Moral Man and Immoral Society* (Louisville, KY: Westminster John Knox Press, 2001), 235 (elevating the social goal of equality over that peace).

70. See Yoder, *When War Is Unjust*, 76.

71. Niebuhr, *Christianity and Power Politics*, 6. Niebuhr mocks the point by suggesting that if 30 percent of the British population had been conscientious objectors, vice 2 percent, then Hitler would not have dared attack Poland.

72. In article 1 of that document, signatories agree to "condemn recourse to war for the solution of international controversies, and renounce it, as an instrument of national policy in their relations with one another." General Treaty for the Renunciation of War [Pact of Paris, aka Kellogg-Briand Pact], August 27, 1928, art. 1, 94 L.N.T.S. 57, 63.

73. U.N. Charter, art. 2, para. 4. The Charter makes an exception for self-defense, in article 51.

74. Aquinas, *Summa Theologica,* ii-ii, q. 29, art. 1, r.o. 1 (citing Augustine, *The City of God*).

CHAPTER 3

1. Exodus 21:23–25. A slightly different iteration is found in Leviticus 24:19–20.

2. 1 Maccabees 13:43–48.

3. To the Tertullianian objection that Jesus's disarming of Peter at Gethsemane was just such a condemnation, I reply in chapter 2, notes 55–60 and accompanying text.

4. Matthew 10:34.

5. As John Eppstein points out, this episode serves as evidence that Christ did not regard military service as sinful *per se*. Eppstein, *The Catholic Tradition of the Law of Nations* (London: Burns Oates & Washbourne, 1935), 14.

6. Luke 3:14.

7. John 2:13–16. The cleansing of the Temple is chronicled elsewhere but in less detail. Matthew 21:12–13; Mark 11:15–17; and Luke 19:45. It has been argued that one person armed only with a whip could not have driven out *all* the iniquitous actors from the Temple, and that therefore Christ must have driven them out by the force of his spirit. C. John Cadoux, *The Early Christian Attitude to War* (New York: Seabury Press, 1982), 35. Whether the moneychangers were driven out by physical force or some other form of force, however, is immaterial. In another passage, taking place just before his capture at Gethsemane, Jesus instructs the disciples to procure for themselves each a purse, bag, and sword. Shown two swords by the disciples he responds, "That is enough." Luke 22:35–38. Although the meaning of this passage is unclear, it suggests that Jesus is advising them that they may have to defend themselves.

8. John 8:11.

9. In the eastern provinces of the Empire, however, the pacifism made possible by the *Pax Romana* in the west was not sustainable, due to the continuing border threats.

Christians are known to have participated in the Thundering Legion of the province of Melitene in present-day Armenia as early as 173 CE. In 202, when Christians were still being persecuted in the west, King Abgar IX of Edessa converted to Christianity and made it the official religion of his kingdom; his forces must therefore have included Christians at the highest level. Roland H. Bainton, *Christian Attitudes Toward War and Peace* (Nashville: Abingdon Press, 1960), 70.

10. Will Durant, *The Story of Civilization*, vol. 3: *Caesar and Christ* (New York: MJF Books, 1944), 654.

11. Durant, *Caesar and Christ*, 655.

12. In Isaiah 2:4.

13. Frederick H. Russell, *The Just War in the Middle Ages* (Cambridge: Cambridge University Press, 1975), 12 (citing Jerome and John Chrysostom). John Chrysostom further considered proper a war "when the soldiers on our side are attacked by the barbarians." Eppstein, *The Catholic Tradition*, 53, citing John Chrysostom, "Homily (VII) on the First Epistle to Timothy." See also Bainton, *Christian Attitudes Toward War*, 86–88.

14. Ambrose, *De Officiis*, i, 27, 129, in Eppstein, *The Catholic Tradition*, 58 (italics removed).

15. Aristotle, *Politics*, in *Great Books of the Western World*, vol. 9: *Aristotle II* (Chicago: Encyclopaedia Britannica, 1952), vii, 14, 1333a; see also *Nicomachean Ethics*, in the same volume, x, 7, 1177b ("we . . . make war that we may live in peace").

16. Augustine, *Answer to Faustus* (Hyde Park, NY: New City Press, 1990), xxii, 74.

17. Augustine, *The City of God*, in *Great Books of the Western World*, vol. 18: *Augustine* (Chicago: Encyclopaedia Britannica, 1952), xix, 7.

18. Augustine, *Answer to Faustus*, xxii, 76; see also Augustine, "Sermon 302," in *Augustine: Political Writings*, eds. E.M. Atkins and R.J. Dodaro (Cambridge: Cambridge University Press, 2001), sec. 15 ("Soldiering doesn't prevent you doing good, but hating does").

19. Bainton, *Christian Attitudes Toward War*, 92 (citing Gustave Combès, *La charité d'après Saint Augustin*).

20. "From Gratian, *Decretum*, part II, causa 23," in *The Ethics of War*, eds. Gregory M. Reichberg et al. (Malden, MA: Blackwell Publishing, 2006), 109–24.

21. "From Raymond of Peñafort, *Summa de casibus poenitentiae*, II, §§ 17–19; William of Rennes, *Apparatus ad summam Raymundi*," in *Ethics of War*, 134–47.

22. Russell, *The Just War in the Middle Ages*, 129 (citing Hostiensis, *Lectura in Decretales Innocentii IV*). The first type, war against infidels, most just. The second type of war, to enforce a judicial order, was just. The third type, resistance of the second, was unjust. The fourth type of war, waged by those with legal authority to repel an injury, was just. The fifth type, waged in opposition to the fourth, was unjust. A privately waged war, the sixth type, was unjust. The seventh type of war, that waged in defense against the sixth, was just. See also Hostiensis, "From *Summa aurea*, On Truce and Peace," in *Ethics of War*, 161–68.

23. Isidore, Archbishop of Seville, wrote in 635 of the need for just war to recover lost goods, or punish an unjust war waged by the other side. Isidore of Seville, *Etymologies*, xviii, 1, 2–3, in *Fontes Historiae Iuris Gentium*, vol. 1., ed. Wilhelm G. Grewe (Berlin: Walter de Gruyter, 1995), 566.

24. Thomas Aquinas, *Summa Theologica*, in *Great Books of the Western World*, vols. 19–20: *Thomas Aquinas* (Chicago: Encyclopaedia Britannica, 1952), ii-ii, q. 40, art. 1.

25. Aquinas, *Summa Theologica*, ii-ii, qq. 41 (strife) and 42 (sedition).

26. Russell, *The Just War in the Middle Ages*, 265 (citing Peter of Auvergne, *Expositio in Politicorum*, vii, 11).

27. Ptolemy of Lucca, *De Regimine Principum* (Philadelphia: University of Pennsylvania Press, 1997), iv, 24, 26.

28. Russell, *The Just War in the Middle Ages*, 266 (citing Giles of Rome, *De Regimine Principum*, iii, 23).

29. Cajetan, "From Commentary to Summa Theologicae II-II, q. 40, a. 1," in *Ethics of War*, 242.

30. A century later, the Spanish Jesuit Luis de Molina would weaken that link, by suggesting the possibility that one could injure another out of "invincible ignorance," thus not incurring guilt, but still finding war permissible for justice, if not for naked retribution. See Luis de Molina, *De iustitia et iure*, ii, 102, 3, in *Ethics of War*, 335. See also Frank Bartholomew Costello, S.J., *The Political Philosophy of Luis de Molina, S.J. (1535–1600)* (Spokane, WA: Gonzaga University Press, 1974), 115.

31. Francisco Suarez, *De Bello*, in *Selections from Three Works of Francisco Suárez, S.J.*, vol. 2 (Oxford: Clarendon Press, 1944), i, 7.

32. Franciscus de Victoria, *De Iure Belli*, in *De Indis et de Iure Belli Relectiones*, vol. 2, ed. Ernest Nys (Washington, DC: Carnegie Institution of Washington, 1917).

33. Suarez, *De Bello*, vii.

34. The United Church of Christ (UCC) is a union largely of German, Swiss, and Hungarian Reformed sects and the Congregational churches that trace their history back to the Puritans and Pilgrims of Massachusetts. The Church of Christ will not be mentioned further in this book because it has no just war doctrine. Its foundational documents, consisting of the Heidelberg Catechism, the Evangelical Catechism of 1929, and the UCC Statement of Faith of 1959, make no mention of the use of force for war, law enforcement, or any other purpose. Furthermore, the UCC's 1985 statement of just war is actually a refutation of it, claiming that "Since Just War criterion itself now rules out war under modern conditions, it is imperative to move beyond Just War thinking to a theology of a Just Peace." General Synod pronouncement and proposal for action on the United Church of Christ as a 'Just Peace Church,' 85–GS-50 (1985), www.ucc.org/theology/justpeace.htm (accessed December 27, 2006).

35. The English church has had its own hierarchy since the Synod of Hertford in 672–673 CE, when English bishops came under the leadership of the Archbishop of Canterbury. This rendered the split somewhat less traumatic than that of Luther and Calvin.

36. Schleitheim Confession, arts. iv and vi, in *The Legacy of Michael Sattler*, ed. John H. Yoder (Scottdale, PA: Herald Press, 1973), 37–40.

37. See Bainton, *Christian Attitudes Toward War*, 142.

38. See, for example, Edward LeRoy Long, Jr., *War and Conscience in America* (Philadelphia: Westminster Press, 1968), 25–26 (articulating Presbyterian just war criteria in the tradition of Augustine and Aquinas).

39. See J.M. Porter, "The Political Thought of Martin Luther," in *Luther: Selected Political Writings*, ed. J.M. Porter (Philadelphia: Fortress Press, 1974), 8.

40. Martin Luther, *Temporal Authority*, in *Luther: Selected Political Writings*, 53–58.

41. Luther, *Temporal Authority*, 65–66.

42. Martin Luther, *Whether Soldiers, Too, Can Be Saved*, in *Luther: Selected Political Writings*, 102 (citing Romans 13:1–4 and 1 Peter 2:13–14).

43. Luther, *Whether Soldiers*, 114.

44. See Martin Luther, *On War Against the Turk*, in *Luther: Selected Political Writings*, 130.

45. The Large Catechism, sec. 181, in *Book of Concord*, www.lcms.org/graphics/assets/media/LCMS/TrigBOC.pdf (accessed January 11, 2008).

46. Augsburg Confession, art. xvi, para. 1, in *Book of Concord* (emphasis added).

47. John Calvin, *Institutes of the Christian Religion* (Philadelphia: Presbyterian Board of Christian Education, 1948), iv, 20, 4.

48. Calvin, *Institutes*, iv, 20, 11.

49. Calvin, *Institutes*, iv, 20, 6.

50. Calvin, *Institutes*, iv, 20, 10. The outlook is further reflected in the Westminster Confession, which views the purpose of the civil magistrate as "for the defense and encouragement of them that are good, and for the punishment of evildoers." Westminster Confession, in Presbyterian Church (U.S.A.), *Book of Confessions* (Louisville, KY: Office of the General Assembly [PCUSA], 2002), xxiii, 1.

51. Calvin, *Institutes*, iv, 20, 11.

52. Calvin, *Institutes*, iv, 20, 12.

53. In contrast, the Second Helvetic Confession, composed by Heinrich Bullinger in 1561 for the Swiss-German Reformed church, empowers the civil magistrate to wage war when necessary: "And if it is necessary to preserve the safety of the people by war, let him [that is the Magistrate] wage war in the name of God; provided he has first sought peace by all means possible, and cannot save his people in any other way except by war." Second Helvetic Confession, xxx, in *Book of Confessions*, sec. 5.256.

54. Westminster Confession, xxv (PCUS)/xxii (UPCUSA), 2 (footnotes omitted), in *Book of Confessions*, sec. 6.128 (emphasis added).

55. Larger Catechism, q. 136 (footnotes omitted), in *Book of Confessions*, sec. 7.246 (emphasis added).

56. Second London Baptist Confession (1689), xxiv, 1–2, www.reformedreader.org/ccc/1689lbc/english/Chapter24.htm (accessed May 10, 2006).

57. Alma 43:29.

58. Moses 5:31. This principle, labeled the Mahan principle in LDS philosophy, is defined as "the abrogation of another's free agency for personal benefit." Mark E. Henshaw, "Murder to Get Gain: LDS Thoughts on U.S. Elements of National Power," in *Wielding the Sword while Proclaiming Peace*, eds. Kerry M. Kartchner and Valerie M. Hudson (Provo, UT: David M. Kennedy Center for International Studies, Brigham Young University, 2004), 71. Note the parallel to Reinhold Niebuhr's definition of evil, which is the "assertion of some self-interest without regard to the whole." Reinhold Niebuhr, *The Children of Light and the Children of Darkness* (New York: Charles Scribner's Sons, 1944), 9.

59. Alma 43:45.

60. Alma 48:7–14.

61. The book of Mormon is one of the books contained within the Book of Mormon.

62. Mormon 3:9–11.

63. See Moroni 9.

64. The Doctrine and Covenants is a collection of divine revelations and declarations delivered from 1823 to 1847, along with three supplements. The vast majority of them were delivered by the founder and first prophet of the Church, Joseph Smith. The Doctrine and Covenants also enjoy the status of canon within the LDS Church.

65. Doctrine and Covenants 98:16.

66. Doctrine and Covenants 98:23–30, 39–43.

67. Doctrine and Covenants 98:31.

68. Doctrine and Covenants 134:8.

69. Doctrine and Covenants 134:11.

70. A prime example of this influence is the article titled "War" in the 1912 *Catholic Encyclopedia*, whose bibliography begins with Thomas Aquinas and Suarez, and ends with Grotius and an American jurist, T.J. Lawrence. See also Oliver O'Donovan, *The Just War Revisited* (Cambridge: Cambridge University Press, 2003) (reflecting an influence as much by secular works as religious).

71. Bainton, *Christian Attitudes toward War*, 173ff.

72. Abbé Charles de St.-Pierre, "Abridgement of the Project for Perpetual Peace" (1713), in *The Human Rights Reader*, ed. Micheline R. Ishay (London: Routledge, 1997), 104–10; Jean-Jacques Rousseau, "Judgment on Perpetual Peace" (1756), in *Human Rights Reader*, 110–14; see also Immanuel Kant, "Perpetual Peace: A Philosophical Sketch" (1795), sec. 2, Second Definitive Article, in *Kant: Political Writings*, ed. Hans Reiss (Cambridge: Cambridge University Press, 1991), 102–5.

73. John Wesley, "Some Observations on Liberty, Occasioned by a Late Tract" (1776), in *Political Writings of John Wesley*, ed. Graham Maddox (Bristol, KY: Thoemmes Press, 1998), 53–84.

74. Bainton, *Christian Attitudes Toward War*, 188–89; William Gribbin, *The Churches Militant: The War of 1812 and American Religion* (New Haven, CT: Yale University Press, 1973), 89.

75. Bainton, *Christian Attitudes Toward War*, 198. In the South, churches generally favored the Confederacy. The Methodist and Presbyterian churches reunited after the war, but the Baptist church did not. Id., 199

76. Bainton, *Christian Attitudes Toward War*, 200.

77. Bainton, *Christian Attitudes Toward War*, 207–10.

78. Eppstein, *The Catholic Tradition*, 132. The postulata itself was never acted upon because, ironically, the Council was interrupted by the Franco-Prussian War.

79. See chapter 2, note 72.

80. O'Donovan, *The Just War Revisited* (2003), 54. Nearly identical language appears in the modern Book of Discipline of the Methodist Church. United Methodist Church, *Book of Discipline* (Nashville: United Methodist Publishing House, 2004), sec. 165(c).

81. James Turner Johnson, *Just War Tradition and the Restraint of War* (Princeton, NJ: Princeton University Press, 1981), 340–41.

82. Gerald Sittser, *A Cautious Patriotism: The American Churches and the Second World War* (Chapel Hill, NC: University of North Carolina Press, 1997).

83. Johnson, *Just War Tradition*, 329 (citing Alfred Vanderpol, *La Doctrine Scholastique du droit de guerre*; James Brown Scott, *The Spanish Origin of International Law*; Eppstein, *The Catholic Tradition*).

84. Johnson, *Just War Tradition*, 330.

85. Reinhold Niebuhr, *Moral Man and Immoral Society* (Louisville, KY: Westminster John Knox Press, 2001), 170.

86. Niebuhr, *Moral Man*, 171–72.

87. Reinhold Niebuhr, *Christianity and Power Politics* (New York: Charles Scribner's Sons, 1940), 9–10.

88. Reinhold Niebuhr, "Must We Do Nothing?" in *War in the Twentieth Century*, ed. Richard B. Miller (Louisville, KY: Westminster/John Knox Press, 1992), 16–17.

89. Charles E. Raynal, "The Relation of the Church to World War II in the Light of the Christian Faith," *The Presbyterian Outlook* (July 24–31, 1995): 4.

90. John Courtney Murray, "Remarks on the Moral Problem of War," in *War in the Twentieth Century* (Louisville, KY: Westminster/John Knox Press, 1992), 252 (citing Pope Pius XII, "Christmas Message, 1944").

91. Pope John XXIII, "Pacem in Terris," in United Nations, *Never Again War! A Documented Account of the Visit to the United Nations of His Holiness Pope Paul VI* (New York: United Nations Office of Public Information, 1965), 112. Paul Ramsey argues that John XXIII left open the possibility of a war to stop an injustice in progress but uncompleted. Paul Ramsey, *The Just War: Force and Political Responsibility* (Lanham, MD: Rowman & Littlefield Publishers, 2002), 192–210. Such an interpretation, however, is too legalistic, for the pope's encyclical suggests no such distinction. John XXIII was simply a pacifist.

92. Pope Paul VI, "Never Again War! Address by His Holiness Pope Paul VI," in *Never Again War!*, 29–43.

93. I am indebted to James Turner Johnson and Lisa Sowle Cahill for their summaries of the wisdom of Ramsey. James Turner Johnson, "Paul Ramsey and the Recovery of the Just War Idea," *Journal of Military Ethics* 1, no. 2 (2002): 136–44; James Turner Johnson, *The War to Oust Saddam Hussein* (Lanham, MD: Rowman & Littlefield Publishers, 2005), 23–26; Lisa Sowle Cahill, *Love Your Enemies: Discipleship, Pacifism, and Just War Theory* (Minneapolis: Fortress Press, 1994), 198–201.

94. Johnson, *Just War Tradition*, 5.

95. James Turner Johnson, *The Holy War Idea in Western and Islamic Traditions* (University Park: Pennsylvania State University Press, 1997); James Turner Johnson, *Morality and Contemporary Warfare* (New Haven, CT: Yale University Press, 1999); Johnson, *The War to Oust Saddam*.

96. Johnson, *Morality and Contemporary Warfare*, 46.

97. *Catechism of the Council of Trent*, On the Fifth Commandment, 280.

98. *Catechism of the Council of Trent*, On the Fifth Commandment, 281.

99. *Catechism of the Catholic Church*, secs. 2307–2308.

100. *Catechism of the Catholic Church*, sec. 2308.

101. *Catechism of the Catholic Church*, sec. 2265.

102. Joseph F. Smith, "President Joseph F. Smith Favors Peace Movement" (September 15, 1914), in *Messages of the First Presidency*, vol. 4, edited by James R. Clark (Salt Lake City: Bookcraft, 1965), 312.

103. David O. McKay, *Gospel Ideals*, 87, in *The Teachings of David O. McKay*, ed. Mary Jane Woodger (Salt Lake City: Deseret Books, 2004), 521.

104. Augsburg Confession, xvi, 2, in *Book of Concord*.

105. Westminster Confession, xxv, 2, in *Book of Confessions*, sec. 6.128.

106. Articles of Religion, xxxvii (1571/1662), in Episcopal Church, *The Book of Common Prayer, 1979*, http://justus.anglican.org/resources/bcp/formatted_1979.htm (accessed January 11, 2008), 875. The 1801 version of the articles of the Episcopal Church states only, "we hold it to be the duty of all men who are professors of the Gospel, to pay respectful obedience to the Civil Authority, regularly and legitimately constituted."

107. Second London Baptist Confession, xxiv, 2. This chapter is nearly identical to that of the Westminster Confession, *supra*.

108. United Presbyterian Church, Confession of Faith (1967), pt. II, sec. A, art. 4(b), in *Book of Confessions*, sec. 9.45 (emphasis added).

109. Southern Baptist Convention, Baptist Faith and Message, art. 19 (1925), art. 16 (1963 and 2000), www.sbc.net/bfm/bfm2000.asp (accessed January 13, 2008).

110. *Book of Discipline*, sec. 165(c).

111. Definition of Aggression, annex to G.A. Res. 3314 (XXIX) (1974).

112. 181st General Assembly (1969), 694, in Presbyterian Church (U.S.A.), *A Composite Review of General Assembly Statements on Peacemaking and the Arms Race* (New York: Office of the General Assembly [PCUSA], 1984), 6–7, following Edward LeRoy Long, Jr., *War and Conscience in America* (Philadelphia: Westminster Press, 1968), 24–29.

113. Ronald H. Stone, "The Justifiable War Tradition," in *The Peacemaking Struggle: Militarism and Resistance,* eds. Ronald H. Stone and Dana Wilbanks (Lanham, MD: University Press of America, 1985), 191.

114. The primary foundational document of the United Methodist Church, the *Book of Discipline*, contains no restatement of specific just war criteria.

115. The following year, the larger Presbyterian Church (USA) concluded its five-year study and issued its policy statement *Christian Obedience in a Nuclear Age*. However, that document contains no restatement or serious analysis of just war criteria.

116. *Catechism of the Catholic Church*, sec. 2309.

117. Michael J. Stelmachowicz, ed., *Peace and the Just War Tradition: Lutheran Perspectives in the Nuclear Age* (New York: Lutheran Council in the USA, 1986).

118. Richard D. Land, "The Crisis in the Persian Gulf and 'Just Wars,'" *Light* (April-June 1991): 2. I would like to thank Jill Martin of the Ethics and Liberty Commission of the Southern Baptist Convention for making this piece available to me. She did so with the express proviso that I disclaim any official SBC status or standing on its part, which I now do.

119. John Mattox has already broken ground in this area. John Mark Mattox, "The Book of Mormon as a Touchstone for Evaluating the Theory of Just War," in *Wielding the Sword*, 57–66.

CHAPTER 4

1. Alberico Gentili, *De Iure Belli* (Oxford: Clarendon Press, 1933), i, 2, 17.

2. But see Hugo Grotius, *De Jure Belli ac Pacis* (Oxford: Clarendon Press, 1925), i, 4, 1, 1 (claiming that private persons can wage war, "as by a traveler against a highwayman"). Grotius, however, blurred the distinction between aggression and defense; the right of an individual to defend himself against an attack on his person is axiomatic, but our discussion is focused on the right to use force for some other purpose, one that Grotius's traveler and highwayman clearly do not have.

3. See Gentili, *De Iure Belli*, i, 3.

4. Augustine, *Answer to Faustus, a Manichean* [*Contra Faustum Manichaeum*] (Hyde Park, NY: New City Press, 1990), xxii, 75.

5. Augustine, *Answer to Faustus*, xxii, 75.

6. Gratian, *Decretum Gratiani*, in *The Ethics of War*, eds. Gregory M. Reichberg et al. (Malden, MA: Blackwell Publishing, 2006), ii, causa 23, q. 1, c. 4 ("in obedience to God or some lawful authority, good men undertaken wars"); id. q. ii, c. 2 ("this kind of war is certainly just which is ordered by God") (both quoting Augustine). Much of Gratian's work is not original to Gratian, but rather, he quotes the works of others. The major contribution of the *Decretum* was that it pulled together all of those disparate sources and memorialized them in an organized restatement of canon law.

7. Gratian, *Decretum Gratiani*, ii, causa 23, q. 4, c. 36; q. 5, c. 9 (both quoting Augustine).

8. Hostiensis, "From Summa Aurea, On Truce and Peace," in *Ethics of War*, 162 ("he is just who takes up the sword with his judge's authority properly intervening, whether by order or consent. . . . Therefore, he who takes up the sword on his own authority is to be smitten by the sword").

9. Thomas Aquinas, *Summa Theologica*, in *Great Books of the Western World*, vols. 19–20: *Thomas Aquinas* (Chicago: Encyclopaedia Brittanica, 1952), ii-ii, q. 40, art. 1.

10. See James Turner Johnson, *Morality and Contemporary Warfare* (New Haven, CT: Yale University Press, 1999), 46.

11. The unsettled question in Thomas's day was whether the ultimate authority to make war rested with the church or the secular authorities. In the Middle Ages the church wielded temporal political power and Pope Gregory VII even explicitly claimed political authority over temporal sovereigns. Pope Gregory VII, "Dictatus Papae," in *Fontes Historiae Iuris Gentium*, vol. 1, ed. Wilhelm G. Grewe (Berlin: Walter de Gruyter, 1995), 289. This set off a power struggle between the church and the Holy Roman Empire for three centuries, which frequently erupted into war. For example, the German Civil War of 1077–1106 began as a dispute over control of the appointment of bishops (the Investiture Controversy) and ended with the capture of Rome itself by the Emperor and the Emperor's subsequent installment of an antipope. This is but one of many examples, the height of the conflict being between Emperor Frederick II and Pope Innocent IV in the thirteenth century. See "Deposition Sentence against Emperor Frederick II," in *Fontes Historiae Iuris Gentium*, vol. 1, 294. The gradual displacement of the church as the primary authority to wage war is visible in the works of Baldus and Bartolus, Albericus of Rosate,

and Cardinal Cajetan. "Baldus de Ubaldis on the Emperor as dominus mundi," in *Fontes Historiae Iuris Gentium*, vol. 1, 344; "Bartolus de Saxoferato on the Emperor as dominus mundi," in *Fontes Historiae Iuris Gentium*, vol. 1, 343; Bartolus de Saxferato, "Tract. Repres., qu. 3, 2, sec. 3," in *Fontes Historiae Iuris Gentium*, vol. 1, 574–575 (finding authority vested in only the pope and Holy Roman Emperor); Angelo Piero Sereni, *The Italian Conception of International Law* (New York: Columbia University Press, 1943), 87 (citing Albericus a Rosate, *In 1. imperium*, Cod. iii, 13, finding such authority in sovereign states outside the Empire, e.g. France and England); Cajetan, "Commentary to Summa Theologicae ii-ii, q. 40, a. 1," in *Ethics of War*, 241–242 (finding authority in the Pope, Holy Roman Emperor, and *any* king or free lord). Cajetan, however, writes from the frame of reference of political authority derived ultimately from God, that is the state is but an instrument of God's work. Victoria, on the other hand, who was a contemporary of Cajetan, denies the temporal authority of the pope over sovereign states, *De Indis*, in *De Indis et de Iure Belli Relectiones*, vol. 2, ed. Ernest Nys (Washington, DC: Carnegie Institution of Washington, 1917), ii, 3, and finds every state to have the authority to wage war, *De Iure Belli*, in *De Indis et de Iure Belli Relectiones*, sec. 5. Thus, by the end of the sixteenth century, the question of papal versus state authority to declare war was settled in favor of the state. Suarez, however, did reserve to the pope the right to *judge* the justness of a given war. Francisco Suarez, *De Bello*, in *Selections from Three Works of Francisco Suárez, S.J.*, vol. 2 (Oxford: Clarendon Press, 1944), ii, 5.

12. See *Catholic Encyclopedia*, "War," sec. III, www.newadvent.org/cathen/index.html (accessed January 8, 2008) (citing Suarez, Molina, and Grotius). The modern *Catechism of the Catholic Church* does not state the principle of proper authority overtly, instead focusing on the function and responsibility of the state to protect the people: "[T]hose who legitimately hold authority . . . have the right to use arms to repel aggressors against the civil community entrusted to their responsibility." *Catechism of the Catholic Church*, sec. 2265.

13. National Conference of Catholic Bishops, *The Challenge of Peace* (Washington, DC: United States Catholic Conference, 1983), para. 87.

14. James M. Childs, Jr., "Nuclear Policy and the Ethics of Anticipation," in *Peace and the Just War Tradition,* ed. Michael J. Stelmachowicz (New York: Lutheran Council in the USA, 1986), 66. In the same volume, Jersild uses the word "authority." Paul Jersild, "On the Viability of the Just War Theory," in *Peace and the Just War Tradition*, 71.

15. John F. Johnson, "Can War Be Just?" *Lutheran Witness* 122, no. 1 (January 2003): 6.

16. 181st General Assembly (1969), 694, in Presbyterian Church (U.S.A.), *A Composite Review of General Assembly Statements on Peacemaking and the Arms Race* (New York: Office of the General Assembly [PCUSA], 1984), 6.

17. Presbyterian Church in America, "Christian Responsibility in a Nuclear Age," www.pcahistory.org/pca/1–439.html (accessed January 13, 2008) (citing Westminster Confession).

18. Episcopal Diocese of Washington, *The Nuclear Dilemma* (Cincinnati: Forward Movement Publications, 1987), 107.

19. 74th General Convention, in Episcopal Peace Fellowship, *Cross Before Flag* (Chicago: Episcopal Peace Fellowship, 2005), 39.

20. United Methodist Council of Bishops, *In Defense of Creation* (Nashville: Graded Press, 1986), 33.

21. Richard D. Land, "The Crisis in the Persian Gulf and 'Just Wars,'" *Light* (April–June 1991): 2.

22. Jersild, "On the Viability of the Just War Theory," 71 (italics removed).

23. Franciscus de Victoria, *De Iure Belli,* sec. 3.

24. A "concurring vote" means that the member either votes in favor of the resolution or abstains.

25. Under Article 25 of the U.N. Charter, members "agree to accept and carry out the decisions of the Security Council." Under Article 48, "The action required to carry out the decisions of the Security Council . . . shall be taken by all the Members . . . or by some of them, *as the Security Council may determine*" (emphasis added).

26. S.C. Res. 678 (1990) (authorizing states to use "all necessary means" to force Iraq to comply with its earlier resolution demanding that Iraq withdraw its forces from Kuwait). The phrase "all necessary means" is a diplomatic euphemism for using military force.

27. S.C. Res. 940 (1994).

28. Land, "The Crisis in the Persian Gulf and 'Just Wars,'" 2.

29. S.C. Res. 751 (1992).

30. S.C. Res. 794 (1992); S.C. Res. 814 (1993).

31. S.C. 161, sec. A, para. 1 (1961); id., sec. B, para. 2 (1961).

32. S.C. Res. 836 (1993).

33. John Mark Mattox argues the point that since Moroni was the leader of his people, it is natural and appropriate for him to also lead them into war, and that therefore the criterion of proper authority is implied. John Mark Mattox, "The Book of Mormon as a Touchstone for Evaluating the Theory of Just War," in *Wielding the Sword while Proclaiming Peace,* eds. Kerry M. Kartchner and Valerie M. Hudson (Provo, UT: David M. Kennedy Center for International Studies, Brigham Young University, 2004), 61. But the same argument may be made of the many wars chronicled in the Old Testament, and writings of the Catholic and Protestant church fathers make no similar claim. Edwin Brown Firmage, whose restatements of just war criteria will appear elsewhere in this volume, does not mention this criterion at all.

34. Doctrine and Covenants 98: 44–45.

35. The *jus fetiale* was an elaborate procedure by which the Roman monarchy and early Republic declared war on another state in order to avenge an injury. First, the head of the College of Fetiales (a select group of priests) traveled to the offending state to request reparation for the injury, swearing an oath to Jupiter attesting to the justness of the demand. If no satisfaction was forthcoming within 33 days, the head of the College returned to the offending state and threatened war, invoking Jupiter and Janus as witnesses. The College as a whole certified the justness of Rome's cause to the Senate. If the Senate passed a decree declaring war, the head of the College traveled to the border of the offending state, declared war, and threw a spear into enemy territory. Livy, *History of Early Rome* i, 32, 6–14, in *Fontes Historiae Iuris Gentium,* vol. 1, 187–88; David J. Bederman, *International Law in Antiquity* (Cambridge: Cambridge University Press, 2001), 231–33; Arthur Nussbaum, *A Concise History of the Law of Nations* (New

York: Macmillan Company, 1954), 10–11; Coleman Phillipson, *The International Law and Custom of Ancient Greece and Rome*, vol. 2 (London: Macmillan and Co., 1911), 332–339.

36. Phillipson, *International Law and Custom of Ancient Greece and Rome*, vol. 2, 198.

37. See Bederman, *International Law in Antiquity*, 222–23.

38. Doctrine and Covenants 98:37.

39. Augustine, *Quaestiones in Heptateuchum*, vi, 10, in *Ethics of War*, 83 (legitimizing ambushes).

40. Isidore of Seville, *Etymologiarum sive Originium*, xviii, 1, 2–3, in *Fontes Historiae Iuris Gentium*, vol. 1, 566. The passage also appears in *Decretum Gratiani*, ii, causa 23, q. 2, c. 1, in *Ethics of War*, 113; see also John Eppstein, *The Catholic Tradition of the Law of Nations* (London: Burns Oates & Washbourne, 1935), 81 (translating the Latin phrase "ex edicto" as "by a formal declaration").

41. Victoria, *De Iure Belli*, sec. 5; Suarez, *De Bello*, ii, 1. Victoria and Suarez focused on "offensive" wars as opposed to "defensive," in which the inherent right of the armed forces to defend the state when an immediate need arose was implied.

42. Suarez, *De Bello*, i, 7 (emphasis added).

43. Gentili, *De Iure Belli*, i, 3.

44. Grotius, *De Jure Belli ac Pacis*, iii, 3, 5.

45. Deuteronomy 20:10.

46. What makes a surprise attack treacherous (the legal term is *perfidious*) is when one invites the confidence of the enemy that a certain person or persons, or place, is "protected," for example, medical, or civilian, with the intent to betray that confidence. Protocol Additional to the Geneva Conventions of 12 August 1949, and Relating to the Protection of Victims of International Armed Conflicts, June 8, 1977 [Protocol I], art. 37, para. 1, 1125 U.N.T.S. 3. On the other hand, ruses intended to mislead the enemy or induce the enemy to act reckless, but which do not violate the confidence described above, are permitted. Id., para. 2. See also Regulations Respecting the Law and Customs of War on Land [the "Hague Regulations"], arts. 23–24, Annex to Convention (IV) respecting the Laws and Customs of War on Land, October 18, 1907, 36 Stat. 2277, 205 CTS 289; Yoram Dinstein, *The Conduct of Hostilities under the Law of International Armed Conflict* (Cambridge: Cambridge University Press, 2004), 198ff.

47. Aquinas, *Summa Theologica*, ii-ii, q. 40, art. 3 (citing Augustine, *Quaestiones in Heptateuchum* x, Super Jos.; Joshua 8:2).

48. *Mishnah Torah*, Sanhedrin 1:5, 2:4; see also Shabtai Rosenne, "The Influence of Judaism on the Development of International Law," *Netherlands International Law Review* 5 (1958): 142–43; Prosper Weil, "Le Judaïsme et le développement du droit international," *Recueil des Cours de l'Academie de Droit International* 151 (1976–III): 293.

49. The distinction between lawful and unlawful combatants is codified in the modern law of armed conflict, specifically the Geneva Convention Relative to the Treatment of Prisoners of War, Aug. 12, 1949 [Geneva Convention III], 75 U.N.T.S. 135, and Additional Protocol I to the Geneva Conventions, June 8, 1977, arts. 43–44, 1125 U.N.T.S. 3. The result of this distinction is that lawful combatants are entitled to the rights of prisoners of war, which includes immunity from prosecution for hostilities, and which unlawful combatants do not have.

50. *Oppenheim's International Law*, vol. 1, 9th ed., eds. Robert Jennings and Arthur Watts (London: Longman Group, 1992), sec. 167.

51. United States Diplomatic and Consular Staff in Teheran (U.S. v. Iran) (Judgment), 1980 I.C.J. 3 (May 24). The Iranian security personnel that were routinely posted around the embassy were conspicuously absent (para. 17), the attack took place over a three-hour period without any government intervention whatsoever (para. 57), and the Iranian government had made efforts to stop attacks on other embassies before and after that of the U.S. embassy (paras. 14 and 20).

52. Teheran Hostages, supra, para. 74.

53. *Oppenheim's International Law*, vol. 1, 9th ed., sec. 145.

CHAPTER 5

1. Plato, *Laws*, in *Great Books of the Western World*, vol. 7: *Plato* (Chicago: Encyclopaedia Brittanica, 1952), i, 628; Plato, *The Republic*, in *Great Books of the Western World*, vol. 7: *Plato*, v, 471; Aristotle, *Politics*, in *Great Books of the Western World*, vol. 9: *Aristotle II* (Chicago: Encyclopaedia Brittanica, 1952), vii, 14, 1333a; Aristotle, *Nicomachean Ethics*, in the same volume, x, 7, 1177b.

2. Plato, *The Republic*, i, 351 (viewing enslavement as the worst injury a state could inflict on another state); Aristotle, *Politics*, vii, 14, 1333b (conquest); Aristotle, *Posterior Analytics*, in *Great Books of the Western World*, vol. 8: *Aristotle I* (Chicago: Encyclopaedia Brittanica, 1952), ii, 11, 94a-94b (raids); Plato, *The Republic*, ii, 373 (wrongful acquisition of property).

3. David J. Bederman, *International Law in Antiquity* (Cambridge: Cambridge University Press, 2001), 222–27; Coleman Phillipson, *The International Law and Custom of Ancient Greece and Rome*, vol. 2 (London: Macmillan and Co., 1911), 182–86.

4. Cicero, *De Re Publica*, in *The Republic and the Laws* (Oxford: Oxford University Press, 1998), iii, 35. See also Cicero, *De Officiis* (Cambridge, MA: Harvard University Press, 1961), i, 11, 35 ("[t]he only excuse . . . for going to war is that we may live in peace unharmed"); id. i, 11, 36 ("it may be gathered that no war is just, unless it is entered upon after an official demand for satisfaction has been submitted").

5. Origen, *Contra Celsum*, iv, 82, in John Eppstein, *The Catholic Tradition of the Law of Nations* (London: Burns Oates & Washbourne, 1935), 43.

6. Ambrose, *De Officiis*, i, 27, 129, in Eppstein, *The Catholic Tradition of the Law of Nations*, 58.

7. Ambrose, *De Officiis*, i, 27, in Eppstein, *The Catholic Tradition of the Law of Nations*, 59 (citing Proverbs 24:11).

8. Augustine, *Quaestiones in Heptateuchum*, vi, 10b, in Eppstein, *The Catholic Tradition of the Law of Nations*, 74.

9. Augustine, *The City of God*, in *Great Books of the Western World*, vol. 18, *Augustine* (Chicago: Encyclopaedia Brittanica, 1952), iv, 6 ("what else is this to be called than great robbery?").

10. Augustine, *The City of God*, iii, 10 ("they were compelled to fight . . . by the necessity of protecting life and liberty").

11. Frederick H. Russell, *The Just War in the Middle Ages* (Cambridge: Cambridge University Press, 1975), 30 (citing Agobard of Lyon, *Liber Apologeticum, Liber pro Filiis et contra Iudith Uxorem Ludovici Pii*, i, 3–4).

12. Russell, *Just War in the Middle Ages*, 30 (citing Hincmar of Reims, *Episola Synodi Carisiacensis*).

13. Gratian, for example, considers the righteousness of war to defend Christian lands against pagan attack as beyond question, a position that today would have holy war overtones (and unnecessary, since a war to defend the homeland from attack by *anyone* is just), but which was necessary to reaffirm during the Crusades. Gratian, *Decretum Gratiani*, ii, causa 23, q. 3, c. 5, in *The Ethics of War*, eds. Gregory M. Reichberg et al. (Malden, MA: Blackwell Publishing, 2006), 114 ("He is full of justice who defends his fatherland from barbarians," citing Ambrose, *De Officiis*).

14. Russell, *Just War in the Middle Ages*, 264–66 (citing Albertus Magnus, *Commentarium Politicorum*, justifying the use of force to establish and defend the polity; Vincent of Beauvais, *Speculum Doctrinale*, presenting war as necessary to preserve liberty and territory and to increase dignity; Ptolemy of Lucca, *De Regimine Principum*, defining purpose and function of armies to defend against external aggression and to assist the prince in preserving justice; Giles of Rome, *De Regimine Principum*, characterizing war as a divine virtue when needed to defend against aggression or to preserve order).

15. Thomas Aquinas, *Summa Theologica*, in *Great Books of the Western World*, vols. 19–20: *Thomas Aquinas* (Chicago: Encyclopaedia Brittanica, 1952), ii-ii, q. 40, art. 1.

16. Thomas Aquinas, *Summa Theologica*, ii-ii, q. 33, arts. 1–2.

17. Thomas Aquinas, *Summa Theologica*, ii-ii, q. 41, art. 1.

18. Thomas Aquinas, *Summa Theologica*, ii-ii, q. 40, art. 1.

19. Thomas Aquinas, *Summa Theologica*, ii-ii, qq. 39 and 42, respectively.

20. Victoria, *De Iure Belli*, in *De Indis et de Iure Belli Relectiones*, vol. 2, ed. Ernest Nys (Washington, DC: Carnegie Institution of Washington, 1917), sec. 5.

21. Victoria, *De Iure Belli*, sec. 13.

22. *Catechism of the Catholic Church*, sec. 2309 (italics in original).

23. National Conference of Catholic Bishops, *The Challenge of Peace* (Washington, DC: United States Catholic Conference, 1983), para. 86.

24. James M. Childs, Jr., "Nuclear Policy and the Ethics of Anticipation," in *Peace and the Just War Tradition*, ed. Michael J. Stelmachowicz (New York: Lutheran Council in the USA, 1986), 67 (implying that attacks on any of the above are just causes for war).

25. Paul Jersild, "On the Viability of the Just War Theory," in *Peace and the Just War Tradition*, 71 (italics in original).

26. John F. Johnson, "Can War Be Just?" *Lutheran Witness* 122, no. 1 (January 2003): 6.

27. 181st General Assembly (1969), 694, in Presbyterian Church (U.S.A.), *A Composite Review of General Assembly Statements on Peacemaking and the Arms Race* (New York: Office of the General Assembly [PCUSA], 1984), 6.

28. Presbyterian Church in America, "Christian Responsibility in a Nuclear Age," www.pcahistory.org/pca/1–439.html (accessed January 13, 2008).

29. 74th General Convention, in Episcopal Peace Fellowship, *Cross Before Flag* (Chicago: Episcopal Peace Fellowship, 2005), 39.

30. United Methodist Church, *The Book of Discipline* (Nashville: United Methodist Publishing House, 2004), para. 165(c).

31. United Methodist Council of Bishops, *In Defense of Creation* (Nashville: Graded Press, 1986), 33.

32. Richard D. Land, "The Crisis in the Persian Gulf and 'Just Wars,'" *Light* (April-June 1991): 2.

33. Alma 43:9.

34. Gordon B. Hinckley, "War and Peace," *Ensign* 33, no. 5 (May 2003): 80 (emphasis added).

35. Francisco Suarez, *De Bello*, in *Selections from Three Works of Francisco Suárez, S.J.*, vol. 2 (Oxford: Clarendon Press, 1944), i, 4; id. iv, 3.

36. Suarez, *De Bello*, i, 4. Indeed, Suarez held that a defensive war could even be mandatory. *Id.* Compare with the Jewish doctrine of *milhemet mitzvah* (mandatory war), a war that the Jewish people are required by God's law to fight, specifically defense against an attack. *Babylonian Talmud*, Sotah 8, 44b; Maimonides, *Mishnah Torah: Hilchot Melachim U'Milchamoteihem* [*The Law of Kings and Their Wars*] (New York: Moznaim Publishing Corporation, 1987), v, 1.

37. *Decretum Gratiani*, ii, causa 23, q. 3, c. 5, in *Ethics of War*, 114.

38. Russell, *Just War in the Middle Ages*, 128–29 (citing Laurentius Hispanus, *Apparatus*, to causa 23, q. 2; Raymond of Peñafort, *Summa de Casibus*, ii, 5, 12, 17).

39. Russell, *Just War in the Middle Ages*, 264 (citing Vincent of Beauvais, *Speculum Doctrinale*, xi, 36).

40. Ptolemy of Lucca, *De Regimine Principum* (Philadelphia: University of Pennsylvania Press, 1997), iv, 24, 5.

41. Giovanni da Legnano, *De Bello, de Represaliis et de Duello*, chap. 26 (Oxford: Oxford University Press, 1917), 246–47.

42. Victoria, *De Iure Belli*, secs. 1 and 3.

43. *Catechism of the Council of Trent*, On the Fifth Commandment, 281.

44. *The Catechism of St. Pope Pius X*, Fifth Commandment, q. 3 (N.p.: The Catholic Primer, 2005), www.catholicprimer.org/vatican_docs/catechism_st_pp_pius_x.pdf (accessed January 13, 2008).

45. Larger Catechism, q. 135, in Presbyterian Church (U.S.A.), *The Book of Confessions* (Louisville, KY: Office of the General Assembly [PCUSA], 2002), sec. 7.245 (citations omitted).

46. Doctrine and Covenants 134:11.

47. *Catechism of the Catholic Church*, sec. 2264.

48. Large Catechism, secs. 179–198 and esp. 181, in *Book of Concord*, www.lcms.org/graphics/assets/media/LCMS/TrigBOC.pdf (accessed January 11, 2008).

49. Large Catechism, sec. 186, in *Book of Concord*.

50. Large Catechism, sec. 189, in *Book of Concord*.

51. *Catechism of the Catholic Church*, sec. 2264.

52. *Catechism of the Catholic Church*, sec. 2265.

53. Martin Luther, *Temporal Authority: To What Extent It Should Be Obeyed*, in *Luther: Selected Political Writings*, ed. J.M. Porter (Philadelphia: Fortress Press, 1974), 54.

54. Doctrine and Covenants 134: 11.

55. *Book of Discipline*, para. 165(c).

56. Robert F. Smylie, "A Presbyterian Witness on War and Peace: An Historical Interpretation," *Journal of Presbyterian History* 59, no. 4 (1981): 502 (citing Minutes of the General Assembly of the Presbyterian Church in the United States of America [1942], 199).

57. Alma 48:10.

58. Joseph F. Smith, "President Joseph F. Smith Favors Peace Movement" (September 15, 1914), in *Messages of the First Presidency*, vol. 4, ed. James R. Clark (Salt Lake City: Bookcraft, 1965), 312 ("within the bounds of justice and mercy and self-protection"); David O. McKay, *Gospel Ideals*, 287, in *The Teachings of David O. McKay*, ed. Mary Jane Woodger (Salt Lake City: Deseret Books, 2004), 522 (describing the first of three conditions that justify a Christian war as an "attempt to dominate and deprive another of his free agency").

59. Cajetan, "From Commentary to Summa Theologicae II-II, q. 40, a. 1," in *Ethics of War*, 241–42; Victoria, *De Iure Belli*, sec. 3.

60. Suarez, *De Bello*, iv, 1.

61. Suarez, *De Bello*, iv, 3.

62. Augustine, *Quaestiones in Heptateuchum*, vi, 10b, in *Ethics of War*, 82. The translation in Eppstein is "to restore what has been unjustly taken by it." Eppstein, *The Catholic Tradition of the Law of Nations*, 74.

63. Isidore of Seville, Etymologiarum sive Originium, xviii, 1, 2–3, in *Fontes Historiae Iuris Gentium*, vol. 1, 566; *Decretum Gratiani*, ii, causa 23, q. 2, c. 1, in *Ethics of War*, 113 (quoting Isidore); Russell, *Just War in the Middle Ages*, 137 (citing Laurentius Hispanus, *Apparatus*, to causa 23 q. 2, which is a commentary on the *Decretum*).

64. Raymond of Peñafort, "From Raymond of Peñafort, *Summa de Casibus Poenitentiae*, ii, §§17–19," in *Ethics of War*, 134.

65. Thomas Aquinas, *Summa Theologica*, ii-ii, q. 40, art. 1.

66. Victoria, *De Iure Belli*, sec. 13. Another Spanish Jesuit, Luis de Molina, cited the recovery of property as one of two kinds of offensive war. Molina's focus, however, was on war to recover property seized innocently, therefore his work is not considered here. Luis de Molina, *De Justitia et Jure* [*On Justice and Law*], tr. ii, disp. 102, sec. 5, in *Ethics of War*, 336.

67. Hugo Grotius, *De Jure Belli ac Pacis* (Oxford: Clarendon Press, 1925), ii, 1, 11; Samuel Pufendorf, *On the Duty of Man and Citizen* (New York: Oxford University Press, 1927), ii, 16, 2.

68. Grotius, *De Jure Belli ac Pacis*, ii, 1, 11.

69. Plato, *Republic*, ii, 373 (attributing unjust seizure of property to greed or lust for wealth).

70. Numbers 21:21–32; for a slightly different account, see Deuteronomy 2:24–34.

71. Russell, *Just War in the Middle Ages*, 21 (citing Augustine, *Quaestiones in Heptateuchum* iv, 44).

72. *Decretum Gratiani,* ii, causa 23, q. 2, c. 3, in *Ethics of War,* 113 (quoting Augustine's passage above).

73. Johannes Althusius, *Politica,* xvi, in *Ethics of War,* 380 (describing one type of defensive cause for war as "the guaranty of free passage").

74. Baltazar Ayala, *De Jure et Officiis Bellicis et Disciplina Militari* (Washington, DC: Carnegie Institution of Washington, 1912), i, 2, 11.

75. Suarez, *De Bello,* iv, 3.

76. For example, the Council authorized the enforcement of embargoes against the rump Yugoslavia (Serbia and Montenegro) during the Yugoslav wars of 1991–1995. S.C. Res. 787, para. 12 (1992); S.C. Res. 820, para. 13 (1993).

77. Franciscus de Victoria, *De Indis,* in *De Indis et de Iure Belli Relectiones,* ed. Ernest Nys (Washington, DC: Carnegie Institution of Washington, 1917), iii, 9 and 12; Francisco Suarez, *De Mediis,* in *Selections from Three Works of Francisco Suárez* (Oxford: Clarendon Press, 1944), i, 2 and 4.

78. Georg Friedrich von Martens, *Summary of the Law of Nations* (Littleton, CO: Fred B. Rothman & Co., 1986), vi, 2, 3.

79. Robert Phillimore, *Commentaries upon International Law* (London: William G. Benning & Co., 1854), iii, 10, 210 (calling the right of self-preservation the "first law of nations"); id., ix, 4, 49; A.G. Heffter, *Le Droit International Public de l'Europe* (Paris: Cotillon, 1857), sec. 113; Johann Kaspar Bluntschli, *Le Droit International Codifié* (Paris: Librairie de Guillaumin & Cie., 1874), sec. 516; Travers Twiss, *The Law of Nations Considered as Independent Political Communities* (Oxford: Clarendon Press, 1875), sec. 29; Edward S. Creasy, *First Platform of International Law* (London: John van Voorst, 1876), sec. 157; Henry Wheaton, *Elements of International Law,* 8th ed., (Boston: Little, Brown, & Co., 1866), secs. 61 and 290; H.W. Halleck, *International Law* (San Francisco: H.H. Bancroft & Co., 1861), xiii, 1–8; id., iv, 19; William Edward Hall, *A Treatise on International Law,* 3d ed. (Oxford: Clarendon Press, 1890), sec. 83; Theodore D. Woolsey, *Introduction to the Study of International Law* (New York: Charles Scribner, 1864), secs. 42–43; id. secs. 111–12.

80. Treaty of Peace (Spain-United States), Dec. 10, 1898 [Treaty of Paris], T.S. 343, 30 Stat. 1754, 11 Bevans 615, 187 CTS 100. The U.S. paid $20 million for the Philippines. Id., art. 3.

81. Deuteronomy 2:30.

82. Ayala, *De Jure,* i, 2, 11.

83. 2 Samuel 10; 1 Chronicles 19.

84. Augustine, *Quaestiones in Heptateuchum,* vi, 10, in Eppstein, *The Catholic Tradition of the Law of Nations,* 74.

85. Thomas Aquinas, *Summa Theologica,* ii-ii, q. 40, art. 1.

86. Cajetan, "Commentary to *Summa Theologicae* II-II, q. 40, a. 1," in *Ethics of War,* 245; Cajetan, "From *Summula,* 'When war should be called just or unjust, licit or illicit,'" in *Ethics of War,* 245–46; Victoria, *De Iure Belli,* sec. 13 (also quoting Augustine); Luis de Molina, "From: *De Iustitia et Iure,*" sec. 1, in *Ethics of War,* 334 (citing Augustine, Aquinas, and Victoria).

87. Pierino Belli, *De Re Militari et Belli Tractatus* (Oxford: Clarendon Press, 1936), ii, 1, 9; Alberico Gentili, *De Iure Belli* (Oxford: Clarendon Press, 1933), i, 20, sec.150

(equating injury with violation of "human" law); Grotius, *De Jure Belli ac Pacis*, ii, 1, 2 and ii, 1, 1, 4; Pufendorf, *On the Duty of Man and Citizen*, ii, 16, 2; Christian Wolff, *Jus Gentium Methodo Scientifica Pertractatum* (Washington, DC: Carnegie Endowment for International Peace, 1934), sec. 617. But see Jean-Jacques Burlamaqui, *The Principles of Natural and Politic Law* (Buffalo, NY: William S. Hein & Co., 2001), ii, 4, 2 (riding both sides of the fence, characterizing a just war as "recovering our undoubted right, or of obtaining satisfaction for a manifest injury").

88. Daryl Charles, *Between Pacifism and Jihad* (Downers Grove, IL: InterVarsity Press, 2005), 144–45.

89. Suarez, *De Bello*, iv, 3.

90. A century earlier, Victoria rejected enlargement of empire and personal glory or convenience of the prince as just causes of war, Victoria, *De Iure Belli*, secs. 11–12. Thomas Hobbes, who in Suarez's time was the major proponent of the theory that war is the natural state of mankind, argues the fallacy of such logic when he writes, "no large or lasting society can be based upon the passion for glory. The reason is that glorying, like honour, is nothing if everybody has it." Thomas Hobbes, *De Cive* [*On the Citizen*], i, 2, in *Ethics of War*, 444. The 1563 treatise of Pierino Belli, a secular work but which draws heavily from ecclesiastical writings of the previous two centuries, is not favorably disposed toward wars waged "for empire and for glory" as opposed to wars of protection. Belli, *De Re Militari*, ii, 1, 7. Even Ayala, who opines that "an honorable war . . . is ever to be preferred to a disgraceful peace" and lists various just causes of war, omits the restoration of honor as one of them. Ayala, *De Jure*, i, 2, 5 and 11.

91. Cicero, *De Re Publica*, iii, 23.

92. Bederman, *International Law in Antiquity*, 222–27; Phillipson, *International Law and Custom of Ancient Greece and Rome*, vol. 2, 182–86.

93. Phillipson, *International Law and Custom of Ancient Greece and Rome*, vol. 2, 195–96.

94. James Brown Scott, *The Spanish Origin of International Law* (Oxford: Clarendon Press, 1934), 75–89; James Brown Scott, *The Catholic Conception of International Law* (Washington, DC: Georgetown University Press, 1934), 437–79.

95. Burlamaqui, *Principles of Natural Law*, ii, 4, 2.

96. Johann Wolfgang Textor, *Synopsis Juris Gentium* (Washington, DC: Carnegie Institution of Washington, 1916), xvii, 10–14.

97. Gérard de Rayneval, *Institutions du droit de la nature et des gens* (Paris: Leblanc, 1803), iii, 2, 1.

98. Wheaton, *Elements of International Law*, secs. 294–95.

99. Heffter, *Le Droit International*, sec. 104; Creasy, *First Platform of International Law*, sec. 164; Bluntschli, *Le Droit International*, sec. 463; Woolsey, *International Law*, secs. 18 and 112(3); George B. Davis, *The Elements of International Law*, 4th ed. (New York: Harper & Bros. Publishers, 1916), 94 (categorizing the right of reputation as a "perfect" right, the denial of which justifies forcible measures of redress).

100. Thomas Aquinas, *Summa Theologica*, ii-ii, q. 37, art. 2; see also q. 38, art. 2.

101. Thomas Aquinas, *Summa Theologica*, ii-ii, q. 39 introduction.

102. Martin Luther, *Whether Soldiers, Too, Can Be Saved*, in *Luther: Selected Political Writings*, 117.

103. Matthew 4:8–10.

104. John 12:1–3.

105. David Von Drehle and R. Jeffrey Smith, "U.S. Strikes Iraq for Plot to Kill Bush," *Washington Post* (June 27, 1993): A1.

106. This case is also distinguishable from that of the U.S. air strikes against Libya in 1986, in response to the Libyan terrorist bombing of a Berlin discotheque frequented by Americans. In that instance the target was not a single person but the U.S. military in general, and specifically directed against persons who had little or no role in military operations against Libya.

107. S.C. Res. 687 (1991).

108. Fourth Consolidated Report of the Director General of the International Atomic Energy Agency under paragraph 16 of S. C. Res. 1051 (1996), para. 74, Appendix to *Note by the Secretary General*, U.N. Doc. S/1997/779 (October 8, 1997).

109. Full disclosure: the author participated in Operation Desert Fox as an Air Force judge advocate deployed in Saudi Arabia.

110. Davis Brown, "Enforcing Arms Control Agreements by Military Force: Iraq and the 800–Pound Gorilla," *Hastings International and Comparative Law Review* 26 (2003): 159–225.

111. Scott Ritter, *Endgame: Solving the Iraq Problem Once and for All* (New York: Simon & Schuster, 1999).

112. In November 1997 the U.S. and Britain begin deploying additional forces to the region. In November 1998 Iraq narrowly avoided U.S. air strikes by agreeing to resume its cooperation.

113. The no-fly zone was established by the Security Council in 1992 (S.C. Res. 781) and extended from military aircraft to all aircraft in 1993 (S.C. Res. 816). In response, the North Atlantic Council launched Operation Deny Flight to enforce it. It was NATO's first military engagement since its inception.

114. Daniel Williams and Ann Devroy, "U.S. Must Escalate Bombing in Bosnia to Boost Credibility," *Washington Post* (April 22, 1994): A2.

CHAPTER 6

1. Luke 3:14.

2. Matthew 5:44. The phrase "do good to those who hate you" appears in some late manuscripts, according to the New International Version.

3. Romans 12:9.

4. Romans 12:17.

5. Romans 12:19.

6. Romans 12:21.

7. Augustine, *Answer to Faustus* (Hyde Park, NY: New City Press, 1990), xxii, 74.

8. Augustine, *The City of God*, in *Great Books of the Western World*, vol. 18: *Augustine* (Chicago: Encyclopaedia Brittanica, 1952), xix, 7.

9. Augustine, "Letter 189: Augustine to Boniface," sec. 6, in *Augustine: Political Writings*, eds. E.M. Atkins and R.J. Dodaro (Cambridge: Cambridge University Press, 2001), 217.

10. Augustine, "Sermon 302: On the Feast of St. Laurence," sec. 15, in *Augustine: Political Writings*, 115 ("Soldering doesn't prevent you doing good, but hating does").

11. Thomas Aquinas, *Summa Theologica*, in *Great Books of the Western World*, vols. 19–20: *Thomas Aquinas* (Chicago: Encyclopaedia Brittanica, 1952), ii–ii, q. 40, art. 1 (quoting Augustine).

12. Thomas Aquinas, *Summa Theologica*, ii–ii, q. 40, art. 1 (emphasis added).

13. *Catechism of the Council of Trent*, On the Fifth Commandment, 280.

14. Franciscus de Victoria, *De Iure Belli*, in *De Indis et de Iure Belli Relectiones*, ed. Ernest Nys (Washington, DC: Carnegie Institution of Washington, 1917), secs. 15–18.

15. Victoria, *De Iure Belli*, sec. 19. This focus would later gain the following of Grotius and Vattel. Hugo Grotius, *De Jure Belli ac Pacis* (Oxford: Clarendon Press, 1925), iii, 12, 1; Emmerich de Vattel, *The Law of Nations or the Principles of Natural Law* (Washington, DC: Carnegie Institution of Washington, 1916), iii, 8, sec. 136.

16. Martin Luther, *Whether Soldiers, Too, Can Be Saved*, in *Luther: Selected Political Writings*, ed. J.M. Porter (Philadelphia: Fortress Press, 1974), 101.

17. Luther, *Whether Soldiers*, 102

18. Luther, *Whether Soldiers*, 113.

19. Luther, *Whether Soldiers*, 114.

20. Francisco Suarez, *De Bello*, in *Selections from Three Works of Francisco Suárez* (Oxford: Clarendon Press, 1944), i, 3.

21. *Catechism of the Catholic Church*, sec. 2302 (quoting Thomas Aquinas, *Summa Theologica* ii–ii, q. 158, art. 1, r.o. 3).

22. National Conference of Catholic Bishops, *The Challenge of Peace* (Washington, DC: United States Catholic Conference, 1983), para. 95.

23. John F. Johnson, "Can War Be Just?" *Lutheran Witness* 122, no. 1 (January 2003): 6.

24. Presbyterian Church in America, "Christian Responsibility in a Nuclear Age," www.pcahistory.org/pca/1–439.html (accessed January 13, 2008). The PCUSA states only that "war must be carried out with the right attitude." 181st General Assembly (1969), 694, in Presbyterian Church (U.S.A.), *A Composite Review of General Assembly Statements on Peacemaking and the Arms Race* (New York: Office of the General Assembly [PCUSA], 1984), 6.

25. 74th General Convention, in Episcopal Peace Fellowship, *Cross Before Flag* (Chicago: Episcopal Peace Fellowship, 2005), 39–40.

26. Episcopal Diocese of Washington, *The Nuclear Dilemma* (Cincinnati: Forward Movement Publications, 1987), 33.

27. Richard D. Land, "The Crisis in the Persian Gulf and 'Just Wars,'" *Light* (April–June 1991): 2.

28. Alma 43:30.

29. For a response comparing retributive justice to vengeance, see the passage from Daryl Charles in chapter 5, note 88 and accompanying text.

30. Farooq Hassan persuasively argues that Tanzania's right to self-defense in international law was extinguished when Uganda renounced its claim on the Kagera Salient. Farooq Hassan, "Realpolitik in International Law: After Tanzanian-Ugandan

Conflict 'Humanitarian Intervention' Reexamined," *Willamette Law Review* 17 (1981): 903. Vietnam's claim of a right to full-scale invasion was weak because a buffer zone could have sufficiently protected Vietnamese territory and the motives of any use of force by a Communist was always suspect in the West, given the history of Soviet expansion and the Korean War.

31. Gary Klintworth, *Vietnam's Intervention in Cambodia in International Law* (Canberra: Australian Government Publishing Service, 1990).

32. *Catechism of the Catholic Church*, sec. 2302 (quoting Thomas Aquinas, *Summa Theologica* ii-ii, q. 158, art. 1, r.o. 3).

33. *The Challenge of Peace*, para. 95.

34. Paul Jersild, "On the Viability of the Just War Theory," in *Peace and the Just War Tradition*, ed. Michael Stelmachowicz (New York: Lutheran Council in the USA, 1986), 71–72 (citing Augustine; italics in original). Childs does not mention of the criterion of right intent in his piece.

35. Johnson, "Can War Be Just?" 6.

36. PCA, "Christian Responsibility."

37. *Cross Before Flag*, 39 (emphasis added).

38. *In Defense of Creation*, 33.

39. Land, "Just Wars," 2.

40. Mormon 3:9–11.

41. Prosecutor v. Fatmir Limaj, Haradin Bala and Isak Musliu, Case. No. IT-03–66–T, Judgment of November 30, 2005.

42. Alma 44:6.

43. Alma 44:19–20.

44. Mormon 4–6.

45. Mormon 5:11.

46. Michael Walzer, *Just and Unjust Wars*, 4th ed. (New York: Basic Books, 2006), 113.

47. Jean Bethke Elshtain, *Just War Against Terror* (New York: Basic Books, 2003), chaps. 10–11.

48. Dino Kritsiotis, "Reappraising Policy Objections to Humanitarian Intervention," *Michigan Journal of International Law* 19 (1998): 1035.

CHAPTER 7

1. John F. Johnson, "Can War Be Just?" *Lutheran Witness* 122, no. 1 (January 2003): 6; 181st General Assembly (1969), 694, in Presbyterian Church (U.S.A.), *A Composite Review of General Assembly Statements on Peacemaking and the Arms Race* (New York: Office of the General Assembly [PCUSA], 1984), 6.

2. Exodus 21:23–25. The principle is also stated in Leviticus 24:19–20 and Deuteronomy 19:20–21.

3. Matthew 5:38–39.

4. Deuteronomy 25:2–3.

5. Augustine, *The City of God*, in *Great Books of the Western World*, vol. 18: *Augustine* (Chicago: Encyclopaedia Brittanica, 1952), iv, 15.

6. Compare John Calvin, *Institutes of the Christian Religion* (Philadelphia: Presbyterian Board of Christian Education, 1948), iv, 20, 12 (warning against arming oneself against a robber unless "driven to it by extreme necessity").

7. Desiderius Erasmus, *The Education of a Christian Prince* (Cambridge: Cambridge University Press, 1997), 106.

8. Franciscus de Victoria, *De Iure Belli*, in *De Indis et de Iure Belli Relectiones*, ed. Ernest Nys (Washington, DC: Carnegie Institution of Washington, 1917), sec. 14 (citing Deuteronomy 25:2). Molina cites this section to arrive at the same conclusion. Molina, "From: *De iustitia et jure*, tr. ii, disp. 102," sec. 7, in *The Ethics of War*, eds. Gregory M. Reichberg et al. (Malden, MA: Blackwell Publishing, 2006), 337.

9. Victoria, *De Iure Belli*, sec. 33. See also Victoria, *De Potestate Civili* [*On Civil Power*], sec. 13, in *Political Writings*, eds. Anthony Pagden and Jeremy Lawrance (Cambridge: Cambridge University Press, 1991), 21.

10. Martin Luther, *Temporal Authority: To What Extent It Should be Obeyed*, in *Luther: Selected Political Writings*, ed. J.M. Porter (Philadelphia: Fortress Press, 1974), 65.

11. Francisco Suarez, *De Bello*, in *Selections from Three Works of Francisco Suárez* (Oxford: Clarendon Press, 1944), iv, 2

12. Suarez, *De Bello*, iv, 8.

13. Victoria, *De Potestate Civili*, sec. 13; Victoria, *De Iure Belli* sec. 33.

14. Hugo Grotius, *De Jure Belli ac Pacis* (Oxford: Clarendon Press, 1925), iii, 1, 4, 2.

15. Samuel von Pufendorf, *On the Duty of Man and Citizen According to Natural Law* (New York: Oxford University Press, 1927), ii, 16, 1.

16. *Catechism of the Catholic Church*, sec. 2309.

17. National Conference of Catholic Bishops, *The Challenge of Peace* (Washington, DC: United States Catholic Conference, 1983), para. 99.

18. James M. Childs, Jr., "Nuclear Policy and the Ethics of Anticipation," in *Peace and the Just War Tradition*, ed. Michael J. Stelmachowicz (New York: Lutheran Council in the USA, 1986), 67.

19. Paul Jersild, "On the Viability of the Just War Theory," *Peace and the Just War Tradition*, 72 (italics in original).

20. Presbyterian Church in America, "Christian Responsibility in a Nuclear Age," www.pcahistory.org/pca/1-439.html (accessed January 13, 2008).

21. 74th General Convention, in Episcopal Peace Fellowship, *Cross Before Flag* (Chicago: Episcopal Peace Fellowship, 2005), 39.

22. Episcopal Diocese of Washington, *The Nuclear Dilemma* (Cincinnati: Forward Movement Publications, 1987), 107.

23. United Methodist Council of Bishops, *In Defense of Creation* (Nashville: Graded Press, 1986), 34.

24. Richard D. Land, "The Crisis in the Persian Gulf and 'Just Wars,'" *Light* (April–June 1991): 2.

25. Alma 48:23–24.

26. Edwin Brown Firmage, "Allegiance and Stewardship: Holy War, Just War, and the Mormon Tradition in the Nuclear Age," *Dialogue: A Journal of Mormon Thought* 16,

no. 1 (1983): 55. Firmage is writing on the just war tradition of the post–Constantine (that is, pre-Mormon) Christian church. This iteration, however, is his own wording.

27. Russia had secured this right from the Ottoman Empire in the Treaty of Kuchuk-Kainardji (Russia-Turkey), July 16, 1774, art. 7, 45 CTS 349, 373.

28. *Challenge of Peace*, para. 99.

29. *Catechism of the Catholic Church*, sec. 1857.

30. *Catechism of the Catholic Church*, sec. 1858.

31. *Catechism of the Catholic Church*, sec. 1858.

32. See Rome Statute of the International Criminal Court, art. 7, U.N. Doc. A/CONF.183/9. In contrast, "genocide" is defined as the same acts, but with the specific intent to destroy a national, ethnic, racial, or religious group. Convention on the Prevention and Punishment of Genocide, Dec. 9, 1948, art. 2, 78 U.N.T.S. 277.

33. In 1 Samuel 4.

34. *Catechism of the Catholic Church*, sec. 1862.

35. *Catechism of the Catholic Church*, sec. 1866. This author cannot conceive any realistic, nontrivial examples of wars whose objects are sloth or lust, that is, desire for physical or corporeal pleasure, and therefore those two sins will not be addressed further.

36. Matthew 5:21–22.

37. *Catechism of the Catholic Church*, sec. 2262; [Lutheran] Large Catechism, sec. 182, in *Book of Concord*, www.lcms.org/graphics/assets/media/LCMS/TrigBOC.pdf (accessed January 11, 2008); [Presbyterian] Larger Catechism, q. 136, in Presbyterian Church (U.S.A.), *The Book of Confessions* (Louisville, KY: Office of the General Assembly [PCUSA], 2002), , sec. 7.246.

38. Treaty of Peace, Friendship and Commerce (China-France), June 9, 1885 [Treaty of Tientsin], arts. 1–2, 76 BFSP 239, 166 CTS 195, 197–98.

39. Treaty of Peace and Convention (France-Siam), October 3, 1893, art. 1, 87 BFSP 187, 179 CTS 149, 150.

40. Treaty of Peace, Friendship, Limits and Settlement (Mexico-United States), February 2, 1848 [Treaty of Guadalupe Hidalgo], arts. 5 and 12, 4 Miller 207, 37 BFSP 567, 102 CTS 29, 36 and 45.

41. Treaty of Peace (Spain-United States), December 10, 1898 [Treaty of Paris], arts. 1–3, T.S. 343, 30 Stat. 1754, 11 Bevans 615, 187 CTS 100, 101.

42. Treaty of Nanking (China-Great Britain), August 29, 1842, 30 BFSP 389, 93 CTS 465, 466. In the same treaty, China ceded Hong Kong to Britain. *Id.* art. 3.

43. Treaty of Peace, Friendship and Commerce (China-Great Britain), June 26, 1858, arts. 10–11, 48 BFSP 47, 119 CTS 163, 167. Opium is mentioned specifically in Agreement respecting the Revision of the Tariff (China-Great Britain), November 8, 1858, Rule 5(1), 119 CTS 175, 177.

44. George Childs Kohn, *Dictionary of Wars* (New York: Checkmark Books, 1999), 454.

45. Davis Brown, "Use of Force Against Terrorism After September 11th: State Responsibility, Self-Defense and Other Responses," *Cardozo Journal of International and Comparative Law* 11 (2003): 25 (citing Osama bin Laden, "Ladenese Epistle: Declaration of War").

46. Kohn, *Dictionary of Wars*, 15.

47. *Catechism of the Catholic Church*, secs. 1812–29.

48. *Catechism of the Catholic Church*, secs. 1805–09.

49. The North American counterpart to the War of Spanish Succession was Queen Anne's War (1702–1713), in which Britain, France, and Spain fought for control of territory.

50. The treaty was actually enacted two years later, during Commodore Perry's second trip. Treaty of Peace and Amity (Japan-United States), March 31, 1854 [Treaty of Kanagawa], 6 Miller 440, 45 BFSP 234, 111 CTS 377, 378.

51. S.C. Res. 713, para. 6 (1991).

52. Abraham Maslow, "A Theory of Human Motivation," *Psychological Review* 50 (1943): 370–96.

53. See Ian Brownlie, *Principles of Public International Law*, 5th ed., chap. 4, sec. 2 (Oxford: Oxford University Press, 1998), 70.

54. Dale Copeland argues that dominant powers are most likely to undertake major war when they fear significant decline, in a theory he labels "dynamic differentials theory." Dale C. Copeland, *The Origins of Major War* (Ithaca, NY: Cornell University Press, 2000),

55. This principle of proportionality is stated in the current international law regulating counter-measures. Responsibility of States for Internationally Wrongful Acts, art. 50(1)(a), Annex to G.A. Res. 56/83 (2001).

CHAPTER 8

1. Sun Tzu, *The Art of War* (Oxford: Oxford University Press, 1963), iii, 9, 17; *The Kautilya Arthasastra* (Bombay: Bombay University Press, 1963), xii, 1; see also *Laws of Manu* (London: Penguin Books, 1991), vii, 172–74.

2. In 1 Samuel 4. Nor did God command the Israelites to make the endeavor. However, after seven months the Philistines returned the Ark to the Israelites with a guilt offering, so prompted by a series of plagues that God inflicted on the Philistines. 1 Samuel 5:1–6, 12.

3. See Francisco Suarez, *De Bello*, in *Selections from Three Works of Francisco Suárez* (Oxford: Clarendon Press, 1944), iv, 40. The commentary in question concerned pt. ii-ii, q. 96, art. 4.

4. Suarez, *De Bello*, iv, 10.

5. Hugo Grotius, *De Jure Belli ac Pacis* (Oxford: Clarendon Press, 1925), ii, 24, 9.

6. *Catechism of the Catholic Church*, sec. 2309.

7. National Conference of Catholic Bishops, *The Challenge of Peace* (Washington, DC: United States Catholic Conference, 1983), para. 98.

8. Paul Jersild, "On the Viability of the Just War Theory," in *Peace and the Just War Tradition*, ed. Michael J. Stelmachowicz (New York: Lutheran Council in the USA, 1986), 72 (italics in original). Childs omits entirely this criterion from his treatment.

9. 74th General Convention, in Episcopal Peace Fellowship, *Cross Before Flag* (Chicago: Episcopal Peace Fellowship, 2005), 39. The Episcopal Diocese of Washington's pamphlet *The Nuclear Dilemma* states only that "[t]here must be a reasonable hope

of success." Episcopal Diocese of Washington, *The Nuclear Dilemma* (Cincinnati: Forward Movement Publications, 1987), 107.

10. United Methodist Council of Bishops, *In Defense of Creation* (Nashville: Graded Press, 1986), 33–34.

11. Richard D. Land, "The Crisis in the Persian Gulf and 'Just Wars,'" *Light* (April–June 1991): 2. This iteration Land places under a criterion of "limited goals."

12. Edwin Brown Firmage, "Allegiance and Stewardship: Holy War, Just War, and the Mormon Tradition in the Nuclear Age," *Dialogue: A Journal of Mormon Thought* 16, no. 1 (1983): 55. See chapter 7, note 26.

13. Suarez, *De Bello*, iv, 10.

14. James F. Childress, "Just-War Criteria," in *War in the Twentieth Century*, ed. Richard B. Miller (Louisville, KY: Westminster/John Knox Press, 1992), 359.

15. *Challenge of Peace*, para. 98.

16. Recounted in 1 Samuel 17.

17. Martin Luther, *Whether Soldiers, Too, Can Be Saved*, in *Luther: Selected Political Writings*, ed. J.M. Porter (Philadelphia: Fortress Press, 1974), 114. See also chapter 6, note 19 and accompanying text.

18. 2 Nephi 5:5; Mosiah 24:23.

CHAPTER 9

1. Cicero, *De Officiis* (Cambridge, MA: Harvard University Press, 1961), i, 34.

2. William of Rennes, "From *Apparatus ad Summam Raymundi*," in *The Ethics of War*, eds. Gregory M. Reichberg et al. (Malden, MA: Blackwell Publishing, 2006), 137.

3. Cajetan, "From *Summula*, 'When war should be called just or unjust, licit or illicit,'" in *Ethics of War*, 248.

4. Francisco Suarez, *De Bello*, in *Selections from Three Works of Francisco Suarez* (Oxford: Clarendon Press, 1944), vi, 5.

5. Suarez, *De Bello*, vii, 3. However, Suarez and Cajetan disagreed on the obligation to accept restitution after hostilities commenced. Id., vii, 4–5.

6. Alberico Gentili, *De Iure Belli* (Oxford: Clarendon Press, 1933), i, 3 (citing Baldus); Samuel Pufendorf, *On the Duty of Man and Citizen* (New York: Oxford University Press, 1927), ii, 16, 3.

7. Thomas Aquinas, *Summa Theologica*, in *Great Books of the Western World*, vols. 19–20: *Thomas Aquinas* (Chicago: Encyclopaedia Britannica, 1952), ii-ii, q. 40, art. 4.

8. Martin Luther, *Whether Soldiers, Too, Can Be Saved*, in *Luther: Selected Political Writings*, ed. J.M. Porter (Philadelphia: Fortress Press, 1974), 113.

9. Luther, *Whether Soldiers*, 114. The phrase "of the devil" is omitted in the Porter edition, but is included in the *Ethics of War* edition, at p. 271 (both works use the same translation).

10. John Calvin, *Institutes of the Christian Religion* (Philadelphia Presbyterian Board of Christian Education, 1948), iv, 20, 12.

11. Calvin, *Institutes*, iv, 20, 12.

12. Desiderius Erasmus, *The Education of a Christian Prince* (Cambridge: Cambridge University Press, 1997), 102.

13. Victoria, *De Iure Belli*, in *De Indis et de Iure Belli Relectiones*, ed. Ernest Nys (Washington, DC: Carnegie Institution of Washington, 1917), sec. 60 (citing Romans 12:18).

14. Suarez, *De Bello*, vi, 5.

15. Hugo Grotius, *De Jure Belli ac Pacis* (Oxford: Clarendon Press, 1925), ii, 24, 1 (italics removed).

16. Emmerich de Vattel, *The Law of Nations or the Principles of Natural Law* (Washington, DC: Carnegie Institution of Washington, 1916), iii, 3, sec. 25.

17. Alma 48:14.

18. Doctrine and Covenants 98:23–31.

19. *Catechism of the Catholic Church*, sec. 2309.

20. National Conference of Catholic Bishops, *The Challenge of Peace* (Washington, DC: United States Catholic Conference, 1983), para. 96.

21. James M. Childs, Jr., "Nuclear Policy and the Ethics of Anticipation," in *Peace and the Just War Tradition,* ed. Michael J. Stelmachowicz (New York: Lutheran Council in the USA, 1986), 66.

22. Paul Jersild, "On the Viability of the Just War Theory," *Peace and the Just War Tradition*, 72.

23. John F. Johnson, "Can War Be Just?" *Lutheran Witness* 122, no. 1 (January 2003): 6.

24. 181st General Assembly (1969), 694, in Presbyterian Church (U.S.A.), *A Composite Review of General Assembly Statements on Peacemaking and the Arms Race* (New York: Office of the General Assembly [PCUSA], 1984), 6.

25. 74th General Convention, in Episcopal Peace Fellowship, *Cross Before Flag* (Chicago: Episcopal Peace Fellowship, 2005), 39.

26. United Methodist Council of Bishops, *In Defense of Creation* (Nashville: Graded Press, 1986), 33.

27. Richard D. Land, "The Crisis in the Persian Gulf and 'Just Wars,'" *Light* (April–June 1991): 2.

28. Edwin Brown Firmage, "Violence and the Gospel: The Teachings of the Old Testament, the New Testament, and the Book of Mormon," *BYU Studies* 25 (1985): 48.

29. *Challenge of Peace*, para. 96.

30. Darrell Cole, *When God Says War Is Right* (Colorado Springs: WaterBrook Press, 2002), 78.

31. Daryl Charles, *Between Pacifism and Jihad* (Downers Grove, IL: InterVarsity Press, 2005), 17ff.

32. James F. Childress, "Just-War Criteria," in *War in the Twentieth Century*, ed. Richard B. Miller (Louisville, KY: Westminster/John Knox Press, 1992), 355.

33. Martin Luther, *On War Against the Turk*, in *Luther: Selected Political Writings*, 121.

CHAPTER 10

1. W. S. Armour, "Customs of Warfare in Ancient India," *Transactions of the Grotius Society* 8 (1922): 76. The Ramayana summed up the principle thus: "It is odious for

Kshattriyas [the warrior caste] to make away with those who cannot defend themselves." Id., 73.

2. *The Laws of Manu* (London: Penguin Books, 1991), vii, 90.

3. L.C. Green, *The Contemporary Law of Armed Conflict* (Manchester: Manchester University Press, 2000), 287.

4. Coleman Phillipson, *The International Law and Custom of Ancient Greece and Rome*, vol. 2 (London: Macmillan and Co., 1911), 221–23.

5. Plato, *The Republic*, in *Great Books of the Western World*, vol. 7: *Plato* (Chicago: Encyclopaedia Brittanica, 1952), v, 470–71.

6. Phillipson, *International Law and Custom of Ancient Greece and Rome*, vol. 2, 229–31.

7. Majid Khadduri, *War and Peace in the Law of Islam* (Baltimore: Johns Hopkins University Press, 1955), 102–4.

8. *Shaybani's Siyar* [*The Islamic Law of Nations*] (Baltimore: Johns Hopkins University Press, 1966), ss. 47 and 1711. The Siyar also memorialized the immunity of women, children, the elderly, and the infirm from attack, but warriors were permitted to burn cities even if protected persons were killed in the process. Id., ss. 29–31, 47, 81, 110–23.

9. In Deuteronomy 20:13–14, God instructs the Israelites that in war they must kill all the men but enslave all the women and children rather than kill them. Though barbaric by our standards, this directive was charitable in its day.

10. 2 Kings 6:22–23.

11. Proverbs 25:21–22.

12. Matthew 5:44.

13. "Peace of God decreed by the Synod of Charroux," art. 2, in *Fontes Historiae Iuris Gentium*, vol. 1, ed. Wilhelm G. Grewe (Berlin: Walter de Gruyter, 1995), 609; see also "Peace of God, proclaimed in an assembly at Charroux, 989," in *The Ethics of War*, eds. Gregory M. Reichberg et al. (Malden, MA: Blackwell Publishing, 2006), 94–95.

14. Raymond of Peñafort, "From Raymond of Peñafort, *Summa de Casibus Poenitentiae*, II," sec. 17, in *Ethics of War*, 134.

15. Raymond, *Summa de Casibus*, in *Ethics of War*, 140–41.

16. Thomas Aquinas, *Summa Theologica*, in *Great Books of the Western World*, vols. 19–20: *Thomas Aquinas* (Chicago: Encyclopaedia Britannica, 1952), ii-ii, q. 41, art. 1.

17. Thomas Aquinas, *Summa Theologica*, ii-ii, q. 64, art. 7 (emphasis added).

18. Franciscus de Victoria, *De Iure Belli*, in *De Indis et de Iure Belli Relectiones*, ed. Ernest Nys (Washington, DC: Carnegie Institution of Washington, 1917), sec. 37.

19. Victoria, *De Iure Belli*, sec. 37.

20. Francisco Suarez, *De Bello*, in *Selections from Three Works of Francisco Suárez* (Oxford: Clarendon Press, 1944), vii, 6.

21. Suarez, *De Bello*, vii, 6.

22. Suarez, *De Bello*, vii, 19.

23. Convention for the Amelioration of the Condition of the Wounded in Armies in the Field, August 22, 1864, 18 Martens Nouveau Recueil (ser. 1) 607, 129 CTS 361.

24. Regulations Respecting the Law and Customs of War on Land, 36 Stat. 2295 [the "Hague Regulations"], Annex to Convention (IV) respecting the Laws and Customs of War on Land, October 18, 1907, 36 Stat. 2277, 205 CTS 289.

25. Geneva Convention for the Amelioration of the Condition of the Wounded and Sick in Armed Forces in the Field, August 12, 1949 [Geneva Convention I], 75

U.N.T.S. 31; Geneva Convention for the Amelioration of the Condition of the Wounded, Sick and Shipwrecked Members of Armed Forces at Sea, August 12, 1949 [Geneva Convention II], 75 U.N.T.S. 85; Geneva Convention Relative to the Treatment of Prisoners of War, August 12, 1949 [Geneva Convention III], 75 U.N.T.S. 135; Geneva Convention Relative to the Protection of Civilian Persons in Time of War, August 12, 1949 [Geneva Convention IV], 75 U.N.T.S. 287; Protocol Additional to the Geneva Conventions of 12 August 1949, and Relating to the Protection of Victims of International Armed Conflicts, June 8, 1977 [Protocol I], 1125 U.N.T.S. 3; Protocol Additional to the Geneva Conventions of 12 August 1949, and Relating to the Protection of Victims of Non-International Armed Conflicts, June 8, 1977 [Protocol II], 1125 U.N.T.S. 609.

26. National Conference of Catholic Bishops, *The Challenge of Peace* (Washington, DC: United States Catholic Conference, 1983), para. 104.

27. Paul Jersild, "On the Viability of the Just War Theory," in *Peace and the Just War Tradition,* ed. Michael J. Stelmachowicz (New York: Lutheran Council in the USA, 1986), 72 (italics in original).

28. John F. Johnson, "Can War Be Just?" *Lutheran Witness* 122, no. 1 (January 2003): 6.

29. 181st General Assembly (1969), 694, in Presbyterian Church (U.S.A.), *A Composite Review of General Assembly Statements on Peacemaking and the Arms Race* (New York: Office of the General Assembly [PCUSA], 1984), 6.

30. 74th General Convention, in Episcopal Peace Fellowship, *Cross Before Flag* (Chicago: Episcopal Peace Fellowship, 2005), 39–40.

31. United Methodist Council of Bishops, *In Defense of Creation* (Nashville: Graded Press, 1986), 34.

32. Richard D. Land, "The Crisis in the Persian Gulf and 'Just Wars,'" *Light* (April–June 1991): 2. Land presents discrimination under the title "limited goals."

33. Edwin Brown Firmage, "Allegiance and Stewardship: Holy War, Just War, and the Mormon Tradition in the Nuclear Age," *Dialogue: A Journal of Mormon Thought* 16, no. 1 (1983): 54–55.

34. While it is true that noncombatants and civilians should be immune from attack, it is not for the reason that war is an official act of government.

35. Presbyterian Church in America, "Christian Responsibility in a Nuclear Age," www.pcahistory.org/pca/1–439.html (accessed January 13, 2008).

36. *Challenge of Peace*, para. 105.

37. James M. Childs, Jr., "Nuclear Policy and the Ethics of Anticipation," *Peace and the Just War Tradition,* 67.

38. Johnson, "Can War Be Just?" 6.

39. Presbyterian Church (U.S.A.), *A Composite Review,* 6.

40. *Cross Before Flag*, 39.

41. *In Defense of Creation*, 34.

42. Land, "Just Wars," 2. Land presents discrimination under the title "limited goals." His discussion of proportionality is devoted to proportionality of cause rather than of means.

43. Firmage, "Allegiance," 54.

44. Edwin Brown Firmage, "Violence and the Gospel: The Teachings of the Old Testament, the New Testament, and the Book of Mormon," *BYU Studies* 25 (1985): 48.

45. Victoria, *De Iure Belli*, sec. 18.

46. This was the objection of the Second Lateran Council to the use of archery in warfare—that such weapons enabled the combatants to attack from a distance without themselves incurring the risk of being attacked. Second Lateran Council, canon 29, www.fordham.edu/halsall/basis/lateran2.html (accessed January 8, 2008). See also G.I.A.D. Draper, "The Interaction of Christianity and Chivalry in the Historical Development of the Law of War," *International Review of the Red Cross* 5 (1965): 19.

CHAPTER 11

1. Thomas Aquinas, *Summa Theologica*, in *Great Books of the Western World*, vols. 19–20: *Thomas Aquinas* (Chicago: Encyclopaedia Brittanica, 1952), ii–ii, qq. 37–41.

2. Thomas Aquinas, *Summa Theologica*, ii–ii, q. 42.

3. Suarez, *De Bello*, in *Selections from Three Works of Francisco Suárez* (Oxford: Clarendon Press, 1944), viii, 2.

4. Charles Macksey, "War," in *The Catholic Encyclopedia* (1917), www.newadvent.org/cathen/index.html (accessed January 8, 2008).

5. Paul Ramsey, *War and the Christian Conscience* (Durham, NC: Duke University Press, 1961), 114.

6. Offered by the Galileans in John 6:15 and by Satan at the temptations of Christ in Matthew 4:8–10.

7. For example, Proverbs 8:15–16.

8. Romans 13:3–4.

9. Augustine, "Letter 153: Augustine to Macedonius," sec. 19, in *Augustine: Political Writings*, eds. E.M. Atkins and R.J. Dodaro (Cambridge: Cambridge University Press, 2001), 82–83.

10. Exodus 20:12. As we shall discover later in this chapter, modern churches classify the duty to obey civil authority within this commandment.

11. Deuteronomy 17:14–20.

12. Mark 12:17.

13. In Mark 13:2 and Luke 21:6. In 70 CE the Romans squelched the Great Jewish Revolt by sieging Jerusalem and destroying the Temple; the Temple was never rebuilt.

14. Romans 13:1, 4, and 7.

15. 1 Peter 2:13–14, 17 (emphasis added).

16. See Daniel 3:8–16; Daniel 6; Acts 5:29.

17. John 8:3–11.

18. John 2:14–17. The cleansing of the Temple is also recounted, in less detail, in Matthew 21:12–13, Mark 11:15–17, and Luke 19:45–46.

19. See Alan Watson, *Jesus and the Law* (Athens, GA: University of Georgia Press, 1996), 76–77.

20. Ambrose, "Letter 50," in *From Irenaeus to Grotius,* eds. Oliver O'Donovan and Joan Lockwood O'Donovan (Grand Rapids, MI: William B. Eerdmans Publishing Company, 1999), 84; see also Ambrose, *De Officiis* i, 28, in *From Irenaeus to Grotius,* 84.

21. Augustine, "Letter 153," sec. 3, in *Augustine: Political Writings,* 73.

22. Augustine, "Letter 153," sec. 17, in *Augustine: Political Writings,* 81.

23. John Chrysostom, "From the Twenty-Fourth Homily on Romans," in *From Irenaeus to Grotius,* 92 (emphasis added).

24. John of Salisbury, *Policraticus,* iii, 15, in *The Stateman's Book of John of Salisbury,* ed. John Dickinson (New York: Alfred A. Knopf, 1927), lxxiii.

25. John of Salisbury, *Policraticus,* viii, 17, in *The Stateman's Book,* 336. John is also an overlooked progenitor of the democratic peace theory, first articulated in modern terms by the Abbé de St.-Pierre and especially Immanuel Kant, who claims that the "republican" form of government is a necessary prerequisite to peace, that is, that autocracies are more warlike than democracies. Immanuel Kant, "Perpetual Peace" (1795), sec. 2, First Definitive Article, in *Kant: Political Writings,* ed. Hans Reiss (Cambridge: Cambridge University Press, 1991), 99–102. See also Michael W. Doyle, "Kant, Liberal Legacies, and Foreign Affairs," Part I, *Philosophy and Public Affairs* 12, no. 3 (1983): 205.

26. John of Salisbury, *Policraticus,* iii, 15, in *The Stateman's Book,* lxxiv.

27. John of Salisbury, *Policraticus,* iii, 15, in *The Stateman's Book,* lxxiii. However, such punishment was limited to situations in which there was no other alternative to curbing their abuses. Id., viii, 18, in *The Stateman's Book,* 356.

28. Thomas Aquinas, *Summa Theologica,* i–ii, q. 90, art. 2.

29. Thomas Aquinas, *Summa Theologica,* i–ii, q. 91, art. 1.

30. Thomas Aquinas, *Summa Theologica,* i–ii, q. 92, art. 1; see also *Id.* i–ii, q. 96, art. 1 (defining the end of law as the common good).

31. Thomas Aquinas, *Summa Theologica,* i–ii, q. 92, art. 1, r.o. 4.

32. Thomas Aquinas, *Summa Theologica,* i–ii, q. 96, art. 4 (emphasis added).

33. Thomas Aquinas, *Summa Theologica,* ii–ii, q. 42, art. 2, r.o. 3.

34. See Thomas Aquinas, *Scripta Super Libros Sententiarum,* ii, dist. 44, q. 2, r.o. 5, in *St. Thomas Aquinas: Political Writings,* ed. R.W. Dyson (Cambridge: Cambridge University Press, 2002), 75.

35. 1 Peter 2:19.

36. Thomas Aquinas, *De Regimine Principum,* vi (London: Sheed and Ward, 1938), 60–61. Franklin Ford attributes the inconsistency with the *Summa* and previous works to an epiphany of political realism, that deposing a tyrant would often bring even greater iniquity. Franklin L. Ford, *Political Murder: From Tyrannicide to Terrorism* (Cambridge, MA: Harvard University Press, 1985), 125. While the experience of the Iraq War might serve to illustrate Ford's assertion, the experience of Kosovo, Cambodia, Uganda, and East Pakistan would seem to disprove it.

37. *Catholic Encyclopedia,* "John Parvus," www.newadvent.org/cathen/index.html (accessed January 8, 2008); Ford, *Political Murder,* 130–32.

38. "Sentence condemning John Petit's proposition, 'Any tyrant,'" Council of Constance, Session 15, July 6, 1415, in *Decrees of Ecumenical Councils,* vol. 1, ed. Norman P. Tanner, S.J. (London: Sheed & Ward, 1990), 432. Specifically, the church rejected

the proposition that "Any tyrant can and ought to be killed, licitly and meritoriously, by any of his vassals or subjects . . . and without waiting for a sentence or a command from any judge."

39. Victoria adopts this position a century later, arguing in favor of the divine necessity of the monarchy. Francisco de Vitoria, *De Potestate Civili* [*On Civil Power*], in *Political Writings,* eds. Anthony Pagden and Jeremy Lawrance (Cambridge: Cambridge University Press, 1991), 3–44. He sidesteps the question of the lawfulness of tyrannicide generally, but his opinion that even the laws of tyrants are binding suggests that he opposes it. Id., q. 3, art 6.

40. Ford, *Political Murder*, 133 (citing Thomas Basin, *History of Louis XI*).

41. Ford, *Political Murder*, 136–37.

42. See Martin Luther, *Temporal Authority: To What Extent It Should Be Obeyed*, in *Luther: Selected Political Writings,* ed. J.M. Porter (Philadelphia: Fortress Press, 1974), 52–53.

43. Martin Luther, *Whether Soldiers, Too, Can Be Saved*, in *Luther: Selected Political Writings*, 105.

44. Luther, *Temporal Authority*, 66; *Whether Soldiers*, 117. This disposition also plays out in the Augsburg Confession, which permits and even subtly encourages civil participation, proclaiming that "lawful civil ordinances are good works of God . . . Therefore, Christians are necessarily bound to obey their own magistrates and laws *save only* when commanded to sin; for then they ought to obey God rather than men." Augsburg Confession xvi, 1 and 6–7, in *Book of Concord*, www.lcms.org/graphics/assets/media/LCMS/TrigBOC.pdf (accessed January 11, 2008) (emphasis added).

45. Luther, *Whether Soldiers*, 108–10.

46. Martin Luther, *Against the Robbing and Murdering Hordes of Peasants*, in *Luther: Selected Political Writings*, 87.

47. For example, in the Schleitheim Confession, arts. iv and vi, in *The Legacy of Michael Sattler*, ed. John H. Yoder (Scottdale, PA: Herald Press, 1973), 37–40.

48. John Calvin, *Institutes of the Christian Religion* (Philadelphia: Presbyterian Board of Christian Education, 1948), iv, 20, 25.

49. Calvin, *Institutes*, iv, 20, 30.

50. Calvin, *Institutes*, iv, 20, 4.

51. Calvin, *Institutes*, iv, 20, 9 ("no government can be happily constituted, unless its first object be the promotion of piety, and that all laws are preposterous which neglect the claims of God"). The role of the civil magistrate as theological enforcer also appears in the 1647 text of the Westminster Confession; among his duties were "that the Truth of God be kept pure, and entire, that all Blasphemies and Heresies be suppressed." Westminster Confession, xxv (PCUS)/xxiii (UPCUSA), 3, footnote, in Presbyterian Church (U.S.A.), *The Book of Confessions* (Louisville, KY: Office of the General Assembly [PCUSA], 2002), sec. 6.129 (edited for dialect).

52. Ford, *Political Murder*, 151–52.

53. John Knox, *The First Blast of the Trumpet*, in *John Knox on Rebellion*, ed. Roger A. Mason, (Cambridge: Cambridge University Press, 1994), 3–47. Knox also opposed Mary's rule on the basis of her being a woman.

54. *John Knox on Rebellion*, 182–95.

55. John Knox, *The Appellation of John Knox*, in *John Knox on Rebellion*, 77.

56. Knox, *Appellation*, 83. See also Scots Confession, xxiv, 2, in *Book of Confessions*, sec. 3.24 (stating that "kings, princes, rulers, and magistrates [are] not only appointed for civil government but also to maintain true religion and to suppress all idolatry and superstition").

57. *Catechism of the Council of Trent*, On the Fourth Commandment, 276.

58. Large Catechism, sec. 151, in *Book of Concord*. The portion of the Catechism on the Fifth Commandment, "Thou shalt not kill," makes no specific provision for killing a tyrant.

59. Augsburg Confession, xvi, 6–7, in *Book of Concord*.

60. Scots Confession, xxiv, in *Book of Confessions*, sec. 3.24. Contrast the Westminster Confession of the following century: "It is the duty of the people to pray for magistrates, . . . *to obey their lawful commands*, and to be subject to their authority, for conscience' sake." Westminster Confession, xxv/xxiii, 4, in *Book of Confessions*, sec. 6.130 (emphasis added).

61. Heidelberg Catechism, q. 104, in *Book of Confessions*, sec. 4.104.

62. Second Helvetic Confession, xxx, in *Book of Confessions*, sec. 5.258.

63. Articles of Religion, xxxvii (1571/1662), in Episcopal Church, *The Book of Common Prayer, 1979*, http://justus.anglican.org/resources/bcp/formatted_1979.htm (accessed January 11, 2008), 876.

64. Christopher Goodman, *How Superior Powers Ought To Be Obeyed By Their Subjects: And Wherein They May Lawfully By God's Word Be Disobeyed And Resisted*, viii and xiii, www.constitution.org/cmt/goodman/obeyed.htm (accessed January 15, 2008).

65. Theodore Beza, *Concerning the Rights of Rulers Over Their Subjects and the Duty Of Subjects Towards Their Rulers*, qq. 5–6, http://fly.hiwaay.net/~pspoole/Beza1.htm (accessed January 15, 2008) (speaking to a right of lower magistrates to rebel against a tyrant *in regimine* but permitting the right of private citizens to do so only against the usurper, and only if the lower magistrates fail to do so).

66. *Catholic Encyclopedia*, "Tyrannicide," citing Domingo Bañez, *De Justitia et Jure* (1595), q. 46, art. 3.

67. James Brown Scott, *The Catholic Conception of International Law* (Washington, DC: Georgetown University Press, 1934), 291 (citing Juan de Mariana, *De Rege et Regis Institutione* [*On the King and the Training of the King*], chap. 6).

68. *Catholic Encyclopedia*, "Tyrannicide." Mariana himself disclaimed any Jesuit official status of the work.

69. Francisco Suarez, *Defensio Fidei Catholicae, et Apostolicae*, in *Selections from Three Works of Francisco Suárez* (Oxford: Clarendon Press, 1944), vi, 6.

70. George Childs Kohn, *Dictionary of Wars* (New York: Checkmark Books, 1999), 425. Estimates of the death toll vary widely.

71. Scott, *Catholic Conception*, 385–89.

72. George Buchanan, *De Jure Regni Apud Scotos*, ii, 47, in *The Powers of the Crown in Scotland*, ed. Charles Flinn Arrowood (Austin: University of Texas Press, 1949), 50.

73. Thomas Jefferson in particular was influenced by Buchanan. See Scott, *Catholic Conception*, 346.

74. Treaty of Peace (Netherlands-Spain), January 30, 1648, 1 CTS 1, 3. This instrument pre-dates the Peace of Westphalia.

75. Doctrine and Covenants 134:1 reads, "We believe that governments were instituted of God for the benefit of man; and that he holds men accountable for their acts in relation to them, both in making laws and administering them, for the good and safety of society."

76. 2 Nephi 2:16 ("Wherefore, the Lord God gave unto man that he should act for himself"). See also Doctrine and Covenants 101:78, which characterizes Agency as the means by which man is held accountable for his sins.

77. Doctrine and Covenants 134:5. See also Doctrine and Covenants 134:2: "We believe that no government can exist in peace, except such laws are framed and held inviolate as will secure to each individual the free exercise of conscience, the right and control of property, and the protection of life."

78. Doctrine and Covenants 134:7–8.

79. Alma 46:3–7, 28–35.

80. Alma 24:1–13.

81. Alma 53:14–18. However, their sons were not considered to be bound by that oath and so they were permitted to take up arms in defense of their parents.

82. Doctrine and Covenants 134:11.

83. Doctrine and Covenants 88:35.

84. Mosiah 29:21–23.

85. Doctrine and Covenants 105.

86. *Catechism of the Catholic Church*, secs. 2242–43 (italics in original).

87. Evangelical Lutheran Church in America, *For Peace in God's World* (August 20, 1995), www.elca.org/socialstatements/peace/ (accessed January 11, 2008), sec. 4(a).

88. Larger Catechism, qq. 127–30, in *Book of Confessions*, secs. 7.237–40 (emphasis added).

89. United Methodist Church, *Book of Discipline*, (Nashville: United Methodist Publishing House, 2004), sec.164(i) (emphasis added).

90. Articles of Religion of the Methodist Church, "Of the Duty of Christians to the Civil Authority," in *Book of Discipline*, sec. 103(3). This article is at the end of the numbered articles, added by legislative enactment in 1939.

91. *Book of Discipline*, sec. 164(f).

92. Southern Baptist Convention, Baptist Faith and Message, art. 17 (2000 text), www.sbc.net/bfm/bfm2000.asp (accessed January 13, 2008). This passage is identical in the corresponding articles of the 1963 and 1925 texts.

93. Articles of Religion, art. 37 (1801 text), in *Book of Common Prayer*, 875.

94. Buchanan, *De Jure Regni*, ii, 10, 10.

95. Buchanan, *De Jure Regni*, ii, 30, 28 (capitalizations removed).

96. Suarez, *Defensio Fidei*, iii, 23.

97. Suarez, *Defensio Fidei*, vi, 4, 19.

98. Suarez, *Defensio Fidei*, vi, 4, 15. Suarez also suggests that the pope, as the best moral authority, should be the arbiter of the justness of an uprising against a legitimate king. Id., vi, 4, 17.

99. Scott, *Catholic Conception*, 427ff.

100. Suarez, *Defensio Fidei*, vi, 4, 13.

101. Scott, *Catholic Conception*, 285, quoting Mariana.

102. Scott, *Catholic Conception*, 286, quoting Mariana.
103. Ibid.
104. Suarez, *Defensio Fidei*, vi, 4, 1.
105. Buchanan, *De Jure Regni*, ii, 34, 32.
106. Suarez, *Defensio Fidei*, vi, 4, 8.
107. Suarez, *Defensio Fidei*, vi, 4, 5.
108. Suarez, *Defensio Fidei*, vi, 4, 6.
109. Suarez, *Defensio Fidei*, vi, 4, 13.
110. *Catechism of the Catholic Church*, sec. 2243.
111. *Catechism of the Catholic Church*, sec. 2237 (original italics removed).
112. Thomas Aquinas, *Summa Theologica*, ii-ii, q. 42, art. 2, r.o. 3.
113. Suarez, *Defensio Fidei*, vi, 4, 9.
114. *Catechism of the Catholic Church*, sec. 2243.
115. Ibid.
116. Suarez, *Defensio Fidei*, vi, 4, 8.
117. *Catechism of the Catholic Church*, sec. 2243.

CHAPTER 12

1. Such operations, usually carried out without the consent of the host state's government, are usually grouped under the heading "Protection of Nationals," as they are most often carried out for the benefit of the intervening state's own nationals.
2. Proverbs 24:11.
3. Jeremiah 22:3.
4. Martin Luther, *Temporal Authority: To What Extent It Should Be Obeyed*, in *Luther: Selected Political Writings*, ed. J.M. Porter (Philadelphia: Fortress Press, 1974), 59.
5. Martin Luther, *Whether Soldiers, Too, Can Be Saved*, in *Luther: Selected Political Writings*, 110.
6. John Calvin, *Institutes of the Christian Religion* (Philadelphia: Presbyterian Board of Christian Education, 1948), iv, 20, 9.
7. Calvin, *Institutes*, iv, 20, 11.
8. Franciscus de Victoria, *De Indis*, in *De Indis et de Iure Belli Relectiones*, ed. Ernest Nys (Washington, DC: Carnegie Institution of Washington, 1917), iii, 13.
9. Victoria, *De Indis*, iii, 15. Victoria makes no mention of foreign intervention against tyranny in *De Iure Belli*.
10. Francisco Suarez, *Defensio Fidei Catholicae, et Apostolicae*, in *Selections from Three Works of Francisco Suárez* (Oxford: Clarendon Press, 1944), iii, 23, 15. It is an interesting reflection of the times that Suarez's contention was based first on "monstrous crimes" against the faith and against priests, *then* against other innocent persons.
11. Suarez, *Defensio Fidei*, iii, 23, 21.
12. See chapter 11, note 108 and accompanying text.
13. Suarez, *Defensio Fidei*, vi, 4, 12 (emphasis added).

14. Jean Bodin, *Six Books of the Commonwealth* (New York: Macmillan Company, 1955), i, 8.

15. Bodin, *Six Books of the Commonwealth*, ii, 4–5.

16. *Vindiciae Contra Tyrannos*, Fourth question, in *A Defence of Liberty Against Tyrants*, ed. Harold J. Laski (New York: Lenox Hill, 1972).

17. Alberico Gentili, *De Iure Belli* (Oxford: Clarendon Press, 1933), i, 16; Hugo Grotius, *De Jure Belli ac Pacis* (Oxford: Clarendon Press, 1925), ii, 25, 8; Samuel von Pufendorf, *De Jure Naturae et Gentium* (Oxford: Clarendon Press, 1934), viii, 6, 14.

18. In September 1815, the emperors of Prussia, Austria, and Russia entered into a treaty that provided for "doing each other reciprocal service, . . . the three allied Princes looking on themselves as merely delegated by Providence to govern three branches of the One family," that is, the three emperors. Treaty of Holy Alliance (Austria, Prussia, Russia), September 11, 1815, art. 2, 65 CTS 199, 201, English translation reprinted in *The Concert of Europe*, ed. René Albrecht-Carrié (New York: Walker and Company, 1968), 34. See also Secret Treaty concerning Common Action Against Revolutionaries (Austria, Prussia, Russia), October 15, 1833, 84 CTS 65, 66. In 1820 and 1821, under the auspices of the Holy Alliance at the Congresses of Troppau and Laibach, Austria intervened in the kingdoms of the Two Sicilies and Sardinia to assist in restoring the monarchy after the Neapolitan Revolt and Piedmontese Revolt, respectively. See Declaration of the Allied Sovereigns of Austria, Prussia and Russia concerning Suppression of Revolutions in the Two Sicilies and Sardinia, May 12, 1821, 8 BFSP 1199, reprinted in *Concert of Europe*, 55–57. Austria would again restore the *status quo* in the Italian Revolts of 1831–1834, during which several Italian states within the Austrian Empire deposed their rulers. Additionally, in 1822, the Congress of Verona awarded a reluctant France the mandate to intervene in the Spanish Civil War of 1820–1823 and restore the absolute monarchy there, which it did (Franco-Spanish War, 1823).

19. Treaty of Kuchuk-Kainardji (Russia-Turkey), July 16, 1774, arts. 7–8, 45 CTS 349, 368.

20. Treaty of Peace (Russia-Turkey) [Treaty of Adrianople], September 14, 1829, 16 BFSP 647, 80 CTS 83, 84. Articles 5 and 6 provided for Serbia, Moldavian, and Wallachian autonomy. Id., arts. 5–6, 80 CTS at 87.

21. Protocols of Conference and Convention respecting Measures to be Taken for the Pacification of Syria (Austria, France, G.B., Prussia, Russia, Turkey), August 3/September 5, 1860, 50 BFSP 6, 122 CTS 487.

22. Treaty from the Settlement of Affairs in the East (Austria-Hungary, France, Germany, Great Britain, Italy, Russia, Turkey), July 13, 1878 [Treaty of Berlin], 69 BFSP 749, 153 CTS 171, 172, English translation reprinted in *American Journal of International Law Supplement* 2 (1908): 401.

23. Henry Wheaton, *Elements of International Law*, eighth ed. (Boston: Little, Brown, & Company, 1866), sec. 69.

24. Robert Phillimore, *Commentaries upon International Law*, vol. 1 (London: William G. Benning & Company, 1854), pt. iv, ch. 1, sec. 394; August-Guilliaume Heffter, *Le Droit International Public de l'Europe* (Paris: Cotillon, 1857), sec. 45(3); Johann Kaspar Bluntschli, *Le Droit International Codifié*, second ed. (Paris: Librairie de

Guillaumin & Cie., 1874), 22 (speaking only to the protection of religious confreres); Edward S. Creasy, *First Platform of International Law* (London: John van Voorst, 1876), sec. 316. Other American works include H.W. Halleck, *International Law* (San Francisco: H.H. Bancroft & Company, 1861), chap. iv, sec. 9; and George Grafton Wilson and George Fox Tucker, *International Law*, second ed. (New York: Silver, Burdett & Company, 1901), sec. 42(d)(3); Ellery C. Stowell, *Intervention in International Law* (Washington, DC: John Byrne & Company, 1921), 86 (acknowledging the body of state practice tending to support the legality of such intervention, but also finding that the state tends to seek other grounds for justifying interventions that are fundamentally humanitarian in nature).

25. Stowell, *Intervention*, 120–22.

26. Treaty of Peace (Spain-United States), December 10, 1898 [Treaty of Paris], art. 1, T.S. 343, 30 Stat. 1754, 11 Bevans 615, 187 CTS 100, 101.

27. Davis Brown, "Iraq and the 800-Pound Gorilla Revisited: Good and Bad Faith, and Humanitarian Intervention," *Hastings International and Comparative Law Review* 28 (2004): 1–24. I agree wholeheartedly with James Turner Johnson's lament that the right of humanitarian intervention did not figure as prominently in the debate as it should have. James Turner Johnson, *The War to Oust Saddam Hussein* (Lanham, MD: Rowman & Littlefield Publishers, 2005), 124.

28. Although the Security Council did not authorize the invasion before it took place, its commendation of ECOWAS after the fact was effectively a retroactive authorization. S.C. Res. 788 (1992).

29. In S.C. Res. 816 (1993), the Council authorized states to use "all necessary measures" to enforce a total no-fly zone over Bosnia and in S.C. Res. 836 (1993) the Council authorized the peacekeeping force in Bosnia (UNPROFOR) to use force to protect Muslim enclaves as well as NATO to provide air power for that purpose.

30. The Security Council specifically authorized an ECOWAS force to enforce a ban on arms and petroleum shipments to Sierra Leone; its support and later commendation of the ECOWAS initiative to restore peace and failure to condemn ECOWAS's invasion of Sierra Leone is tantamount to an approval of it. See S.C. Res. 1132 (1997); S.C. Res. 1162 (1998).

31. Grotius writes, "If . . . it should be granted that even in extreme need subjects cannot justifiably take up arms . . ., nevertheless it will not follow that *others* may not take up arms *on their behalf*." Grotius, *De Jure Belli ac Pacis*, ii, 25, 8, 3 (emphasis added).

32. See chapter 11, notes 86, 88, and 75–85 and accompanying text, respectively.

33. Pontifical Council for Justice and Peace, *Compendium of the Social Doctrine of the Church* (Vatican City: Roman Catholic Church, 2004), sec. 506 (italics in original, citations omitted, quoting John Paul II, "Message for the 2000 World Day of Peace"). See also United States Conference of Catholic Bishops, *The Harvest of Justice Is Sown in Peace* (Washington, DC: U.S. Conference of Catholic Bishops, 1993), 38–39. This position is consistent with that of the American Catholic Bishops in the 1980s, who stated that, "War is permissible only to confront 'a real and certain danger,' i.e., to protect innocent life, to preserve conditions necessary for decent human existence, and to secure basic human rights." National Conference of Catholic Bishops, *The Challenge of Peace* (Washington, DC: United States Catholic Conference, 1983), sec. 86(a).

34. 210th General Assembly, "Just Peacemaking and the Call for International Intervention for Humanitarian Rescue," PC(USA) Minutes, 1998, 455, reprinted in *Social Witness Policy Compilation*, chap. 4, "Peacemaking," http://index.pcusa.org/NXT/gateway.dll/socialpolicy/chapter00000.htm?fn=default.htm$f=templates$3.0 (accessed January 11, 2008).

35. Gordon B. Hinckley, "War and Peace," *Ensign* 33, no. 5 (May 2003): 80. This statement was made by the president of the Mormon Church.

36. United Methodist Church, *Book of Discipline*, (Nashville: United Methodist Publishing House, 2004), sec. 165(c) (emphasis added).

37. Evangelical Lutheran Church in America, *For Peace in God's World* (August 20, 1995), http://www.elca.org/socialstatements/peace (accessed January 11, 2008), sec. 4(b).

38. 210th General Assembly, "Just Peacemaking and the Call for International Intervention for Humanitarian Rescue," supra note 34.

39. U.S. Conference of Catholic Bishops, "Statement of President," March 24, 1999, www.usccb.org/comm/archives/1999/99–064a.shtml (accessed January 11, 2008).

40. Evangelical Lutheran Church in America, "Statement by the Presiding Bishop on the Crisis in the Balkans," April 9, 1999, www.elca.org/ob/kosovo.html (accessed January 11, 2008).

41. Episcopal Church, "Remarks by the Presiding Bishop on the NATO Bombing Campaign," March 26, 1999, www.episcopalchurch.org/1275_1329_ENG_HTM.htm (accessed January 11, 2008).

42. PC(USA) Commissioners' Resolution 98–8, "Concerning Kosovo," www.pcusa.org/pcusa/ga210/comres98/cr08.html (accessed January 11, 2008) (calling on the Security Council "to consider the appropriateness of immediate international intervention as a humanitarian measure").

43. Pontifical Council, *Compendium of the Social Doctrine*, sec. 506.

44. U.N. Charter, art. 42.

45. Thomas M. Franck, *Recourse to Force* (Cambridge: Cambridge University Press, 2002), 149–50.

46. Franck, *Recourse to Force*, 166–67.

47. Franck, *Recourse to Force*, 169.

48. Nicholas J. Wheeler, *Saving Strangers* (Oxford: Oxford University Press, 2000), 78.

49. Independent International Commission on Kosovo, *The Kosovo Report* (Oxford: Oxford University Press, 2000), chap. 6.

50. The son of Idi Amin, Taban, enjoyed a similar form of notoriety.

51. Kenneth M. Pollack, *The Threatening Storm: The Case for Invading Iraq* (New York: Random House, 2002), 124.

52. Ian Brownlie, *International Law and the Use of Force by States* (Oxford: Clarendon Press, 1963), 338–39; Oscar Schachter, *International Law in Theory and Practice* (Dordrecht: Martinus Nijhoff Publishers, 1991), 125.

53. Indeed, the same is true of collective self-defense, but no reasonable person would argue that Kuwait should not have been liberated from invasion by Iraq on the basis that Lebanon was not liberated from occupation by Syria.

54. Here we treat the term "murder" according to its most common meaning, which is a deliberate killing motivated by hate or the prospect of gain. Labeling other

processes that result in deaths, for example, legalizing abortion or the applying capital punishment within a reasonably fair legal system, as "murder" confuses the argument and is counterproductive.

55. Michael Walzer, *Arguing about War* (New Haven, CT: Yale University Press, 2004), 81.

CHAPTER 13

1. John C. Ford, S.J., "The Morality of Obliteration Bombing," *Theological Studies* 5, no. 3 (1944): 267.

2. Ford, "The Morality of Obliteration Bombing," 293–95.

3. Second Calhoun Commission, "Atomic Warfare and the Christian Faith," *Social Action* (May 15, 1946): 11. The Federal Council of Churches is now the National Council of Churches.

4. Second Calhoun Commission, "Atomic Warfare," 13, note 6.

5. Second Calhoun Commission, "Atomic Warfare," 14.

6. Dun Commission, "The Christian Conscience and Atomic War," *Christianity and Crisis* (December 11, 1950): 165.

7. Indeed, two of the members, including the namesake of the Calhoun Commissions, refused to sign the document. Charles E. Raynal, "The Response of American Protestantism to World War II and Atomic Weapons," in *Peace, War and God's Justice,* eds. Thomas D. Parker and Brian J. Fraser (Toronto: United Church Publishing House, 1989), 158.

8. Paul Ramsey, "The Limits of Nuclear War," in *The Just War* (Lanham, MD: Rowman & Littlefield, 1983), 211–58; see also Paul Ramsey, *War and the Christian Conscience* (Durham, NC: Duke University Press, 1961), 226–27.

9. National Conference of Catholic Bishops. *The Challenge of Peace* (Washington, DC: United States Catholic Conference, 1983), sec. 147 (citing Pope Pius XII, "Address to the VII Congress of the World Medical Association").

10. *Challenge of Peace*, secs. 151–52.

11. *Challenge of Peace*, secs. 174 and 189. This position was not new; the 183rd General Assembly of the Presbyterian Church came to the same conclusion in 1971. See Presbyterian Church (U.S.A.), *Christian Obedience in a Nuclear Age* (Louisville, KY: Office of the General Assembly [PCUSA], 1988), 6.

12. The Lutheran Church's social statement *Peace and Politics* was the first post-NCCB document in print but it was not widely disseminated, nor was the Presbyterian document of 1988, *Christian Obedience in a Nuclear Age*. The Methodist and Episcopal documents of 1986 and 1987, *In Defense of Creation* and *The Nuclear Dilemma*, respectively, gained a somewhat wider audience.

13. Lutheran Church in America, *Peace and Politics* (New York: Lutheran Church in America, 1984), 1. The definition of the term "crime against humanity" at the time was, in part, "murder, extermination, enslavement, deportation, and other inhumane acts committed against any civilian population." Charter of the International Military Tribunal

(France, Great Britain, United States, U.S.S.R.), August 8, 1945, art. 6(c), 82 U.N.T.S. 279. The position that the use of nuclear weapons by a defending state against an aggressor state is a crime against humanity is very much a stretch, as it does not account for the necessary element of the criminal mind, as the common crime of murder does.

14. United Methodist Council of Bishops, *In Defense of Creation* (Nashville: Graded Press, 1986), 47–48.

15. PCUSA, *Christian Obedience*, 27.

16. Lutheran Church, *Peace and Politics*, 6.

17. Episcopal Diocese of Washington, *The Nuclear Dilemma* (Cincinnati: Forward Movement Publications, 1987), 21.

18. Episcopal Diocese, *Nuclear Dilemma*, 20.

19. PCUSA, *Christian Obedience*, 6.

20. Methodist Bishops, *In Defense of Creation*, 15 and 46–49.

21. Episcopal Diocese, *Nuclear Dilemma*, 111.

22. Matthew 5:21–22 (murder and anger); Matthew 5:27–28 (adultery and lust).

23. Lutheran Church, *Peace and Politics*, 7.

24. Ford, "The Morality of Obliteration Bombing," 289ff.

25. Thomas Aquinas, *Summa Theologica*, in *Great Books of the Western World*, vols. 19–20: *Thomas Aquinas* (Chicago: Encyclopaedia Brittanica, 1952), ii-ii, q. 64, art. 7.

26. Franciscus de Victoria, *De Iure Belli*, in *De Indis et de Iure Belli Relectiones*, ed. Ernest Nys (Washington, DC: Carnegie Institution of Washington, 1917), sec. 37.

27. Episcopal Diocese, *Nuclear Dilemma*, 108 (emphasis added).

28. Methodist Bishops, *In Defense of Creation*, 64–65.

29. George H. Brand, "Toward a Just Defense," in *Peace and the Just War Tradition*, ed. Michael J. Stelmachowicz (New York: Lutheran Council in the USA, 1986), 38.

30. Reinhold Niebuhr defines evil as "the assertion of some self-interest without regard to the whole." In contrast, good seeks to bring self-interest under the discipline of a more universal law. Reinhold Niebuhr, *The Children of Light and the Children of Darkness* (New York: Charles Scribner's Sons, 1944), 9.

31. In Paul Jersild, "On the Viability of the Just War Theory," in *Peace and the Just War Tradition*, 78.

32. Second Calhoun Commission, "Atomic Warfare," 12. Ford expressly rejected this argument as tantamount to a motivation of revenge. Ford, "The Morality of Obliteration Bombing," 282 and 296. While Ford makes a fair point, his argument seems oblivious to the counterpoints that: (1) customary international law recognizes a right of "belligerent reprisal," which is a deliberate violation of the law of war in retaliation for the enemy's violation, for the purpose of deterring further violations; and (2) the Germans were fighting for a grossly unjust cause, a point to which we shall return momentarily. However, Ford's point that the "they did it first" argument does not withstand scrutiny is conceded in this particular instance, because of the targeting of civilians.

33. Michael Walzer, *Just and Unjust Wars*, fourth ed. (New York: Basic Books, 2006), 255.

34. Walzer, *Just and Unjust Wars*, 258.

35. Ford shows, by the Allies' own documents, that the Allies' strategy went beyond simply targeting industrial centers in order to cripple the German war machine; rather,

it was to undermine the morale of and terrorize the German civilian population. Ford, "The Morality of Obliteration Bombing," 294.

36. Walzer, *Just and Unjust Wars*, 258.

37. Ford, "The Morality of Obliteration Bombing," 301.

38. Ramsey, *War and the Christian Conscience*, 186. We shall turn to Ramsey's qualification of this statement momentarily.

39. Walzer, *Just and Unjust Wars*, 264 ("had the Japanese exploded an atomic bomb over an American city . . . the action would clearly have been a crime").

40. Michael Walzer, *Arguing about War* (New Haven, CT: Yale University Press, 2004), 40; see also Walzer, *Just and Unjust Wars*, 259.

41. Walzer, *Just and Unjust Wars*, 266.

42. Walzer argues that unconditional surrender was not a necessary demand against Japan as it was against Germany, on the ground that the Japanese ideology was a "more ordinary form of military expansion." Walzer, *Just and Unjust Wars*, 267–68. I disagree with this assertion. Japan's racism and belief in its own ethnic superiority was no less virulent than that of the Nazis, and the Japanese government had no more regard for the basic principles of peaceful coexistence than its German counterpart. There is no significant distinction between the two ideologies.

43. Ramsey, *War and the Christian Conscience*, 186. In today's world, the closest analog might be a state in which the large majority of the population supported a policy to destroy Israel, that is, cause it to cease to exist, and who would willingly participate in the effort.

44. Ramsey, *War and the Christian Conscience*, 188.

45. Ibid.

46. John 18:36.

47. *Challenge of Peace*, sec. 15 (emphasis added).

48. See Sigval M. Berg, "Toward a Christian Ethic on Peace and War," in *Peace and the Just War Tradition*, 31 (placing "the sanctity of life" on par with the "the dignity, uniqueness, and equality of all persons," among other things).

CHAPTER 14

1. First Calhoun Commission, "The Relation of the Church to the War in the Light of the Christian Faith," *Social Action* 10, no. 10 (1944): 33.

2. Revelation 19:11.

3. James Turner Johnson makes much of this point in his complaint that the Catholic Church has moved proper authority to a lower priority. James Turner Johnson, *The War to Oust Saddam Hussein* (Lanham, MD: Rowman & Littlefield Publishers, 2005), 28–29.

4. James Turner Johnson, "Just War Thinking in Recent American Religious Debates over Military Force," in *The Price of Peace*, eds. Charles Reed and David Ryall (Cambridge: Cambridge University Press, 2007), 96–97.

5. National Conference of Catholic Bishops, *The Challenge of Peace* (Washington, DC: United States Catholic Conference, 1983), sec. 68.

6. George Weigel, *Tranquillitas Ordinis* (Oxford: Oxford University Press, 1987); see also George Weigel, "The Development of Just War Thinking in the post-Cold War World: an American Perspective," in *The Price of Peace* (Cambridge: Cambridge University Press, 2007), 20.

Bibliography

Albrecht-Carrié, René, ed. *The Concert of Europe*. New York: Walker and Company, 1968.

Aristotle. *Nicomachean Ethics* (c. 350 BCE), translated by W.D. Ross, 333–436 in *Great Books of the Western World*, vol. 9: *Aristotle II*. Chicago: Encyclopaedia Brittanica, 1952.

———. *Politics* (c. 350 BCE), translated by Benjamin Jowett, 437–548 in *Great Books of the Western World*, vol. 9: *Aristotle II*. Chicago: Encyclopaedia Brittanica, 1952.

———. *Posterior Analytics* (c. 350 BCE), translated by G.R.G. Mure, 95–137 in *Great Books of the Western World*, vol. 8: *Aristotle I*. Chicago: Encyclopaedia Brittanica, 1952.

Aquinas, Thomas, Saint. *De Regimine Principum, ad Regem Cypri* [*On the Governance of Rulers, to the King of Cyprus*] (1267), edited and translated by Gerald B. Phelan. London: Sheed and Ward, 1938.

———. *The Summa Theologica* (1265–1273), translated by Fathers of the English Dominican Province, in *Great Books of the Western World*, vols. 19–20: *Thomas Aquinas*. Chicago: Encyclopaedia Brittanica, 1952. A complete version of the same translation is available online at www.newadvent.org/summa (accessed January 11, 2008).

———. *The Political Ideas of St. Thomas Aquinas: Representative Selections*, edited by Dino Bigongliari. New York: Hafner Publishing Company, 1953.

———. *Aquinas: Selected Political Writings*, edited by A.P. D'Entrèves, translated by J.G. Dawson. Oxford: Basil Blackwell, 1954.

———. *St. Thomas Aquinas: Political Writings*, edited by R.W. Dyson. Cambridge: Cambridge University Press, 2002.

Armour, W.S. "Customs of Warfare in Ancient India," *Transactions of the Grotius Society* 8 (1922): 71–88.

Augustine, Saint, Bishop of Hippo. *The City of God* [*De Civitate Dei*] (c. 413–426 CE), translated by Marcus Dods, 127–618 in *Great Books of the Western World*, vol. 18: *Augustine*. Chicago: Encyclopaedia Brittanica, 1952.

———. *The Political Writings of St. Augustine*, edited by Henry Paolucci. Washington, DC: Regnery Publishing, 1962.

————. *Answer to Faustus, a Manichean [Contra Faustum Manichaeum]* (398 CE), translated by Roland Teske, S.J., edited by Boniface Ramsey. Hyde Park, NY: New City Press, 1990.

————. *Augustine: Political Writings*, edited by Ernest L. Fortin and Douglas Kries. Indianapolis: Hackett Publishing Company, 1994.

————. "Letter 138: Augustine to Marcellinus" (c. 411 CE), 30–43 in *Augustine: Political Writings*, edited by E.M. Atkins and R.J. Dodaro. Cambridge: Cambridge University Press, 2001.

————. "Letter 153: Augustine to Macedonius" (c. 413 CE), 71–88 in *Augustine: Political Writings*, edited by E.M. Atkins and R.J. Dodaro. Cambridge: Cambridge University Press, 2001.

————. "Letter 189: Augustine to Boniface" (417 CE), 214–18 in *Augustine: Political Writings*, edited by E.M. Atkins and R.J. Dodaro. Cambridge: Cambridge University Press, 2001.

————. "Sermon 302: On the Feast of St. Laurence" (n.d.), 107–19 in *Augustine: Political Writings*, edited by E.M. Atkins and R.J. Dodaro. Cambridge: Cambridge University Press, 2001.

————. *Augustine: Political Writings*, edited by E.M. Atkins and R.J. Dodaro. Cambridge: Cambridge University Press, 2001.

Ayala, Balthazar. *Three Books on the Law of War and on the Duties Connected with War and on Military Discipline [De Jure et Officiis Bellicis et Disciplina Militari Libri III]* (1582), edited by John Westlake, translated by John Pawley Bate. 2 vols. Washington, DC: Carnegie Institution of Washington, 1912.

The Babylonian Talmud (c. 500 CE), translated by I. Epstein. 18 vols. London: Soncino Press, 1936.

Bainton, Roland H. *Christian Attitudes Toward War and Peace: A Historical Survey and Critical Re-evaluation*. Nashville: Abingdon Press, 1960.

Bederman, David J. *International Law in Antiquity*. Cambridge: Cambridge University Press, 2001.

Belli, Pierino. *De Re Militari et Belli Tractatus [A Treatise on Military Matters and Warfare]* (1563), translated by Herbert C. Nutting. 2 vols. Oxford: Clarendon Press, 1936.

Benson, Ezra Taft. "The Lord's Base of Operations," *The Improvement Era* 65, no. 6 (June 1962): 454–56.

Beza, Theodore. *Concerning the Rights of Rulers Over Their Subjects and the Duty Of Subjects Towards Their Rulers* (1574), translated by Henry-Louis Gonin, edited by Patrick S. Poole. http://fly.hiwaay.net/~pspoole/Beza1.htm (accessed January 15, 2008).

Bluntschli, Johann Kaspar. *Le Droit International Codifié*, second ed., translated (from German to French) by M.C. Lardy. Paris: Librairie de Guillaumin & Cie., 1874.

Bodin, Jean. *Six Livres de la République [Six Books of the Commonwealth]* (1576), edited and translated by M.J. Tooley. New York: Macmillan Company, 1955.

The Book of Mormon. Salt Lake City: Church of Jesus Christ of Latter-day Saints, 1981.

Brand, George H. "Toward a Just Defense," 37–53 in *Peace and the Just War Tradition: Lutheran Perspectives in the Nuclear Age*, edited by Michael J. Stelmachowicz. New York: Lutheran Council in the USA, 1986.

Brown, Davis. "Use of Force against Terrorism after September 11th: State Responsibility, Self-Defense and Other Responses," *Cardozo Journal of International and Comparative Law* 11 (2003): 1–53.

———. "Enforcing Arms Control Agreements by Military Force: Iraq and the 800–Pound Gorilla," *Hastings International and Comparative Law Review* 26 (2003): 159–225.

———. "Iraq and the 800–Pound Gorilla Revisited: Good and Bad Faith, and Humanitarian Intervention," *Hastings International and Comparative Law Review* 28 (2004): 1–24.

Brownlie, Ian. *International Law and the Use of Force by States*. Oxford: Clarendon Press, 1963.

———. *Principles of Public International Law*, fifth ed. Oxford: Oxford University Press, 1998.

Brutus, Junius [pseudonym]. *Vindiciae Contra Tyrannos*, in *A Defence of Liberty Against Tyrants: A Translation of the Vindiciae Contra Tyrannos*, 1689 translation, edited by Harold J. Laski. New York: Lenox Hill, 1972.

Buchanan, George. *The Powers of the Crown in Scotland* [*De Jure Regni Apud Scotos*] (1579), translated by Charles Flinn Arrowood. Austin, TX: University of Texas Press, 1949.

Burlamaqui, Jean-Jacques. *The Principles of Natural and Politic Law* [*Principes du droit Naturel et Politique*] (1792), translated by Nugent. Buffalo: William S. Hein & Co., 2001.

Cadoux, C. John. *The Early Christian Attitude to War: A Contribution to the History of Christian Ethics* (1919). New York: Seabury Press, 1982.

Cahill, Lisa Sowle. *Love Your Enemies: Discipleship, Pacifism, and Just War Theory*. Minneapolis: Fortress Press, 1994.

Cajetan, Cardinal [Tomaso de Vio]. *Commentary to Summa Theologicae* (1517), 241–45 in *The Ethics of War*, edited by Gregory M. Reichberg et al. Malden, MA: Blackwell Publishing, 2006.

———. *Summula*, "When War Should Be Called Just or Unjust, Licit or Illicit" (1524), 245–50 in *The Ethics of War*, edited by Gregory M. Reichberg et al. Malden, MA: Blackwell Publishing, 2006.

Calhoun Commission, First. "The Relation of the Church to the War in the Light of the Christian Faith," *Social Action* 10, no. 10 (1944): 3–79.

Calhoun Commission, Second. "Atomic Warfare and the Christian Faith," *Social Action* (May 15, 1946): 5–24.

Calvin, John. *Institutes of the Christian Religion* (1536), translated by John Allen. 2 vols. Philadelphia: Presbyterian Board of Christian Education, 1948.

Catechism of the Catholic Church. Vatican City: Libreria Editrice Vaticana, 1993. A complete, official English translation is online at www.vatican.va/archive/catechism/ccc_toc.htm (accessed January 11, 2008).

The Catechism of the Council of Trent (1566), translated by J. Donovan. Baltimore: F. Lucas, Jr., 1829.

The Catechism of St. Pope Pius X (c. 1880). N.p.: The Catholic Primer, 2005. www.catholicprimer.org/vatican_docs/catechism_st_pp_pius_x.pdf (accessed January 13, 2008).

The Catholic Encyclopedia (1917). www.newadvent.org/cathen/index.html (accessed January 8, 2008).

Central Intelligence Agency. *The World Factbook.* www.cia.gov/library/publications/the-world-factbook/geos/us.html (accessed January 10, 2008).

Charles, J. Daryl. *Between Pacifism and Jihad: Just War and Christian Tradition.* Downers Grove, IL: InterVarsity Press, 2005.

Childress, James F. "Just-War Criteria," 351–72 in *War in the Twentieth Century: Sources in Theological Ethics*, edited by Richard B. Miller. Louisville, KY: Westminster/John Knox Press, 1992.

Childs, James M., Jr. "Nuclear Policy and the Ethics of Anticipation," 54–69 in *Peace and the Just War Tradition: Lutheran Perspectives in the Nuclear Age*, edited by Michael J. Stelmachowicz. New York: Lutheran Council in the USA, 1986.

Cicero, Marcus Tullius. *De Re Publica* [*The Republic*] (51 BCE), 1–94 in *The Republic and the Laws*, translated by Niall Rudd. Oxford: Oxford University Press, 1998.

———. *De Officiis* [*On Moral Duties*] (44 BCE), translated by Walter Miller. Cambridge, MA: Harvard University Press, 1961.

Clausewitz, Carl von. *On War*, first ed. (1832), edited and translated by Michael Howard and Peter Paret. New York: Alfred A. Knopf, 1993.

Cole, Darrell. *When God Says War Is Right.* Colorado Springs: WaterBrook Press, 2002.

The Consolidated Treaty Series, edited by Clive Parry. 231 vols. Dobbs Ferry, NY: Oceana Publications, 1969.

Copeland, Dale C. *The Origins of Major War.* Ithaca, NY: Cornell University Press, 2000.

Costello, Frank Bartholomew, S.J. *The Political Philosophy of Luis de Molina, S.J. (1535–1600).* Spokane, WA: Gonzaga University Press, 1974.

Creasy, Edward S. *First Platform of International Law.* London: John van Voorst, 1876.

Davis, George B. *The Elements of International Law*, fourth ed., revised by Gordon E. Sherman. New York: Harper & Bros. Publishers, 1916.

Decrees of the Ecumenical Councils, edited by Norman P. Tanner, S.J. 2 vols. London: Sheed & Ward, 1990.

Dinstein, Yoram. *The Conduct of Hostilities under the Law of International Armed Conflict.* Cambridge: Cambridge University Press, 2004.

Doyle, Michael W. "Kant, Liberal Legacies, and Foreign Affairs," Part I, *Philosophy and Public Affairs* 12, no. 3 (1983), 205-35.

Draper, G.I.A.D. "The Interaction of Christianity and Chivalry," *International Review of the Red Cross* 5 (1965): 3–23.

Dun Commission. "The Christian Conscience and Atomic War," *Christianity and Crisis* (December 11, 1950): 161–68.

Durant, Will. *The Story of Civilization*, vol. 3: *Caesar and Christ.* New York: MJF Books, 1944.

Elshtain, Jean Bethke. *Just War Against Terror: The Burden of American Power in a Violent World.* New York: Basic Books, 2003.

Episcopal Church. *The Book of Common Prayer, 1979.* http://justus.anglican.org/resources/bcp/formatted_1979.htm (accessed January 11, 2008).

Episcopal Diocese of Washington. *The Nuclear Dilemma: A Christian Search for Understanding.* Cincinnati: Forward Movement Publications, 1987.

Episcopal Peace Fellowship. *Cross Before Flag: Episcopal Statements on War and Peace*, revised ed. Chicago: Episcopal Peace Fellowship, 2005.

Evangelical Lutheran Church in America. *For Peace in God's World* (August 20, 1995). www.elca.org/socialstatements/peace (accessed January 11, 2008).

Eppstein, John. *The Catholic Tradition of the Law of Nations.* London: Burns Oates & Washbourne, 1935.

Erasmus, Desiderius. *The Education of a Christian Prince* (1516), translated and edited by Lisa Jardine. Cambridge: Cambridge University Press, 1997.

Firmage, Edwin Brown. "Allegiance and Stewardship: Holy War, Just War, and the Mormon Tradition in the Nuclear Age," *Dialogue: A Journal of Mormon Thought* 16, no. 1 (1983): 47–61.

———. "Violence and the Gospel: The Teachings of the Old Testament, the New Testament, and the Book of Mormon," *BYU Studies* 25 (1985): 31–53.

Fontes Historiae Iuris Gentium, edited by Wilhelm G. Grewe. 3 vols. Berlin: Walter de Gruyter, 1995.

Ford, Franklin L. *Political Murder: From Tyrannicide to Terrorism.* Cambridge, MA: Harvard University Press, 1985.

Ford, John C., S.J. "The Morality of Obliteration Bombing," *Theological Studies* 5, no. 3 (1994): 261–309.

Franck, Thomas M. *The Power of Legitimacy among Nations.* New York: Oxford University Press, 1990.

———. *Recourse to Force: State Action against Threats and Armed Attacks.* Cambridge: Cambridge University Press, 2002.

Gentili, Alberico. *De Iure Belli Libri Tres* [*The Law of War in Three Books*] (1612), translated by John C. Rolfe. 2 vols. Oxford: Clarendon Press, 1933.

Goodman, Christopher. *How Superior Powers Ought To Be Obeyed By Their Subjects: And Wherein They May Lawfully By God's Word Be Disobeyed And Resisted* (1558), edited by Patrick S. Poole. www.constitution.org/cmt/goodman/obeyed.htm (accessed January 15, 2008).

Gratian. *Concordia Discordantium Canonum* [*Decretum Gratiani*] (c. 1140), 109–24 in *The Ethics of War*, edited by Gregory M. Reichberg et al. Malden, MA: Blackwell Publishing, 2006.

Green, L.C. *The Contemporary Law of Armed Conflict*, second ed. Manchester: Manchester University Press, 2000.

Gribbin, William. *The Churches Militant: The War of 1812 and American Religion.* New Haven, CT: Yale University Press, 1973.

Grotius, Hugo. *De Jure Belli ac Pacis Libri Tres* [*Three Books on the Law of War and Peace*] (1646 edition), translated by Francis W. Kelsey. 2 vols. Oxford: Clarendon Press, 1925.

Hall, William Edward. *A Treatise on International Law*, third ed. Oxford: Clarendon Press, 1890.

Halleck, H.W. *International Law; or, Rules Regulating the Intercourse of State in Peace and War.* San Francisco: H.H. Bancroft & Co., 1861.

Hamilton, Edith. *Mythology*. New York: Little, Brown & Company, 1942.

Hassan, Farooq. "Realpolitik in International Law: After Tanzanian-Ugandan Conflict 'Humanitarian Intervention' Reexamined," *Willamette Law Review* 17 (1981): 859–912.

Heffter, August-Guilliaume [Wilhelm]. *Le Droit International Public de l'Europe*, translated (from German to French) by Jules Bergson. Paris: Cotillon, 1857.

Hinckley, Gordon B. "War and Peace," *Ensign* 33, no. 5 (May 2003): 78–81.

Holmes, Arthur F., ed. *War and Christian Ethics*, second ed. Grand Rapids, MI: Baker Academic, 2005.

Homer. *The Iliad* (c. 550 BCE), translated by Samuel Butler, 1–179 in *Great Books of the Western World*, vol. 4: *The Iliad of Homer and the Odyssey*. Chicago: Encyclopaedia Britannica, 1952.

Huntington, Samuel P. "The Clash of Civilizations," *Foreign Affairs* 72, no. 3 (1993): 22–49.

Independent International Commission on Kosovo. *The Kosovo Report: Conflict, International Response, Lessons Learned*. Oxford: Oxford University Press, 2000.

International Court of Justice Reports, 1980–2004.

Ishay, Micheline R., ed. *The Human Rights Reader: Major Political Essays, Speeches, and Documents from the Bible to the Present*. London: Routledge, 1997.

Jersild, Paul. "On the Viability of the Just War Theory," 70–87 in *Peace and the Just War Tradition: Lutheran Perspectives in the Nuclear Age*, edited by Michael J. Stelmachowicz. New York: Lutheran Council in the USA, 1986.

John of Salisbury, *Policraticus* (1159), in *The Statesman's Book of John of Salisbury*, edited and translated by John Dickinson. New York: Alfred A. Knopf, 1927.

John XXIII, Pope. *Pacem in Terris: Encyclical Letter* (April 11, 1963), 81–124 in United Nations, *Never Again War! A Documented Account of the Visit to the United Nations of His Holiness Pope Paul VI*. New York: United Nations Office of Public Information, 1965.

Johnson, James Turner. *Ideology, Reason, and the Limitation of War: Religious and Secular Concepts 1200–1740*. Princeton, NJ: Princeton University Press, 1975.

———. *Just War Tradition and the Restraint of War: A Moral and Historical Inquiry*. Princeton, NJ: Princeton University Press, 1981.

———. *Can Modern War Be Just?* New Haven, CT: Yale University Press, 1984.

———. "Just War Thinking in Recent American Religious Debates over Military Force," 76–97 in *The Price of Peace: Just War in the Twenty-First Century*, edited by Charles Reed and David Ryall. Cambridge: Cambridge University Press, 1987.

———. *The Quest for Peace: Three Moral Traditions in Western Cultural History*. Princeton, NJ: Princeton University Press, 1987.

———. *The Holy War Idea in Western and Islamic Traditions*. University Park, PA: Pennsylvania State University Press, 1997.

———. *Morality and Contemporary Warfare*. New Haven, CT: Yale University Press, 1999.

———. "Paul Ramsey and the Recovery of the Just War Idea," *Journal of Military Ethics* 1, no. 2 (2002): 136–144.

———. *The War to Oust Saddam Hussein: Just War and the New Face of Conflict*. Lanham, MD: Rowman & Littlefield Publishers, 2005.

Johnson, John F. "Can War Be Just?" *Lutheran Witness* 122, no. 1 (January 2003): 4–7. Also available at www.lcms.org/graphics/assets/ media/LCMS/jan03.pdf (accessed September 18, 2006).

Journal of Discourses, edited by G.D. Watt. 26 vols. Salt Lake City: Deseret Books, 1974.

Kant, Immanuel. *Kant: Political Writings*, edited by Hans Reiss, translated by H.B. Nisbet, second ed. Cambridge: Cambridge University Press, 1991.

Kartchner, Kerry M. and Valerie M. Hudson, eds. *Wielding the Sword while Proclaiming Peace*. Provo, UT: David M. Kennedy Center for International Studies, Brigham Young University, 2004.

The Kautilya Arthaśāstra (c. 350 BCE-150 CE), translated and edited by R.P. Kangle. 3 vols. Bombay: Bombay University Press, 1963.

Khadduri, Majid. *War and Peace in the Law of Islam*. Baltimore: Johns Hopkins University Press, 1955.

Klintworth, Gary. *Vietnam's Intervention in Cambodia in International Law*. Canberra: Australian Government Publishing Service, 1990.

Knox, John. *The First Blast of the Trumpet* (1558), 3–47 in *John Knox on Rebellion*, edited by Roger A. Mason. Cambridge: Cambridge University Press, 1994.

———. *The Appellation of John Knox* (1558), 72–114 in *John Knox on Rebellion*, edited by Roger A. Mason. Cambridge: Cambridge University Press, 1994.

———. *John Knox on Rebellion*, edited by Roger A. Mason. Cambridge: Cambridge University Press, 1994.

Kohn, George Childs. *Dictionary of Wars*, revised ed. New York: Checkmark Books, 1999.

Kritsiotis, Dino. "Reappraising Policy Objections to Humanitarian Intervention," *Michigan Journal of International Law* 19 (1998), 1005–50.

Land, Richard D. "The Crisis in the Persian Gulf and 'Just Wars,'" *Light* (April-June 1991): 2–4.

The Laws of Manu (c. 500 BCE), translated by Wendy Doniger and Brian Smith. London: Penguin Books, 1991.

League of Nations Treaty Series, 1928.

Legnano, Giovanni da. *De Bello, de Represaliis et de Duello* [*On War, on Reprisals, and on Duelling*] (1360), edited by Thomas Erskine Holland, translated by James Leslie Brierly. Oxford: Oxford University Press, 1917.

Long, Edward LeRoy, Jr. *A Survey of Christian Ethics*. New York: Oxford University Press, 1967.

———. *War and Conscience in America*. Philadelphia: Westminster Press, 1968.

Luther, Martin. *Temporal Authority: To What Extent It Should Be Obeyed* (1523), translated by J.J. Schindel, 51–69 in *Luther: Selected Political Writings*, edited by J.M. Porter. Philadelphia: Fortress Press, 1974.

———. *Against the Robbing and Murdering Hordes of Peasants* (1525), translated by Charles M. Jacobs, 85–88 in *Luther: Selected Political Writings*, edited by J.M. Porter. Philadelphia: Fortress Press, 1974.

———. *Whether Soldiers, Too, Can Be Saved* (1526), translated by Charles M. Jacobs, 101–19 in *Luther: Selected Political Writings*, edited by J.M. Porter. Philadelphia: Fortress Press, 1974.

————. *On War Against the Turk* (1529), translated by Charles M. Jacobs, 121–31 in *Luther: Selected Political Writings*, edited by J.M. Porter. Philadelphia: Fortress Press, 1974.

Lutheran Church in America. *Peace and Politics: Adopted by the Twelfth Biennial Convention*. New York: Lutheran Church in America, 1984.

Maimonides, Moses. *Mishneh Torah: Hilchot Melachim U'Milchamoteihem* [*The Laws of Kings and Their Wars*] (c. 1170–80), translated by Rabbi Eliyahu Touger. New York: Moznaim Publishing Corporation, 1987.

Martens, Georg Friedrich von. *Summary of the Law of Nations, Founded on the Treaties and Customs of the Modern Nations of Europe* [*Primae Lineae Iuris Gentium Europaerum Practici*] (1795), translated by William Cobbett. Littleton, CO: Fred B. Rothman & Co., 1986.

Maslow, Abraham H. "A Theory of Human Motivation," *Psychological Review* 50 (1943): 370–96.

Mattox, John Mark. "The Book of Mormon as a Touchstone for Evaluating the Theory of Just War," 57–66 in *Wielding the Sword while Proclaiming Peace,* edited by Kerry M. Kartchner and Valerie M. Hudson. Provo, UT: David M. Kennedy Center for International Studies, Brigham Young University, 2004.

McKay, David O. *The Teachings of David O. McKay*, edited by Mary Jane Woodger. Salt Lake City: Deseret Books, 2004.

Messages of the First Presidency of the Church of Jesus Christ of Latter-day Saints, 1833–1964, edited by James R. Clark. 6 vols. Salt Lake City: Bookcraft, 1965.

Miller, Richard B., ed. *War in the Twentieth Century: Sources in Theological Ethics*. Louisville, KY: Westminster/John Knox Press, 1992.

The Mishnah, translated by Herbert Danby. Oxford: Oxford University Press, 1933.

Murray, John Courtney, S.J. "Remarks on the Moral Problem of War," 247–71 in *War in the Twentieth Century: Sources in Theological Ethics,* edited by Richard B. Miller. Louisville, KY: Westminster/John Knox Press, 1992.

National Conference of Catholic Bishops. *The Challenge of Peace: God's Promise and Our Response*. Washington, DC: United States Catholic Conference, 1983.

The New Oxford Annotated Bible, New Revised Standard Version, edited by Michael D. Coogan, third ed. Oxford: Oxford University Press, 2001.

Niebuhr, H. Richard. "War as the Judgment of God," 47–55 in *War in the Twentieth Century: Sources in Theological Ethics*, edited by Richard B. Miller. Louisville, KY: Westminster/John Knox Press, 1992.

Niebuhr, Reinhold. *Christianity and Power Politics*. New York: Charles Scribner's Sons, 1940.

————. *The Children of Light and the Children of Darkness*. New York: Charles Scribner's Sons, 1944.

————. "Must We Do Nothing?" 12–18 in *War in the Twentieth Century: Sources in Theological Ethics,* edited by Richard B. Miller. Louisville, KY: Westminster/John Knox Press, 1992.

————. *The Nature and Destiny of Man* (1941–43). 2 vols. Louisville, KY: Westminster John Knox Press, 1996.

————. *Moral Man and Immoral Society: A Study in Ethics and Politics* (1932). Louisville, KY: Westminster John Knox Press, 2001.

Nussbaum, Arthur. *A Concise History of the Law of Nations*, revised ed. New York: Macmillan Company, 1954.

O'Donovan, Oliver. *The Just War Revisited*. Cambridge: Cambridge University Press, 2003.

O'Donovan, Oliver and Joan Lockwood O'Donovan, eds. *From Irenaeus to Grotius: A Sourcebook in Christian Political Thought*. Grand Rapids, MI: William B. Eerdmans Publishing Company, 1999.

Oppenheim's International Law, vol. 1, ninth ed., edited by Robert Jennings and Arthur Watts. London: Longman Group, 1992.

Paul VI, Pope. "Never Again War! Address by His Holiness Pope Paul VI," 29–43 in United Nations, *Never Again War! A Documented Account of the Visit to the United Nations of His Holiness Pope Paul VI*. New York: United Nations Office of Public Information, 1965.

Phillimore, Robert. *Commentaries upon International Law*. 4 vols. London: William G. Benning & Co., 1854.

Phillipson, Coleman. *The International Law and Custom of Ancient Greece and Rome*. 2 vols. London: Macmillan and Co., 1911.

Plato. *The Republic* (c. 360 BCE), translated by Benjamin Jowett, 295–441 in *Great Books of the Western World*, vol. 7: *Plato*. Chicago: Encyclopaedia Brittanica, 1952.

————. *Laws* (c. 360 BCE), translated by Benjamin Jowett, 640–799 in *Great Books of the Western World*, vol. 7: *Plato*. Chicago: Encyclopaedia Brittanica, 1952.

Pontifical Council for Justice and Peace. *Compendium of the Social Doctrine of the Church*. Vatican City: Roman Catholic Church, 2004.

Presbyterian Church in America. "Christian Responsibility in a Nuclear Age" (n.d.). www.pcahistory.org/pca/1-439.html (accessed January 13, 2008).

Presbyterian Church (U.S.A.). *A Composite Review of General Assembly Statements on Peacemaking and the Arms Race*. New York: Office of the General Assembly [PCUSA], 1984.

————. *Christian Obedience in a Nuclear Age: A Policy Statement Adopted by the 200th General Assembly*. Louisville, KY: Office of the General Assembly [PCUSA], 1988.

————. *The Book of Confessions*. Louisville, KY: Office of the General Assembly [PCUSA], 2002.

————. *Social Witness Policy Compilation* (n.d.). http://index.pcusa.org/NXT/gateway.dll/socialpolicy/chapter00000.htm?fn=default.htm$f=templates$3.0 (accessed January 11, 2008).

Ptolemy of Lucca. *De Regimine Principum* [*On the Government of Rulers*] (c. 1301), translated by James M. Blythe. Philadelphia: University of Pennsylvania Press, 1997.

Pufendorf, Samuel von. *De Officio Hominis et Civis Juxta Legem Naturalem Libri Duo* [*On the Duty of Man and Citizen According to Natural Law in Two Books*] (1682), translated by Frank Gardner Moore. 2 vols. New York: Oxford University Press, 1927.

————. *De Jure Naturae et Gentium Libri Octo* [*The Law of Nature and Nations in Eight Books*] (1672), translated by C.H. Oldfather and W.A. Oldfather. 2 vols. Oxford: Clarendon Press, 1934.

Ramsey, Paul. *War and the Christian Conscience: How Shall Modern War Be Conducted Justly?* Durham, NC: Duke University Press, 1961.

———. *Speak Up for Just War or Pacifism: A Critique of the United Methodist Bishops' Pastoral Letter "In Defense of Creation."* University Park, PA: Pennsylvania State University Press, 1988.

———. *The Just War: Force and Political Responsibility* (1968). Lanham, MD: Rowman & Littlefield Publishers, 2002.

Raymond of Peñafort. *Summa de Casibus Poenitentiae* (1224–26), 134–47 in *The Ethics of War*, edited by Gregory M. Reichbert et al. Malden, MA: Blackwell Publishing, 2006.

Raynal, Charles E. "The Response of American Protestantism to World War II and Atomic Weapons," 145–60 in *Peace, War and God's Justice*, edited by Thomas D. Parker and Brian J. Fraser. Toronto: United Church Publishing House, 1989.

———. "The Relation of the Church to World War II in the Light of the Christian Faith," *The Presbyterian Outlook* (July 24–31, 1995): 4–6.

Rayneval, Gérard de. *Institutions du Droit de la Nature et des Gens*, second ed. Paris: LeBlanc, 1803.

Reichberg, Gregory M., Henrik Syse and Endre Begby, eds. *The Ethics of War: Classic and Contemporary Readings*. Malden, MA: Blackwell Publishing, 2006.

Rosenne, Shabtai. "The Influence of Judaism on the Development of International Law," *Netherlands International Law Review* 5 (1958): 119–49.

Rubin, Barry. "Religion and International Affairs," 20–34 in *Religion, the Missing Dimension of Statecraft*, edited by Douglas Johnston and Cynthia Sampson. New York: Oxford University Press, 1994.

Rummel, Rudolph J. *Death by Government*. New Brunswick, NJ: Transaction Publishers, 2007.

Russell, Frederick H. *The Just War in the Middle Ages*. Cambridge: Cambridge University Press, 1975.

Schachter, Oscar. *International Law in Theory and Practice*. Dordrecht: Martinus Nijhoff Publishers, 1991.

Scott, James Brown. *The Catholic Conception of International Law*. Washington, DC: Georgetown University Press, 1934.

———. *The Spanish Origin of International Law*. Oxford: Clarendon Press, 1934.

Sereni, Angelo Piero. *The Italian Conception of International Law*. New York: Columbia University Press, 1943.

Shaybani's Siyar [*The Islamic Law of Nations*] (c. 800), translated by Majid Khadduri. Baltimore: Johns Hopkins University Press, 1966.

Sittser, Gerald. *A Cautious Patriotism: The American Churches and the Second World War*. Chapel Hill, NC: University of North Carolina Press, 1997.

Smylie, Robert F. "A Presbyterian Witness on War and Peace: An Historical Interpretation," *Journal of Presbyterian History* 59, no. 4 (1981): 498–516.

Southern Baptist Convention. *Baptist Faith and Message* (1925–2000). www.sbc.net/bfm/bfm2000.asp (accessed January 13, 2008).

Stark, Rodney. *The Victory of Reason: How Christianity Led to Freedom, Capitalism, and Western Success*. New York: Random House, 2005.

Stelmachowicz, Michael J., ed. *Peace and the Just War Tradition: Lutheran Perspectives in the Nuclear Age*. New York: Lutheran Council in the USA, 1986.

Stone, Ronald H. "The Justifiable War Tradition," 185–95 in *The Peacemaking Struggle: Militarism and Resistance*, edited by Ronald H. Stone and Dana Wilbanks. Lanham, MD: University Press of America, 1985.

Stowell, Ellery C. *Intervention in International Law*. Washington, DC: John Byrne & Co., 1921.

Suarez, Francisco. *Defensio Fidei Catholicae, et Apostolicae* [*A Defence of the Catholic and Apostolic Faith*] (1613), 647–725 in *Selections from Three Works of Francisco Suárez, S.J.*, vol. 2, translated by Gwladys L. Williams, Ammi Brown and John Waldron. Oxford: Clarendon Press, 1944.

———. *De Bello* [*On War*] (1621), 797–865 in *Selections from Three Works of Francisco Suárez, S.J.*, vol. 2, translated by Gwladys L. Williams, Ammi Brown and John Waldron. Oxford: Clarendon Press, 1944.

———. *De mediis, quibus ad convertendos, vel coercendos infidels nonapostatas uti licet* [*On the means, which may be used for the conversion and coercion of unbelievers who are not apostates*] (1621), 737–95 in *Selections from Three Works of Francisco Suárez, S.J.*, vol. 2, translated by Gwladys L. Williams, Ammi Brown and John Waldron. Oxford: Clarendon Press, 1944.

———. *Selections from Three Works of Francisco Suárez, S.J.*, translated by Gwladys L. Williams, Ammi Brown and John Waldron. 2 vols. Oxford: Clarendon Press, 1944.

Sun-Tzu. *The Art of War* (c. 400–320 BCE), translated by Samuel B. Griffith. Oxford: Oxford University Press, 1963.

Textor, Johann Wolfgang. *Synopsis Juris Gentium* [*Synopsis of the Law of Nations*] (1680), translated by John Pawley Bate. Washington, DC: Carnegie Institution of Washington, 1916.

Triglot Concordia [*Book of Concord*]: *The Symbolical Books of the Evangelical Lutheran Church* (1584), translated by Evangelical Lutheran Synod of Missouri. www.lcms.org/graphics/assets/media/LCMS/TrigBOC.pdf (accessed January 11, 2008).

Twiss, Travers. *The Law of Nations Considered as Independent Political Communities: On the Rights and Duties of Nations in Time of War*, second ed. Oxford: Clarendon Press, 1875.

United Methodist Church. *The Book of Discipline of the United Methodist Church, 2004*. Nashville: United Methodist Publishing House, 2004.

United Methodist Council of Bishops. *In Defense of Creation: The Nuclear Crisis and a Just Peace*. Nashville: Graded Press, 1986.

United Nations Treaty Series, 1946–1977.

United States Conference of Catholic Bishops. *The Harvest of Justice Is Sown in Peace*. Washington, DC: U.S. Conference of Catholic Bishops, 1993.

Vattel, Emmerich de. *The Law of Nations or the Principles of Natural Law* [*Le Droit des Gens, ou Principes de la Loi Naturelle*] (1758), translated by Charles G. Fenwick. 3 vols. Washington, DC: Carnegie Institution of Washington, 1916.

Victoria, Franciscus de [Francisco de Vitoria]. *De Indis* [*On the Indians*] (1557), 115–62 in *De Indis et de Iure Belli Relectiones*, vol. 2, edited by Ernest Nys, translated by John Pawley Bate. Washington, DC: Carnegie Institution of Washington, 1917.

————. *De Iure Belli* [*On the Law of War*] (1557), 163–87 in *De Indis et de Iure Belli Relectiones*, vol. 2, edited by Ernest Nys, translated by John Pawley Bate. Washington, DC: Carnegie Institution of Washington, 1917.

————. *De Potestate Civili* [*On Civil Power*] (c. 1528), 3–44 in *Political Writings*, edited by Anthony Pagden and Jeremy Lawrance. Cambridge: Cambridge University Press, 1991.

————. *Political Writings*, edited by Anthony Pagden and Jeremy Lawrance. Cambridge: Cambridge University Press, 1991.

Waltz, Kenneth N. *Man, the State and War: A Theoretical Analysis*. New York: Columbia University Press, 1954.

Walzer, Michael. *Arguing about War*. New Haven, CT: Yale University Press, 2004.

————. *Just And Unjust Wars: A Moral Argument with Historical Illustrations*, fourth ed. New York: Basic Books, 2006.

Washington Post, 1993–94.

Watson, Alan. *Jesus and the Law*. Athens, GA: University of Georgia Press, 1996.

Webster, Alexander F.C. *The Pacifist Option: The Moral Argument Against War in Eastern Orthodox Theology*. San Francisco: International Scholars Publications, 1998.

————. "Justifiable War as a 'Lesser Good' in Eastern Orthodox Moral Tradition," *St. Vladimir's Theological Quarterly* 47, no. 1 (1990): 3–57.

Webster, Alexander F.C. and Darrell Cole. *The Virtue of War: Reclaiming the Classic Christian Traditions East and West*. Salisbury, MA: Regina Orthodox Press Inc, 2004.

Weigel, George. *Tranquillitas Ordinis: The Present Failure and Future Promise of American Catholic Thought on War and Peace*. Oxford: Oxford University Press, 1987.

————. "The development of Just War Thinking in the post-Cold War World: an American Perspective," 19–36 in *The Price of Peace: Just War in the Twenty-First Century*, edited by Charles Reed and David Ryall. Cambridge: Cambridge University Press, 2007.

Weil, Prosper. "Le Judaïsme et le développement du droit international," *Recueil des Cours de l'Academie de Droit International* 151 (1976–III): 253–335.

Wesley, John. *Political Writings of John Wesley*, edited by Graham Maddox. Bristol: Thoemmes Press, 1998.

Wheeler, Nicholas J. *Saving Strangers: Humanitarian Intervention in International Society*. Oxford: Oxford University Press, 2000.

William of Rennes. *Apparatus ad Summam Raymundi* [*Commentary on the Summa of Raymond*] (c. 1250), 134–47 in *The Ethics of War*, edited by Gregory M. Reichberg et al. Malden, MA: Blackwell Publishing, 2006.

Wheaton, Henry. *Elements of International Law*, eighth ed., edited by Richard Henry Dana, Jr. Boston: Little, Brown, & Co., 1866.

Wilson, George Grafton and George Fox Tucker. *International Law*, second ed. New York: Silver, Burdett & Co., 1901.

Wolff, Christian. *Jus Gentium Methodo Scientifica Pertractatum* [*The Law of Nations Treated According to the Scientific Method*] (1764), translated by Joseph H. Drake. 2 vols. Washington, DC: Carnegie Endowment for International Peace, 1934.

Woolsey, Theodore D. *Introduction to the Study of International Law*. New York: Charles Scribner, 1864.

Wright, Quincy. *A Study of War*, second ed. Chicago: University of Chicago Press, 1965.

Yoder, John H., ed. *The Legacy of Michael Sattler*. Scottdale, PA: Herald Press, 1973.

Yoder, John H. *When War is Unjust: Being Honest in Just-War Thinking*. Minneapolis: Augsburg Publishing House, 1984.

———. *The Politics of Jesus*, second ed. Grand Rapids, MI: William B. Eerdmans Publishing Company, 1994.

Index

About the Author

Davis Brown is director of the Just War Theory Project, a worldwide, multi-disciplinary initiative of the Academic Council on the United Nations System to reevaluate the role of war, intervention, and rebellion in maintaining world public order. He is also an attorney, a member of the United Methodist Church, and a former visiting scholar at George Washington University Law School. He currently teaches in the Department of Politics at the University of Virginia.